1770 – 1790 Census
of the
Cumberland Settlements

1770–1790
CENSUS OF THE
CUMBERLAND SETTLEMENTS

Davidson, Sumner and Tennessee Counties
(In What is Now Tennessee)

Compiled by
RICHARD CARLTON FULCHER

Baltimore
GENEALOGICAL PUBLISHING CO., INC.
1987

Table of Contents

Introduction

Davidson County Census. 1

Sumner County Census. 136

Tennessee County Census 185

References - Davidson County. . . 195

References - Sumner County. . . . 230

References - Tennessee County . . 242

Bibliography. 245

Appendix. 247

INTRODUCTION

There has always been a serious obstacle to family historians tracing Tennessee ancestry - that being the loss of early enumerations of the inhabitants of the Tennessee Country. Our earliest extant Federal Census includes only the 1810 Census of Rutherford County, and an incomplete 1820 Census. From the time of the first settlement at the French Lick, the present site of Nashville, Tennessee, in the winter of 1779-80, the area now called Tennessee became the cross-roads of a great western migration. The gap of 40 years between settlement and 1820 without even a crude index of settlers presents a formidable obstacle to research.

The purpose of this compilation is to identify as many families as possible in the western North Carolina settlements along the Cumberland River, through which ran the many trails of western expansion. Originally, this area was a part of Washington County, North Carolina, from which Davidson County was formed in 1783, to encompass all the area between the western slopes of the Cumberland Mountains to the Tennessee and Duck Rivers. Subsequently, two counties were carved from Davidson County - Sumner and Tennessee Counties. Today, this area represents all or part of some 40 counties in Tennessee.

As new counties were created, then sub-divided into still more counties on a rapid scale, early settlers were found to be in changing official jurisdictions. The researcher is faced with the problem of having several jurisdictions in which to search for ancestral records, even though his ancestor may have moved around very little, if at all. Consider that a settler on Round Lick Creek or its tributaries, which might be located in Wilson or Smith County today, may have actually purchased the land when the area was known as Sumner County, but the deed would be recorded in Davidson County. This confusion of jurisdiction, along with the recording of marriages, wills, and deeds in the County Court Minutes instead of Marriage, Will, or Deed books, presents greater research problems. To deal with these problems, I have divided this enumeration into three sections, one each for DAVIDSON, SUMNER, and TENNESSEE counties, in order to more closely identify the inhabitants with the actual area they settled, and I have included substantially all public record references found on each individual during the period 1770 to 1790.

The 3 sections of the Census are followed by a **Reference List** to identify the references used to compile the Census; and that list is followed by a **Bibliography** giving more detailed description of some of the references cited in the Census. Lastly, I include an **Appendix** to elaborate on records on a few of the early settlers.

As with any project of this magnitude, there is always the chance of error. In doing your research, please check the cited original sources for accuracy. I would greatly appreciate your bringing errors or needed changes to my attention.

I wish to thank Mrs. Robert E. Shelhart, reference librarian for the Williamson County Public Library in Franklin, Tennessee, for the tremendous help she has always generously provided, especially when I started this project.

I hope this compilation will help make your family research more productive.

Richard C. Fulcher

Part One

THE INHABITANTS OF RECORD
BETWEEN THE YEARS 1770 AND 1790,
IN THE CUMBERLAND SETTLEMENTS OF
WASHINGTON COUNTY, NORTH CAROLINA,
KNOWN AFTER APRIL 14, 1783, AS
DAVIDSON COUNTY, NORTH CAROLINA
(NOW THE CUMBERLAND BASIN OF TENNESSEE)

[description of references follows census]

A

ACUFF, Timothy - assignee of North Carolina land grant for 640 acres on Stone's River, March 7, 1786: [ref. 1].

ADAMS, ____ - killed by Indians during their attack on Brown's Station in 1788: [ref. 2].

AHERRON, John - was acquitted in Nov., 1890, of murdering Christian Destow: [ref. 3].

ALEXANDER, Ebeneezer - summoned for Davidson Co. jury duty, Nov., 1790: [ref. 4].

ALFORD, William - purchased land on Elk Fork, 1790: [ref. 5].

ALFRED, John (heirs of) - sold land in 1789, on Spring Creek, north side of Cumberland River (Sumner Co. at the time; afterwards Wilson Co.): [ref. 6].

ALLARD, Hardy - 1787 Davidson Co. tax roll with 1 taxable person: [ref. 7].

ALLEN, Jim - was a lawyer in Nashville before 1797/98, but failing in business, he went off with the Indians and became an interpretor at the Chickasaw Agency on the Natchez Trace: [ref. 8].

ALLEN, Samuel - plaintiff vs. Allen Rice in Superior Court of Law and Equity for Davidson and Sumner Co., held in Nashville, Nov. 1790: [ref. 9].

ALLEN, William - came to the Cumberland area to hunt in 1771, with Mansker. He was captured by Indians: [ref. 10].

ALLERTON/ALLERSON, Alexander - listed in North Carolina Act of 1784, as one of the settlers on the Cumberland who had died their prior to the passage of this Act, which granted 640 acres to their heirs or devisees (without any price to be paid to the public): [ref. 11].

ALLISON, David - attorney; admitted to Courts held in May 1788, at Greeneville under the authority of North Carolina: [ref. 12a]. Clerk pro tempore of Superior Court of Law and Equity for Davidson Co., May Term, 1789: [ref. 12b].

ALLISON, John - North Carolina land grant; 228 acres on Cumberland River, Sept. 15, 1787: [ref. 13].

ALL(A)WAY, Archelaus - signer of the Cumberland Compact in
May, 1780: [ref. 14].
ALSTON, Philip - before moving to the Cumberland Settlements,
he had lands on Bayou Pierce in the Mississippi Territory
or Florida: [ref. 15a]. He came to the Cumberland with
trader Turnbull from Natchez (he fled according to one
source): [ref. 15b]. Afterward he returned then moved
to Mexico where he became Empressario: [ref. 15c]. Signer
of the Cumberland Compact in May, 1780. He resided at
Freeland Station in 1784, when he executed his power of
attorney to Thomas Mosley (of the same place): [ref. 15d].
ALSTON, Thomas W. - signer of the Cumberland Compact in May,
1780: [ref. 16].
ALSTONS - sold preemptions and removed to land between Walnut
Hills and Natchez: [ref. 17].
ANDERSON, Daniel - land purchases on Murfree's Fork, Caleb's
Creek, and Red River (the last afterward in Tennessee Co.;
then Robertson Co.): [ref. 18a]. Purchased land on Drake's
Creek in 1789 (Sumner Co. at the time): [ref. 18b].
ANDERSON, Henry - 1787 Davidson Co. tax roll with 1 taxable:
[ref. 19].
ANDERSON, John - signer of the Cumberland Compact in May,
1780: [ref. 20].
ANDERSON, Luke - participated in Capt. Shannon's attack on
Indian raiding party in 1787: [ref. 21].
ANDERSON, Matthew - signer of the Cumberland Compact in May,
1780: [ref. 22]. (See also, Part Two, Sumner Co. for Matthew
Anderson.)
ANDERSON, William - summoned for Davidson Co. jury duty in
May, 1790: [ref. 23]. (See also, Part Two, Sumner Co.,
for William Anderson.)
ARMSTRONG, Andrew - purchased land on north side of Cumberland
River in 1788: [ref. 24].
ARMSTRONG, Francis - arrived with the Donelson flotilla, April
24, 1780: [ref. 25a]. Signer of the Cumberland Compact,
May, 1780. Sued by Daniel Hogan & wife for debt of Indian
corn before the Committee of the Cumberland Association,
Mar. 4, 1783: [ref. 25b]. Listed in North Carolina Preemption
Act of 1784, as one who stayed and defended the Cumberland
Settlements, and entitled to make his preemption entry without
any price to be paid to the public: [ref. 25c]. North
Carolina land grant; 640 acres on Richland Creek, April
17, 1786: [ref. 25d]. 1787 Davidson Co. tax roll with 2
taxables. He fell upon a party of Indians near Gantt's
Station; ran them off and recovered 5 horses in 1790: [ref.
25e].
ARMSTRONG, James - North Carolina land grant; March 14, 1786;
7200 acres on Stone's River: [ref. 26].

DAVIDSON COUNTY

ARMSTRONG, John - purchased Lot 61 in Town of Nashville, April 8, 1785: [ref. 27].

ARMSTRONG, Martin - purchased ½ Lot 37, and Lot 45 in Town of Nashville, April 8, 1785: [ref. 28a]. North Carolina land grant of 2670 acres on Thompson Creek, Sept. 15, 1787: [ref. 28b]. Also purchased land on Caney Fork River, Dec. 8, 1788 (at the time in Sumner Co., afterwards Smith Co.): [ref. 28c]. Recorded shipping load of produce to Natchez in winter of 1788-89: [ref. 28d].

ARMSTRONG, Mary - see Capt. William Armstrong.

ARMSTRONG, Thomas - North Carolina land grant; March 7, 1786; 640 acres on Stone's River: [ref. 29]. (See also Capt. William Armstrong)

ARMSTRONG, Capt. William - D.A.R. membership on this line. Born 10 May 1737, in PA; lived in Orange Co., NC during Revolution; married Jane Lapsley, who was born ca. 1745 and died after 1773. North Carolina land grant for 3840 acres on the Cumberland River: [ref. 30a]. 1787 Davidson Co. tax roll; 1 taxable person. Summoned for Davidson Co. jury duty, Nov. 1788: [ref. 30b]. He died 20 June 1788, in Tennessee: [ref. 30c]. Children: Thomas ARMSTRONG, b. 5 May 1767; m. (1st) Susannah PRATT, (2nd) Fannie ANDERSON, and (3rd) Elizabeth ANDERSON. James ARMSTRONG, b. 25 Dec. 1768; m. Mary MEBANE. Mary ARMSTRONG, b. 23 Dec. 1771; m. Alexander TIMMINS. Wm. Lapsley ARMSTRONG, b. 10 Mar. 1773; m. Mary CAVITT.

ARMSTRONG, Wm. Lapsley - see Capt. William Armstrong.

ARMSTRONG, Thomas - (heirs of) sold land in 1790, on Yellow Creek (at the time Tennessee Co., afterwards Robertson, then Montgomery and/or Dickson Cos.): [ref. 31].

ARRINGTON, Charles - "of Sumner Co." purchased of Philemon Thomas of Fayette Co., VA, heir of Wm. Nelson, Pvt.; Feb. 4, 1789, 200 acres on Red River (at the time Tennessee Co.): [31b].

ASHE, Col. John Baptist - no evidence found of settling on the Cumberland, but he did receive North Carolina land grant, March 14, 1788, for 4457 acres on Tennessee River: [ref. 32] D.A.R. membership on this line. His child was Samuel Porter ASHE, who married Mary SHEPPARD.

ASHE, Samuel - North Carolina land grant, March 14, 1788, for 1508 acres on Thompson Creek: [ref. 33].

ASHE, Samuel Porter - see Col. John Baptist Ashe.

ASPIC (ESPEY?), Alexander - listed in North Carolina Act of 1784, as one of the Cumberland settlers who had died there prior to passage of this Act, which granted 640 acres to his heirs or devisees without any price to be paid to the public: [ref. 34].

ASTILL, ____ - killed by Indians in the summer of 1788, a few miles west of Nashville: [ref. 35a]. Another source records his death as Oct. 1787: [ref. 35b].

ASTON, Philip - came to the Cumberland Settlements in 1783: [ref. 36]. (As no other record is found, could this source referred to Philip Alston?)
ATKINS, John - (heirs of) sold land in 1790, on Spencer's Creek (at the time Sumner Co., afterwards Wilson Co.): [ref. 37].
AYER, William - summoned for Sumner Co. jury duty, 1790, for the Superior Court of Law and Equity: [ref. 38].

B

BACOTE, Peter - North Carolina land grant; March 14, 1786, on Duck River: [ref. 1].
BADSBY, John - (heirs of) sold land in 1790, on Spring Creek (at the time Sumner Co., then, Wilson Co.): [ref. 2].
BAILEY, Ethelred - (heirs of) sold land in 1788, on Hickman Creek (at the time, Sumner Co., then, Smith Co.): [ref. 3].
BAKER, A. - 1787 Davidson Co. tax roll; 1 taxable: [ref. 4].
BAKER, Betsy - daughter of Charles Baker (see below).
BAKER, Charity - daughter of Charles Baker (see below).
BAKER, Charles - summoned for Davidson Co. jury duty, Nov. 1790: [ref. 5a]. His will dated Aug. 1796, mentioned his wife Elizabeth and children: Zachariah, Isaac, Nancy (Constable), Betsy (Ball), Charrity (Perry), and Nathan: [ref. 5b].
BAKER, Elizabeth - wife of Charles Baker (see above).
BAKER, Elizabeth C. - see Col. Joshua Baker.
BAKER, Capt. John - purchased land on Round Lick Creek in 1790 (at the time Sumner Co., then either Wilson or Sumner Co.): [ref. 6].
BAKER, John - came to the Cumberland area with 20 adventurers from NC, Rockbridge in VA, and New River, to hunt in 1769, and afterwards returned with Mansker: [ref. 7]
BAKER, Col. Joshua - D.A.R. membership on this line. Born 11 Mar. 1763, in Frederick Co., VA; listed on 1787 Davidson Co. tax roll with 1 taxable. Defendant in suit brought by Joseph Robideaux, 28 Oct. 1788, in Superior Court of Law & Equity: [ref. 8a]. Married 9 June 1790, Susanah Lewis (b. 13 Sept. 1768; d. 24 Nov. 1813). He died 14 Apr. 1816, in Nashville, TN. Child: Elizabeth C., b. 22 May, 1791; (other children born after 1791): [ref. 8b].
BAKER, Nancy - daughter of Charles Baker (see above).
BAKER, Nathan - son of Charles Baker (see above).
BAKER, Nicholas - 1787 Davidson Co. tax roll; 1 taxable: [ref. 9a]. Mentioned as deceased in will of Anthony Hart, proved May 25, 1795, in Davidson Co. Also mentioned was his wife Sarah Baker: [ref. 9b].

BAKER, Obediah - purchased land in 1788, on Smith Fork of Caney Fork River (Sumner Co., then Smith Co.): [ref. 10].

BAKER, Reuben - 1787 Davidson Co. tax roll with 1 taxable: [ref. 11].

BAKER, Sarah - mentioned as wife of Nicholas Baker in the will of Anthony Hart: [ref. 12].

BAKER, Susannah - plaintiff vs. Robert Nelson, whom she sued for slander, May, 1790. He had said of her, "...the said Susannah, that she, at a place called and known by the name of Heaton's Old Station, was delivered of a Bastard, which Bastard she murdered." Nelson was found guilty: [ref. 13]. (See also, Col. Joshua Baker.)

BAKER, Zachariah - son of Charles Baker (see beforementioned).

BALENDER, Jethro - (heirs of) sold land in 1790, on Spring Creek (Sumner Co.; then Wilson Co.): [ref. 14].

BALESTINE, Jessie - killed by Indians late in 1780, at Mansker's Lick: [ref. 15].

BAILSTON, Jesse - listed in North Carolina Act of 1784, as one of the settlers on the Cumberland who died prior to the passage of the Act, which granted 640 acres to his heirs or devisees without any payment to be made to the public: [ref. 16]. (See Jessie BALESTINE, above)

BALLARD, Burnell - (heirs of) sold land in 1790, on Yellow Creek (Tennessee Co. at the time; then Robertson, the Montgomery or Dickson Cos.): [ref. 17].

BARKER, Samuel - (heirs of) sold land in Tennessee Co. in 1789: [ref. 18].

BARNETT, ____ - killed by Indians in 1783, while surveying soon after the commissioners came out (1784): [ref. 19].

BARNETT, Mary - see Josiah Payne.

BARNETT, Peter - killed by Indians in 1786, on the waters of Blooming Grove Creek, below present site of Clarksville (afterwards, Tennessee, then Montgomery Co.): [ref. 20].

BARNETT, Robert - 1787 Davidson Co. tax roll with 1 taxable. Married Margaret Young, July 31, 1789: [ref. 21].

BARRELL, Thomas - North Carolina land grant, Sept. 15, 1787: [ref. 22].

BARRETT, William - signer of the Cumberland Compact, May, 1780: [ref. 23].

BARROW, John - listed in the North Carolina Preemption Act of 1784, as one who stayed and defended the Cumberland Settlements, and entitled to make his preemption entry without any price to be paid to the public: [ref. 24]. 1787 Davidson Co. tax roll with 1 taxable.

BARTON, Samuel - signer of the Cumberland Compact, May, 1780, and member of the Committee of the Cumberland Association, Jan. 1783: [ref. 25a]. Listed in the North Carolina Preemption Act of 1784, as one who stayed and defended the Cumberland Settlements, and entitled to make his preemption entry without any price to be paid to the public: [ref. 25b]. Wounded by Indians a few days before the Battle of the Bluffs: [ref. 25c]. Purchased land in 1789, on Round Lick Creek (Sumner Co. at the time; then Wilson or Smith Co.): [ref. 25d].

BAY, Sgt. Andrew - purchased land in 1787, on Spencer's Creek (Sumner Co., then Wilson Co.): [ref. 26].

BEARD, David - summoned for jury duty from Sumner Co., Nov. 1788, before the Superior Court of Law & Equity: [ref. 27].

BEARD, Lewis - assignee of North Carolina land grant, March 7, 1786, on Harpeth River: [ref. 28].

BEATIE, David - summoned for Davidson Co. jury duty in Nov. 1790: [ref. 29].

BELEW, Capt. Benjamin - is believed to have left the Donelson flotilla at the mouth of the Ohio River and went either to the Illinois country or to Natchez. See Bellew entries in Sumner Co. section of this work.

BELL, Elizabeth - see Robert Nelson.

BELL, George - North Carolina land grant, April 17, 1786, for 640 acres on Red River (afterwards, Tennessee Co.): [ref. 30].

BELL, Hugh Ferguson - D.A.R. membership on this line. Born 1753, on the sea; married 1786, Margaret Montgomery, who died in 1839: [ref. 31a]. 1787 Davidson Co. tax roll; 2 taxables. Wounded by Indians on 20 January 1789: [ref. 31b]. Purchased 125 acres from James Bosley on south side of Cumberland River, April 5, 1789: [ref. 31c]. He died 1849, in Clarksville, Montgomery Co., Tn. Child: William Bell, b. 1787.

BELL, Mrs. Hugh Ferguson (Margaret Montgomery) - sister of Col. John Montgomery: [ref. 32].

BELL, John - purchased 75 acres from James Bosley, Mar. 26, 1787: [ref. 33]. 1787 Davidson Co. tax roll; 2 taxables.

BELL, Robert - purchased land on Duck River, June 30, 1788: [ref. 34].

BELL, William - son of Hugh Ferguson Bell (see above).

BENNETT, Henry - (heirs of) sold land in 1790, on the east side of Stone's River: [ref. 35].

BERNARD, John - referred to as "old," was beheaded by Indians in 1780, and his head carried away. He was, at the time, making improvements at Freeland's Station, then called Denton's Lick: [ref. 36a]. He was listed in the North Carolina Act of 1784, as one of the settlers on the Cumberland who had died there prior to passage of this Act, which granted 640 acres to his heirs or devisees without any price to be paid to the public: [ref. 36b].

BERRY, Thomas - North Carolina land grant, Nov. 15, 1787, on Indian Creek (afterwards Sumner, then Smith Co.): [ref. 37].

BETTIS, Jno. - (heirs of) sold land in 1789, on Caney Fork River (at the time Sumner Co., then Smith and/or White and/or Warren Cos.): [ref. 38].

BICKLEY, Elizabeth - married Jacob Guice in Davidson Co. (see hereafter).
BIDKEY (or BIDLACK), Nathaniel - signer of the Cumberland Compact, May, 1780: [ref. 38b].
BIRD, William - summoned from Sumner Co. for jury duty on the Superior Court of Law and Equity, Nov. 1790: [ref. 39].
BISWELL, James - killed by Indians after January 1, 1787: [ref. 40].
BIZWELL, James - purchased Lot 28 in the Town of Nashville, July 8, 1788: [ref. 41].
BLACK, William - purchased land in 1789, on Drake's Creek (Sumner Co. at the time): [ref. 42].
BLACKBURN, John - killed in Sept. 1789, near Buchanan's Station by Indians who scalped him and left a spear sticking out of his body: [ref. 43].
BLACKAMORE (variously, BLACKEMORE, BLACKMORE) - see also, Sumner Co. section of this work.
BLACKAMORE, George Dawson - 1787 Davidson Co. tax roll with 1 taxable: [ref. 44]. See also, Sumner Co. section of this work for additional information.
BLACKAMORE, John - North Carolina land grant, April 17, 1786, on Dry Creek: [ref. 45a]. 1787 Davidson Co. tax roll with 8 taxables [ref. 45b].
BLACKAMORE, John, Jr. - signer of the Cumberland Compact in May, 1780: [ref. 46].
BLACKAMORE, Capt. John (J.), Sr. - led the "Clinch River Company," who joined the Donelson flotilla March 5, 1779, at the mouth of Clinch River and arrived with the flotilla at French Lick (site of Nashville), April 24, 1780: [ref. 47a]. Signer of the Cumberland Compact in May, 1780: [ref. 47b]. Qualified as a member of the Cumberland Committee, Jan. 18, 1783: [ref. 47c]. Listed in the North Carolina Preemption Act of 1784, as one of the settlers on the Cumberland, who had died there prior to the passage of the Act, whose heirs and devisees were entitled to 640 acres without any price to be paid to the public: [ref. 47d].
BLACKAMORE, Thomas - 1787 Davidson Co. tax roll with 2 taxables: [ref. 48a]. Purchased 227 acres from John Marney, February 21, 1788, on White's and Heaton's Creeks: [ref. 48b]. Summoned for Davidson Co. jury duty, May, 1789: [ref. 48c].
BLACKAMORE, William - 1787 Davidson Co. tax roll with 2 taxables: [ref. 49a]. Purchased 640 acres in Davidson Co. from Eusebius Bushnell, Oct. 7, 1788: [ref. 49b].
BLACKEMORE - see BLACKAMORE.
BLACKMAN, George - summoned from Sumner Co. for jury duty on the Superior Court of Law and Equity, May, 1790: [ref. 50].

BLAIR, James - purchased land on Mill Creek, 1790: [ref. 51].

BLAIR, Samuel - was in Buchanan's Fort during Indian attack, Sept. 30, 1792: [ref. 52a]. Had his powder horn shot off by Indians, 30 Dec. 1793: [ref. 52b].

BLAIR, Thomas - 1787 Davidson Co. tax roll with 1 taxable: [ref. 53].

BLEDSOE - see Sumner Co. section of this work.

BLEDSOE, Col. Anthony - see Sumner Co. section of this work for information.

BLEDSOE, Col. Isaac - see Sumner Co. section of this work for information.

BLOUNT, John - assignee of heirs of Tobias Sledham, 1789: [ref. 54]. Believe this individual did not settle on the Cumberland, but was only acting as land purchasing agent.

BLOUNT, John Gray - North Carolina land grant, Sept. 15, 1787, on the Tennessee River: [ref. 55a]. Land grants also on the Cumberland and Harpeth Rivers: [ref. 55b]. Land purchase on Blooming Grove Creek (then Tennessee Co.) and Cumberland River, 1790: [ref. 55c]. As no other records are found in this period suggesting residency, this is probably the same John Gray Blount of Washington, North Carolina on the Forks of the Tar River, who was one of the original shareholders of the Transylvania lands with the Hendersons and other North Carolinians. He had probably acquired his interest in western lands when he accompanied Daniel Boone on his explorations and settlement of Boonesborough: [ref. 55d].

BLOUNT, Capt. Reading - though he had a North Carolina land grant, dated March 14, 1786, on the Tennessee River, and another land purchase in Davidson Co. in 1788, this individual like possibly his brother above, did not settle in the Cumberland, but resided in Beaufort County, North Carolina: [ref. 56].

BLOUNT, William - North Carolina land grant, March 14, 1786, on the Tennessee River: [ref. 57].

BODEY (BODIE), William - 1787 Davidson Co. tax roll; 1 taxable: [ref. 58a]. Married in Davidson Co., June 14, 1790, to Jennie Lane: [ref. 58b].

BOIN (see, also, BOWEN)

BOIN, William - summoned from Sumner Co. jury duty in Superior Court of Law and Equity meeting in Nashville, Nov. 1788: [ref. 59]. Excused as juror, Nov. 1788.

BOLEN, Jane - witness in court case, Nov. 1790: [ref. 60].

BOND, William - purchased land on Harpeth River in 1788: [ref. 61].

BONN (BUNN/possibly BONE), James - purchased land in 1790, on Shackler's Creek of the Cumberland River: [ref. 62].

BONNER, James - purchased land in 1788 on Round Lick Creek (Sumner Co. at the time): [ref. 63].

BOOKER, Kasper - listed in the North Carolina Act of 1784, as one who was either too young to receive a preemption under the Preemption Act of 1782, or was one of those to come into the Cumberland Settlements afterward, and stayed and defended the settlements, and now entitled to 640 acres: [ref. 64].

BOONE, James - purchased land in 1789, on the North Fork of Sycamore Creek (Tennessee Co. at the time; then Robertson Co.): [ref. 65].

BOREN (variously, BORIN), Bazel (variously, B.) - 1787 Davidson Co. tax roll with 1 taxable: [ref. 66a]. Summoned from Tennessee Co. for jury duty in 1790: [ref. 66b].

BORIN, John - 1787 Davidson Co. tax roll with 1 taxable: [ref. 67].

BORIN, Stephen - summoned from Tennessee Co. for jury duty in 1790: [ref. 68].

BORIN, William - 1787 Davidson Co. tax roll with 1 taxable: [ref. 69].

BOSLEY (variously BOSELY), Beal - purchased 50 acres in Davidson Co., April 8, 1789, from Sam'l and Elizabeth Martin: [ref. 70].

BOSLEY, Capt. James - of Maryland; married 12 Dec. 1783, Rebecca Maclin, dau. of Wm. Macklin and Sarah Clack. She died 1787, without issue: [ref. 71a]. Purchased Lot 55 in the Town of Nashville, 6 July 1785, from Wm. Mecklin (sic): [ref. 71b]. 1787 Davidson Co. tax roll with 17 taxables: [ref. 71c]. NC land grant, July 10, 1788: [ref. 71d].

BOSLEY, John - summoned for Davidson Co. jury duty, May 1790: [ref. 72].

BOSLEY, Rebecca - see Rebecca Maclin.

BOUCHER, Ensign William - purchased land in 1790, on Barton's Creek (in Sumner Co. at the time; then Wilson Co.): [ref. 73].

BOUCHER, Kasper - arrived with the Donelson flotilla, April 24, 1780: [ref. 74].

BOURLAND, John - purchased land, May 5, 1789, on the Middle Fork of Red River (Tennessee Co. at the time): [ref. 75].

BOWEN, John - North Carolina land grant, Oct. 8, 1787, on Stuart's Creek: [ref. 76].

BOWEN, Thomas - 1787 Davidson Co. tax roll with 1 taxable: [ref. 77].

BOWEN, William - mortally injured by a buffalo in February, 1777. He was with a party including his wife, John Duncan, and James Ferguson. He was left in camp at Deacon's Pond where Palmyra now stands, where he died, apparently of malnutrition. His wife left him and took up with Ferguson: [ref. 78].

BOWEN, William - assignee of North Carolina land grant, July 10, 1788, on the Cumberland River: [ref. 79a]. He was born in Fincastle Co., VA; the grandchild of Quakers of

Welsh descent in Pennsylvania. Appointed Capt. of militia in Washington Co., VA in 1777. He and his wife, the former Mary Henry Russell built their home in 1788 on Mansker's Creek in what is now Sumner Co.: [ref. 79b].

BOWMAN, Mr. - killed by Indians after January 1, 1787, in Sumner or Davidson Co.: [ref. 80].

BOWMAN, William - assignee of North Carolina land grant, March 7, 1786, on Stone's River: [ref. 81a]. Summoned for Sumner Co. jury duty, Nov. 1788, in the Superior Court of Law and Equity meeting in Nashville: [ref. 81b].

BOYCE, Seth - (heirs of) sold land on East Fork of Turnbull Creek in 1788: [ref.82].

BOYD, Ann - see Robert Boyd.

BOYD, Catherine - see Robert Boyd.

BOYD, Francis - see Robert Boyd.

BOYD, James - 1787 Davidson Co. tax roll with 1 taxable: [ref.83].

BOYD, John - D.A.R. membership on his line. Born 2 May 1764 in Halifax Co., VA: [ref. 84a]. Came with Donelson flotilla April 24, 1780: [ref. 84b]. Signer of the Cumberland Compact in May, 1780: [ref. 84c]. Recorded his stock mark before the Committee of the Cumberland Association on May 3, 1783, thus: A crop and a slit in the right ear, and two slits in the left, one on each side of the point of the ear, and brands thus - IB: [ref. 84d]. Purchased Lot 1 in Town of Nashville, Aug. 16, 1784: [ref. 84e]. 1787 Davidson Co. tax roll with 2 taxables: [ref. 84f]. One source referred to him as "Old Johnnie Boyd," who grew watermelons in his corn patch near French Lick Station in 1787: [ref. 84g].

BOYD, John - married Mary Boyd, Sept. 1, 1790, in Davidson Co.: [ref. 85a]. 1787 Davidson Co. tax roll with 1 taxable: [ref. 85b].

BOYD, John - see Robert Boyd.

BOYD, Lettice - see Robert Boyd.

BOYD, Margaret - married William Murry in Davidson Co. on Mar. 31, 1790: [ref. 86].

BOYD, Mary - see Robert Boyd.

BOYD, Newsom Robert - see Robert Boyd.

BOYD, Robert - summoned for Davidson Co. jury duty, Nov. 1790: [ref. 87a]. He had land on Drake's Creek (Sumner Co.), and also on Trumpet Creek in Iredale Co., NC, according to his will, proven in Davidson Co., Jan. 7, 1794. His wife was Ann _____, and his children were: John; Lettice Chambers; Newsom Robert; Catherine McConnell; Sarah Blair, wife of Peter Blair; Mary; Francis Edmondson; and William: [ref. 87b].

BOYD, William - see Robert Boyd.

BOYERS, H. - 1787 Davidson Co. tax roll with 1 taxable: [ref. 88].

BOYLES, H. - 1787 Davidson Co. tax roll with 1 taxable: [ref. 89].

BRADFORD, Henry - 1787 Davidson Co. tax roll with 2 taxables: [ref. 90].

BRADLEY, Edward, Jr. - signer of the Cumberland Compact in May, 1780: [ref. 91].

BRADLEY, Edward, Sr. - signer of the Cumberland Compact in May, 1790: [ref. 92].

BRADLEY, Gee - North Carolina land grant, Sept. 15, 1787, on the Cumberland River: [ref. 93].

BRADLEY, James - signer of the Cumberland Compact in May, 1780: [ref. 94].

BRADSHAW, H. (Hugh) - 1787 Davidson Co. tax roll with 1 taxable: [ref. 95a]. Purchased 300 acres on the Cumberland River from Samuel Vernor, July 8, 1788: [ref. 95b].

BRADSHER, Jno. - see Lawson Bradsher.

BRADSHER, Lawson - (heir of Jno. Bradsher) sold land in Davidson Co. in 1790: [ref. 96].

BRALSTON, Jesse - listed in the North Carolina Preemption Act of 1784, as one of the settlers on the Cumberland who had died there, whose heirs or devisees were to receive 640 acres without any price to be paid to the public: [ref. 97].

BRANKS, Robert - North Carolina land grant, Oct. 8, 1787, on the Cumberland River: [ref. 98].

BRYANTS, came to Mansker's Lick in Nov., 1775, with Casper Mansker: [ref. 99].

BREAKY, Andrew - "of Davidson Co." assignee of North Carolina land grant, May 3, 1786, on Red River (afterwards Tennessee Co.): [ref. 100].

BRAND, John - executed bond to Wm. Webber on attachment against the estate of Webber before the Committee of the Cumberland Association, June 7, 1783: [ref. 101].

BREEZE, Richard - listed in the North Carolina Preemption Act of 1784, who had either been in the settlements by June 1, 1780, and too young for a preemption, or, a settler arriving after June 1, 1780. Both categories were to receive 640 acres without any price to be paid to the public: [ref. 102].

BREHON, James G. - land purchase, Nov. 1788, on Caney Fork (Sumner Co. at the time; then Smith Co.): [ref. 103].

BRIGANCE, John - land purchased in Sumner Co. in 1790: [ref. 104]. (See also, Sumner Co. section of this work.)

BRISTON, James - purchased land in 1789, on Goose Creek on north side of the Cumberland River (Sumner Co. at the time; then Smith Co.): [ref. 105].

BROADBENT, Richard - purchased land, Sept. 27, 1788, on Murfree's Fork: [ref. 106].

BROCK, John - pursued, with Capt. Robertson, the Indian raiding party that came to Freeland's Station in May, 1780: [ref. 107].

BROCK, Joseph - North Carolina land grant, Oct. 8, 1787, on the Red River (afterward, Tennessee Co.), and the Cumberland River: [ref. 108a]. Purchased land in 1788, on Sulphur Fork (then Tennessee Co., afterwards, Robertson or Montgomery Co.): [ref. 108b].

BROOK, Cash - accompanied the Mansker Party in 1769/70, taking articles to Fort Natchez to sell: [ref. 109].

BROWN, ____ - referred to as "son of Mrs. Brown," was captured by Indians near Nashville: [ref. 110].

BROWN, ____ - referred to as "son of John Brown," was killed by Indians in 1788, during an attack on Brown's Station, located on the west fork of Mill Creek: [rerf. 111].

BROWN, Daniel - son of Thomas Brown, mentioned in his father's estate division in 1795: [ref. 112]. See Thomas Brown, hereafter.

BROWN, George - legatee of James Brown (see hereafter).

BROWN, James - (heirs of) sold land in 1789, on Cedar Creek on the south side of the Cumberland River (Sumner Co. at the time; then Wilson Co.): [ref. 113a]. An estate division for a James Brown, deceased, was filed in Davidson Co. in 1797. Joseph Brown and George Brown were legatees of the estate. James Brown's military grant #1065, for 640 acres, was sold to William Brown for the "express purpose of redeeming his mother and brothers and sister out of Creek and Cherokee Indian (captivity) for the sum of (20 or 70)? pounds Virginia currency.": [ref. 113b]. Milly Brown, who purchased land in 1789, on Cedar Creek, was an heir of James Brown (see hereafter).

BROWN, Mrs. James (Jane) - survivor of an Indian massacre: [ref. 114].

BROWN, John - was sued by Humphrey Hogan for the recovery of a kettle, before the Committee of the Cumberland Association, Mar. 4, 1783: [ref. 115a]. North Carolina land grant, April 17, 1786, on the south side of the Cumberland River: [ref. 115b]. A son of John Brown was killed by Indians in 1788, during an attack on Brown's Station, located on the west fork of Mill Creek: [ref. 115c]. John Brown was killed by Indians near Holly Tree Gap, in what is now Williamson County, while locating a grant with Hugh Tenin and Grimes, both of whom were also killed: [ref. 115d]. According to one source, he left a wife ____ Erwin, and two children, and his widow afterwards married James Campbell: [ref. 115e].

BROWN, Joseph - son of James Brown (see hereafter).

BROWN, Moses - killed by Indians near Brown's Station on Richland Creek in 1785: [ref. 118].

BROWN, Thomas - 1787 Davidson Co. tax roll with 3 taxables: [ref. 119a]. Division of estate in Davidson Co., Jan. 1795, lists share to each heir: Stephen Hopton; Joseph Dunam (married Mary Brown); Philip Pipkin (married Margaret Brown); Seth Hargrove; Thomas Brown; and Daniel Brown: [ref. 119b].

BROWN, William - 1787 Davidson Co. tax roll with 1 taxable: [ref. 120a]. Wounded by Indians about 20 July, 1789: [ref. 120b].

BROWNEN, John - (heirs of) sold land in 1790, on Spring Creek: [ref. 121].

BRYAN, James - North Carolina land grant, Sept. 15, 1787, on the south side of the Cumberland River: [ref. 122a]. Summoned for Davidson Co. jury duty, Nov. 1788: [ref. 122b].

BRYAN, John - (heirs of) sold land in 1790, on Stones River: [ref. 123].

BRYANT, James - summoned for Davidson Co. jury duty in 1788: [ref. 124a]. He was in Buchanan's Fort during an Indian attack, Sept. 30, 1792: [ref. 124b].

BUCHANAN, Alexander - joined the Robertson party at Powell's Valley and came overland to the French Lick. He was mortally wounded by Indians during their attack on French Lick Station (also known as the first Buchanan Station) on April 2, 1781, and he died shortly after: [ref. 125a]. He was listed in the North Carolina Preemption Act of 1784, as one of the settlers on the Cumberland who had died there prior to passage of the Act, which granted 640 acres to his heirs or devisees without any price to be paid to the public: [ref. 125b]. He was the son of John Buchanan, Sr. and brother of Maj. John Buchanan, Jr. and Samuel Buchanan.

BUCHANAN, Archibald - D.A.R. membership on this line. Born 1748, in Augusta Co., Virginia: [ref. 126a]. Listed on the 1787 Davidson Co. tax roll with 2 taxables: [ref. 126b]. He was married before 1800, to Patsey Motney: [ref. 126c]. His will, proved in Davidson Co. in 1806, mentions his children: Martha (Steel); Lilly (Wells); Mary (Jones); Rebecca (Shannon); Nancy (Drew); Ellen; James B.; and his brother, Robert Buchanan; and his grandchildren "The sons and daughters of my daughter, Martha Steel": [ref. 126d].

BUCHANAN, Ellen - see Archibald Buchanan, above.

BUCHANAN, James, Jr. - signer of the Cumberland Compact in May, 1780: [ref. 127].

BUCHANAN, James, Sr. - signer of the Cumberland Compact in May, 1780: [ref. 128].

BUCHANAN, James - see Archibald Buchanan, beforementioned.

BUCHANAN, Jane - see John Buchanan, Sr., beforementioned.

BUCHANAN, Maj. John, Jr. - D.A.R. membership on this line.
   Born Jan. 12, 1759, in Harrisburg, Pennsylvania. Married
   (1st) Mary Kennedy, who died in childbirth: [ref. 129a].
   Ordered by the Committee of the Cumberland Association
   on April 1, 1783, to lay off a road with Capt. Daniel
   Williams, from Nashborough toward Mansker's Station: [ref.
   129b]. Listed on the 1787 Davidson Co. tax roll with 1
   taxable. Land purchase on Cedar Lick Creek, 1788: [ref.
   129c]. Summoned for Davidson Co. jury duty, Nov. 1788:
   [ref. 129d].
BUCHANAN, John - listed in the North Carolina Preemption
   Act of 1784, as one of the settlers on the Cumberland,
   who was either too young to receive a grant under the
   Preemption Act of 1782, but had stayed in the settlements,
   or, a settler arriving after June 1, 1780, who was still
   in the settlements; both of whom were entitled to 640 acres:
   [ref. 130].
BUCHANAN, John, Sr. - D.A.R. membership on this line. Born
   ca. 1738, in Ireland. Married Jane Trindle ca. 1758, who
   died after 1787. Migrated to Pennsylvania to North Carolina;
   then came to the Watauga Settlements before coming to the
   Cumberland Settlements: [ref. 131a]. Built a station at
   French Lick, (later called Fort Nashborough), in 1779:
   [ref. 131b]. In 1787/88, he was living in his station
   on Mill Creek when killed by Indians in his own house while
   sitting with his wife by the fireplace: [ref. 131c]. His
   children were: John, b. 12 Jan. 1759; Alexander; Samuel;
   Nancy (m. James Mulherron); and Jane (m. James Todd): [ref.
   131d].
BUCHANAN, John - son of John Buchanan, Jr.; born 15 May 1787:
   [ref. 132].
BUCHANAN, Lilly - see Archibald Buchanan.
BUCHANAN, Marcha - married John Kirkpatrick in Davidson Co.
   on Sept. 6, 1789: [ref. 133].
BUCHANAN, Martha - see Archibald Buchanan.
BUCHANAN, Mary - see Archibald Buchanan.
BUCHANAN, Nancy - see Archibald Buchanan.
BUCHANAN, Nancy - see John Buchanan, Sr.
BUCHANAN, Rebecca - see Archibald Buchanan.
BUCHANAN, Sally - see Maj. John Buchanan.
BUCHANAN, Samuel - son of John Buchanan, Sr.; 1787 Davidson
   Co. tax roll with 1 taxable. Killed by Indians in 1787,
   while plowing after moving to the new Buchanan station:
   [ref. 134a]. Estate settlement filed in Davidson Co.,
   1796: [ref. 134b].
BUCHANAN, Sarah - married Ephraim Pratt in Davidson Co. on
   June 28, 1790: [ref. 135].
BUCKLE, Thomas - (heirs of) sold land in 1790, on White's
   Creek: [ref. 136].
BUDD, Samuel - North Carolina land grant, Feb. 18, 1786,
   on the Cumberland River: [ref. 137].
BURGESS, Thos. - signer of the Cumberland Compact in May,
   1780: [ref. 138].

BURGESS, William - signer of the Cumberland Compact in May, 1780: [ref. 139].
BURNS, Joshua - (heirs of) sold land in 1789, on Bear Creek: [ref. 140].
BURTON, Robert - North Carolina land grant, June 13, 1787, on Smith Creek: [141].
BUSH (see also, Sumner Co. section of this work).
BUSH, John - North Carolina land grant, March 14, 1786, on the south side of the Cumberland River: [ref. 142].
BUSHART, Hannah - married Thomas Murrey in Davidson Co., Oct. 12, 1790: [ref. 143].
BUSHNELL, Eusebius (Eusaubius) - purchased Lot 28 in Town of Nashville from Lardner Clark, June 30, 1786: [ref. 144a]. 1787 Davidson Co. tax roll with 2 taxables: [144b].   Died in 1789: [ref. 144c].
BUSHONGS (variously, BUSHONEY), Andrew - signer of the Cumberland Compact in May, 1780: [ref. 145].
BUTCHER, G. - 1787 Davidson Co. tax roll with 1 taxable: [ref. 146].
BUTTS, Archibald - North Carolina land grant, March 7, 1786, on the Cumberland River: [ref. 147].
BUXTON, William - North Carolina land grant, March 7, 1786, on the Cumberland River: [ref. 148].
BYRNES (BYRNES), James - North Carolina land grant, Oct. 8, 1787, on Kasper Creek: [ref. 149].   1787 Davidson Co. tax roll with 1 taxable.

C

CAFFREY, John - arrived with his family in the Donelson flotilla, April 24, 1780: [ref. 1a].   Signer of the Cumberland Compact in May, 1780: [ref. 1b].   He was wounded in the thigh by Indians in the Summer of 1780, near the Bluff: [ref. 1c].   He went to Mansker's Station when John Donelson left for Kentucky: [ref. 1d].
CAFFREY (variously, CUFFEY), Peter - purchased Lot 35 in the Town of Nashville, Aug. 16, 1784: [ref. 2a].   His wife and child were taken prisoner by Indians four miles from Nashville on February 25, 1792: [ref. 2b].
CAFFREY, Rachel - married George Walker in Davidson Co. on Aug. 9, 1790: [ref. 3].
CAGE, William - purchased Lot 40 in the Town of Nashville, Aug. 16, 1784: [ref. 4].   (See his biography in the Sumner Co. section of this work.)
CAIN, James - arrived with his family in the Donelson flotilla, April 24, 1780: [ref. 5a].   Signer of the Cumberland Compact in May, 1780: [ref. 5b].

CAIN, Jesse - 1787 Davidson Co. tax roll with 1 taxable: [ref. 6].

CALLAWAY, John - signer of the Cumberland Compact in May, 1780: [ref. 7].

CALLENDER, Thomas - "of the County of New Hanover in ye town of Wilmington, North Carolina" purchased land in Davidson Co. in 1787: [ref. 8a]. North Carolina land grant, March 14, 1786, for 3840 acres on the north side of the Cumberland River: [ref. 8b]. As no further record during this period is found on this indvidual, it is believed by this compiler, that he was not an actual settler in the Cumberland during this time period.

CALLEY, William - signer of the Cumberland Compact in May, 1780: [ref. 9].

CAMERON, Charles - signer of the Cumberland Compact in May, 1780: [ref. 10].

CAMPBELL, Alexander - summoned for Davidson Co. jury duty, Nov. 1790: [ref. 11].

CAMPBELL, Charles - signer of the Cumberland Compact in May, 1780: [ref. 12].

CAMPBELL, John - North Carolina land grant, March 14, 1786, for 2560 acres on the south side of the Cumberland River: [ref. 13a]. While a resident of "Guilford County, North Carolina," he purchasedd land in Davidson Co. on Sept. 6, 1787: [ref. 13b]. The record is unclear if this individual was an actual resident of the Cumberland Settlements during this time period.

CAMPBELL, Joshua - defendant before the Superior Court of Law and Equity during May term, 1790: [ref. 14].

CAMPBELL, Michael - purchased land in 1790, on Barton's Creek (Sumner Co. at the time; afterwards, Wilson Co.): [ref. 15].

CAMPBELL, Philip - purchased land in 1790, on Barton's Creek (Sumner Co. at the time; then Wilson Co.): [ref. 15].

CANNON, James - purchased land in 1788, on Red River (Tennessee Co. beginning that year; afterwards, Robertson and/or Montgomery Co.): [ref. 17].

CANNON, Lewis - purchased land in 1789, on the north side of the Cumberland River: [ref. 18].

CANYER, William - listed in the 1787 Davidson Co. tax roll with 1 taxable: [ref. 20].

CARD, Joseph - purchased land at the head of Turnbull's Creek in 1788: [ref. 21].

CARMICK, Eunice - see Eunice Williams.
CARNAHAN, Andrew - 1787 Davidson Co. tax roll with 1 taxable:
[ref. 22a].   Summoned for Davidson Co. jury duty, Nov.
1790: [22b].
CARR, John - son of William Carr, was at Clark's Station,
Kentucky, in 1780, and came to the Cumberland Settlement
in 1783: [ref. 23].
CARR, Robert - 1787 Davidson Co. tax roll with 1 taxable:
[ref. 24].
CARR, William - was at Clark's Station in Kentucky in 1780,
and came to the Cumberland Settlements in 1783.   Father
of John Carr: [ref. 25].
CAROTHERS, Ezekial - Inventory of estate recorded, July 1794,
in Davidson Co., by Robert and Susannah Carothers,
Administrator and Administratrix: [ref. 26].
CARTER, John - purchased land in 1788, on Lick Creek: [ref.
27].
CARTWRIGHT, Anne - see Robert Cartwright.
CARTWRIGHT, David - see Robert Cartwright.
CARTWRIGHT, Elizabeth - see Robert Cartwright.
CARTWRIGHT, J. - 1787 Davidson Co. tax roll with 1 taxable:
[ref. 28].
CARTWRIGHT, Jacob - see Robert Cartwright.
CARTWRIGHT, James - see Robert Cartwright.
CARTWRIGHT, Jesse - see Robert Cartwright.
CARTWRIGHT, John H. - see Robert Cartwright.
CARTWRIGHT, Joseph - North Carolina land grant, June 6, 1788,
for 640 acres on the north side of the Cumberland River:
[ref. 29].
CARTWRIGHT, Justinian - constable to the Davidson Co. Grand
Jury, Nov. 1788: [ref. 30].
CARTWRIGHT, Robert - D.A.R. membership on this line.   Born
Feb. 22, 1722, in Princess Anne Co., VA; married (1st)
Anne Huggins; (2nd) Mary Hunter; (3rd) Anne Pembroke in
1764, in Princess Ann Co. (born 1741; died 1825).   He resided
in the Watauga Settlements during the Revolution: [ref.
31a].   He and his family arrived in the Cumberland
Settlements in the Donelson flotilla, April 24, 1780: [ref.
31b].   Signer of the Cumberland Compact in May, 1780: [ref.
31c].   North Carolina land grant: [ref. 31d].   Purchased
320 acres on Dry Creek on March 29, 1788, from Thomas
Kilgore: [ref. 31e].   Children: William, b. July 4, 1746,
d. in infancy; Martha, b. May 14, 1750; Mary, b. Aug. 11,
1753, married Jas. H. Wallace; Anne, b. June 2, 1755, married
Thomas Nelson; Susanna, b. Sept. 1757, d. Aug. 1759; Robert,
b. Dec. 7, 1759, d. March 23, 1776; John H., b. Feb. 26,
1762, d. 1780; Penny, b. Feb. 28, 1765, d. in infancy;
Jacob, b. Feb. 22, 1767, married Patience Hobdy; Thomas,

(continued next page)

CARTWRIGHT, Robert - (continued)

    b. Nov. 20, 1768, married Nancy Christian; James, b. Feb. 14, 1770, married (1st) Frances Thompson; married (2nd) Mrs. Kittrel; William H., b. Oct. 4, 1773, d. young; Elizabeth, b. Sept. 1776, d. 1864, married James Rutherford; Robert, married Elizabeth Lawson; David, born 1782; and Jesse, born 1787: [ref. 31f].

CARTWRIGHT, Martha - see Robert Cartwright.

CARTWRIGHT, Mary - see Robert Cartwright.

CARTWRIGHT, Penny - see Robert Cartwright.

CARTWRIGHT, Robert - see Robert Cartwright.

CARTWRIGHT, Robert - see Robert Cartwright.

CARTWRIGHT, Susanna - see Robert Cartwright.

CARTWRIGHT, Thomas - see Robert Cartwright.

CARTWRIGHT, William - see Robert Cartwright.

CARTWRIGHT, William - settled first at Donelson's Station at Clover Bottom, where he planted corn with Donelson and Ragan. He then moved to Mansker's Station when Donelson's Station was broken up due to Indian problems: [ref. 32a]. He was killed by Indians at Clover Bottom during a corn gathering expedition: [ref. 32b].

CARTWRIGHT, William H. - see Robert Cartwright.

CARVER, David - listed in the North Carolina Preemption Act of 1784, as one of the settlers on the Cumberland who had died there, whose heirs or devisees were to receive 640 acres without any price to be paid to the public: [ref. 33].

CARVER, Ned - killed by Indians in either July or August, 1780, about five miles above Nashville on a bluff on the north side of the Cumberland. His wife and two children escaped and came to Nashville: [ref. 34a]. Listed in the North Carolina Preemption Act of 1784, as one of the settlers to the Cumberland who had died there, and whose heirs and devisees were to receive 640 acres without any price to be paid to the public: [ref. 34b].

CARVIN, _____ - a widow who was married to Edward Swanson at Fort Nashboro: [ref. 35].

CARVIN, Edward - listed in the North Carolina Preemption Act of 1784, as one of the settlers on the Cumberland who died there, and whose heirs or devisees were entitled to 640 acres without any price to be paid to the public: [ref. 36].

CARVIN, William - North Carolina land grant, April 17, 1786, for 640 acres on the north side of the Cumberland River: [ref. 37].

CASHAW, Rebecca - was married to Francis Rordine in Davidson Co. on March 9, 1790: [ref. 38].

CASTELLO (variously, CASTILLO, CASTILIO), John, Sr. - witness
to a lawsuit before the Committee of the Cumberland
Association, March 4, 1783: [ref. 39a]. Listed in the
North Carolina Preemption Act of 1784, as one of the settlers
on the Cumberland, who had either been too young on June
1, 1780, for a grant, or, a settler, arriving after June
1, 1780, who had remained in the settlements. Both
categories were to recieve 640 acres without any price
to be paid to the public: [ref. 39b].
CASTILLO, Pierce - listed in the North Carolina Preemption
Act of 1784, as one of the settlers on the Cumberland who
had stayed and defended the settlements, and was entitled
to 640 acres without any price to be paid to the public:
[ref. 40].
CASTLEMAN (variously, CASSELMAN), Andrew - 1787 Davidson
Co. tax roll with 1 taxable: [ref. 41].
CASTLEMAN, Benjamin - 1787 Davidson Co. tax roll with 1
taxable: [ref. 42a]. He was in the company including Capt.
Rains, pursuing Indians to the Muscle Shoals, who had
attacked the settlements in 1787: [ref. 42b].
CASTLEMAN, Jacob - signer of the Cumberland Compact in May,
1780: [ref. 43a]. 1787 Davidson Co. Tax roll with 1 taxable:
[ref. 43b]. Assignee of North Carolina land grant, Sept.
15, 1787, for 640 acres on Stone's Lick Creek: [ref. 43c].
Summoned for Davidson for jury duty, Nov. 1788: [ref. 43d].
CASTLEMAN, John - had a son, Joseph, who was killed by Indians
in the Sumner of 1781: [ref. 44a]. 1787 Davidson Co. tax
roll with 1 taxable: [ref. 44b]. He helped defend Buchanan
Station during an Indian attack on Sept. 20, 1792: [ref.
44c].
CASTLEMAN, Joseph - son of John, was killed by Indians in
the Summer of 1781: [ref. 45].
CASTLEMAN, Robert - son of John Castleman, was killed by
Indians ca. 1781: [ref. 46].
CASTLEMAN, Robin - helped defend Buchanan Station during
an Indian attack, Sept. 20, 1792: [ref. 47].
CATHAM, Edward - purchased land on Little Harpeth River,
Nov. 16, 1788, from William Newell: [ref. 48].
CATHERINE, Peter - attachment against the estate of, by Andrew
Keller before the Committee of the Cumberland Association,
April 2, 1783: [ref. 49]. (See also, Peter Catron - could
this be the same individual?)
CATRON, Francis - signer of the Cumberland Compact, May 1780:
[ref. 50].
CATRON, Peter - signer of the Cumberland Compact, May, 1780:
[ref. 51a]. North Carolina land grant, April 17, 1786,
for 640 acres on Mill Creek: [ref. 51b].

CATRON, Philip - signer of the Cumberland Compact, May, 1780: [ref. 52a]. Wounded in the breast by Indians while riding from Freeland's Station to the Bluff in 1780, so that he spat blood, but he recovered: [ref. 52b]. North Carolina land grant, April 17, 1786, for 640 acres on Mill Creek: [ref. 52c].

CHARLEVILLE, Charles - died in 1780, at the age of 84, at the Great French Lick Trading Post: [ref. 53].

CHESNIER, Jacques - purchased of Timothy Demunbre (sic), July 17, 1788, 1000 acres of land on the north side of the Cumberland River: [ref. 54].

CHILD, Francis - North Carolina land grant, March 14, 1786, for 3840 acres on Caney Creek: [ref. 55].

CHILDERS (variously, CHILDRESS), John - summoned for Davidson Co. jury duty, Nov. 1790: [ref. 56].

CHOAT, Valentine - purchased land in 1790, on Station Camp Creek (Sumner Co. at the time): [ref. 57]. See also Sumner Co. section of this work.

CIMBERLIN, Jacob - signer of the Cumberland Compact, May, 1780: [ref. 58].

CIVIL, Jacob - a free negro and son of Jack Civil, was captured by Indians at Clover Bottom in 1780: [ref. 60].

CLACK, William - was killed by Indians, May 16/17, 1792, while returning from Court on the Cumberland: [ref. 61].

CLARK, Lardner - 1787 Davidson Co. tax roll with 1 taxable: [ref. 62a]. Summoned for Davidson Co. jury duty, 1788: [ref. 62b]. Had first dry goods store in Nashville.

CLARK, Thomas - North Carolina land grant, March 14, 1786, for 2560 acres on the Cumberland River: [ref. 63].

CLARK, Vashal - purchased land on Barton's Creek in 1788: [ref. 64].

CLARK, Sgt. William - purchased land in 1789, on Goose Creek (possibly Sumner Co.): [ref. 65].

CLAYTON, (boy) - captured from the fort, and after running from his captors, he was caught and scalped and killed on Richland Creek west of Nashville, shortly after the Battle of Buchanan's Station, April 2, 1781: [ref. 66].

CLAYTON, _____ - killed by Indians on Taylor's Trace, Sept. 30, 1792: [ref. 67].

CLAYTON, Seward - brother of the boy Clayton mentioned above, remained in captivity with the Indians for several years and after returning to Nashville, he was killed by Indians while with Jonathan Gee, two miles east of the present city of La Vergne, Tennessee: [ref. 68].

CLYERS, James - (heirs of) sold land in 1789, on Station Camp Creek, north of the Cumberland River (Sumner Co. at the time): [ref. 69].

CLYERS, John - (heirs of) sold land in 1789, on Station Camp Creek (at the time Sumner Co.): [ref. 70].
COATING, John - victim of assault; Davidson Co. Court Case, May, 1790: [ref. 71].
COBB, William - (heirs of) sold land in 1790, on Blooming Grove Creek (at the time Tennessee Co., afterwards, Montgomery Co.): [ref. 72].
COCHRAN, John - 1787 Davidson Co. tax roll with 1 taxable: [ref. 73].
COCHRAN, William - assignee of the heirs of Allen Murdock, land in Davidson Co., 1790: [ref. 74]
COCK, William - produced license to practice as an attorney before the Superior Court of Law and Equity, May term, 1789: [ref. 75].
COCKE, Phines - arrived with the Donelson flotilla, April 24, 1780: [ref. 76].
COCKRILL, Ann Robertson Johnson - D.A.R. membership on this line. Born Feb. 10, 1757, in Wake Co., NC: [ref. 77a] Married (1st) Nehemiah Johnson, who was killed by the falling of a tree: [ref. 77b]. After her husband's death, Ann came to the Cumberland Settlement with her three children on the Donelson flotilla, April 24, 1780: [ref. 77c]. She married (2nd) John Cockrill in 1780. She was listed in the North Carolina Preemption Act of 1784, as one of the settlers who had stayed and defended the settlements and entitled to 640 acres without any price to be paid to the public: [ref. 77d]. Children: (by Nehemiah Johnson) Mary "Polly", b. May 17, 1772; married (1st) Gen. Isaac Roberts, (2nd) Mr. Stevens: Elizabeth, married (1st) Nehemiah Courtney, (2nd) Daniel Evans: Charity, married Reuben Parks. Her children by John Cockrill were: John, Jr. (III), b. July 8, 1781: Ann "Nancy", b. Feb. 1, 1783: Sterling R., b. March 7, 1785; died in infancy: James, b. Jan. 28, 1787: Mark, b. Dec. 2, 1788: Susanna, b. Sept. 2, 1790: and other children born after 1790. Ann was the sister of James, Mark, and John Robertson.
COCKRILL, Ann "Nancy" - see Ann Robertson Johnson Cockrill.
COCKRILL, James - see Ann Robertson Johnson Cockrill.
COCKRILL, Maj. John - arrived with the Donelson flotilla, April 24, 1780: [ref. 78a]. He recorded his stock mark before the Committee of the Cumberland Association on Feb. 11, 1783, which was a "crop off the right ear, and under kell in the left.":[ref. 78b]. He was married to the widow Ann Johnson (see her biography). He was named in the North Carolina Preemption Act of 1784, as one of the settlers who had stayed and defended the settlements and entitled to 640 acres without any price to be paid to the public:

(continued next page)

COCKRILL, John - (continued)
[ref. 78c]. North Carolina land grant, April 17, 1786, for 640 acres on Mill Creek: [78d]. 1787 Davidson Co. tax roll with 1 taxable: [78e]. Fired upon by Indians and had his horse killed in 1788: [ref. 78f].

COCKRILL, John, Jr. - see Ann Robertson Johnson Cockrill.

COCKRILL, Mark - see Ann Robertson Johnson Cockrill.

COCKRILL, Sterling R. - see Ann Robertson Johnson Cockrill.

COCKRILL, Susannah - see Ann Robertson' Johnson Cockrill.

COLCHESTER, John - (heirs of) sold land in 1788, on Red River: [ref. 79].

COLE, James - son-in-law of James Drumgold, came to the Cumberland Settlements from Natchez in 1783: [ref. 80].

COLEMAN, Spill - signer of the Cumberland Compact, May, 1780: [ref. 81].

COLLINS, William - arrived with the Donelson flotilla, April 24, 1780: [ref. 82a]. Listed in the North Carolina Preemption Act of 1784, as one of the settlers who had stayed and defended the Cumberland Settlements and entitled to 640 acres without any price to be paid to the public: [ref. 82b].

COLLINSWORTH, Miss - taken prisoner by the Indians, Feb. 17, 1792, on the Chickasaw Trace: [ref. 83].

COLLINSWORTH, Mrs. - killed by Indians Feb. 17, 1792, on the Chickasaw Trace: [ref. 84].

COLLINSWORTH, James - administrator of the estate of William Collinsworth, deceased, in Davidson Co., 1795: [ref. 85].

COLLINSWORTH, John - killed by Indians Feb. 17, 1792, on the Chickasaw Trace: [ref. 86].

COLLINSWORTH, Olive - orphan of William Collinsworth, deceased, 1795, who afterward married William Shute in Davidson Co., 7 Jan. 1801: [ref. 87].

COLLINSWORTH, William - North Carolina land grant, April 17, 1788, for 640 acres on Little Harpeth River: [ref. 88a]. His estate administered by James Collinsworth in Davidson Co., 1795, the proceedings of which mention orphan, Olive Collinsworth: [ref. 88b].

COLYEARS, William - killed by Indians after Jan. 1, 1787: [ref. 89].

COMSTOCK (variously, CUMSTOCK), Thomas - North Carolina land grant, Oct. 8, 1787, for 100 acres on the Cumberland River: [ref. 90a]. Purchased land in 1788, on the Sulphur Fork of Red River (Tennessee County in 1788, then Robertson Co.): [ref. 90b].

CONDRY, Dennis - arrived with the Donelson flotilla, April 24, 1780: [ref. 91a]. Listed in the North Carolina Preemption Act of 1784, as one of the settlers who stayed and defended the Cumberland Settlements and entitled to 640 acres without any price to be paid to the public: [ref. 91b].

CONDRY, John - signer of the Cumberland Compact, May, 1780: [ref. 92].

CONNER, William - 1787 Davidson Co. tax roll with 1 taxable: [ref. 93].

CONRAD, Philip - came from Kentucky, where he had been a member of Capt. Logan's Company in 1779: [ref. 94a]. He was killed in the spring of 1780, by a falling tree where Bass' Tan Yard later stood: [ref. 94b]. Listed in the North Carolina Preemption Act of 1784, as one of the settlers to the Cumberland who had died there, whose heirs or devisees were entitled to 640 acres without any price to be paid to the public: [ref. 94c].

CONSELLEA, Harmon - signer of the Cumberland Compact, May, 1780: [ref. 95].

CONTES, C. - 1787 Davidson Co. tax roll with 1 taxable: [ref. 96].

COOKE, James - signer of the Cumberland Compacat, May, 1780: [ref. 97].

COOK(E), Phineas - listed in the North Carolina Preemption Act of 1784, as one of the settlers being either too young at the time of the Preemption Act of 1782 to receive a grant, or one arriving after the passage of the Act, who stayed and defended the settlements, and entitled to 640 acres: [ref. 98]. (See also; Phenix COX, p. 24; and Phines COCKE, p. 21.)

COOKE, William - kept the records of the Superior Court of Law and Equity during the May session of 1789: [ref. 99a]. Produced license to practice as an attorney during the same session: [ref. 99b].

COON, Prudence - was married to Elijah Gower in Davidson Co., Dec. 22, 1790: [ref. 100].

COONROD (variously, COUNROD), Nicholas - signer of the Cumberland Compact, May, 1780: [ref. 101a]. 1787 Davidson Co. tax roll with 3 taxables: [ref. 101b]. Purchased 68 acres of Isaac Linsey, July 9, 1788: [ref. 101c].

COOPER, James - 1787 Davidson Co. tax roll with 1 taxable: [ref. 102].

COOPER, William - listed in the North Carolina Preemption Act of 1784, as one of the settlers on the Cumberland, who had died there prior to the passage of the Act, whose heirs or devisees were entitled to 640 acres without any price to be paid to the public: [ref. 103].

CORBIN, Arthur - land purchase in 1790, on Yellow Creek: [ref. 104].

COTTON, John - arrived with the Donelson flotilla, April 24, 1780: [ref. 105a]. Defendant in Court held in Davidson Co., Nov. 1790: [ref. 105b].

COURTNEY, Nehemiah - married Elizabeth Johnston in Davidson Co., Oct. 14, 1790: [ref. 106].

COUTS, Chrisley - summoned for jury duty from Tennessee County
by the Superior Court of Law and Equity meeting in Nashville,
May, 1789: [ref. 107].
COWAN, John - signer of the Cumberland Compact, May, 1780:
[ref. 108].
COWER, Ned - came to the Cumberland area to hunt in 1769,
in the company of 20 adverturers from North Carolina, Rock
Bridge in Virginia, and New River: [ref. 109a]. He was
killed by Indians according to one source: [109b].
COX, Edward - North Carolina land grant, Oct. 8, 1787, for
640 acres on Mill Creek: [ref. 110].
COX, John - 1787 Davidson Co. tax roll with 1 taxable: [ref.
111].
COX, Phenix - plaintiff in lawsuit against Stephen Ray for
breach of contract, heard before the Committee of the
Cumberland Association, Aug. 5, 1783: [ref. 112a]. 1787
Davidson Co. tax roll with 1 taxable: [ref. 112b].
COX, Thomas - signer of the Cumberland Compact, May, 1780:
[ref. 113a]. 1787 Davidson Co. tax roll with 1 taxable:
[ref. 113b].
CRAFFORD - see CRAWFORD.
CRADDOCK, Capt. John - purchased 3200 acres of Samuel Jones,
Feb. 22, 1786: [ref. 114a]. Purchased land in 1788, on
the West Fork of Red River (Tennessee Co. in 1788, afterwards
Montgomery Co.): [ref. 114b].
CRAIGHEAD, Rev. Thomas B. - 1787 Davidson Co. tax roll with
2 taxables: [ref. 115a]. Purchased 200 acres on Cumberland
River, May 10, 1789, from Lardner Clark: [ref. 115b].
CRANE, John - 1787 Davidson Co. tax roll with 1 taxable:
[ref. 116].
CRANE, Lewis - helped build Heaton's Station, which was
finished in 1779: [ref. 117a]. Listed in the North Carolina
Preemption Act of 1784, as one of those who had settled
on the Cumberland in 1780 and stayed to defend the
settlements, and were entitled to 640 acres without any
price to be paid to the public: [ref. 117b].
CRAWFORD, George - 1787 Davidson Co. tax roll with 1 taxable:
[ref. 118].
CRAWFORD, Hugh - summoned for jury duty from Sumner Co. by
the Superior Court of Law and Equity meeting in Nashville,
Nov. 1790: [ref. 119]. See, also, the Sumner Co. section
of this work.
CREPPS, Christian - purchased 25 acres on the Cumberland
River from James Bosley, Mar. 21, 1787: [ref. 120].
CROCKETT, Andrew - D.A.R. membership on this line. Born
1746, in Augusta Co., VA: [ref. 121a]. North Carolina
land grant, April 17, 1786, for 640 acres on the Little
Harpeth River (afterwards, Williamson Co.): [ref. 121b].
Children: James, b. 9 Dec. 1770, m. Martha Bell; Samuel,
b. 1 Nov. 1772, m. Joanna Sayers; John, b. 1777; Nancy,
b. 30 March 1780; Polly; Robert; and Andrew: [ref. 121c].

CROCKETT, Andrew - see Andrew Crockett
CROCKETT, James - see Andrew Crockett.
CROCKETT, James - signer of the Cumberland Compact, May, 1780: [ref. 122a]. North Carolina land grant, April 17, 1786, for 640 acres on Little Harpeth River: [ref. 122b].
CROCKETT, John - see Andrew Crockett.
CROCKETT, John - North Carolina land grant, April 17, 1786, for 640 acres on the Little Harpeth River (afterwards Williamson Co.): [ref. 123].
CROCKETT, Nancy - see Andrew Crockett.
CROCKETT, Polly - see Andrew Crockett.
CROCKETT, Robert - one of a company of adventurers from North Carolina, Rock Bridge in Virginia, and New River, who came to the Cumberland to hunt in 1769. He was killed by Indians near the headwaters of Roaring River and the Caney Fork: [ref. 124].
CROCKETT, Samuel - see Andrew Crockett.
CROCKETT, Samuel - summoned for jury duty from Tennessee Co. by the Superior Court of Law and Equity meeting in Nashville, Nov. 1790: [ref. 125].
CROW, D. - 1787 Davidson Co. tax roll with 1 taxable: [ref. 126].
CROW, John - signer of the Cumberland Compact, May, 1780: [ref. 127a]. North Carolina land grant, April 17, 1786, for 640 acres on White's Creek: [ref. 127b].
CRUTCHER, Anthony - purchased Lot 31 in the Town of Nashville, July 26, 1784: [ref. 128]
CRUTCHER, John A. - summoned for Davidson Co. jury duty, Nov. 1788: [ref. 129].
CRUTCHER, Thomas - 1787 Davidson Co. tax roll with 1 taxable: [ref. 130a]. Summoned for Davidson Co. jury duty, Nov. 1788: [ref. 130b].
CRUTCHER, William - purchased Lot 19 in the Town of Nashville, July 26, 1784: [ref. 131a]. Wounded by Indians on the waters of Blooming Grove (below the present site of Clarksville) in 1786. They left him for dead with a knife sticking out of his body, but he recovered: [ref. 131b]. 1787 Davidson Co. tax roll with 1 taxable.: [ref. 131c]. Purchased land in 1790, on the Sulphur Fork of Red River (Tennessee Co. at the time; then Robertson Co.): [ref. 131d].
CRUTCHFIELD, John - listed in the North Carolina Preemption Act of 1784, as one of the settlers on the Cumberland who died there, whose heirs or devisees were entitled to 640 acres without any price to be paid to the public: [ref. 132].
CRUTCHFIELD, William - arrived in the Cumberland Settlements with his family on board the Donelson flotilla, April 24, 1780, in the company of three other families, according to his son: [ref. 133].

CULBERSON, John - witness for plaintiff (Cox vs. Ray), before
the Committee of the Cumberland Association, Aug. 5, 1783:
[ref. 134].
CUFFEY, Capt. - negro; was killed by Indians, March 20, 1791,
on his master's plantation: [ref. 135]. See Caffrey.
CUMSTOCK - see COMSTOCK.
CURTIS (variously, CURTICE), Rice - summoned for Davidson
Co. jury duty, May, 1789: [ref. 136].
CURTIS, John - appointed Constable for the Court, May, 1789:
[ref. 137a]. He was killed by Indians, Jan. 7, 1792, near
the Cumberland River: [ref. 137b].

D

DANIEL, James - summoned for Davidson Co. jury duty, Nov.
1788: [ref. 1]
DARDEN, John - land purchase, 1789: [ref. 2].
DAUGHERTY, George - signer of the Cumberland Compact, May,
1780: [ref. 3].
DAUGHERTY, Henry - signer of the Cumberland Compact, May,
1780: [ref. 4].
DAUGHERTY, Joseph - signer of the Cumberland Compact, May,
1780: [ref. 5].
DAVIDSON, Joseph - purchased land of Thos. McFarland on April
7, 1788: [ref. 6].
DAVIDSON, Parmelia - married George McLane in Davidson Co.,
July 20, 1789: [ref. 7].
DAVIS, Ammon - see Frederick Davis.
DAVIS, Ciddy - see Frederick Davis.
DAVIS, Elizabeth - see Frederick Davis.
DAVIS, Elizabeth - see Frederick Davis.
DAVIS, Elisha - see Frederick Davis.
DAVIS, Elisha - purchased land of Silas Lenton: [ref. 8].
DAVIS, Fanny - see Frederick Davis.
DAVIS, Frederick - D.A.R. lineage on this line. Born 22
Sept. 1748, in NC; m. Fanny Grieves, Aug. 9, 1769, in
Pasquotank Co., NC: [ref. 9a]. Purchased land of Cartwright
in Davidson Co.: [ref. 9b]. Summoned for Davidson Co.
jury duty, Nov., 1790: [ref. 9c]. Children: John, b. July
30, 1770, m. Dora Gleaves; James, b. 1775, m. Mary Leah;
Ammon, m. Sally Roberts; Elisha, b. ca. 1781, m. Mary Sarah
Fry; Ciddy, b. 1772, m. Jonathan Robertson; Elizabeth,
m. Daniel Hamner; and Nancy, b. March 19, 1787: [ref. 9d].

DAVIS, James - see Frederick Davis.
DAVIS, John - see Frederick Davis.
DAVIS, Moses - (heirs of) sold land in 1789, on Spencer's Creek (Sumner Co. at the time, then Wilson Co.): [ref. 10].
DAVIS, Nancy - see Frederick Davis.
DAW, Jeffery - (heirs of) sold land in 1789, on Sulphur Fork of Red River (Tennessee Co. at the time, then Robertson Co.): [ref. 11].
DAWSON, John - summoned from Sumner Co. for jury duty on the Superior Court of Law and Equity meeting in Nashville in 1790: [ref. 12].
DEADRICK, John - defendant in case before the Superior Court of Law and Equity, Nov. 1790: [ref. 13].
DEAL, Thos. - purchased land, Jan. 21, 1790: [ref. 14].
DEASON, (variously, DESON, DECEAN), Samuel - signer of the Cumberland Compact, May, 1780: [ref. 15a]. Defendant in suit brought by Michael Shaver for breach of contract, before the Committee of the Cumberland Association, June 1783: [ref. 15b]. Defendant in action brought by George Freeland for trespass, before the Committee of the Cumberland Association, July 1, 1783. Witnesses testified Deason had whipped a negro (apparently belonging to Freeland), who had thrown a clod at his little girl and had struck her leaving a mark: [ref. 15c]. Purchased of James Bosley, Jan. 1, 1789, 100 acres on the Cumberland River: [ref. 15d].
DEASON, ____ - "little girl" of Samuel Deason (see above).
DELANEY, James - 1787 Davidson Co. tax roll with 1 taxable: [ref. 16a]. Purchased land in 1788, on Clear Branch (possibly, Clear Fork of Smith Fork; at the time in Sumner Co., afterwards, Smith Co.): [ref. 16b].
DEMONBREUM, Timothe (Jacques Timothey Boucher Sieur de Montbreun) - D.A.R. membership on this line. Born 23 March 1747, in Boucherville, Canada; married Nov. 26, 1766, Margaret Therese Archange Gilbert: [ref. 17a]. Plaintiff in case vs. Anthony Crutcher before the Superior Court of Law and Equity, Oct. 1788: [ref. 17b].
DENNING (variously, DENNINGS), Robert - purchased Lot 72 in the Town of Clarksville from William Polk, Sept. 15, 1786 (Tennessee Co. in 1788; then Montgomery Co.): [ref. 18a]. 1787 Davidson Co. tax roll with 1 taxable: [ref. 18b].
DENTON, John - signer of the Cumberland Compact, May, 1780: [ref. 18c].
DENTON, ____ - son of Joseph Denton, was killed by Indians during their attack on Brown's Station in 1788: [ref. 19].
DENTON, Jonathan - participated in the attack on Coldwater, and Indian town near Muscle Shoals, in 1789: [ref. 20].
DENTON, Joseph - signer of the Cumberland Compact, May, 1780: [ref. 21]. His son was killed by Indians (see above).

DESHA (variously, DeSHEA), Robert - summoned from Sumner Co. for jury duty on the Superior Court of Law and Equity meeting in Nashville, Nov. 1788, and was subsequently fined for failing to appear: [ref. 22].

DESON - see DEASON.

DESTOW, Christian - was shot opposite his heart and killed instantly on the 26th day of Sept. 1790. "The wound was of the breath of half an inch and depth of 4 inches." John Aherrin was charged with his murder, but was acquitted: [ref. 23].

DEVER, Jno. - purchased land in 1790, on the upper fork of Marrowbone Creek: [ref. 24].

DICKINSON, Henry - land sold by his heir, Mason Dickinson, in 1789, on Big Cedar Creek (possibly, Sumner Co. at the time; then Wilson Co.): [ref. 25].

DICKINSON, John - purchased land on White's Creek from heirs of Thomas Morrow in 1790, and in August, 1790, purchased land on Flynn's Creek (possibly, Sumner, then Smith, then Jackson Cos.): [ref. 26].

DICKINSON, Mason - heir of Henry Dickinson; see above.

DILLON, John - (heirs of) sold land in 1790, on White's Creek: [ref. 27].

DOBBINS (variously, DOBINS), William - purchased land of James Allen: [ref. 28a]. Purchased land on White's Creek, 1789: [ref. 28b].

DOCKERTY, Robert - signer of the Cumberland Compact, May 1780: [ref. 29].

DODGE (variously, DOGE), John - plaintiff in case vs. Anthony Crutcher before the Superior Court of Law and Equity, 28 Oct. 1788: [ref. 30].

DODGE, Richard - signer of the Cumberland Compact, May, 1780. 1787 Davidson Co. tax roll with 1 taxable.

DONALDSON, Jacob - 1787 Davidson Co. tax roll with 1 taxable: [ref. 31].

DONALDSON, James - came to the Cumberland Settlements from Natchez in 1783: [ref. 32a]. 1787 Davidson Co. tax roll with 3 taxables: [ref. 32b]. James Donaldson, "late of Davidson County, North Carolina, was tried and acquitted in November, 1788, for the robbery of 2 swivel guns (small cannon) from a boat on the Mississippi River, belonging to Peter Tardivo and Isreal Todd, the alleged robbery having occurred on the 29th day of December, 1784: [ref. 32c]. Inventory of the estate delivered to Court, July, 1796, by James Hamilton, Administrator: [ref. 32d].

DONELSON, Col. John, Sr. - D.A.R. membership on this line. He led the river flotilla to the Cumberland Settlements, arriving April 24, 1780: [ref. 33a]. Subsequently built a fort at the Clover Bottom at Stone's River: [ref. 33b]. Signer of the Cumberland Compact, May, 1780: [ref. 33c].

(continued next page)

DONELSON, Col. John, Sr. - (continued)

    Following Indian atrocities in the area, Donelson removed
with his in-laws to Kentucky in 1781 or 1782, settling
at Davies Station in Lincoln Co., near Whitley's Station,
in which resided James and Samuel Davies. In 1782, he
was a commissioner to treat with the Indians, and attended
the Treaty at Nashville. In the fall of 1785, he and his
family moved back to the Cumberland Settlements, and he
went to the Big Bend of the Tennessee River as a Georgia
commissioner. The next spring, he left the Big Bend for
home; went to the old settlement in VA to settle some
matters, then proceeded toward the Cumberland via Kentucky.
While in the company of John Telly and a man named Leach,
he was wounded in the abdomen and one of his knees, just
after passing the Big Spring. He had Leach to push in
his protruding bowels, and soon ate heartily of bread and
buffalo tongue, and died within an hour after. He was
buried near the spring: [ref. 33d]. Children: Alexander,
b. 1749; Mary, born 1751, m. Capt. John Caffery; Catherine,
b. 1752, m. Col. Thomas Hutchings; Stockley, b. 1753, m.
Mrs. Elizabeth Glasgow Martin; Jane, b. 1754, m. Col. Robert
Hays; John II, b. 7 April 1755, m. Mary Purnell; William,
b. 1758, m. Charity Dickerson; Samuel, b. 1758, m. Mary
Smith; Severn, b. 1763, m. Elizabeth Rucker; Rachel, b.
1767, m. (1st) Lewis Robards, (2nd) Andrew Jackson; Leven,
b. 1769: [ref. 33e].
DONELSON, Capt. John, Jr. (II) - son of Col. John Donelson,
    Sr., (see above), came to the Cumberland Settlements on
    the Donelson flotilla, 24 April, 1780, with his bride,
    Mary Purcell: [ref. 34a]. 1787 Davidson Co. tax roll with
    3 taxables: [ref. 34b]. Land grant: [ref. 34c].
DONELSON, Leven - see Col. John Donelson, Sr.
DONELSON, Mary - see Col. John Donelson, Sr.
DONELSON, Rachel - see Col. John Donelson, Sr.
DONELSON, Samuel - see Col. John Donelson, Sr.
DONELSON, Severn - see Col. John Donelson, Sr.
DONELSON, Stokley (Stockley) - see Col. John Donelson, Sr.
DONELSON, Leven - see Col. John Donelson, Sr.
DONELSON, William - son of Col. John Donelson, Sr., listed
    in 1787 Davidson Co. tax roll with 12 taxables: [ref. 35a].
    North Carolina land grant, April 19, 1788: [ref. 35b].
    Summoned for Davidson Co. jury duty, May, 1789: [ref. 35c].
    North Carolina Land Grant: [ref. 35d]
DONELY (variously, DONNALLY), James - North Carolina land
    grant, Sept. 24, 1787, for 274 acres on Richland Creek:
    [ref. 36a]. Purchased land on Clear Branch of the Cumberland
    River, 1790: [ref. 36b].

DOUGLAS, William - son of Edward Douglas, purchased land
in 1788, on Barton's Creek (Sumner Co. at the time, then
Wilson Co.): [ref. 37].   See Douglas family in the Sumner
Co. section of this work.
DOUGHERTY, George - purchased Lot 26 in the Town of Nashville,
Aug. 16, 1784: [ref. 38].   See, also, DAUGHTERY.
DOZER (variously, DOZIER), James - sold land between the
Stone's and Cumberland River in 1790: [ref. 39].
DRAKE, Benjamin, Sr. - came with the Heaton party to the
French Lick, arriving Dec. 24, 1779: [ref. 40a].   Signer
of the Cumberland Compact in May, 1780: [ref. 40b].   Member
of the first Grand Jury, Oct. 7, 1783: [ref. 40c].   1787
Davidson Co. tax roll with 2 taxables: [ref. 40d].
Participated in the attack on Coldwater, an Indian town
near Muscle Shoals in 1787: [ref. 40e].   Land Grants: [ref.
40f].
DRAKE, Benjamin, Jr. - 1787 Davidson Co. tax roll with 1
taxable: [ref. 41a].   Summoned for Davidson Co. jury duty,
May, 1789: [ref. 41b].
DRAKE, Elizabeth - wife of John Drake, mentioned in deed:
[ref. 42].
DRAKE, Isaac - signer of the Cumberland Compact in May, 1780:
[ref. 43].
DRAKE, John - signer of the Cumberland Compact, May, 1780:
[ref. 44a].   1787 Davidson Co. tax roll with 1 taxable:
[ref. 44b].   Wife Elizabeth mentioned in deed - North
Carolina land grant, April 17, 1788: [ref. 44c].
DRAKE, Jonathan - D.A.R. membership on this line.   Born ca.
1740 in VA; married ca. 1770: [ref. 45a].   Purchased lot
from the Trustees of the Town of Nashville: [ref. 45b].
North Carolina land grant: [ref. 45c].   Children: Robert;
and Sarah, b. 25 Jan. 1783: [ref. 45d].
DRAKE, Joseph - came to the Cumberland area in 1769 to hunt
with 20 adventurers from North Carolina, Rock Bridge in
Virginia, and the New River.   He returned with Mansker
in 1771: [ref. 46].
DRAKE, Robert - see Jonathan Drake.
DRAKE, Sarah - see Jonathan Drake.
DRAKE, Susan - was married to James Leeper in 1780, at Fort
Nashborough, being the first marriage celebrated there:
[ref. 47].
DRAKE, Susannah - wife of Benjamin Drake mentioned in deed:
[ref. 48].
DREW, John - purchased land in 1789, on Goose Creek (Sumner
Co. at the time; then Smith Co.): [ref. 49a].   Purchased
land of Jas. Bosley: [ref. 49b].
DRUMGOLD, James - father-in-law to James Cole, came to the
Cumberland Settlements in 1783: [ref. 50].

DUFFEY (variously, DUFFEE), Cornelias - plaintiff in lawsuit, Nov. 1790: [ref. 51].

DUFFLESEN, John - summoned for Davidson Co. jury duty, Nov. 1790: [ref. 52].

DUKHAM, John - signer of the Cumberland Compact, May, 1780: [ref. 53].

DUNBAR, Samuel - failed to appear as witness for the State in Court, May, 1790: [ref. 54].

DUNBAR, Thomas - summoned from Tennessee Co. for jury duty by the Superior Court of Law and Equity, in 1790: [ref. 55].

DUNCAN, D. - 1787 Davidson Co. tax roll with 1 taxable: [ref. 56].

DUNCAN, John - listed with Samuel Duncan in 1787 Davidson Co. tax roll with 2 taxables: [ref. 57].

DUNCAN, "Big John" - was with William Bowen when Bowen was trampled by a buffalo while hunting near Palmyra. Bowen's wife left him sick and took up with James Ferguson, and Bowen apparently died of malnutrition: [ref. 58].

DUNCAN, John - 1787 Davidson Co. tax roll with 1 taxable: [ref. 59].

DUNCAN, Martin - 1787 Davidson Co. tax roll with 1 taxable: [ref. 60a]. Participated in the attack on Coldwater, the Indian town near Muscle Shoals, in 1787: [ref. 60b]. Summoned from Tennessee Co. for jury duty by the Superior Court of Law and Equity, May, 1790: [ref. 60c].

DUNCAN, Samuel - listed with John Duncan on the 1787 Davidson Co. tax roll with 2 taxables: [ref. 61].

DUNCAN, William - 1787 Davidson Co. tax roll with 1 taxable: [ref. 62a]. Summoned from Tennessee Co. for jury duty by the Superior Court of Law and Equity, May, 1790: [ref. 62b].

DUNHAM, Daniel, Sr. - witness in suit (Hamilton vs. Martin) brought before the Committee of the Cumberland Association, May 6, 1783: [ref. 63a]. Killed by Indians at Dunham Station, 1 mile west of Johnston's Lick on the present site of Belle Meade Mansion, in 1787 or 1788. He was scalped and chopped, and the station destroyed: [ref. 63b].

DUNHAM, Donl - North Carolina land grant: [ref. 64].

DUNHAM, John - arrived with the Donelson flotilla, April 24, 1780: [ref. 65a]. Signer of the Cumberland Compact, May, 1780: [ref. 65b]. Elected Ensign of militia at Freeland's Station, Mar. 15, 1783: [ref. 65c]. Defendant in suit brought by David Gwin, before the Committee of the Cumberland Association, June, 1783: [ref. 65d]. Listed in the North Carolina Preemption Act of 1784, as one of the settlers on the Cumberland in 1780, who had stayed and defended the Settlements, and entitled to 640 acres without any price to be paid to the public: [ref. 65e]. Land grant: [ref. 65f].

DUNHAM, Joseph - as a small boy, escaped Indians, with his
brother William, and fled to Freeland's Station to raise
the alarm after Mr. Bernard was killed at Denton's Lick:
[ref. 66a]. He was killed by Indians where the plantation
of Mr. Irwin later stood on Richland Creek: [ref. 66b].
DUNHAM (variously DUNAM), Joseph - mentioned as heir in the
Division of the estate of Thomas Brown, deceased, filed
in Davidson Co., Jan. 1795 (bequest in right of his wife):
[ref. 67].
DUNHAM, William - with his brother, Joseph, ran to Freeland's
Station to raise the alarm when Indians killed Mr. Bernard
at Denton's Lick: [ref. 68a]. Killed by Indians where
the plantation of Mr. Irwin later stood on Richland Creek:
[ref. 68b].
DUNN, Elizabeth - married William Hudson, Oct. 15, 1789,
in Davidson Co.: [ref. 69].
DUNNAGIN, Joseph - signer of the Cumberland Compact, May,
1780: [ref. 70].
DUNNING, Robert - summoned from Tennessee Co. for jury duty
by the Superior Court of Law and Equity, in 1790: [ref.
71].
DUNOHO (variously, DONOHO, DUNIHOO), Thomas - North Carolina
land grant: [ref. 72].
DURAT (variously, DERAQUE), John - a half-breed, who helped
defend Buchanan's Station during the Indian attack of Sept.
30, 1792: [ref. 73].

E

EADER - negro, who was taken prisoner by Indians after attack
on Zeigler's Station, June 26, 1792: [ref. 74].
EATON - see HEATON.
EDGAR & TAIT - purchased land of Sanders: [ref. 75].
EDMONDSON (variously, EDMISTON, EDMESTON), Francis - daughter
of Robert Boyd (see beforementioned).
EDMONDSON, John - listed with William, Robert, and Robert
Edmiston (sic) on the 1787 Davidson Co. tax roll with 4
taxables: [ref. 76a]. Summoned for Davidson Co. jury duty,
Nov. 1788: [ref. 76b]. Purchased land of Isaac Lensey:
[ref. 76c].
EDMONDSON, Robert - 1787 Davidson Co. tax roll (see John
Edmondson). Wounded in the arm by Indians at Neeley's
Bend in 1787: [ref. 77].
EDMONDSON, Robert - 1787 Davidson Co. tax roll (see John
Edmondson). Summoned for Davidson Co. jury duty, Nov.
1788: [ref. 78].

EDMONDSON, Thomas - signer of the Cumberland Compact, May, 1780: [ref. 79a]. Land grant: [ref. 79b].
EDMONDSON, William - 1787 Davidson Co. tax roll (see John Edmondson). Land grant: [ref. 80].
ELLIOTT, ____ - 1787 Davidson Co. tax roll with 1 taxable: [ref. 81].
ELLIOTT, Falkner - 1787 Davidson Co. tax roll with 1 taxable: [ref. 82].
ELLIOTT, John - North Carolina land grant: [ref. 83].
ELLIOTT, Tilpa? - purchased land on Caleb's Creek in Tennessee County in 1790: [ref. 84].
ELLIOTT, Zebpa? - purchased land in 1790, on Spring Creek (Sumner Co. at the time; then Wilson Co.): [ref. 85].
ELLIS, Joel - wounded by Indians, June 26, 1792, at Zeigler's Station: [ref. 86].
ELLIS, William - arrived with the Donelson flotilla, April 24, 1780: [ref. 87a]. Listed in the North Carolina Preemption Act of 1784, as one of the settlers on the Cumberland in 1780, who stayed and defended the settlements and was entitled to 640 acres without any price to be paid to the public: [ref. 87b]. Plaintiff in a suit before the Superior Court of Law and Equity, Nov. 1790: [ref. 87c].
ENGLISH, Joshua - (heirs of) sold land in 1789, on Spring Creek (Sumner Co. at the time; then Wilson Co.): [ref. 88].
ERVIN (variously, ERLIN, ERSIN, IRVIN), Andrew - arrived with the Donelson flotilla, April 24, 1780: [ref. 89a]. Listed in the North Carolina Preemption Act of 1784, as one of the settlers on the Cumberland in 1780, who had stayed and defended the settlements, and who was entitled to 640 acres without any price to be paid to the public: [ref. 89b].
ESEINS, Jobe - heir of Thomas Eseins, sold land on Yellow Creek (afterwards, Tennessee Co.; then Robertson Co.): [ref. 90].
ESEINS, Thomas - see Jobe Eseins, abovementioned.
ESKRIDGE, John - participated in the attack by men from the Cumberland Settlements, on Coldwater, an Indian town near the Muscle Shoals: [ref. 91].
ESKRIDGE, Moses - participated in the attack by men from the Cumberland Settlements, on Coldwater, an Indian town near the Muscle Shoals: [ref. 92].
ESPEY, George - signer of the Cumberland Compact, May, 1780: [ref. 93a]. Killed by Indians on Drake's Creek in 1782: [ref. 93b]. Listed in the North Carolina Preemption Act of 1784, as one of the settlers on the Cumberland who died there, whose heirs or devisees were entitled to 640 acres without any price to be paid to the public: [ref. 93c].

ESPEY, James - signer of the Cumberland Compact, May, 1780:
[ref. 94a]. Defendent in a suit brought by Samuel Martin
for a debt, before the Committee of the Cumberland
Association, June, 1783: [ref. 94b]. Listed in the North
Carolina Preemption Act of 1784, as one of the settlers
on the Cumberland in 1780, who had stayed and defended
the settlements and was entitled to 640 acres without any
price to be paid to the public: [ref. 94c]. 1787 Davidson
Co. tax roll with 1 taxable: [94d]. 2 land grants: [ref.
94e].
ESPEY, John - arrived with the Donelson flotilla, April 24,
1780: [ref. 95].
ESPEY, Robert - arrived with the Donelson flotilla, April
24, 1780: [ref. 96a]. Signer of the Cumberland Compact,
May, 1780: [ref. 96b]. He was security for Samuel Barton,
entry taker, Oct. 7, 1783: [ref. 96c]. Served on the first
Grand Jury: [ref. 96d]. One source states he was killed
by Indians near Cross's Old Field, however, as the source
gives the date of death as 1780, this may have been another
of the same name: [ref. 96e].
ESTER, William - (heirs of) sold land in 1789, on Lick Creek
on the south side of the Cumberland River: [ref. 97].
ESTES, Samuel - (heirs of) sold land in 1790: [ref. 98].
EUMAN, E. - 1787 Davidson Co. tax roll with 1 taxable: [ref.
99].
EVAN, Jesse - 1787 Davidson Co. tax roll with 1 taxable:
[ref. 100].
EVANS, Maj. - commanded a battalion of troops raised for
the protection of Davidson Co. in 1787: [ref. 101].
EVANS (variously, EVINS), Evins - signer of the Cumberland
Compact, May, 1780: [102].
EVANS, John - signer of the Cumberland Compact, May, 1780:
[ref. 103a]. Listed in the North Carolina Preemption Act
of 1784, as one of the settlers on the Cumberland in 1780,
who stayed and defended the settlements, and entitled to
640 acres without any price to be paid to the public: [ref.
103b]. 1787 Davidson Co. tax roll with 1 taxable: [ref.
103c]. North Carolina land grant: [ref. 103d].
EVANS, Jonathan - signer of the Cumberland Compact, May,
1780: [ref. 104].
EVANS, Polly - married William Nash in Davidson Co., June
5, 1790: [ref. 105].
EVANS, Robert - with John Rains, Jr., captured an Indian
and brought him back to Nashville: [ref. 106].
EVANS, Thomas - land grant: [ref. 107].
EVERETT (variously, EVERITT, EVERITTE), Drusila - married
Robert Mitchell in Davidson Co., June 1, 1789: [ref. 108].
EVERETTE, James - killed by Indians, June 8, 1792, at Gowen's
place: [ref. 109].

EVERITT, John - was a farmer, who resided two miles north of the later site of the old Asylum for the Insane in Nashville. He had four daughters, the oldest of which gave the alarm when the younger three daughters were killed by Indians. He also had a son, Thomas H. Everitt: [ref. 110].
EVERITT, Thomas H. - son of John Everitt (see above).
EWING (variously, EWEN, EWIN), Alexander - D.A.R. membership on this line. Born March 10, 1752, in VA; resided in Prince George Co., VA during the Revolution. Married ca. 1788, Sarah Smith, in Cumberland Co., VA. She was born 12 Aug. 1761: [ref. 111a]. 1787 Davidson Co. tax roll with 3 taxables: [ref. 111b]. Children: William, Randel, Alexander, and Lucinda, who was born Dec. 10, 1792: [ref. 111c].
EWING, Alexander - see Alexander Ewing, Sr.
EWING, Amelia - see Alexander Ewing, Sr.
EWING, Andrew (Sr.) - D.A.R. membership on this line. Born 15 March, 1740, in Buckingham Co., VA; married Dec. 11, 1760, to Susannah Shannon, who was born Dec. 26, 1737, in Philadelphia, PA: [ref. 112a]. Signer of the Cumberland Compact, May, 1780: [ref. 112b]. He recorded his stock mark with the Committee of the Cumberland Association on Feb. 11, 1783, which was "A crop off each ear, and upper kell in each.": [ref. 112c]. Purchased a lot from the Trustees of the Town of Nashville: [ref. 112d]. 1787 Davidson Co. tax roll with 1 taxable: [ref. 112e]. Elected first clerk of the Committee of the Cumberland Association, Jan. 7, 1783: [ref. 112f]. He died 30 April, 1813, near Nashville: [ref. 112g]. His will also mentions William, Wilson Edly, and Andrew B. Ewing, sons of Edley Ewing; and Edley and Andrew Montgomery, sons of William Montgomery: [ref. 112h]. Children: Andrew, Jr., b. July 1768, m. Sarah Hickman; Margaret, b. Jan. 4, 1770, m. 1787, Andrew Castleman; William, b. 29 Nov. 1771; Amelia, b. Jan. 7, 1774, m. Moses Speer; Nathan, b. Feb. 17, 1776; and Elizabeth, b. Mar. 14, 1779, m. Thomas Shannon: [ref. 112i].
EWING, Andrew, Jr. - see Andrew Ewing, Sr.
EWING, Elizabeth - see Andrew Ewing, Sr.
EWING, John - purchased land of Tho. Hickman, Sheriff in Davidson Co.: [ref. 113].
EWING, Lucinda - see Alexander Ewing Sr.
EWING, Margaret - see Andrew Ewing, Sr.
EWING, Nathan - see Andrew Ewing, Sr.
EWING, William - see Andrew Ewing, Sr.
EWING, William - see Andrew Ewing, Sr.
EXHEART, D. - 1787 Davidson Co. tax roll with 1 taxable: [ref. 114]. (Could this be Earheart or Farhart - see David FARHART).

F

FANE, David - listed in the North Carolina Preemption Act of 1784, as one of the settlers on the Cumberland in 1780, who had died there, and whose heirs or devisees were entitled to 640 acres without any price to be paid to the public: [ref. 1].

FARHART, David - purchased land of Isaac Lensey: [ref. 2]. See D. Exheart.

FARGIN, George - (heirs of) sold land in 1788, on Mill Creek: [ref.3].

FARGIN, Jethroe - heir of George Fargin: [ref. 4].

FEELING (variously, FELIN, PHELAN, PHELIN), Samuel - trespass charges brought against him by Terrel before the Committee of the Cumberland Association were dismissed, Mar. 4, 1783: [ref. 5a]. Purchased land of Russell Gowen, April 3, 1787: [ref. 5b].

FENNER, Richard - D.A.R. membership on this line. Married Ann Geddy: [ref. 6a]. Purchased land in 1789, on Spring Creek: [ref. 6b]. North Carolina land grants: [ref. 6c]. Child: Dr. Robert Fenner: [ref. 6d].

FENNER, Robert - son of Richard Fenner, above. North Carolina land grants: [ref. 7].

FERGUS, James - North Carolina land grant: [ref. 8].

FERGUSON, James - was in hunting party with William Bowen and John Duncan: [ref. 9a]. He was afterward killed by Indians near Henry's Station, March 10, 1794: [ref. 9b].

FINALSON (variously, FINDELSTONE), George or Richard - Frenchman who helped defend Buchanan Station during the Indian attack of Sept. 30, 1792: [ref. 10a]. Another source listed his name as Richard Findelstone: [ref. 10b].

FISHER, Frederick - D.A.R. membership on this line. Born 1762, in Augusta Co., VA. Married Mary Fisher: [ref. 11a]. Purchased land on White's Creek in 1790: [ref. 11b]. Died April 24, 1846, in Marshall Co., TN. Child: Jacob Fisher, b. 1787: [ref. 11c].

FISHER, Archibald - summoned from Sumner Co. for jury duty by the Superior Court of Law and Equity, May 1790: [ref. 12].

FISHER, Jacob - see Frederick Fisher.

FLANCY, Daniel - 1787 Davidson Co. tax roll with 1 taxable: [ref. 13].

FLANRY, Daniel - North Carolina land grant: [ref. 14].

FLEMING, William - signer of the Cumberland Compact, May, 1780: [ref. 15].

FLETCHER, Thomas - signer of the Cumberland Compact, May, 1780: [ref. 16a]. Recorded his stock mark in the Minutes of the Committee of the Cumberland Association on Feb.

(continued next page)

FLETCHER, Thomas - (continued)
    11, 1783, thus: "A crop and hole in the right ear, and
an under kell in the left, and brands thus - TF.": [ref.
16b]. His sheriff's deputation cancelled, and then he
was elected Sheriff of the Cumberland District, Mar. 15,
1783, by the Committee of the Cumberland Association: [ref.
16c]. Witness in a lawsuit (Keller vs. Martin), before
the Committee of the Cumberland Association, May 6, 1783:
[ref. 16d]. According to one source, he was killed by
Indians near the mouth of the Harpeth River in April, 1787:
[ref. 16e]. Another source gives the date of his death
as 1791: [ref. 16f]. He had a son killed by Indians at
the same time: [ref. 16g].
FLETCHER, ____ - son of Thomas Fletcher; see above.
FLOOD, David - arrived with the Donelson flotilla, April
24, 1780: [ref. 17a]. Listed in the North Carolina
Preemption Act of 1784, as one of the settlers to the
Cumberland in 1780, who had stayed and defended the
settlements and was entitled to 640 acres without any price
to be paid to the public: [ref. 17b].
FLOWRON, Richard - North Carolina land grant: [ref. 18].
FLYNN, George - plaintiff vs. Israel Harman, accused of
"loosing canoe of plaintiff," before the Committee of the
Cumberland Association, April 1, 1783: [ref. 19a]. Purchased
land of the Trustees of Nashville: [ref. 19b].
FOLK, Christopher - (heirs of) sold land in 1788: [ref. 20].
FORD, Isaac - listed in 1787 Davidson Co. tax roll with Lewis
and John Ford; 3 taxables: [ref. 21].
FORD, Col. James - participated in the expedition against
the Indians at Muscle Shoals in June 1787: [ref. 22a].
Summoned from Tennessee Co. for jury duty by the Superior
Court of Law and Equity, May, 1790: [ref. 22b]. Defendant
in law-suit: [ref. 22c].
FORD, John - listed on the 1787 Davidson Co. tax roll with
Isaac and Lewis Ford; 3 taxables: [ref. 23a]. North Carolina
land grant: [ref. 23b]. Purchased land in Sumner Co. where
"Virginia line crosses Puncheon Camp Creek (afterward,
Smith Co.): [ref. 23c]. Purchased land on Mill Creek
(Davidson Co.), in 1789: [ref. 23d].
FORD, Lewis - listed with John and Isaac Ford on the 1787
Davidson Co. tax roll with 3 taxables: [ref. 24].
FORDE, John - purchased land of Jas. Bosley: [ref. 25].
FOREMAN, John - purchased lot of the Trustees of Nashville
in 1786: [ref. 26a]. North Carolina land grants: [ref.
26b].
FORT, Catherine - see Elias Fort, hereafter.
FORT, Elias, Jr. - see Elias Fort, hereafter.

FORT, Elias, Sr. - D.A.R. membership on this line. Born July, 1730, in North Carolina; married May 24, 1758, to Sarah Sugg, who was born 1738: [ref. 27a]. Purchased land in 1788, on Smith Fork of the Caney Fork River (at the time Sumner Co., then Smith Co.): [ref. 27b]. He died in Robertson Co.: [ref. 27c]. Children: William, b. June 23, 1759, m. Elizabeth Hillard; Josiah, b. Sept. 8, 1762, m. (1st) Piety Horn, (2nd) Selah Horn; Sugg, b. 1774, m. Catherine Prince; Obedience, m. Maj. David Smith; Elizabeth, m. Eppa Lawson; Ester, m. Burwell Jackson; Catherine, m. Mather Williams; Milbrey, m. William DeLocke: [ref. 27d].

FORT, Elizabeth - see Elias Fort, Sr.

FORT, Ester - see Elias Fort, Sr.

FORT, Josiah - see Elias Fort, Sr.

FORT, Milbrey - see Elias Fort, Sr.

FORT, Obedience - see Elias Fort, Sr.

FORT, Sugg - see Elias Fort, Sr.

FORT, William - see Elias Fort, Sr.

FOSTER, Anthony - D.A.R. membership on this line. Born March 13, 1741, in VA. Married 1760, in Fairfax, Culpepper Co., VA to Rose Coleman, who was born 1742: [ref. 28a]. Defender of the Western Settlements of Watauga, Holston, and Clinch: [ref. 28b]. Purchased land in Davidson Co. in 1788: [ref. 28c]. Died in Nashville, Tennessee, Nov. 3, 1816. Children: Anthony; John; Robert, b. July 18, 1769, m. Ann S. Hubbard; Thomas, Edmund, Sarah, Hannah, (daughter) m. Mr. Read; (daughter) m. Mr. Compton; (daughter) m. Mr. Ray; (daughter) m. Mr. Long: [ref. 28d].

FOSTER, Anthony - see Anthony Foster, Jr.

FOSTER, Edmund - see Anthony Foster, Jr.

FOSTER, J. - wounded by Indians about Jan. 20, 1789: [ref. 29].

FOSTER, James - arrived with the Donelson flotilla, April 24, 1780: [ref. 30a]. Signer of the Cumberland Compact, May, 1780: [ref. 30b]. Listed in the North Carolina Preemption Act of 1784, as one of the settlers on the Cumberland in 1780, who stayed and defended the settlements, and entitled to 640 acres without any price to be paid to the public: [ref. 30c]. 1787 Davidson Co. tax roll with 1 taxable: [ref. 30d]. North Carolina land grant: [ref. 30e].

FOSTER, John - see Anthony Foster, Jr.

FOSTER, Robert - see Anthony Foster, Jr.

FOSTER, Sarah - see Anthony Foster, Jr.

FOSTER, Thomas - see Anthony Foster, Jr.

FOSTER, _____ - 4 daughters of Anthony Foster, Jr. whose names are unknown at present. See father's entry above for marriage information.

FOWLER, James - listed in the North Carolina Preemption Act of 1784, as one of the settlers to the Cumberland who had died there, whose heirs or devisees were entitled to 640 acres without any price to be paid to the public: [ref. 31].

FRANCISES, George - North Carolina land grant: [ref. 32].

FRANKLIN, Isaac - see James Franklin, (Sr.).

FRANKLIN, James - see James Franklin, (Sr.).

FRANKLIN, James (Sr.) - D.A.R. membership on this line. Born 1755; married Jane Lauderdale; resided in Virginia during the Revolution: [ref. 33a]. Came to the Cumberland Settlements with the Donelson flotilla, April 24, 1780, and afterwards helped Mansker build his Station near what is now Goodlettsville, Tennessee. He made a settlement in the autumn of 1783, with James McCain, Elmore Douglass, Charles Carter, and others on the west side of Big Station Camp Creek at the upper Nashville Road crossing: [ref. 33b]. There are two James Franklins listed in the North Carolina Preemption Act of 1784; one who died in the Cumberland Settlements prior to the passage of the Act, and whose heirs were entitled to 640 acres without any price to be paid to the public; and one who stayed and defended the settlements and entitled to 640 acres without any price to be paid to the public: [ref. 33c]. It is unclear to this compiler which one is father or son. James Franklin was summoned from Sumner Co. for jury duty on the Superior Court of Law and Equity in 1788: [ref. 33d]. Children: Isaac, b. May 26, 1789; James; John; William, b. Sept 15, 1794: [ref. 33e].

FRANKLIN, John - see James Franklin (Sr.).

FRANKLIN, William - see James Franklin (Sr.).

FRAZIER, (variously, FRAZER, FRAZOR), Daniel - arrived with the Mansker party in the winter of 1779, and helped in the building of Mansker's Station near what is now Goodlettsville, Tennessee: [ref. 34a]. North Carolina land grants: [ref. 34b].

FRAZIER, George - purchased land in 1788, on Sycamore Creek (Tennessee Co. at the time; then Robertson Co.): [ref 35a]. Summoned from Tennessee Co. for jury duty on Superior Court of Law and Equity, 1789: [ref. 35b].

FRAZIER, James - summoned from Sumner Co. for jury duty on the Superior Court of Law and Equity in 1788: [ref. 36a]. Released from jury duty in Oct., 1788: [ref. 36b].

FRAZIER, John - was with a survey party on Defeated Creek in what is now Smith Co., on March 2, 1786, when attacked by Indians: [ref. 37a]. 1787 Davidson Co. tax roll with 1 taxable: [ref. 37b].

FREELANDS - sold preemption and removed to lands between Walnut Hills and Natchez: [ref. 38].

FREELAND, Capt. George - was with the Robertson party which explored the area of the French Lick in 1778-79, and was one of those left to plant corn while Robertson returned to the bring the first settlers: [ref. 39a]. He helped built Freeland's Station, a short distance west of the French Lick in late 1779. He apparently returned to the Holston River area for his family, as he is found among those on the Donelson flotilla which arrived at the French Lick, April 24, 1780: [ref. 39b]. Member of the Committee of the Cumberland Association, Jan, 1783: [ref. 39c]. He recorded his stock mark in the Minutes of the Committee of the Cumberland Association on Feb. 11, 1783, thus: "A crop off the left ear, and a swallow fork in the right, and brand thus - CF.": [ref. 39d]. Listed in the North Carolina Preemption Act of 1784, as one of the settlers to the Cumberland in 1780, who stayed and defended the settlements, and entitled to 640 acres without any price to be paid to the public: [ref. 39e]. North Carolina land grant, Feb. 27, 1788: [ref. 39f]. Received other land grants: [ref. 39g].

FREELAND, Jacob - helped build Freeland's Station, which was located a short distance west of the French Lick in 1779. He apparently returned to the Holston River area for his family, as he is found among those arriving at the French Lick with the Donelson flotilla on April 24, 1780: [ref. 40a]. Signer of the Cumberland Compact, May, 1780: [ref. 40b].

FREELAND, James - signer of the Cumberland Compact, May, 1780: [ref. 41a]. Listed in the North Carolina Preemption Act of 1784, as one of the settlers to the Cumberland in 1780, who stayed and defended the settlements, and entitled to 640 acres without any price to be paid to the public: [ref. 41b].

FREELAND, Samuel - purchased land of Russell Gowen: [ref. 42a]. 1787 Davidson Co. tax roll with 1 taxable: [ref. 42b].

FRENCH, George - killed by Indians, August 1, 1791: [ref. 43].

FRENCH, Thomas - 1787 Davidson Co. tax roll with 1 taxable: [ref. 44].

FRIZE(?), Lesois - signer of the Cumberland Compact, May, 1780: [ref. 45].

G

GAIS (variously, GUISE), Christopher, Jr. - listed along with Christopher Gais, Sr., and Jonathan Gais, in the North Carolina Preemption Act of 1784, as settlers on the Cumberland, who either had arrived in the settlements after June 1, 1780, and stayed; or, were too young to receive a preemption under the Preemption Act of 1782: [ref. 1].
GAIS, Christopher, Sr. - see Christopher Gais, Jr. [ref. 2].
GAIS, Jonathan - see Christopher Gais, Jr. [ref. 3].
GALLASPY, William - 1787 Davidson Co. tax roll with 1 taxable: [ref. 4].
GALLOWAY, John - listed in the North Carolina Preemption Act of 1784, as one of the settlers on the Cumberland who had died there, whose heirs or devisees were entitled to 640 acres of land without any price to be paid to the public: [ref. 5].
GAMBERT, Bradley - summoned for Davidson Co. jury duty, Nov. 1788: [ref. 6]. (See Bradley Gamble below - could this be the same individual?)
GAMBLE, Bradley - purchased land on the road to Holston, Nov. 1789: [ref. 7]. (See Bradley Gambert, above.)
GAMBLE, Edmon - found "not guilty" of charges brought against him before the Superior Court of Law and Equity, May, 1790: [ref. 8].
GAMBLE, Edward - purchased land in Nov. 1789, on the south side of Red River (Tennessee Co., then Montgomery Co.): [ref. 9].
GAMBLE, Elizabeth - married Richard Shaffer in Davidson Co., Oct. 21, 1789: [ref. 10].
GAMBLE, Josiah - signer of the Cumberland Compact, May, 1780: [ref. 11a]. Defendant charged with slander against Ephriam Payton, the appeal of which was abated by the death of the defendant: [ref. 11b].
GARRARD - see GERRARD.
GAUSNEW, William - listed in the North Carolina Preemption Act of 1784, as one of the settlers on the Cumberland who had died there, and whose heirs or devisees were entitled to 640 acres without any price to be paid to the public: [ref. 12].
GAUSWAY, William - listed in the North Carolina Preemption Act of 1784, as one of the settlers on the Cumberland who had died there, and whose heirs or devisees were entitled to 640 acres without any price to be paid to the public: [ref. 13].
GEE, Capt. John - purchased land in 1788, on Caney Fork River (Sumner co. at the time; then, Smith County): [ref. 14].

GEE, Jonathan - sent on a scout with Clayton Powell from Buchanan's Station, Sept. 29, 1792, and was killed by Indians on Taylor's Trace: [ref. 15].

GEIOCH, William - signer of the Cumberland Compact, May, 1790: [ref. 16].

GENTRY, John - 1787 Davidson Co. tax roll with 1 taxable: [ref. 17].

GENTRY, Nicholas - listed in the North Carolina Preemption Act of 1784, as one of the settlers on the Cumberland who had died there, and whose heirs or deivsees were entitled to 640 acres without any price being paid to the public: [ref. 18].

GENTRY, Randal - killed by Indians in April, 1787: [ref. 19].

GETER, Argolas (variously, Archilas) - purchased land of Jonathan Drake: [ref. 20a]. 1787 Davidson Co. tax roll with 1 taxable: [ref. 20b].

GERRARD (variously, GARRARD), Charles - North Carolina land grant: [ref. 21a]. Purchased land in 1788, on Round Lick Creek (Sumner Co. at the time; then Wilson or Smith Co.): [ref. 21b].

GERVIN, David - listed in the North Carolina Preemption Act of 1784, as one of the settlers on the Cumberland who had died there, and whose heirs or devisees were entitled to 640 acres without any price to be paid to the public: [ref. 22].

GIBSON, Gad (Gadi) - summoned from Tennessee Co. for jury duty on the Superior Court of Law and Equity, May, 1790, but was fined for failing to appear: [ref. 23].

GIBSON, John - arrived with the Donelson flotilla, April 24, 1780: [ref. 24a]. Signer of the Cumberland Compact, May, 1780: [ref: 24b]. Defendant in lawsuit brought by Julius Sanders over gambling debt before the Committee of the Cumberland Association, May 6, 1783: [ref. 24c]. Listed in the North Carolina Preemption Act of 1784, as one of the settlers on the Cumberland in 1780, who stayed and defended the settlements, and entitled to 640 acres without any price to be paid to the public: [ref. 24d]. 1787 Davidson Co. tax roll with 1 taxable: [ref. 24e]. Purchased land of the Trustees of Nashville: [ref. 24f]. Summoned from Tennessee Co. for jury duty on the Superior Court of Law and Equity, May, 1789: [ref. 24g]. He was killed by Indians near Nashville, June 14, 1791: [ref. 24h]. His heirs sold his land in 1790?, on Blooming Creek (Tennessee Co. at the time; then Montgomery Co.): [ref. 24i]. (Note the discrepancy in date of death and date heirs sold land.)

GIBSON, Jourdan - mentioned in lawsuit (Jas. McCain vs. Wm. Graham) before the Committtee of the Cumberland Association, 1 April, 1783: [ref. 25]. (See also, Sumner Co. section)

GIBSON, W. - came to the Cumberland Settlements in 1786, and settled at Bledsoe's Lick (afterward, Sumner Co.): [ref. 26].

GILBERT, John - purchased land in 1788, on Red River (Tennessee Co. after Nov. 1788): [ref. 27].

GILKEY, John - listed in the North Carolina Preemption Act of 1784, as one of the settlers on the Cumberland who had died there, whose heirs or devisees were entitled to 640 acres without any price to be paid to the public: [ref. 28a]. Will probated, Dec. 12, 1796, mentions that he was a resident "of Fort Nash and province of North Carolina.."; bequeaths to wife all of the estate of her first husband lands in (Redford?) Co., NC; mentions her children by her first husband, and his sons Robert Gilkey and Samuel Gilkey: [ref. 28b].

GILKEY, Robert - sickened and died in 1780; was the first settler to die a natural death: [ref. 29a]. His slave was fired upon by Indians in 1780: [ref. 29b].

GILL, Peter - killed by Indians at the Battle of the Bluffs, April 2, 1781: [ref. 30].

GILLESPY (variously, GILLASPY), George - purchased land in 1790, on Barton's Creek (Sumner Co. at the time; afterwards, Wilson Co.): [ref. 31].

GILLESPIE, William - summoned for Davidson Co. jury duty, Nov. 1788: [ref. 32a]. Received 2 land grants: [ref. 32b].

GILLILAND, Hugh - 1787 Davidson Co. tax roll with 2 taxables: [ref. 33].

GILMORE, Charles - purchased land in 1789, on the south side of Sycamore Creek: [ref. 34].

GIVENS, James - signer of the Cumberland Compact, May, 1780: [ref. 35].

GIVENS, Robert - signer of the Cumberland Compact, May, 1780: [ref. 36].

GLASGOW, Col. James - "of County Dobbs, North Carolina," received North Carolina land grant in 1787, and three additional grants: [ref. 37].

GLASGOW, Hon. James - purchased land in 1788, on Caney Fork River (Sumner Co, then Smith Co.): [ref. 38].

GLASS, Roger - shot through the thigh by Indians in 1783: [ref. 39].

GLAZE, Michael - summoned for jury duty on the Superior Court of Law and Equity, Nov. 1788: [ref. 40].

GLEAVES, Michael - 1787 Davidson Co. tax roll with 1 taxable: [ref. 41a]. Fined for failure to appear for jury duty by the Superior Court of Law and Equity, Nov. 1788: [ref. 41b]. Purchased land of L. Steel: [ref. 41c].

GLOSTER, Thomas - purchased land in 1789, on Sulphur Fork of Red River (then Tennessee Co., afterward, Robertson Co.): [ref. 42].

GODFREY, William - purchased land in 1790, on Flynn's Creek (Sumner Co. at the time, then Smith, then Jackson Cos.): [ref. 43].

GOINS (variously, GOIN, GOINGS), David - killed by Indians at Mansker's Station in 1780/81. He had slept late on the morning Mansker's Station was broken up and was shot in bed by Indians shooting through the portholes: [ref. 44a]. William Goings (sic) was granted administration of his estate by the Committee of the Cumberland Association, Mar. 4, 1783: [ref. 44b]

GOINS, William - administrator of the estate of David Goins, deceased (see above).

GOODLOE, Robert - signer of the Cumberland Compact, May, 1780: [ref. 45].

GOODWIN, Nathan - purchased land in 1788, on Caney Fork River (Sumner Co. as of Nov. 1788; afterwards, Smith Co.): [ref. 46].

GORDAN, Charles - 1789 Davidson Co. tax roll: [ref. 47].

GORDAN, Thomas - was with the Mansker party taking goods by boat to sell at Fort Natchez in 1769/70: [ref. 48].

GOWEN, William - signer of the Cumberland Compact, May, 1780: [ref. 49a]. Plaintiff in lawsuit against John Gibson concerning cattle belonging to the estate of David Gower, deceased, before the Committee of the Cumberland Association, July 1, 1783: [ref. 49b]. Member of the first Grand Jury, Oct. 7, 1783: [ref. 49c]. North Carolina land grant: [ref. 49d].

GOWER, Abel, Jr. - killed by Indians on the Cumberland River near Clover Bottom, while bringing harvested crops grown in the fields there: [ref. 50a]. Listed in the North Carolina Preemption Act of 1784, whose heirs or devisees were entitled to 640 acres without any price to be paid to the public: [ref. 50b].

GOWER, Abel, Sr. - arrived with the Donelson flotilla, April 24, 1780: [ref. 51]. killed by Indians at the same time as his son, Abel Gower, Jr. above.

GOWER, Elijah - married Prudence Coon in Davidson Co., 22 Dec. 1790: [ref. 52a]. Estate inventory recorded Oct. 1795, in Davidson Co.: [ref. 52b].

GOWER, Engley - married Thomas Russell in Davidson Co., Nov. 13, 1780: [ref. 53].

GOWER, Nancy - daughter of Abel Gower, Sr., came with her father to the Cumberland Settlement aboard the Donelson flotilla, April 24, 1780: [ref. 54].

GOWER, Russell - arrived with the Donelson flotilla, April 24, 1780: [ref. 55a]. Signer of the Cumberland Compact, May, 1780: [ref. 55b]. Witness for the plaintiff (Sanders vs. Thompson), before the Committee of the Cumberland Association, May 6, 1783: [ref. 55c]. Purchased a lot in the Town of Nashville: [ref. 55d].

GRACE, James - (heirs of) sold land in 1790, on Barton's Creek (Sumner Co. at the time, then Wilson Co.): [ref. 56].
GRAGG, Samuel - purchased land, Nov. 2, 1789, on Persimmon Branch: [ref. 57].
GRAHAM (variously, GRAHAMS), William - defendant in a lawsuit brought by James Graham against him for the recovery of a bed, heard before the Committee of the Cumberland Association, April 1, 1783: [ref. 58a]. North Carolina land grant: [ref. 58b].
GRAMER, John - 1787 Davidson Co. tax roll with 1 taxable: [ref. 59].
GRANT, Squire - 1787 Davidson Co. tax roll with 4 taxables: [ref. 60].
GRAY, James - heir of John Gray (see below).
GRAY, John - his heirs, James and Joseph Gray sold his land in 1789, on Spring Creek (Sumner Co. at the time, then Wilson Co.): [ref. 61a]. The heirs sold in 1790, his land between Blooming Grove Creek and the Cumberland River (Tennessee Co. at the time; then Montgomery Co.): [Ref. 61b].
GRAY, Joseph - heir of John Gray (see above).
GRAY, Randolph - (heirs of) sold land in 1790, on the West Fork of Red River (Tennessee Co. at the time; then Montgomery Co.): [ref. 62].
GREEN, George - signer of the Cumberland Compact, May, 1780: [ref. 63].
GREEN, James - signer of the Cumberland Compact, May, 1780: [ref. 64].
GREEN, Jonathan - signer of the Cumberland Compact, May, 1780: [ref. 65].
GREEN, Lewis - resided in Washington Co., NC on the Clinch River. On the way to the Cumberland Settlements, he sickened and died at a camp called Blue Springs, ca. November, 1783. His nuncupative will given to the Court by his daughter, Sarah, on 7 April, 1785. He requested bequests be given to his children: Zachariah Green; Mary, the wife of Matthew Payne; and Sarah, the wife of Josiah Payne. He said there were several married children who had moved away: [ref. 66].
GREEN, Mary - daughter of Lewis Green and wife of Matthew Payne (see father's sketch).
GREEN, Sarah - daughter of Lewis Green and wife of Josiah Payne (see her father's sketch).
GREEN, Thos. - summoned for Davidson Co. jury duty in 1788: [ref. 67a]. Purchased land from Thomas Hickman, Sheriff: [ref. 67b].

GREEN, William - signer of the Cumberland Compact, May, 1780:
[ref. 68a]. Listed in the North Carolina Preemption Act
of 1784, as one of the settlers on the Cumberland who had
died there, and whose heirs were entitled to 640 acres
without any price to be paid to the public: [ref. 68b].

GREEN, William - purchased land, Oct. 1, 1789, on the Sulphur
Fork of Red River (Tennessee Co. at the time; then Robertson
Co.): [ref. 69].

GREEN, Zachariah - son of Lewis Green (see beforementioned).

GREER, James West - North Carolina land grant: [ref. 70].

GREER, Zachariah - signer of the Cumberland Compact, May,
1780: [ref. 71].

GRIGG, Samuel - summoned from Sumner Co. for jury duty on
the Superior Court of Law and Equity, Nov. 1790: [ref.
72].

GRIMES, Perley - signer of the Cumberland Compact, May, 1780:
[ref. 73].

GROSS , Richard - signer of the Cumberland Compact, May,
1780: [ref. 74].

GUBBINS, William - North Carolina land grants: [ref. 75].

GUFFY, Alexander - listed with Henry Guffy on the 1787 Davidson
Co. tax roll with 2 taxables: [ref. 76]

GUFFY, Henry - listed with Alexander Guffy on the 1787 Davidson
Co. tax roll (see beforementioned).

GUICE (variously, GUISE, GAIS), Jacob - married Elizabeth
Bickley in Davidson Co. on Feb. 2, 1789: [ref. 77].

GUTHRIE, Henry - D.A.R. membership on this line. Born 10
Dec. 1754, in Hanover, VA: [ref. 78a]. Signer of the
Cumberland Compact, May, 1780: [ref. 78b]. He did not
marry until 1796: [ref. 78c].

GWNS (sic), Edward - purchased land in 1788, on Barton's
Creek (Sumner Co. after Nov. 1788; then Wilson Co.): [ref.
79].

GWIN, David - brought suit against John Dunam for detaining
a bed, before the Committee of the Cumberland Association,
Mar. 4, 1784: [ref. 80].

H

HACKSAW, James - (heirs of) sold land in 1789, on Madeson
Creek : [ref. 1].

HADLEY, Capt. - brought a company of soldiers to the Cumberland
Settlements in 1787, which became part of Evan's Battalion,
and remained 2 years. Among the Company was Valentine
Sevier: [ref. 2].

HADLEY, Joshua - D.A.R. membership on this line. Born July 13, 1753, in Fayetteville, NC; m. 1786, to Hannah Holmes, who was born 1768, the daughter of Gov. Holmes of VA. He died 8 Feb. 1830, in Williamson Co., TN: [ref. 3a]. North Carolina land grants: [ref. 3b]. Children: William, born 1787; (several children born after 1790).

HADLEY, William - see Joshua Hadley.

HADSOCK, Josiah - (heirs of) sold land in 1789, which bordered the corner of Hardy Murfree's land: [ref. 4].

HAGGARD, James - killed by Indians during their attack on Brown's Station in 1788: [ref. 5].

HAGGARD, Mrs. James - killed by Indians at the same time as her husband; see above.

HAGGARD, John - summoned from Tennessee Co. for jury duty on the Superior Court of Law and Equity, Nov. 1790: [ref. 6].

HAGGARD, John - killed by Indians at Brown's Station in 1788: [ref. 7a]. Supplemental inventory of estate sale filed in Davidson Co., July 1794: [ref. 7b].

HAQUE - erected a cotton machine on Mill Creek, at which some persons were killed by Indians: [ref. 8].

HAINEY, Bartnet - signer of the Cumberland Compact, May, 1780: [ref. 9].

HAINEY, Robert - signer of the Cumberland Compact, May, 1780: [ref. 10].

HAINEY, Thomas - listed in the North Carolina Preemption Act of 1784, as one of the settlers on the Cumberland who died there, and whose heirs were entitled to 640 acres without any price to be paid to the public: [ref. 11].

HAIR, David - (heirs of) sold land in 1788, located on the north side of the Cumberland River: [ref. 12].

HALL, James - 1787 Davidson Co. tax roll with 1 taxable: [ref. 13a]. Killed by Indians after Jan. 1, 1787: [ref. 13b].

HALL, Richard - killed by Indians after Jan. 1, 1787: [ref. 15].

HALL, William - signer of the Cumberland Compact, May, 1780: [ref. 16].

HALL, William - came to the Cumberland Settlements in 1786, and settled at Bledsoe's Lick: [ref. 17a]. Killed by Indians near the locust land about Bledsoe's Lick in 1787: [ref. 17b].

HAMBLETON, Thomas - purchased land in 1789, on Drake's Creek (Sumner Co. at the time): [ref. 18].

HAMILTON, Elijah - purchased land of P. Lockett: [ref. 19].

HAMILTON, George - wounded by Indians in Feb., 1788, during their attack on Bledsoe's Station: [ref. 20].

HAMILTON, James - signer of the Cumberland Compact, May, 1780: [ref. 21].

HAMILTON, John - plaintiff in lawsuit against Samuel Martin for breach of contract concerning land improvement, heard before the Committee of the Cumberland Association, May 5, 1783: [ref. 22a]. Also, plantiff on behalf of his daughter, Elonar Hamilton, against Mr. & Mrs. Isaac Bledsoe, Mr. & Mrs. James McCain, and Mr. & Mrs. James Lynn, for slander and defamation, heard before the Committee of the Cumberland Association, July 1, 1783: [ref. 22b]. Released as juror, Oct. 1788: [ref. 22c]. Summoned from Sumner Co. for jury duty on the Superior Court of Law and Equity, Nov. 1788: [ref. 22d].

HAMILTON, Thomas - purchased land on the south side of the Cumberland River in 1788: [ref. 23a]. Summoned from Sumner Co. for jury duty on the Superior Court of Law and Equity meeting in Nashville in 1788: [ref. 23b].

HAMILTON, William - purchased a lot on the Town of Nashville, July 30, 1785: [ref. 24].

HAMPTON & HAY - purchased land of Bushnell & Dobbins: [ref. 25].

HAMPTON, Adam - 1787 Davidson Co. tax roll with 3 taxables: [ref. 26a]. Summoned for Davidson Co. jury duty, Nov. 1788: [ref. 26b]. North Carolina land grants: [ref. 26c].

HAMPTON, Thomas - defendant in lawsuit brought by John Irvin, which was continued, Nov. 1790: [ref. 27a]. Plaintiff in court against John Boyd and James Foster for trespass and assault, Nov. 1790. Defendants found not guilty: [ref. 27b].

HANCOCK, Isham - purchased land Nov. 1788, on the Caney Fork River (Sumner Co. at the time; then Smith Co.): [ref. 28].

HAND, Levi - purchased lot in the Town of Nashville: [ref. 29].

HANDLEY, Samuel - 1787 Davidson Co. tax roll with 1 taxable: [ref. 30a]. North Carolina land grant: [ref. 30b].

HANKINS, Josiah - helped Thomas Kilgore build his station: [ref. 31].

HANLEY, James - was with James Robertson in early 1779, on his first trip to the French Lick area: [ref. 32a]. He was the only one of Robertson's party, who hadn't settled in (the Cumberland Settlements) by 1780: [ref. 32b].

HANNA, John - purchased land in 1790, on Flynn's Creek (Sumner Co. at the time; then Smith; then Jackson Cos.): [ref. 33].

HANNAH, Jos. - 1787 Davidson Co. tax roll with 2 taxables: [ref. 34].

HANSELL, Charles - (heirs of) sold land on Mill Creek in 1790: [ref. 35].

HARAMOR?, Elizabeth - was the married daughter of Jonathan Jennings (see his sketch).

HARDEMAN, _____ - first appeared as a tax payer in Davidson
   Co. in 1788: [ref. 36].
HARDEMAN, Baily - see Thomas Hardeman.
HARDEMAN, Blackston - see Thomas Hardeman.
HARDEMAN, Constant - see Thomas Hardeman.
HARDEMAN, Dorothy - see Thomas Hardeman.
HARDEMAN, Eleazor - see Thomas Hardeman.
HARDEMAN, Elizabeth - see Thomas Hardeman.
HARDEMAN, Franklin - see Thomas Hardeman.
HARDEMAN, John - see Thomas Hardeman.
HARDEMAN, Lewis - see Thomas Hardeman.
HARDEMAN, Nancy - see Thomas Hardeman.
HARDEMAN, Nicholas - see Thomas Hardeman.
HARDEMAN, Peter - see Thomas Hardeman.
HARDEMAN, Pitt - see Thomas Hardeman.
HARDEMAN, Susannah - see Thomas Hardeman.
HARDEMAN, Thomas - see Thomas Hardeman.
HARDEMAN, Thomas - D.A.R. membership on this line. Born
   Jan. 8, 1750, in Albemarle Co., VA. Married (1st) Mary
   Perkins, who was born Aug. 10, 1754, in Henry Cove, VA.
   Lived in Washington Co., NC during the Revolution. Married
   (2nd) in 1799, Susan Perkins: [ref. 37a]. North Carolina
   land grant: [ref. 37b]. He died June 4, 1835, in Davidson
   Co., TN: [ref. 37c]. Children: Nicholas; Nancy, b. 1774;
   John; Constant, b. Jan. 3, 1778; Eleazor, b. Dec. 1, 1779;
   Thomas; Dorothy, b. May 15, 1786; Baily; Susannah, died
   young; Peter; Elizabeth; Franklin; Pitt; and Blackston,
   b. Mar. 24, 1790: [ref. 37d].
HARDIN (variously, HARDON), B. - 1787 Davidson Co. tax roll
   with 1 taxable: [ref. 38].
HARDIN, Henry - signer of the Cumberland Compact, May, 1780:
   [ref. 39].
HARDIN, Martin (variously, Martain) - signer of the Cumberland
   Compact, May, 1780: [ref. 40a]. 1787 Davidson Co. tax
   roll with 1 taxable: [ref. 40b].
HARDIN, John - summoned from Sumner Co. for jury duty on
   the Superior Court of Law and Equity, meeting in Nashville,
   Nov. 1788: [ref. 41a]. Excused as juror in Nov. 1788:
   [ref. 41b]. Kept the records of the Superior Court of
   Law and Equity, May term, 1789: [ref. 41c]. Purchased
   land in 1790, on Spencer's Creek (Sumner Co. at the time;
   then Wilson Co.): [ref. 41d].
HARGET, Frederick - purchased land on the East Fork of Stone's
   River in 1788: [ref. 42a]. North Carolina land grant:
   [ref. 42b].
HARGROVE, William - North Carolina land grant: [ref. 43].
HARLEY, Joseph - purchased land in 1788, on Collin's River
   (Sumner Co. from Nov. 1788; then Smith; then Jackson or
   Overton; then White Cos.): [ref. 44].

HARLIN (variously, HARLAN), Joshua - married Mary Smith in
Davidson Co., Nov. 17, 1789: [ref. 45].
HARLIN, Silas - signer of the Cumberland Compact, May, 1780:
[ref. 46].
HARMAN, Israel - sued by Geo. Flynn, April 1, 1783, before
the Committee of the Cumberland Association, for "loosing
of a canoe, property of the plaintiff." The commitee found
for the plaintiff in damages of 40 shillings, 9 pence:
[ref. 47].
HARMON (variously, HARMAND), Anthony - 1787 Davidson Co.
tax roll with 1 taxable: [ref. 48a]. Filed suit against
Russell Gower before the Superior Court of Law and Equity,
Nov. 1788: [ref. 48b].
HARNEY, Thomas - listed in the North Carolina Preemption
Act of 1784, as one of the settlers on the Cumberland who
died there, and whose heirs were entitled to 640 acres
without any price to be paid to the public: [ref. 49].
HARPER, Robert - purchased land, Dec. 21, 1789, on Madeson
Creek: [ref. 50].
HARRELL, Peter - purchased land in 1790, on the West Fork
of Red River (Tennessee Co. at the time; then Montgomery
Co.): [ref. 51].
HARRINGTON, Abijah - married Sarah Marrs in Davidson Co.
on Nov. 19, 1789: [ref. 52].
HARRIS, James - arrived with the Donelson flotilla, April
24, 1780: [ref. 53a]. Defense witness in case (Freeland
vs. Deson), heard before the Committee of the Cumberland
Association, July 1, 1783: [ref. 53b]. Listed in the North
Carolina Preemption Act of 1784, as one of the settlers
on the Cumberland in 1780, who had stayed and defended
the settlements and entitled to 640 acres without any price
to be paid to the public: [ref. 53c]. 1787 Davidson Co.
tax roll with 1 taxable: [ref. 53d].
HARRIS, John (Sr.) - defendant in court case before the
Committee of the Cumberland Association, April 1, 1783,
accused of killing a mare belonging to William Loggans
by the felling of a tree: [ref. 54a]. He was also accused
by Frederick Stump of killing his mare by the felling of
a tree before the beforementioned Committee during the
same session: [ref. 54b]. Defendant in lawsuit brought
by Ruben Messeeker before the beforementioned Committee,
Aug. 5, 1783: [ref. 54c]. Received NC land grant: [ref.
54d]. Killed by Solomon White on 13 June, 1786, who hit
him on the head with a cutting pole "inflicting a mortal
wound of the depth of 1/4 inch," and John Harris "died
instantly." Solomon White was convicted of manslaughter:
[ref. 54e].
HARRISON, James - came to the settlements in 1786, and settled
at Bledsoe's Lick (afterwards, Sumner Co.): [ref. 55].
HARRISON, Reuben, Jr. - called "grey-headed"; arrived with
the Donelson flotilla, Apr. 24, 1780: [ref. 56].

HARRISON, Reuben, Jr. - arrived with the Donelson flotilla, April 24, 1780: [ref. 57].

HARRISON, Thomas - (heirs of) sold land on Mill Creek in 1790: [ref. 58].

HARROD, Barnard - 1787 Davidson Co. tax roll with 1 taxable: [ref. 59].

HARROD, Barnet - witness for the plaintiff (Daniel Hogan vs. Obediah Terrell) heard before the Committee for the Cumberland Association, May 6, 1783: [ref. 60].

HARROD, James - may have been the same James Harrod who came to the Cumberland from Illinois to hunt with Michael Stoner in 1767: [ref. 61a]. Signer of the Cumberland Compact, May, 1780: [ref. 61b]. Daniel Hogan was granted the administration of James Harrod's estate by the Committee of the Cumberland Association, Mar. 4, 1783. Hogan was husband of Harrod's widow: [ref. 61c].

HARROLD, Robert - 1787 Davidson Co. tax roll with 1 taxable: [ref. 62].

HARRY, ____ killed by Indians, June 29, 1791, on Red River (Tennessee Co., then either Montgomery or Robertson Co.): [ref. 63].

HARRY, ____ - killed by Indians, July 18, 1791, in Sumner Co.: [ref. 64].

HART, Anthony - purchased land in 1790, on Sycamore Creek: [ref. 65a]. North Carolina land grants: [ref. 65b]. Will proved, May 25, 1795, in Davidson Co. mentions wife Susannah; and children - William and Susannah Martin Hart: [ref. 65c].

HART, John - (heirs of) sold land in 1788, on Leaper's Fork (Davidson; afterwards, Williamson Co.): [ref. 66].

HART, Nathaniel - signer of the Cumberland Compact, May, 1780: [ref. 67]. (See also, Simpson Hart, p. 156.)

HAUSKINS, Josiah - from Kilgore's Fort; was killed by Indians: [ref. 68].

HAW, Daniel - North Carolina land grant: [ref. 69].

HAWLEY, William - (heirs of) sold land on Sycamore Creek of the Cumberland River in 1789: [ref. 70].

HAWTHORNE, Noah - signer of the Cumberland Compact, May, 1780: [ref. 71].

HAY, David - commanded group of the settlement men, going by water on the punitive expedition against the Indian town, Coldwater. The party were ambushed while enroute by Indians: [ref. 72a]. 1787 Davidson Co. tax roll with 3 taxables: [ref. 72b].

HAY, Joseph - killed by Indians on Lick Branch near the Sulphur Springs in 1780: [ref. 73a]. Listed in the North Carolina Preemption Act of 1784, as one of the settlers on the Cumberland who had died there, and whose heirs were entitled to 640 acres without any price to be paid to the public: [ref. 73b].

HAYBERT, Samuel - North Carolina land grant: [ref. 74].
HAYES, James - "late of Sumner Co.," was accused of stealing
the horse of Phillip Shackler, May, 1789: [ref. 75].
HAYES, Nancy - married Robert White in Davidson Co., Jan.
7, 1789: [ref. 76].
HAYES, Nathaniel - signer of the Cumberland Compact, May,
1780: [ref. 77].
HAYES, Samuel - signer of the Cumberland Compact, May, 1780:
[ref. 78].
HAYS, Elizabeth - see Robert Hayes.
HAYS, Hugh - North Carolina land grant: [ref. 79].
HAYES, John - summoned for Davidson Co. jury duty on the
Superior Court of Law and Equity, Nov. 1790: [ref. 80].
HAYS, Narcissa - see Robert Hays.
HAYS, Patsy - see Robert Hays.
HAYS, Rachel - see Robert Hays.
HAYS, Robert - D.A.R. membership on this line. Born ca.
1758 in NC; married Jane Donelson in Davidson Co., Jan.
27, 1786: [ref. 81a]. Purchased land from Anthony Crutcher,
6 Jan. 1785: [ref. 81b]. 1787 Davidson Co. tax roll with
4 taxables: [ref. 81c]. Received North Carolina land grants:
[ref. 81d]. In June, 1787, he participated in punitive
expedition against Indians at Coldwater, an Indian town
near Muscle Shoals: [ref. 81e]. He died prior to Sept.
18, 1819, at Hayesboro, Tennessee: [ref. 81f]. Children:
Stokely, b. 1788; Samuel; Patsy; Elizabeth; Narcissa; and
Rachel: [ref. 81g].
HAYS, Samuel - son of Robert Hays; established a Station
on Stone's River in 1783: [ref. 82a]. North Carolina land
grant: [ref. 82b]. Summoned from Sumner Co. as a juror
on the Superior Court of Law and Equity, meeting in
Nashville, Nov., 1788: [ref. 82c]. Fined for not attending
as juror by the same Court, Nov. 1788: [ref. 82d]. Inventory
of his estate filed with the Court in Davidson Co., Aug.
25, 1794, by Elizabeth Hayes, "relic" : [ref. 82e]. Estate
division recorded in Davidson Co., Mar. 29, 1795. Andrew
Jackson, Esq. was appointed "Special Guardian" of "Legattees
and Mrs. Hays, widow.": [ref. 82f].
HAYS, Stokely - see Robert Hays.
HAYS, William - killed by Indians in Davidson or Sumner Co.
after Jan. 1, 1787: [ref. 83].
HEATON, Amos - built his Station on the north side of the
Cumberland River, 1779/80: [ref. 84a]. Listed in the North
Carolina Preemption Act of 1784, as one of the settlers
on the Cumberland River in 1780, who stayed and defended
the settlements, and who was entitled to 640 acres without
any price to be paid to the public: [ref. 84b]. North
Carolina land grant: [ref. 84c]. 1787 Davidson Co. tax
roll with Robert Heaton, listing 5 taxables: [ref. 84d].

(continued next page)

HEATON, Amos - (continued)

Will proved in Davidson Co., Mar. 4, 1795; mentions his
wife Elizabeth and children: Robert; Enoch; Thomas;
Elizabeth, m. Cain; Polly; and Sally: [ref. 84e].
HEATON, Enoch - son of Amos Heaton; married Ruth Topp in
Davidson Co., Oct. 20, 1789: [ref. 85].
HEATON, Elizabeth - see Amos Heaton.
HEATON, Polly - see Amos Heaton.
HEATON, Robert - son of Amos Heaton; listed on 1787 Davidson
Co. tax roll with Amos Heaton and 5 taxables: [ref. 86a].
North Carolina land grant: [ref. 86b].
HEATON, Sally - see Amos Heaton.
HEATON, Thomas - see Amos Heaton.
HENDERSON, James - Morgan Henderson, heir of James Henderson,
sold his land in 1789, on Barren River on the east side
of the Cumberland River (ref. 87].
HENDERSON, John - North Carolina land grants: [ref. 88].
HENDERSON, Morgan - heir of James Henderson (see above).
HENDERSON, Nathaniel - signer of the Cumberland Compact,
May, 1780: [ref. 89]
HENDERSON, Pleasant - signer of the Cumberland Compact,
May, 1780: [ref. 90].
HENDERSON, Richard - signer of the Cumberland Compact, May,
1780: [ref. 91].
HENDRICKS, Joseph - shot and had his arm broken by Indians
at the Battle of the Bluffs, April 2, 1781: [ref. 92a].
Wounded with broken arm by Indians, while in the company
of John Tucker, returning from Freeland's Station to the
bluff in Feb. 1782: [ref. 92b].
HENDRICKS, Thomas - signer of the Cumberland Compact, May,
1780: [ref. 93a]. Acquitted of horse stealing before the
Superior Court of Law and Equity, May, 1789: [ref. 93b].
HENNIS, Ben Bury - (heirs of) sold land in 1790, on the
West Fork of Red River (Tennesee Co. at the time; then
Montgomery Co.): [ref. 94].
HENRY, ____ - summoned from Tennessee Co. for jury duty on
the Superior Court of Law and Equity meeting in Nashville,
May, 1790: [ref. 95].
HENRY, Hugh - had a boat in the Donelson flotilla which was
sunk then raised, and arrived at French Lick, April 24,
1780: [ref. 96a]. Listed with Isaac Henry on the 1787
Davidson Co. tax roll with 2 taxables: [ref. 96b].
HENRY, Isaac - listed with Hugh Henry on the 1787 Davidson
Co. tax roll with 2 taxables: [ref. 97].
HENRY, Mary - a widow, who arrived with her family aboard
the Donelson flotilla, April 24, 1780: [ref. 98].
HENRY, Thomas - summoned for jury duty on the Superior Court
of Law and Equity, Nov. 1790: [ref. 99].

HERALD, Robert - summoned for jury duty on the Superior Court
of Law and Equity, Nov. 1790: [ref. 100].
HERD, Charles - helped defend Buchanan's Station during the
Indian attack of Sept. 30, 1792: [ref. 101].
HERN, Drewry - his heir, George Hern, sold his land in 1788,
on Barton's Creek (Sumner Co., then Wilson Co.): [ref.
102].
HERN, George - heir of Drewry Hern (see above).
HEROD, Jenny - married to John Tucker by James Shaw, Trustee,
at Fort Nashborough: [ref. 103]. (See, also, HARROD).
HERRELL, James - estate of, was administered by Daniel Hogan,
who produced inventory of estate, March 4, 1783, to the
Committee of the Cumberland Association: [ref. 104a]. Heirs
of sold land in 1790, on Barton's Creek (Sumner Co. at
the time; then Wilson Co.): [ref. 104b].
HERRINGTON, Elisha - purchased land in 1790, on Dickson (sic)
Creek (Sumner Co. at the time; then Smith Co.): [ref. 105].
HEYKANOL, Benjamin - killed by Indians June 29, 1791, near
Bledsoe's Lick (Sumner Co.): [ref. 106].
HICKMAN, _____ - 1788 Davidson Co. tax roll: [ref. 107].
HICKMAN, Charles - killed by Indians April 1, 1791, on Duck
River: [ref. 108].
HICKMAN, Edwin - purchased land with Lewis Hickman from B.
W. Pollock in 1786: [ref. 109a]. Summoned for jury duty
on the Superior Court of Law and Equity, Nov., 1788: [ref.
109b]. North Carolina land grants: [ref. 109c]. Estate
division filed in Davidson Co., July, 1794, on behalf of
his wife Elizabeth and orphans: [ref. 109d].
HICKMAN, Edmund - surveyor, killed by Indians on Piney River
(now Hickman Co.): [ref. 110].
HICKMAN, Elizabeth - see William Hickman.
HICKMAN, Elliott - see William Hickman.
HICKMAN, Jemima - see William Hickman.
HICKMAN, Lewis - purchased land with Edwin Hickman from B.
W Pollock in 1786: [ref. 111].
HICKMAN, Lucy - see William Hickman.
HICKMAN, Martha - see William Hickman.
HICKMAN, Mildred - see William Hickman.
HICKMAN, Nancy - see William Hickman.
HICKMAN, Sarah - see William Hickman.
HICKMAN, Susan - see William Hickman.
HICKMAN, Thomas - son of William Hickman (see following).
Sheriff of Davidson Co. in Nov. 1788: [ref. 112a]. North
Carolina land grants: [ref. 112b]. Killed by Indians
according to the historian, Haywood: [ref. 112c].
HICKMAN, William, Jr. - son of William Hickman, Sr. (see
following). Summoned for Davidson Co. jury duty, Nov.
1788: [ref. 113].

HICKMAN, William, Sr. - D.A.R. membership on this line. Born 1730, Spotsylvania Co., VA; married Ann (last name unknown). He died 1787 in Davidson Co. Children: Edwin; Thomas, m. Miss Dudley; Elliott; William, m. Ann ___; Lucy, m. Gen'l Sam Miller; Sarah, m. Andrew Ewing; Nancy, m. John Childress; Marth, m. Dan. Hill; Elizabeth, m. Oliver Williams; Susan, m. Roger Sappington, M. D.; Mildred, m. Will Smith; and Jemima, m. W. L. Marr: [ref. 114].
HILL, Green - of Franklin Co., NC, received a North Carolina land grant June 25, 1787, which was located in Davidson Co.: [ref. 115a]. D.A.R. membership on this line. According to several sources, the family did not settle in the area until 1799: [ref. 115b].
HINDS, Hamilton - listed with James, Thomas, and William Hinds on the 1787 Davidson Co. tax roll with 3 taxables: [ref. 116].
HINDS, James - 1787 Davidson Co. tax roll with Hamilton, Thomas, and William Hinds: [ref. 117].
HINDS, John - purchased land in 1789, on Yellow Creek on the south side of the Cumberland River: [ref. 118].
HINDS, Thomas - listed with Hamilton, James, and William Hinds on the 1787 Davidson Co. tax roll: [ref. 119].
HINDS, William - listed with Hamilton, James, and Thomas Hinds on the 1787 Davidson Co. tax roll: [ref. 120].
HINES, Thomas - signer of the Cumberland Compact, May, 1780: [ref. 121].
HINSON, William - signer of the Cumberland Compact, May, 1780: [ref. 122].
HOBSON, John - signer of the Cumberland Compact, May, 1780: [ref. 123].
HODGE, Francis - signer of the Cumberland Compact, May, 1780: [ref. 124a]. Listed in the North Carolina Preemption Act of 1784, as one of the settlers on the Cumberland in 1780, who stayed and defended the settlements, and entitled to 640 acres without any price to be paid to the public: [ref. 124b]. 1787 Davidson Co. tax roll with 1 taxable: [ref. 124c].
HOGAN, Daniel - arrived with the Donelson flotilla, April 24, 1780: [ref. 125a]. Signer of the Cumberland Compact, May, 1780: [ref. 125b]. Served as administrator of the estate of James Herrod, deceased, before the Committee of the Cumberland Association, Mar. 1783: [ref. 125c]. He and his wife sued James Todd, before the Cumberland Association, May 4, 1783: [ref. 125d]. Listed in the North Carolina Preemption Act of 1784, as one of the settlers on the Cumberland in 1780, who had stayed and defended the settlements, and entitled to 640 acres without any price to be paid to the public: [ref. 125e]. 1787 Davidson Co. tax roll with 1 taxable: [ref. 125f]. Purchased land in 1789, on Sulphur Fork (probably Tennessee Co., then Robertson Co.): [ref. 125g]. North Carolina land grant: [ref. 125h].

HOGAN, Edward - shot through the arm during an Indian ambush of his party going by boat on the punitive expedition against the Indian town of Coldwater, near Muscle Shoals in 1787: [ref. 126].

HOGAN, Humphrey - was with the Mansker party in 1769/70, taking articles to sell at Fort Natchez: [ref. 127a]. According to one source, he came with the Heaton party to the Cumberland Settlements, arriving Dec. 24, 1779: [ref. 127b]. Another source indicates he arrived with the Donelson flotilla, April 24, 1780: [ref. 127c]. Signer of the Cumberland Compact, May 1780: [ref. 127d]. Listed in the North Carolina Preemption Act of 1784, as one of the settlers on the Cumberland in 1780, who had stayed and defended the settlements, and entitled to 640 acres without any price to be paid to the public: [ref. 127e]. Brought lawsuit against Stephen Ray before the Committee of the Cumberland Association, Mar. 4, 1783: [ref. 127f]. Also, brought suit against John Brown, Isaac Mayfield, and Mayfield's mother, for the recovery of a kettle lent to them by Hogan, which was left in his custody by Richard Henderson: [ref. 127g]. Ordered by the Committee of the Cumberland Association, April 1, 1783, to help lay off a road between Heatonsburg and Mansker's Station: [ref. 127h]. His heirs sold his land in 1790, on the Sulphur Fork of Red River (Tennessee Co. at the time): [ref. 127i].

HOGAN, Richard - came to the Cumberland area in 1777, with Thomas Spencer from Kentucky: [ref. 128a]. Summoned from Sumner Co. for jury duty on the Superior Court of Law and Equity, meeting in Nashville, Nov. 1788: [ref. 128b].

HOGGATT (variously HOGGOTT, HOGGERT), Mr. - was special messenger between the Cumberland settlers and the Creek Indian Chief McGillevray in the spring of 1788: [ref. 129].

HOGGATT, James - purchased land of Donl. Oglesby in 1785: [ref. 130a]. Purchased land of Jas. Bosley: [ref. 130b]. North Carolina land grants: [ref. 130c]. Summoned for Davidson Co. jury duty on the Superior Court of Law and Equity, Oct., 1788: [ref. 130d]. Married Grizzel Nesset, Sept. 8, 1790, in Davidson Co.: [ref. 130e].

HOLLEY, Dixon - purchased land on the south fork of Harpeth River in 1788: [ref. 131].

HOLLEY, Nathaniel - purchased land in 1789, on Clear Branch near Sulphur Fork (Possibly Tennessee Co.): [ref. 132a]. North Carolina land grant: [ref. 132b].

HOLLIDAY (variously, HOLLADAY, HOLLODAY), John - came to the Cumberland area to hunt with Thomas S. Spencer from Kentucky in 1777: [ref. 133a]. Signer of the Cumberland Compact, May, 1780: [ref. 133b].

HOLLIS, James, Sr. - elected lieutenant of defense at "Heatons-burg" (Heaton's Station) in 1783: [ref. 134a]. Brought charges before the Committee of the Cumberland Association on Jan. 7, 1783, against Joshua and Eneas Thomas for threatening his life: [ref. 134b]. North Carolina land grant: [ref. 134c]. Listed on the 1787 Davidson Co. tax roll with John, Joshua, and Samuel Hollis: [ref. 134d].

HOLLIS, John - listed with James, Joshua, and Samuel Hollis on the 1787 Davidson Co. tax roll: [ref. 135].

HOLLIS, Joshua - listed with James, John, and Samuel Hollis on the 1787 Davidson Co. tax roll: [ref. 136a]. Married Mary Wilheim in Davidson Co., Aug. 19, 1789: [ref. 136b].

HOLLIS, Samuel - arrived with the Donelson flotilla, April 24, 1780: [ref. 137a]. Listed in the North Carolina Preemp-tion Act of 1784, as one of the settlers on the Cumberland, who was too young for a preemption grant under the Preemption Act of 1782, but now entitled to 640 acres: [ref. 137b].

HOLLIS, Sarah - married William Hooper in Davidson Co., March 4, 1789: [ref. 138].

HOLLODAY - (see HOLLIDAY).

HOMES, Hardy - North Carolina land grant: [ref. 139].

HOOD, David - was severely wounded and scalped by Indians at French Lick in 1782, but he survived: [ref. 140a]. He died of fever soon after the Nickajack expedition and was buried in the Robertson graveyard: [ref. 140b].

HOOD, Robin - helped defend Buchanan's Station during the Indian attack of Sept. 30, 1792: [ref. 141].

HOOD, William - signer of the Cumberland Compact, May, 1780: [ref. 142a]. Killed by Indians in the Summer of 1781, just outside the fort at Freeland's Station: [ref. 142b]. Listed in the North Carolina Preemption Act of 1784, as one of the settlers on the Cumberland, who had died there, and whose heirs were entitled to 640 acres without any price to be paid to the public: [ref. 142c].

HOOPER, Aeneas (variously, Ennis, Enos) - D.A.R. membership on this line. Born ca. 1760, Edgefield District, SC; was married in Davidson Co.,1796, to Annie Young, who was born 1775; d. 1807. He died in 1800, in Davidson Co. Children: Hulda; and Claiborne, b. Apr. 21, 1799: [ref. 143]. (It is unclear if this individual was actually in the Cumberland Settlements during the period for this census.)

HOOPER, Absalom - came from Natchez to the Cumberland Settle-ments in the latter part of 1783: [ref. 144a]. North Caro-lina land grant: [ref. 144b]. 1787 Davidson Co. tax roll with 7 taxables: [ref. 144c]. Purchased land of Saml. Vernor: [ref. 144d].

HOOPER, Claiborne - see Aeneas Hooper.
HOOPER, Hulda - see Aeneas Hooper.
HOOPER, William - married Sarah Hollis in Davidson Co., Mar.
4, 1789: [ref. 146].
HOPE, Adam - D.A.R. membership on this line. Born Nov. 1,
1761, in Washington Co., VA; married ca. 1785, in Washington
Co., VA: [ref. 147a]. Purchased land of Jason Thompson:
[ref. 147b]. Children: Adam, Jr.; and Samuel, b. July
29, 1790: [ref. 147c].
HOPE, Adam, Jr. - see Adam Hope.
HOPE, John - 1787 Davidson Co. tax roll with 1 taxable: [ref.
148a]. Purchased land of John Johnston and Lardner Clark
[ref. 148b].
HOPE, Samuel - see Adam Hope.
HOPKINS, Lacey - purchased land in 1790, on Yellow Creek:
[ref. 149a]. Admitted to bar in Nashville to practice
law, Nov. 1790: [ref. 149b].
HOPPER, _____ - came with the Heaton party to the Cumberland
Settlements, arriving Dec. 24, 1779: [ref. 150].
HORNBERGER, Phil - 1787 Davidson Co. tax roll with 1 taxable:
[ref. 151].
HORNER, Charles - purchased land of Isadore Scarrott: [ref.
152].
HOSER, Jacob - purchased land on Stone's River, 1789: [ref.
153].
HOSKINS, Joseph - killed by Indians at Kilgore's Station:
[ref. 154].
HOSKINS, Josiah - killed by Indians in early 1784: [ref.
155].
HOWARD, John - 1787 Davidson Co. tax roll with 1 taxable:
[ref. 156].
HOWARD, Joshua - elected Capt. of militia at Freeland's Station
in 1783: [ref. 157a]. North Carolina land grant: [ref.
157b].
HOWDISHALL, Henry - arrived with the Donelson flotilla, April
24, 1780: [ref. 158a]. Listed in the North Carolina
Preemption Act of 1784, as one of the settlers on the
Cumberland in 1780, who stayed and defended the settlements,
and entitled to 640 acres without any price to be paid
to the public: [ref. 158b]. Killed by Indians near Gen.
Rutherford's, 14 April, 1793: [ref. 158c].
HOWELL, John - purchased land on Lick Creek of the Cumberland
River: [ref. 159].
HUBBARD (variously, HUBARD), Zebulon - summoned from Sumner
Co. for jury duty on the Superior Court of Law and Equity
meeting in Nashville, 1790: [ref. 160].
HUDSON, William - married Elizabeth Dunn in Davidson Co.,
on Oct. 15, 1789: [ref. 161].

HUGHLETT, William - North Carolina land grant: [ref. 162].
HUGHES, ___ - came to the Cumberland area to hunt in 1777, with Mansker. They were attacked by Indians but escaped: [ref. 163].
HUMPHRIES, David - land purchase in 1788, on Mulherrin Creek (Sumner Co.; then Smith Co.): [ref. 164].
HUNT, Memucan - though this individual was the assignee of Samuel Glaze, heir of Corporal Jonathan Glaze, for a land grant on the West Fork of the Harpeth River in 1785, he did not settle in the Cumberland. He died in 1808, in Granville Co., NC. (See D.A.R. membership information on this line.)
HUNTER, Capt. - killed by Indians, Jan. 20, 1789: [ref. 165].
HUNTER, James - witness to the will of John Hunter, dated Mar. 7, 1788, and probated in Davidson Co.: [ref. 166].
HUNTER, John - purchased land of Bushnell & Dobbins; and Jonathan Drake and wife: [ref. 167a]. His will was proven in Davidson Co., April, 1789. In it is mentioned his wife Mary: [ref. 167b].
HUNTER Mary - wife of John Hunter (see above).
HURLEY, John - purchased land on Duck River in 1790: [ref. 168].
HUSTON, Ben - 1787 Davidson Co. tax roll with 1 taxable: [ref. 169].
HUSTON, Chamberlain - purchased land, Aug. 26, 1788, on Barton's Creek (Sumner Co.; then Wilson Co.): [ref. 170].
HUTCHENS, James - purchased land in 1789, on Barton's Creek (Sumner Co. at the time; then Wilson Co.): [ref. 171].
HUTCHINGS, Betty - daughter of Capt. Thomas Hutchings.
HUTCHINGS, Christopher - son of Capt. Thomas Hutchings.
HUTCHINGS, Jennie - daughter of Capt. Thomas Hutchings.
HUTCHINGS, John - son of Capt. Thomas Hutchings.
HUTCHINGS, Lemuel - son of Capt. Thomas Hutchings.
HUTCHINGS, Mary - daughter of Capt. Thomas Hutchings.
HUTCHINGS, Rachel - daughter of Capt. Thomas Hutchings.
HUTCHINGS, Stokely - son of Capt. Thomas Hutchings.
HUTCHINGS, Thomas - son of Capt. Thomas Hutchings.
HUTCHINGS, Capt. Thomas - D.A.R. membership on this line. Born 1750, in Pittsylvania Co., VA; married 1768, in Pittsylvania Co. to Katherine Donelson, who was born 1750. Resided in Pittsylvania Co. during the Revolution: [ref. 172a]. This family arrived at French Lick with the Donelson flotilla, April 24, 1780: [ref. 172b]. They first settled at Donelson's Fort in Clover Bottom, then removed to Mansker's Station when the Indian threat caused Donelson to break up his station: [ref. 172c]. Children: John, m. Miss Smith; Lemuel, m. Miss Owin; Thomas; Stokeley, m. Elizabeth Atwood; Christopher, m. Louise Ann Edwards; Rachel; Mary; Betty; and Jennie: [ref. 172d].

I

ILOR, M. - 1787 Davidson Co. tax roll with 1 taxable: [ref. 1].
INGLES, John - North Carolina land grant: [ref. 2].
IRESON, ___ - killed by Indians at Richland Creek, while on a surveying expedition soon after the Commissioners came out: [ref. 3].
IRVIN, John - plaintiff in court case against Thomas Hampton, before the Superior Court of Law and Equity, Nov. 1790: [ref. 4].
ISBELL, Thomas - North Carolina land grant: [ref. 5].
ISLER, Melcher - purchased land from A. Hamilton: [ref. 6]. (See ILOR.)
IVEY, Curtis - North Carolina land grant: [ref. 7].

J

JACKSON, Andrew - appointed attorney in behalf of the Davidson Co. Supreme Court of Law, Nov. 1788: [ref. 1a]. Was with Col. Elijah Robertson in the pursuit of Indians who had attacked Robertson's Station in 1789: [ref. 1b].
JACKSON, Jno. - North Carolina land grant which also refers to Robertson Jackson: [ref. 2].
JACKSON, Joseph - signer of the Cumberland Compact, May, 1780: [ref. 3].
JACKSON, Robertson - referred to on a North Carolina land grant with Jno. Robertson: [ref. 4].
JAMES, Daniel - listed with Edward James on the 1787 Davidson Co. tax roll with 2 taxables: [ref. 5a]. Purchased land of the Trustees of Nashville: [ref. 5b].
JAMES, Edward - listed with Daniel James on the 1787 Davidson Co. tax roll with 2 taxables: [ref. 6].
JAMES, John - (heirs of) sold land in 1788, on Caney Fork River (Sumner Co.; then Smith Co.): [ref. 7].
JAMES, Thomas - came to the Cumberland Settlements in 1783, from Natchez: [ref. 8a]. 1787 Davidson Co. tax roll with 7 taxables: [ref. 8b]. Purchased land of Jonathan and Mrs. Drake: [ref. 8c].
JAMESON (variously, JAMISON, JIMERSON), Thos. - purchased land of A. Crutcher: [ref. 9].
JARROT, Daniel - signer of the Cumberland Compact, May, 1780: [ref. 10].
JEFRISS (variously, JEFFREYS), Thomas - signer of the Cumberland Compact, May, 1780: [ref. 11].

JENKINS (variously, JINKINS), Josiah - (heirs of) sold land
in 1790, on Yellow Creek: [ref. 12].
JENKINS, Wm. - North Carolina land grant: [ref. 13].
JENNINGS (variously, JINNINGS), Edward - was appointed by
the court to inquire of damages sustained by plaintiff
in lawsuit, Nov. 1790: [ref. 14]
JENNINGS, Edmund - was 25 years old when he started with
James Robertson in Oct. 1779, going overland to the French
Lick. His father and family came to the settlement aboard
the Donelson flotilla which arrived April 24, 1780: [ref.
15]
JENNINGS, John - North Carolina land grant, 1786: [ref. 16].
JENNINGS, Jonathan - arrived with the Donelson flotilla,
April 24, 1780: [ref. 17a]. His son ran during an Indian
attack, but didn't return: [ref. 17b]. Signer of the
Cumberland Compact, May, 1780: [ref. 17c]. His will was
signed July 6, 1784, "having this day received several
wounds from the Indians." It mentions his wife though
not named, and children: William; Edmund; Elizabeth Harmore;
Mary; Uggy; Anne; Susanah; and "Jonathan who was scalped
by Indians" and "rendered incapable of getting his living.":
[ref. 17d]. It was believed to be Delaware Indians who
gave Jonathan Jennings his mortal wounds: [ref. 17e]. Listed
in the North Carolina Preemption Act of 1784, as one of
the settlers on the Cumberland who had died there, and
whose heirs were entitled to 640 acres without any price
to be paid to the public: [ref. 17f].
JENNINGS, Mrs. Jonathan - see references by historian, Haywood:
[ref. 18]
JEREGAN, Gardner - sold land to Howell Tatum in 1789: [ref.
19].
JOHNS, James - described as "old," came with the Donelson
flotilla, April 24, 1780: [ref.20a]. He helped build
Renfroe's Fort on Red River: [ref. 20b]. He and his wife
were killed by Indians at Battle Creek: [ref. 20c]. Listed
in the North Carolina Preemption Act of 1784, as one of
the settlers on the Cumberland who had died there, and
whose heirs were entitled to 640 acres without any price
to be paid to the public: [ref. 20d].
JOHNS, Mrs. James - killed by Indians at Battle Creek at
the same time her husband was killed: [ref. 21].
JOHNS, Randol - assignee of the heirs of Andrew Littleworth
in a Davidson Co. land transaction: [ref. 22].
JOHNS, Richard - 1787 Davidson Co. tax roll with 1 taxable:
[ref. 23].
JOHNSON, Archibald - (heirs of) sold land in 1790, on Dry
Fork of the West Fork of Red River (Tennessee Co. at the
time; then Montgomery Co.): [ref. 24].

JOHNSON, Charity - see Ann Robertson Johnson Cockrill.
JOHNSON, David - witnessed Lancelot Johnson's deed, 1790: [ref. 25].
JOHNSON, Elizabeth - see Ann Robertson Johnson Cockrill.
JOHNSON, Isaac - signer of the Cumberland Compact, May, 1780: [ref. 26a]. Fired upon by Indians in 1782, while returning to the Bluff from Kilgore's Station in the company of Samuel Martin: [ref. 26b]. Recorded his stock mark with the Committee of the Cumberland Association, June 26, 1783, - "A swallow fork in the right ear, and an under kell in the right.": [ref. 26c]. Defense witness in case of Spencer vs. Todd, heard before the Committee of the Cumberland Association, May 6, 1783: [ref. 26d]. Listed in the North Carolina Preemption Act of 1784, as one of the settlers on the Cumberland in 1780, who stayed and defended the Settlements and entitled to 640 acres without any price to be paid to the public: [ref. 26e].
JOHNSON, Lancelot - purchased land in 1790, on the west side of Red River (Tennessee Co.; then Montgomery Co.): [ref. 27].
JOHNSON, Mary "Polly" - see Ann Robertson Johnson Cockrill.
JOHNSON, Nehemiah - see Ann Robertson Johnson Cockrill.
JOHNSON, Thomas - purchased land on Cripple Creek of Stone's River in 1788: [ref. 28].
JOHNSON, W. - killed by Indians on Barren River in 1780: [ref. 29].
JOHNSON, William - summoned from Tennessee Co. for jury duty on the Superior Court of Law and Equity, May, 1789: [ref. 30].
JOHNSON, Ann - listed in the North Carolina Preemption Act of 1784, as one of the settlers on the Cumberland in 1780, who stayed and defended the Settlements, and entitled to 640 acres without any price to be paid to the public: [ref. 31]. See Ann Robertson Johnson Cockrill.
JOHNSTON, Daniel - arrived with the Donelson flotilla, April 24, 1780: [ref. 32a]. Signer of the Cumberland Compact, May, 1780: [ref. 32b]. Killed by Indians during the pursuit of an Indian raiding party, while camped with Capt. Wm. Pruett's Company on Duck River in 1783: [ref. 32c].
JOHNSTON, Elizabeth - married Nehemiah Courtney in Davidson Co., Oct. 14, 1790: [ref. 33].
JOHNSTON, Isaac - arrived with the Donelson flotilla, April 24, 1780: [ref. 34a]. Signer of the Cumberland Compact, May, 1780: [ref. 34b]. Witness in lawsuit (Hamilton vs. Martin) heard before the Committee of the Cumberland Association, May 6, 1783: [ref. 34c]. Served on the Grand Jury, Oct. 7, 1783: [ref. 34d]. North Carolina land grants: [ref. 34e]. Summoned for Davidson Co. jury duty, Nov.

(continued next page)

JOHNSTON, Isaac - (continued)

1788: [ref. 34f]. Purchased land of William Collinsworth: [ref. 34g]. (Note: the distinct possibility exists that Isaac Johnston and Isaac Johnson may be confused in the records.)

JOHNSTON, John - North Carolina land grant: [ref. 35a]. Purchased land of John Hope: [ref. 35b].

JOHNSTON, John - a lad who was captured by Indians in March, 1787, and held captive several years: [ref. 36].

JOHNSTON, Thomas - summoned from Tennessee Co. for jury duty on the Superior Court of Law and Equity, Nov. 1790: [ref. 37].

JOHNSTON, William - listed in the North Carolina Preemption Act of 1784, as one of the settlers on the Cumberland who died there, and whose heirs were entitled to 640 acres without any price to be paid to the public: [ref. 38].

JOHNSTON, William - 1787 Davidson Co. tax roll with 1 taxable: [ref. 39].

JOINER, Nancy - witness for plaintiff (Freeland vs. Deson) before the Committee of the Cumberland Association, July 1, 1783: [ref. 40].

JONEER, Stephen - (heirs of) sold land in 1790, on Barton's Creek (Sumner Co. at the time; then Wilson Co.): [ref. 41].

JONES, Mrs. - survivor of the Battle Creek massacre: [ref. 42].

JONES, Abraham - listed in the North Carolina Preemption Act of 1784, as one of the settlers on the Cumberland who died there, and whose heirs were entitled to 640 acres without any price to be paid to the public: [ref. 43].

JONES, Ambrose - North Carolina land grants: [ref. 44].

JONES, Cheziah - testified in lawsuit (Humphrey Hogan vs. Stephen Ray) before the Committee of the Cumberland Association, May 6, 1783: [ref. 45].

JONES, Hardy - North Carolina land grant: [ref. 46].

JONES, Jacob - listed in the North Carolina Preemption Act of 1784, as one of the settlers on the Cumberland who had died there, and whose heirs were entitled to 640 acres without any price to be paid to the public: [ref. 47].

JONES, James - listed with John Jones on the 1787 Davidson Co. tax roll: [ref. 48].

JONES, John - listed with James Jones on the 1787 Davidson Co. tax roll: [ref. 49a]. Purchased land in 1788, on Caney Fork River (Sumner Co.; then Smith Co.): [ref. 49b].

JONES, Mollie - was taken prisoner by the Indians on June 26, 1792, at Zeigler's Station (Sumner Co.): [ref. 50].

JONES, Robert - killed by Indians in 1787, near the house of David Wilson (Wilson's Station in what was Sumner Co. after Nov. 1788): [ref. 51].

JONES, Samuel - North Carolina land grant: [ref. 52].
JONES, Stephen - his land sold by Thomas Jones, his heir, in 1789; and sold land in 1790, on Mill Creek: [ref. 53].
JONES, Thomas - heir of Stephen Jones (see above).
JOCELYN (variously, JOSLIN), Benjamin - 1787 Davidson Co. tax roll with 1 taxable: [ref. 54a]. He was helping Southerlin Mayfield build wolf pens at Mayfield's Station on Mill Creek in 1788, when Indians attacked the party and killed Mayfield and one of his sons. Jocelyn escaped by out-running his pursuers: [ref. 54b]. Purchased land on the east fork of Stones River in 1789: [ref. 54c]. He purchased land of Bushnell & Dobbins: [ref. 54d].

K

KARR (variously, CARR), Robert - North Carolina land grant: [ref. 1].
KEDAR, Capt. Ballard - purchased land in 1788, on Caney Fork (Sumner; then Smith Co.): [ref. 2].
KEEFE, Thomas - wounded by Indians, June 26, 1792, at Zeigler's Station: [ref. 3].
KEINDEN, Cornelius - wounded by Indians in Feb., 1791, at Sugar Camp near Bledsoe's Lick (Sumner Co. at the time): [ref. 4].
KELAR (variously KELLAR, KELLOW), Adon - signer of the Cumberland Compact, May, 1780: [ref. 5].
KELLAR (variously, KELLOW), Andrew - arrived with the Donelson flotilla, April 24, 1780: [ref. 6a]. Brought suit against John Dunham for breach of contract before the Committee of the Cumberland Association, Mar. 4, 1783: [ref. 6b]. He brought suit against James Foster for trespass in the killing of a steer: [ref. 6c]. Listed in the North Carolina Preemption Act of 1784, as one of the settlers on the Cumberland in 1780, who stayed and defended the settlements, and entitled to 640 acres without any price to be paid to the public: [ref. 6d].
KELLS, John - listed in the North Carolina Preemption Act of 1784, as one of the settlers on the Cumberland in 1782, too young to receive a preemption, but having become of age was entitled to 640 acres: [ref. 7].
KENDRICK, John - taken prisoner by Indians near Fort Nashborough in 1780: [ref. 8].
KENDRICKS, Jane - husband of, killed near Winchester's Mill in 1789: [ref. 9].

KENNEDY, Abraham - see John Kennedy, Sr.
KENNEDY, George - killed by Indians at French Lick (first Buchanan Station) during the Battle of the Bluffs, April 2, 1781: [ref. 10a]. Listed in the North Carolina Preemption Act of 1784, as one of the settlers on the Cumberland who had died there, and whose heirs were entitled to 640 acres without any price to be paid to the public: [ref. 10b].
KENNEDY, George, Jr. - killed at the Battle of the Bluffs, April 2, 1781: [ref. 11].
KENNEDY, Hettie - see Robert Campbell Kennedy.
KENNEDY, John - son of John Kennedy (Sr.); see above. Arrived with his family at the French Lick on the Donelson flotilla, April 24, 1780: [ref. 12a]. Listed in the North Carolina Preemption Act of 1784, as one of the settlers on the Cumberland who was too young to receive a preemption in 1784, but having come of age, was entitled to 640 acres: [ref. 12b]. He produced the Inventory of the estate of Wm. Simpson, deceased, to the Court, Jan., 1797, in right of his wife: [ref. 12c]
KENNEDY, John (Sr.) - arrived with the Donelson flotilla, April 24, 1780: [ref. 13a.]. Listed in the North Carolina Preemption Act of 1784, as one of the settlers on the Cumberland in 1780, who stayed and defended the settlements, and entitled to 640 acres without any price to be paid to the pubic: [ref. 13b]. His will was proven in Davidson Co., Jan. 3, 1786; which does not mention his wife, but mentions the following children: John; Abraham; Marget; and Mary: [ref. 13c]. See also the Inventory of his estate: [ref. 13d].
KENNEDY, Marget - see John Kennedy (Sr.).
KENNEDY, Mary - see John Kennedy (Sr.).
KENNEDY, Risby - killed by Indians at Mansker's Lick in the winter of 1780: [ref. 14].
KENNEDY, Robert Campbell - D.A.R. membership on this line. Married Esther Edmondson. 1787 Davidson Co. tax roll with 1 taxable: [ref. 15a]. Child: Hettie, m. Robert Huston McEwen: [ref. 15b].
KENNEDY, Robin - helped defend Buchanan's Station during the Indian attack, Sept. 30, 1792: [ref. 16].
KENNEDY, William - helped defend Buchanan's Station during the Indian attack of Sept. 30, 1792: [ref. 17].
KERBY (variously, KIRBY), Henry - signer of the Cumberland Compact, May, 1780: [ref. 18].
KEYKENDALL (variously, KUYKENDALL, KYRKENDALL), Benjamin - member of the first Grand Jury, Oct. 7, 1783: [ref. 19a]. Summoned from Sumner Co. for jury duty on the Superior Court of Law and Equity in 1790: [ref. 19b].

KEYKENDALL, Joseph - summoned from Sumner Co. for jury duty on the Superior Court of Law and Equity, Nov. 1791, and was fined for failure to appear. He made affidavit to the Court of his being prevented by the Indians making excursions into the settlements where he lived, which was judged sufficient for him to be exempted: [ref. 20].

KEYKENDALL, Simon - summoned from Sumner Co. for jury duty on the Superior Court of Law and Equity, meeting in Nashville, Nov., 1788: [ref. 21].

KEYWOOD, ____ - a hunter who escaped an Indian ambush in which Miliken was killed, in April, 1780, at Richland Creek: [ref. 22].

KILGORE, Thomas - D.A.R. membership on this line. Born 1715 in VA; married Pheobe Lee in VA: [ref. 23a]. He settled on Red River in the winter of 1780, and built Kilgore's Station: [ref. 23b]. Summoned from Sumner Co. for jury duty on the Superior Court of Law and Equity, meeting in Nashville, in 1788: [ref. 23c]. North Carolina land grant: [ref. 23d]. Died 1824 in Robertson Co., Tennessee. Children: Pheobe Lee, m. Damon Moore; Lydia; m. James Yates, Sr.; Florence "Frances", m. Thomas Gunn; Gabriel; Thomas; and Anice "Alice", m. (1st) John Strother, m. (2nd) William Payne: [ref. 23e].

KIMBERLIN, Michael - signer of the Cumberland Compact, May, 1780: [ref. 24].

KING, Martin - signer of the Cumberland Compact, May, 1780: [ref. 25].

KIRKPATRICK, Capt. - killed by Indians about the 20th of January, 1788: [ref. 26].

KIRKPATRICK, Maj. - with Col. Mansker and a guard of 100 men, protected 22 families coming to the Cumberland Settlements by way of Knoxville in the fall of 1788: [ref. 27]

KIRKPATRICK, John - according to D.A.R. records, the son of John Kirkpatrick and Margaret Jane Wilkins. 1787 Davidson Co. tax roll with 3 taxables: [ref. 28a]. Married Martha Buchanan in Davidson Co., Sept. 6, 1789: [ref. 28b]. Purchased land of James Bosley: [ref. 28c].

KNOX, Henry - came to the Cumberland area to hunt in 1771, with Mansker: [ref. 29].

KNOX, James - came to the Cumberland area to hunt in 1771, with Mansker: [ref. 30].

KOEN, John - North Carolina land grant: [ref. 31].

L

LAMB, Col. Gedian - (heirs of) sold land in 1790, on the south side of Cumberland River: [ref. 1].

LAMBERT, Aaron - purchased land in 1790, on Sycamore Creek (Tennessee Co.; then Robertson Co.): [ref. 2].

LANCASTER, Jno. - listed with William Lancaster in the 1787 Davidson Co. tax roll with 2 taxables: [ref. 3].

LANCASTER, Martha - married Hy (sic) Turney, (possibly, Henry Turney), Dec. 13, 1788, in Davidson Co.: [ref. 4].

LANCASTER, William - listed with Jno. Lancaster in the 1787 Davidson Co. tax roll with 1 taxable.

LANE, Henry - found guilty of assault upon John Coating, Nov., 1788: [ref. 5].

LANE, Jennie - married William Bodie in Davidson Co., June 14, 1790: [ref. 6].

LANIER (variously, LENEAR, LENEIR, LENIER, LENIRE), James - listed with Henry Lanier on the 1787 Davidson Co. tax roll with 4 taxables: [ref. 7a]. Defendant in Court, 1788: [ref. 7b]. Purchased land of James Robertson; and purchased land of Julius Sanders: [ref. 7c]. He sold land to Henry Lanier: [ref. 7d]. His heirs sold his land in 1789, on Round Lick Creek (Sumner Co.; then Smith Co.): [ref. 7e].

LANIER, Henry - see James Lanier.

LANIER, Isaac - and family arrived with the Donelson flotilla, April 24, 1780: [ref. 8].

LANIER, Isham - purchased land of Henry Lenear: [ref. 9].

LANIER, Robert - (heirs of) sold land in 1789, on Murfree's Fork on the north side of Stone's River: [ref. 10].

LARIMAN, D. - was beheaded by Indians at Freeland's Station: [ref. 11].

LARRIMORE, Edward - listed in the North Carolina Preemption Act of 1784, as one of the settlers who died in the defense of the Cumberland Settlements, whose heirs were entitled to 640 acres without any price to be paid to the public: [ref. 12a]. He was killed before receiving preemption land, which was confiscated when he became entitled to it to pay the debts of his estate: [ref. 12b].

LASAVOUR, Isaac - listed in the North Carolina Preemption Act of 1784, as one of those who died in the defense of the Cumberland Settlements, whose heirs were entitled to 640 acres without any price to be paid to the public: [ref. 13].

LASH, Christopher - purchased land on Stone's River in 1790, from the heirs of John Bryan: [ref. 14].

LATIMER (variously, LATIMORE) - see Sumner Co. section of
this work.
LATIMER, Witheral - purchased land of Bushnell and Dobbins:
[ref. 15]. See Sumner County section of this work for
the LATIMER family.
LATIMORE, Thomas - helped defend Buchanan's Station during
the Indian attack on the station on September 20, 1792:
[ref. 16].
LAWRENCE, Adam - summoned from Sumner Co. for jury duty on
the Superior Court of Law and Equity, meeting in Nashville,
Nov. 1788. He was fined for failure to appear: [ref. 17a].
Purchased land, July 7, 1789, on the North Fork of Red
River (Tennessee Co. at the time): [ref. 17b].
LAWRENCE, Nathaniel - North Carolina land grant: [ref. 18].
LEATON (variously, LEIGHTON), William - signer of the Cumber-
land Compact, May, 1780: [ref. 19a]. He was sued by Jesse
Sumers (sic) for a debt before the Committee of the Cumber-
land Association, Mar. 4, 1783; and he was sued by Samuel
Martin, May 6, 1783, before the same body: [ref. 19b].
Listed in the North Carolina Preemption Act of 1784, as
one of those who had died in the defense of the Settlements,
whose heirs were entitled to 640 acres without any price
to be paid to the public: [ref. 19c]. See **Appendix.**
LEE, Hardy - (heirs of) sold land in 1790: [ref. 20].
LEE, Timothy - (heirs of) sold land in 1790, on the East
Fork of Blooming Grove Creek (Tennessee Co. at the time;
then Montgomery Co.): [ref. 21].
LEE, James - purchased land in 1790: [ref. 22].
LEEPER (variously, LEAPER, LEIPER), George - signer of the
Cumberland Compact, May, 1780: [ref. 23].
LEEPER, Hugh - signer of the Cumberland Compact, May, 1780:
[ref. 24a]. He witnessed the will of James Leeper: [ref.
24b]. He married Ruth Long (see John Long). North Carolina
land grant: [ref. 24c].
LEEPER, James - D.A.R. membership on this line. Born ca.
1755 in NC. Came to the Cumberland Settlements from Kentucky: [ref. 25a]. Signer of the Cumberland Compact, May,
1780: [ref. 25b]. Married Susan Drake in 1780; theirs
being the first marriage celebrated at Fort Nashborough.
Member of Capt. Benjamin Logan's Company in 1779. He was
mortally wounded at the Battle of the Bluffs, April 2,
1781. Susan, his wife, was born 1763, and was accidentally
killed in 1784, by the discharge of a rifle which fell
from its rack over the door. The couple had one child,
Sarah Jane, who was born after James Leeper's death: [ref.
25c].

LEEPER, Robertson - listed on a North Carolina land grant with Hugh Leeper: [ref. 26].

LEEPER, Sarah Jane - daughter of James Leeper and Susan Drake, was born ca. July, 1781. She married Alexander Smith in 1798: [ref. 27].

LEFEVER, Catherine - plaintiff in lawsuit against Robert Espey and wife, heard before the Committee of the Cumberland Association, May 6, 1783: [ref. 28].

LEFEVER, Isaac - killed by Indians at Clover Bottom: [ref. 29].

LEIR, James - (heirs of) sold land in 1789, on Round Lick Creek (Sumner Co. at the time; then Smith Co.): [ref. 30].

LENEAR - see LANIER.

LENIER - see LANIER.

LEONEY - see LOONEY.

LEVI, Mathew - (heirs of) sold land in 1789, on Goose Creek (Sumner Co. at the time; then Smith Co.): [ref. 34].

LEWELLEN, Abednego - purchased land of the Trustees of Nashville, July 29, 1784: [ref. 35a]. Killed by Indians in 1789, while hunting with Evan Shelby, Hugh F. Bell, and Col. Tenen: [ref. 35b].

LEWIS, Hugh - listed with Thomas Lewis on the 1787 Davidson Co. tax roll with 2 taxables: [ref. 36].

LEWIS, J. N. - purchased land of B. W. Pollock: [ref. 37].

LEWIS, James - see Col. Joel Lewis.

LEWIS, John - see Col. Joel Lewis.

LEWIS, Col. Joel - D.A.R. membership on this line. Born Aug. 28, 1760, in Albermarle Co., VA; married Miriam Eastman. Lived in Surry Co., NC during the Revolution. Children: Sarah, b. Feb. 16, 1787; James, b. 1788; John, b. 1790: [ref. 38a]. North Carolina land grant: [ref. 38b].

LEWIS, Sarah - see Col. Joel Lewis.

LEWIS, T. Wm. - purchased land of James Robertson: [ref. 39].

LEWIS, Thomas - listed with Hugh Lewis on the 1787 Davidson Co. tax roll with 2 taxables: [ref. 40].

LIGHTHOLDER, Christopher - by his will proven April, 1789, and witnessed by Oliver Williams and Aquilla Carmack, he left all his estate to the support of the Methodist Church: [ref. 41].

LINCH - see LYNCH.

LINDSAY - see LINDSEY.

LINDSEY (variously, LINDSAY, LINDSLEY, LINSEY), - sold preemptions and removed to lands between Walnut Hills and Natchez: [ref. 42].

LINDSEY, James - 1787 Davidson Co. tax roll with 1 taxable: [ref. 43].

LINDSEY, Isaac - came to the Cumberland area to hunt and trap with 4 others from South Carolina in 1767, finding Michael Stoner and Harrod also hunting in the area: [ref. 44a]. He helped build Heaton's Station during the fall and winter of 1779, one half mile below Nashville on the north side of the Cumberland River: [ref. 44b]. Signer of the Cumberland Compact, May, 1780: [ref. 44c]. Member of the Committee of the Cumberland Association, Jan. 7, 1783: [ref. 44d]. Elected member of the Inferior Court of Pleas and Quarter Sessions, Oct. 6, 1783: [ref. 44e]. Security on bond for Daniel Williams, who was elected first sheriff: [ref. 44f]. North Carolina land grant: [ref. 44g]. State witness in May, 1790, before the Superior Court of Law and Equity: [ref. 44h].
LINN - see LYNN.
LINTON, Silas - North Carolina land grant: [ref. 45].
LITTLEWORTH, Andrew - (heirs of) sold land in 1788: [ref. 46].
LOCKHART, Pleasant - purchased land of John Marney: [ref. 47a]. Inventory of sale of chattel estate recorded in Davidson Co., Jan. 1795: [ref. 47b].
LOGAN, Benjamin - North Carolina land grant: [ref. 48].
LOGAN, William - arrived with the Donelson flotilla, April 24, 1780: [ref. 49a]. Signer of the Cumberland Compact, May, 1780: [ref. 49b]. Plaintiff in lawsuit against James Todd, John Harris, and Thomas McFarland, concerning the killing of his mare by the felling of a tree, brought before the Committee of the Cumberland Association, April 1, 1783: [ref. 49c].
LOGGANS (variously, LOGGINS), William - came by land and settled at Heaton's Station: [ref. 50a]. North Carolina land grant: [ref. 50b]. 1787 Davidson Co. tax roll with 1 taxable: [ref. 50c]. He was in the party commanded by Capt. Rains pursuing the Indians to Muscle Shoals, who had attacked the settlements in 1787: [ref. 50d]. Served as juror, Nov. 1788: [ref. 50e].
LOGGANS, Samuel - found not guilty of the charge of perjury against John Madole, brought against him by the State, before the Superior Court of Law and Equity, Nov. 1788: [ref. 51].
LOGUE, Civens - see John Logue.
LOGUE, David - see John Logue.
LOGUE, Ellinor - see John Logue.
LOGUE, Ellinor - see John Logue.
LOGUE, John - will proven in Davidson Co., Oct. 1793, listing his wife Ellinor, and children: Mary; Marget; Ruth; Ellinor; Manassah; Civens; and David: [ref. 52].
LOGUE, Manassah - see John Logue.
LOGUE, Marget - see John Logue.

LOGUE, Mary - see John Logue.
LOGUE, Ruth - see John Logue.
LONG, Nicholas - purchased land of Jacob Mathews: [ref. 53].
LONG, Ruth - daughter of John Long and June Henry, married
    Hugh Leeper (beforementioned). D.A.R. membership on this
    line: [ref. 54].
LONG, William - 1787 Davidson Co. tax roll with 1 taxable:
    [ref. 55].
LONGHAIR - a Chickasaw chief and his son were killed in May,
    1789, near Clinch River, while accompanying Judge McNairy
    on his rounds through the settlements: [ref. 56].
LOOMAS, Jonathan - North Carolina land grant: [ref. 57].
LOONEY (variously, LUNEY, LUNA), David - purchased property
    from the Trustees of Nashville, Aug. 16, 1784: [ref. 58].
LOONEY, Jon - signer of the Cumberland Compact, May, 1780:
    [ref. 59].
LOONEY, Peter - arrived with the Donelson flotilla, April
    24, 1780: [ref. 60a]. Signer of the Cumberland Compact,
    May, 1780: [ref. 60b]. Listed in the North Carolina
    Preemption Act of 1784, as one of the settlers on the
    Cumberland in 1780, who had stayed and defended the
    Settlements and entitled to 640 acres without any price
    to be paid to the public: [ref. 60c]. Summoned from Sumner
    Co. for jury duty on the Superior Court of Law and Equity,
    Nov. 1788: [ref. 60d]. Purchased land in 1790, on Station
    Camp Creek (then Sumner Co.): [ref. 60e].
LOONEY, Robert - summoned from Sumner Co. for jury duty on
    the Superior Court of Law and Equity, Nov. 1788: [ref.
    61].
LOVE, Joseph - 1787 Davidson Co. tax roll with 1 taxable:
    [ref. 62].
LOVE, Josiah - purchased land of Robert Nelson: [ref. 63a].
    He was attorney for the heirs of Freeland in May, 1790:
    [ref. 63b].
LUCAS, Abigail - daughter of Robert Lucas (see hereafter).
LUCAS, Andrew - security for Samuel Barton, who was elected
    Entry Taker for the Committee of the Cumberland Association,
    Oct. 1, 1783: [ref. 64a]. Purchased land of the Trustees
    of Nashville; and purchased land of James Bosley: [ref.
    64b]. Wounded by Indians at the headwaters of Drake's
    Creek: [ref. 64c]. 1787 Davidson Co. tax roll with 1
    taxable: [ref. 64d].
LUCAS, Asenath - daughter of Robert Lucas, married a Stewart
    (see Robert Lucas).
LUCAS, Betsy - orphan of David Lucas, deceased (see hereafter).
LUCAS, David - his orphan children: Nansey, Betsey, and Leah
    are mentioned in the Minutes of the Superior Court of Law
    and Equity in 1795: [ref. 65].

LUCAS, Edward - signer of the Cumberland Compact, May, 1780: [ref. 66a]. He was heir-at-law of Robert Lucas, deceased, and claimed preemption of 640 acres on the east fork of Richland Creek, adjoining James Robertson, near the head of a little branch including the spring and improvement: [ref. 66b]. Purchased land of Thomas Molloy: [ref. 66c].

LUCAS, George - son of Robert Lucas (see hereunder).

LUCAS, Isaac - had his thigh broken by an Indian bullet in 1781: [ref. 67a]. Killed at the attack on Freeland's Station: [ref. 67b]. Listed in the North Carolina Preemption Act of 1784, as one of the settlers who had died in the defense of the Cumberland Settlements, and whose heirs were entitled to 640 acres without any price to be paid to the public: [ref. 67c].

LUCAS, Leah - daughter of David Lucas (see above).

LUCAS, Nansy - daughter of David Lucas (see above).

LUCAS, Polly - daughter of Robert Lucas (see hereafter).

LUCAS, Rebecca - daughter of Robert Lucas (see hereafter).

LUCAS, Robert - was mortally wounded at the Battle of the Bluffs, April 2, 1781, and died several days later: [ref. 68a] Estate inventory filed in Davidson Co.. in 1797, records that "his death occurred in the year 1780 (sic)," but "the situation of this county was such that no administration of the effects could be had." This record also mentions his sons: Edward; George; and William; and daughters: Rebecca Sappington; Sarah Hamilton; Asenath Stewart; Polly and Abigail. His wife Sarah was administrix: [ref. 68b].

LUCAS, Sarah - daughter of Robert Lucas, married a Hamilton (see Robert Lucas).

LUCAS, Sarah - defense witness in the case (Freeman vs. Deson) before the Committee of the Cumberland Association, July 1, 1783: [ref. 69a]. Failed to appear as a witness for the defense before the Superior Court of Law and Equity, Nov. 1790: [ref. 69b].

LUCAS, Smith - failed to appear as a defense witness before the Superior Court of Law and Equity, Nov. 1790: [ref. 70].

LUCAS, Rebecca - daughter of Robert Lucas, married a Sappington (see Robert Lucas).

LUCAS, William - son of Robert Lucas (see above).

LUMSDEN (variously, LUMEDIN), John - listed in the North Carolina Preemption Act of 1784, as one of the settlers who died in the defense of the Cumberland Settlements, whose heirs were entitled to 640 acres without any price to be paid to the public: [ref. 71].

LUMSDAY, James - an account against the estate of, was proved before the Committee of the Cumberland Association, Jan. 7, 1783: [ref. 72].

LUMSLEY, James - killed by Indians at Mansker's Station: [ref. 73].

LUPER, John - 1787 Davidson Co. tax roll with 1 taxable: [ref. 74].

LUSK, William - plaintiff in lawsuit against Nathan Holly before the Superior Court of Law and Equity, Nov., 1790: [ref. 75a]. Summoned from Tennessee Co. for jury duty before the beforementioned court, 1790: [ref. 75b].

LYLES, Hugh - 1787 Davidson Co. tax roll with 1 taxable: [ref. 76].

LYNCH (variously, LINCH), David - came to the Cumberland area to hunt in 1777 with Mansker. He took the shingles and was carried back to the settlement from which he had come by Isaac Bledsoe: [ref. 77].

LYNCH, William - was with the same hunting party as David Lynch (see above).

LYNN (variously, LINN), Adam - 1787 Davidson Co. tax roll with 1 taxable: [ref. 78a]. North Carolina land grants: [ref. 78b].

LYNN, James - signer of the Cumberland Compact, May, 1780: [ref. 79a]. Elected Ensign of Militia at Mansker's Station in 1783: [ref. 79b]. Sued by John Hamilton in behalf of his daughter, Elonar, for slander, before the Committee of the Cumberland Association, July 1, 1783, but the suit was dismissed by plaintiff: [ref. 79c].

LYTLE, Archibald - purchased land in 1789, on Caney Fork (Sumner Co.; then Smith Co.): [ref. 80a]. North Carolina land grants: [ref. 80b]. (See D.A.R. membership information on Archibald Lytle.)

LYTLE, William - purchased property of the Trustees of the Town of Nashville, April 8, 1785: [ref. 81]. (See also comments concerning D.A.R with Archibald Lytle above.)

M

McADAMS, John - signer of the Cumberland Compact, May, 1780: [ref. 1a]. Recorded his stock mark in the Minutes of the Committee of the Cumberland Association, Feb. 11, 1783, thus: "A crop off the right ear and whole (sic) through it, and a swallow fork in the left." [ref. 1b]. Witness for the plaintiff (White vs. Rains & Noble), heard before the Cumberland Committee, Mar. 4, 1783: [ref. 1c]. Defendant in action brought by Julius Sanders, May 6, 1783, concerning Indian corn owed to plaintiff: [ref. 1d]. Elected first constable at Fort Nashboro, Oct. 7, 1783: [ref. 1e].

McADOO (variously, McADOE), Arthur - arrived with the Donelson
    flotilla, April 24, 1780: [ref. 2a]. Signer of the
    Cumberland Compact, May, 1780: [ref. 2b]. North Carolina
    land grant: [ref. 2c]. Listed in the North Carolina
    Preemption Act of 1784, as one of the settlers on the
    Cumberland in 1780, who stayed and defended the settlements,
    and entitled to 640 acres without any price to be paid
    to the public: [ref. 2d].
McADOO, James - signer of the Cumberland Compact, May, 1780:
    [ref. 3a]. Listed in the North Carolina Preemption Act
    of 1784, as one of the settlers on the Cumberland who stayed
    and defended the settlements, and entitled to 640 acres
    without any price to be paid to the public: [ref. 3b].
McALLISTER, James - 1787 Davidson Co. tax roll with 1 taxable:
    [ref. 4].
McINTOSH (variously, McANTOSH), Ben - 1787 Davidson Co. tax
    roll with 1 taxable: [ref. 5].
McINTOSH - listed with Thomas McIntosh on the 1787 Davidson
    Co. tax roll with 2 taxables: [ref. 6].
McINTOSH, Thomas - listed with Charles McIntosh on the 1787
    Davidson Co. tax roll: [ref. 7].
McCAIN (variously, McKAIN, McKANE), Ephriam, Jr. - summoned
    for Davidson Co. jury duty on the Superior Court of Law
    and Equity, May, 1790: [ref. 8].
McCAIN, James - made settlement with James Franklin, Elmore
    Douglass, Charles Carter, and others, on the west side
    of Big Station Camp Creek where the upper Nashville road
    crossed the creek, in the fall of 1783. He informed John
    Carr that all Cumberland settlers who could get horses
    after the Indian atrocities went to Kentucky: [ref. 9a].
    He recorded his stock mark in the Minutes of the Committee
    of the Cumberland Association, Aug. 27, 1783; thus: "A
    crop off each ear, and an under and over kell in each."
    :[ref. 9b]. Filed suit against William Graham to recover
    a bed, heard before the beforementioned Committee, April
    1, 1783: [ref. 9c]. Elected first Constable at Mansker's
    Station, Oct. 7, 1783: [ref. 9d]. Summoned from Sumner
    Co. for jury duty on the Superior Court of Law and Equity,
    May, 1790: [ref. 9e]
McCAIN, Thomas - 1787 Davidson Co. tax roll with 1 taxable:
    [ref. 10a]. Killed by Indians in 1789; his estate settlement
    filed in Davidson Co.: [ref. 10b].
McCAMMENTS, William - purchased land with William McCamments
    from Frederick Stump: [ref. 11].
McCAMMENTS, William - purchased land with Hugh McCamments
    from Frederick Stump (see above).

McCANN, Nathaniel - North Carolina land grant: [ref. 12].
McCARTNEY, Charles - signer of the Cumberland Compact, May, 1780: [ref. 13].
McCARTY, Jacob - 1787 Davidson Co. tax roll: [ref. 14a]. Summoned from Tennessee Co. for jury duty on the Superior Court of Law and Equity in 1790: [ref. 14b].
McCAY, David - (heirs of) sold land in 1791, on Stone's River: [ref. 15].
McCLAIN, Thomas - fined for failing to appear for jury duty on the Superior Court of Law and Equity, Nov. 1788: [ref. 16].
McCLURE, Nathan - North Carolina land grant: [ref. 17].
McCONNELL, Catherine - see Catherine Boyd.
McCORMICK, William - claimed preemption of 640 acres "on Harpeth River beginning near the Little Fork above the Nobs, running down both sides of the river including spring and improvements and marked on a tree near the spring ID: [ref. 18].
McCRORY (variously, MacRORY, McRORY), Hugh - helped defend Buchanan's Station during the Indian attack of Sept. 30, 1792. He heard cows running and raised the alarm: [ref. 19]. See Capt. Thomas McCrory.
McCRORY, James - purchased land on Cripple Creek of Stone's River in 1788: [ref. 20a]. He was fired upon by Indians on Oct. 3, 1792, north of the Cumberland River: [ref. 20d].
McCRORY, John - wounded during an Indian attack in 1790 (possibly at Brown's Station): [ref. 21a]. He helped defend Buchanan's Station during the Indian attack of Sept. 30, 1792, at which time he killed the chief leader, a Shawnee: [ref. 21b].
McCRORY, Robert - killed by Indians while in the company of Capt. Gordon in June 1794: [ref. 22a]. A supplemental inventory of his estate was filed in Davidson Co. in 1797: [ref. 22b]. See Capt. Thomas McCrory.
McCRORY, Robert - filed the estate inventory of Thomas McCrory in Davidson Co., April 1796: [ref. 23].
McCRORY, Capt. Thomas - D.A.R. membership on this line. See the Tennessee Chapter D.A.R. records on this family which include several early Cumberland settlers. His children were: James, Hugh, Robert, John, Thomas, William, and Ester. He died in North Carolina in 1788, but record unclear if he were in the Cumberland Settlements.
McCRORY, Thomas - helped defend Buchanan's Station during the Indian attack of September 30, 1792: [ref. 24a]. Estate inventory filed in Davidson Co., April, 1796, by Robert McCrory: [ref. 24b]. See Capt. Thomas McCrory.
McCUESTION (variously, McQUESTION), James - purchased land on Cripple Creek of Stone's River: [ref. 25].

McCULLOCH (variously, McCULLOUCH), Benjamin - purchased land
    in 1788, on Caney Fork River (Sumner Co.; then Smith Co.):
    [ref. 26].
McCULLOCH, Samuel - purchased land of J. B. Ashe: [ref. 27].
McCUTCHEN (variously, McCUTCHAM, McCUTCHAM), Elizabeth - wife
    of John McCutchen (see hereafter).
McCUTCHEN, Elizabeth - wife of William McCutchen (see
    hereafter).
McCUTCHEN, Grizzel - child of William McCutchen (see hereafter).
McCUTCHEN, James - mentioned as a brother of Patrick and John
    McCutchen in the will of John: [ref. 28]. See **Appendix**.
McCUTCHEN, Jane - daughter of William McCutchen (see hereafter).
McCUTCHEN, John - was fined for failing to appear as a juror
    on the Superior Court of Law and Equity, Nov. 1788: [ref.
    29a]. His will, proven in Davidson Co., Jan. 30, 1789,
    mentions his wife Elizabeth, and son, Hugh, and "other younger
    children." His brothers, Patrick and James McCutchen, were
    executors: [ref. 29b].
McCUTCHEN, Patrick - signer of the Cumberland Compact, May,
    1780: [ref. 30a]. Listed with Samuel and James on the 1787
    Davidson Co. tax roll with 3 taxables: [ref. 30b]. Executor
    of the will of John McCutchen, his brother (see above).
    North Carolina land grant: [30c]. Married Hannah Marshall
    in Davidson Co. on Mar. 24, 1789: [ref. 30d].
McCUTCHEN, Samuel - signer of the Cumberland Compact, May,
    1780: [ref. 31a]. Listed with Patrick and James McCutchen
    on the 1787 Davidson Co. tax roll. North Carolina land
    grant: [ref. 31b].
McCUTCHEN, William - will proven in Davidson Co., April, 1789;
    mentions his wife Elizabeth and children, Grizzel and Jane.
    Also mentions his land on Mill Creek adjoining Southerlin
    Mayfield: [ref. 32]. See **Appendix**.
McDANIEL, Allen - (heirs of) sold land in 1790, on Mill Creek:
    [ref. 33].
McDANIEL, John - (heirs of) sold land in 1790, between Blooming
    Creek and Cumberland River (Tennessee Co. at the time; then
    Montgomery Co.): [ref. 34].
McDOWELL, John - 1787 Davidson Co. tax roll with 1 taxable:
    [ref. 35].
McDOWELL, Joseph - purchased land on Mill Creek in 1788: [ref.
    36a]. North Carolina land grant: [ref. 36b].
McELWRATH, Joseph - summoned from Sumner Co. for jury duty
    on the Superior Court of Law and Equity, May, 1790: [ref.
    37].
McENTIRE (variously, McINTIRE, McINTYRE), Alexander - purchased
    land of the Trustees of Nashville: [ref. 38].
McEWEN, Cyrus - see William McEwen.
McEWEN, David - see William McEwen.
McEWEN, Ephriam - see William McEwen.

McEWEN, James - son of William McEwen (see below).
McEWEN, Jane - daughter of William McEwen (see below).
McEWEN, Margaret - daughter of William McEwen (see below).
McEWEN, William - D.A.R. membership on this line. Born 1744, in Scotland; married Sarah Kerr in Salisbury, Rowan Co., NC, on Oct. 24, 1776: [ref. 39a]. Purchased land of Samuel Barton: [ref. 39b]. Died in Williamson Co., TN, Feb. 1816. Children: Jane, b. Aug. 4, 1780, m. John Goff; David, b. ca. 1783; Margaret, b. 1785, m. Thomas Goff; Ephraim; James, b. 1793; and Cyrus, b. June 5, 1801: [ref. 39c].
McFADDEN, Andrew - released from forfeiture of his recognizance, Nov. 1788: [ref. 40].
McFADDEN, David - listed with James McFadden on the 1787 Davidson Co. tax roll with 1 taxable: [ref. 41].
McFADDEN, Capt. James - named overseer of a road cut from Maulding's Station to Mansker's Station, by the Committee of the Cumberland Association, April 1, 1783: [ref. 42a]. Member of the first Grand Jury, Oct. 7, 1783: [ref. 42b]. Listed with David McFadden on the 1787 Davidson Co. tax roll with 2 taxables: [ref. 42c]. North Carolina land grant: [ref. 42d].
McFARLAND, ____ - wounded by Indians, July 15, 1792, at Dripping Spring: [ref. 43].
McFARLAND, John - witness in a lawsuit (Wm. Mitchell vs. Geo. Mansker) before the Committee of the Cumberland Association, April 1, 1783: [ref. 44a]. 1787 Davidson Co. tax roll with 1 taxable: [ref. 44b]. Purchased land of the Trustees of the town of Nashville, Aug. 16, 1784: [ref. 44c].
McFARLAND, Thomas - defendant in a lawsuit brought by William Loggan before the Committee of the Cumberland Association, April 1, 1783, for the killing of Loggan's mare by "felling of a tree.": [ref. 45a]. 1787 Davidson Co. tax roll with 1 taxable: [ref. 45b]. North Carolina land grant: [ref. 45c]. Estate inventory filed in Davidson Co., July 3, 1796: [ref. 45d].
McFARLIN, James - 1787 Davidson Co. tax roll with 2 taxables: [ref. 46].
McFARLIN, Thomas - purchased land of John Foremand: [ref. 47]. (See Thomas McFarland).
McGAUGHY (variously, McGAUGHS), Miss - killed by Indians at Hickman's Station in 1789: [ref. 48]. (See McGough - is this the same family?)
McGAVOCK, Cynthia - see James McGavock, Sr.
McGAVOCK, David - North Carolina land grant: [ref. 49a]. First appeared as a taxpayer in Davidson Co. on the 1789 tax roll: [ref. 49b]. (See James McGavock, Sr.)
McGAVOCK, Hugh - see James McGavock, Sr.

McGAVOCK, James - see James McGavock, Sr.
McGAVOCK, James, Sr. - D.A.R. membership on this line. Born
    1728, in County Antrim, Ireland; married Mary Cloyd in
    Rockbridge Co., VA, 1790: [ref. 50a]. First appeared in
    Davidson Co. as a taxpayer on the 1787 tax roll: [ref.
    50b]. North Carolina land grant: [ref. 50c]. Purchased
    land of Freeland and wife: [ref. 50d]. Children: Hugh,
    b. 1761, m. Nancy Kent; David, b. 1763, m. (1st) Elizabeth
    McDowell, m. (2nd) Mrs. Mary Hubble; James, b. 1764, m.
    Mary Crockett; Randal, b. 1766, m. Sarah D. Rodgers;
    Margaret, m. Col. Joseph Kent; Mary, b. 1769, m. Philip
    Grimes in 1798; Cynthia, b. 1776, m. Gen. Geo. Cloyd; Joseph,
    b. 1780, m. Margaret Graham; and Sally, b. 1787: [ref.
    50e].
McGAVOCK, Joseph - see James McGavock, Sr.
McGAVOCK, Margaret - see James McGavock, Sr.
McGAVOCK, Mary - see James McGavock, Sr.
McGAVOCK, Randal - see James McGavock, Sr.
McGAVOCK, Sally - see James McGavock, Sr.
McGAVOCK, William - North Carolina land grant: [ref. 51].
McGOWAN, Samuel - 1787 Davidson Co. tax roll with 1 taxable:
    [ref. 52].
McGOUGH, John - 1787 Davidson Co. tax roll with 1 taxable:
    [ref. 53].
McLANE (variously, McLEAN), Ephriam - "of Davidson Co."
    received North Carolina land grant, Dec. 25, 1787: [ref.
    54a]. 1787 Davidson Co. tax roll with 1 taxable: [ref.
    54b].
McLANE, Ephriam - listed as "2nd" in the 1787 Davidson Co.
    tax roll with 1 taxable: [ref. 55].
McLANE, George - married Parmelia Davidson in Davidson Co.,
    July 20, 1789: [ref. 56].
McLEAN, Ephriam - purchased land of Green Hill [ref. 57a].
    Received North Carolina land grants: [ref. 57b].
McMURRAY (variously, McMURREY, McMURRY), Samuel - signer
    of the Cumberland Compact, May, 1780: [ref. 58a]. NC land
    grant: [ref. 58b]. According to one source, he helped
    defend Buchanan's Station during an Indian attack: another
    source states he was killed by Indians on Mar. 25, 1792,
    during an attack on Buchanan's Station: [ref. 58c].
McMURRAY, Thomas - North Carolina land grant: [ref. 59].
McMURRAY, William - signer of the Cumberland Compact, May,
    1780: [ref. 60].
McMURTRY (variously, McMYRTRY, McMYRTY), John - signer of
    the Cumberland Compact, May, 1780: [ref. 61a]. Listed
    in the North Carolina Preemption Act of 1784, as one of
    the settlers on the Cumberland who had died there in defense
    of the settlements, whose heirs were entitled to 640 acres
    without any price to be paid to the public: [ref. 61b].

McMURRAY, Samuel - signer of the Cumberland Compact, May, 1780: [ref. 62].

McMURRAY, William - signer of the Cumberland Compact, May, 1780: [ref. 63].

McNAIRY, Judge John - presided over the Superior Court of Law and Equity for the Davidson County session held in Nashville, beginning November, 1788: [ref. 64a]. His party was attacked by Indians on the west side of Clinch River in May, 1789: [ref. 64b].

McNIGHT (variously, McKNIGHT), Robert - 1787 Davidson Co. tax roll with 1 taxable: [ref. 65].

McNIGHT, William - 1787 Davidson Co. tax roll with 1 taxable: [ref. 66].

McNEES (variously, McNEESE, possibly, McNISH), Benjamin - purchased land in 1789, on the north side of Sulphur Fork (Tennessee Co.; then Montgomery Co.): [ref. 67].

McSEA (possibly, MAXEY), John - 1787 Davidson Co. tax roll with 1 taxable: [ref. 68].

McSPADDEN, ____ - 1787 Davidson Co. tax roll with 1 taxable: [ref. 69].

McVAY, John - signer of the Cumberland Compact, May, 1780: [ref. 70].

McWHISTER, William - 1787 Davidson Co. tax roll with 1 taxable: [ref. 71].

McWHORTER, George - summoned for Davidson County jury duty, May, 1790, on the Superior Court of Law and Equity: [ref. 72].

McWHORTER, William - signer of the Cumberland Compact, May, 1780: [ref. 73].

MACLIN (variously, MACLEN), Ann - see William Maclin.

MACLIN, Dolly - see William Maclin.

MACLIN, Elizabeth - see William Maclin.

MACLIN, James - see William Maclin.

MACLIN, John - see William Maclin.

MACLIN, Mary - see William Maclin.

MACLIN, Rebecca - see William Maclin.

MACLIN, Sackfield - see William Maclin.

MACLIN, Sarah - see William Maclin.

MACLIN, William - D.A.R. membership on this line. Born in Brunswick Co., VA; married Sarah Clack: [74a]. Listed on the 1787 Davidson Co. tax roll with 7 taxables: [ref. 74b]. Purchased land of the Trustees of the Town of Nashville, July 8, 1785: [ref. 74c]. Children: Ann, b. 1755, m. Richard Bolling Cross; Mary, b. 1757, m. Gen. Wm. Cocke; Dolly, b. 1758, m. Jonathan Robertson; Sarah, b. 1759, m. Col. Elijah Robertson; John, b. 1760, m. Sarah Taylor; William, b. 1761, m. ____ Parker; Jane, b. 1763, m. ____ Clack; Elizabeth, b. 1765, m. Gen. Landon Carter; Rebecca, b. 1767, m. Capt. James Bosley; Sackfield, b. 1769; and James b. 1769: [ref. 74d].

MACLIN, William - see William Maclin.
MACY, John - clerk pro loc tempore for the Superior Court of Law and Equity for Davidson Co., Nov. 1788: [ref. 75].
MADOLE, John - found not guilty of perjury before the Superior Court of Law and Equity, Nov. 1788: [ref. 76].
MAHON (variously, MAHAN), Archibald - purchased land in 1789, on the Sulphur Fork of Red River (Tennessee Co.; then Robertson Co.): [ref. 77a]. Summoned from Tennessee Co. for jury duty on the Superior Court of Law and Equity, May, 1790: [ref. 77b].
MANESI, James - summoned for Davidson Co. jury duty on the Superior Court of Law and Equity, Nov., 1790: [ref. 78].
MANIFEE (variously, MENEFEE, MENIFEE), James - attacked by Indians in 1780, while hunting: [ref. 79a]. Wounded by Indians during the Battle of the Bluffs, April 24, 1781: [ref. 79b].
MANIFEE, Jarrott - North Carolina land grant: [ref. 80].
MANIFEE, Jonas - arrived with the Donelson flotilla, April 24, 1780: [ref. 81a]. Listed in the North Carolina Preemption Act of 1784, as one of the settlers on the Cumberland in 1780, who stayed and defended the settlements, and entitled to 640 acres without any price to be paid to the public: [ref. 81b]. Summoned for Davidson Co. jury duty on the Superior Court of Law and Equity, Nov., 1788: [ref. 81c].
MANSKER (variously, MANSCO), Capt. Gasper (variously, Casper, Kasper, Kaspar) - was an early hunter to the Cumberland area: [ref. 82a]. Signer of the Cumberland Compact, May, 1780: [ref. 82b]. He built a fort called Mansker's Station on the west side of Mansker's Lick in 1779, and it was the first fort burned by the Indians. He rebuilt his fort near the present site of Goodlettsville, Tennessee. He was wounded by Indians at the Battle of the Bluffs, April 2, 1781: [ref. 82c]. Elected Lieutenant of militia at his station in 1783: [ref. 82d]. He recorded his stock mark in the Minutes of the Committee of the Cumberland Association, May, 1, 1783, thus: "A crop off the right ear, and a slit in the dewlap of the cattle, and brands thus - KM in a circle.": [ref. 82e]. Summoned from Sumner Co. for jury duty on the Superior Court of Law and Equity, May, 1789: [ref. 82f].
MANSKER, George - defendant in a lawsuit brought by William Mitchell before the Committee of the Cumberland Association, April 1, 1783: [ref. 83].
MARLEY, Robert - North Carolina land grants: [ref. 84].
MARLIN, Archibald - 1787 Davidson Co. tax roll with 1 taxable: [ref. 85].
MARNEY, Elizabeth - wife of John Marney, was administratrix of John Turner's estate in behalf of Turner's children: [ref. 86].

MARNEY, John - granted the administration of the estate of
John Turner, deceased, by the Committee of the Cumberland
Association, Feb. 5, 1783: [ref. 87a]. Purchased land
of Joshua Howard: [ref. 87b].
MARRS, Sarah - married Abijah Harrington in Davidson Co.,
Nov. 19, 1789: [ref. 88].
MARSHALL, Hannah - married Patrick McCutchen in Davidson
Co., Mar. 24, 1789: [ref. 89].
MARSHALL, John - 1787 Davidson Co. tax roll with 1 taxable:
[ref. 90].
MARSHALL, William - 1787 Davidson Co. tax roll with 1 taxable:
[ref. 91a]. North Carolina land grant: [ref. 91b].
MARTIN (variously, MARTEN), Alexander - North Carolina land
grant: [ref. 92].
MARTIN, Andrew - was a guard for Southerlin Mayfield at
Mayfield's Station, and was killed by Indians during their
attack on the Station in 1788: [ref. 93].
MARTIN, Archibald - summoned from Davidson Co. for jury duty
on the Superior Court of Law and Equity, Nov. 1790: [ref.
94].
MARTIN, Delilah - married Mitchell O'Neal in Davidson Co.,
March 5, 1790: [ref. 95].
MARTIN, George - summoned from Sumner Co. for jury duty on
the Superior Court of Law and Equity, May, 1790: [ref.
96].
MARTIN, Joseph - 1787 Davidson Co. tax roll with 1 taxable:
[ref. 97a]. Summoned for Davidson Co. jury duty on the
Superior Court of Law and Equity, Nov., 1788: [ref. 97b].
Tennessee County Coroner: [ref. 97c]. Purchased land of
Loggins and of Samuel Martin: [ref. 97d].
MARTIN, Samuel - signer of the Cumberland Compact, May, 1780:
[ref. 98a]. Captured by Indians in 1782, while returning
to the Bluff from Kilgore's Station. He remained in
captivity 10 or 11 months, then returned elegantly dressed
with two valuable horses and silver spurs. It was whispered
that he had aided the Indians and shared in the plunder:
[ref. 98b]. Elected 1st Lieutenant of militia at Fort
Nashborough, 1783: [ref. 98c]. Listed on the 1787 Davidson
Co. tax roll with 2 taxables: [ref. 98d]. Was a peace
offer messenger between Cumberland Settlements and Creek
Chief McGillevray prior to 1788: [ref. 98e]. Purchased
land of the Trustees of Nashville, April 8, 1785: [ref.
98f]. North Carolina land grant: [ref. 98g]. Purchased
land of James Bosley and of James Martin: [ref. 98h]. (The
records are unclear whether the beforementioned references
to Samuel Martin are for one or more individuals.)

MARTIN, Thomas - purchased land of Andrew Lucas, Jan. 6,
1785: [ref. 99a]. Summoned from Sumner Co. for jury duty
on the Superior Court of Law and Equity, 1790: [ref. 99b].
MARTIN, William - purchased land, April 23,, 1782, on Bledsoe's
Creek (afterwards Sumner Co.): [ref. 100a]. Led a Company
of men pursuing Indians, who had attacked settlements on
Bledsoe's Creek in 1787: [ref. 100b].
MARY - negro woman killed by Indians during the attack on
Zeigler's Station, June 26, 1792: [ref. 101].
MASON, John - (heirs of) sold land in 1790, on the east fork
of Blooming Grove Creek (Tennessee Co.; then Montgomery
Co.): [ref. 102].
MASON, Philip - formerly of Pennsylvania, was a young man
when killed by Indians in 1784. He and Philip Trammell
had killed a deer and were skinning it at the head of White's
Creek, when the Indians fired upon them. Mason was wounded,
and the Indians carried off the venison. Trammell got
assistance from Eaton's Station and followed the Indians.
Catching up with them, another fight ensued, and Mason
received a second fatal wound. He had lived with his family
of 7 to 9 brothers and sisters near Kilgore's Station:
[ref. 103].
MASON, Samuel - helped build Kilgore's Station on Red River
in the winter of 1780: [ref. 104a]. He was elected Constable
at Maulding's Station of Oct. 7, 1783: [ref. 104b].
MASSIE, Peter - known as the "weeping prophet," came to the
settlments in 1790. He died at the house of Mr. Hodge
near Nashville in December, 1791: [ref. 105].
MATHEWS, Jacob - North Carolina land grant: [ref. 106].
MAULDING (variously, MALDING, MAUDLIN, MAULDON), Ambrose
- helped build Kilgore's Station on Red River in the winter
of 1780: [ref. 107a]. Elected Lieutenant of militia at
Maulding's Station in 1783: [ref. 107b]. Killed by Indians
at Kilgore's Station: [ref. 107c].
MAULDING, James - proved an account against the estate of
Richard Stanton, deceased, before the Committee of the
Cumberland Association, Mar. 4, 1783: [ref. 108a]. Purchased
property of the Trustees of the Town of Nashville: [ref.
108b].
MAULDING, Moat - ordered by the Committee of the Cumberland
Association, April 1, 1783, to help lay off a road from
Mansker's Station to Maulding's Station: [ref. 109].
MAULDING, Morton - signer of the Cumberland Compact, May,
1780: [ref. 110].
MAULDING, Moses - helped build Kilgore's Station on Red River
in the winter of 1780: [ref. 111a]. He was killed by Indians
at Kilgore's Station: [ref. 111b].

MAXEY, Jesse - signer of the Cumberland Compact, May, 1780: [ref. 112a]. North Carolina land grant: [ref. 112b]. Wounded, scalped, and left for dead by the Indians, who left a knife sticking out of his body in Feb. 1788, at Asher's Station, but he recovered: [ref. 112c].

MAXWELL, Mrs. - was married to James Freeland by James Shaw, Trustee, at Fort Nashboro: [ref. 113].

MAXWELL, Daniel - listed in the North Carolina Preemption Act of 1784, as one of the settlers who had been killed in the defense and settlement of the Cumberland Settlements, whose heirs were entitled to 640 acres without any price to be paid to the public: [ref. 114].

MAXWELL, David - signer of the Cumberland Compact, May, 1780: [ref. 115a]. Listed in the North Carolina Preemption Act of 1784, as one of the settlers who had died in the defense and settlement of the Cumberland Settlements, whose heirs were entitled to 640 acres without any price to be paid to the public: [ref. 115b]. Moses and William Maxwell were his heirs mentioned in his estate division filed in Davidson Co., 1796: [ref. 115c].

MAXWELL, James - summoned for Davidson Co. jury duty, Nov. 1790: [ref. 116a]. Prosecutor in the Superior Court of Law and Equity, May, 1790: [ref. 116b].

MAXWELL, Jesse - North Carolina land grant: [ref. 117].

MAXWELL, John - taken prisoner by Indians near the mound (near French Lick) in 1780: [ref. 118].

MAXWELL, Moses - with William Maxwell, was heir to David Maxwell (see abovementioned): [ref. 119].

MAXWELL, William - summoned from Sumner Co. for jury duty before the Superior Court of Law and Equity, Nov., 1788; and was subsequently fined for failing to appear: [ref. 120].

MAYFIELD, ____ - daughter of James Mayfield and wife of John Brown was killed by Indians ca. 1792, a few months prior to her husband's death by Indians: [ref. 121].

MAYFIELD, George - son of Southerlin Mayfield, was captured by Indians in 1788, during their attack on Mayfield's Station, at which time his father and brother were killed. He was taken to the Creek Nation. He escaped years later and became an interpretor to Andrew Jackson: [ref. 122].

MAYFIELD, Isaac - arrived with the Donelson flotilla, April 24, 1780: [ref. 123a]. Listed in the North Carolina Preemption Act of 1784, as one of the settlers on the Cumberland at the time of the 1782 Preemption Act, who were too young at the time to receive land, but who were now entitled to 640 acres: [ref. 123b].   1787 Davidson

(continued next page)

MAYFIELD, Isaac - (continued)

Co. tax roll with 1 taxable: [ref. 123c]. He was killed
by Indians on July 6, 1794, within 5 miles of Nashville,
while standing guard for his son-in-law, who was hoeing
corn.   Eight musket balls pierced his body, and he was
scalped, and a bayonet thrust through his face, and 2 bloody
tomahawks were left near his body: [ref. 123d].

MAYFIELD, James - came from Jefferson Co., VA to the Cumberland
Settlements: [ref. 124a]. He was killed by Indians at
Heaton's Station in 1780: [ref. 124b]. Listed in the North
Carolina Preemption Act of 1784, as one of the settlers
killed in defense of the Cumberland Settlements, whose
heirs were entitled to 640 acres without any price to be
paid to the public: [ref. 124c]. His son Micajah Mayfield,
filed his power of attorney to his brother, Isaac Mayfield,
to   settle   the   estate   of   his   father,   James   Mayfield
"preempted." He also mentioned their younger brothers,
Elijah and Elisha: [ref. 124d]. North Carolina land grant:
[ref. 124e].   His wife, at the time of his death, was
Ellender (last name unknown), who remarried afterward to
John Glenn, who was also killed by Indians: [ref. 124f].
James Mayfield's children listed in Davidson County Court
Minutes in 1810, included Micajah, Isaac, Southerlin, Elijah,
Elisha, and a daughter who married John Haggard, and a
daughter who married John Brown: [ref. 124g].

MAYFIELD, John - son of Southerlin Mayfield, was mentioned
in a deposition by John Marion, entered in evidence in
a lawsuit in Williamson County, Tennessee, 1824.   Marion
stated that John Mayfield lived in Davidson Co. at the
time: [ref. 125].

MAYFIELD, Margaret - wife of Southerlin Mayfield, married
John Gibson, after the death of Southerlin: [ref. 126].

MAYFIELD,   Southerlin   -   son   of   James   Mayfield   (see
beforementioned), was assignee of two North Carolina land
grants: [ref. 127a].   He built a station on a branch of
the Mill Creek which was burned by Indians about 1786,
and subsequently, he entered into a contract with John
Haggard, John Campbell, and Benjamin Joslin to build another
Station.   Upon completion, the families of these men along
with Mayfield's family moved into the Fort.   Shortly
thereafter, while burning logs to plant the first crop
and building wolf pens about 1/2 mile from the Fort, Indians
ambushed the party and killed Mayfield, along with his
son, William, and a guard, Andrew Martin. His son, George,
was captured (see beforementioned).   In a few days, at
the request of Mrs. Mayfield, everyone left the station:

(continued next page)

MAYFIELD, Southerlin - (continued)

[ref. 127b]. Account of estate sale filed in Davidson
Co. in 1796: [ref. 127c].
MEARS, James - North Carolina land grant: [ref. 128].
MEARS, William - 1787 Davidson Co. tax roll with 1 taxable:
[ref. 129].
MELDRUM, George - plaintiff in lawsuit against Lardner Clark,
heard before the Superior Court of Law and Equity, May,
1790: [ref. 130].
MENEES (variously, MENNES, MENISS, MINISS, MINUS), James
- purchase land of Jas. Scott: [ref. 131].
MENEES, Ben - 1787 Davidson Co. tax roll with 1 taxable:
[ref. 132a]. Purchased land in 1789, on the west side
of the Sulphur Fork of Red River (Tennessee Co., then
Robertson Co.): [ref. 132b].
MENEES, James - purchased lot 32 of the Trustees of the Town
of Nashville, April 7, 1786: [ref. 133a]. Purchased land
of Jas. Scott: [ref. 133b]. Summoned for Davidson Co.
jury duty on the Superior Court of Law and Equity, Nov.,
1788: [ref. 133c].
MESSEEKER, Ruben - plaintiff in lawsuit against John Harris,
Sr. for a debt, heard before the Committee of the Cumberland
Association, Aug. 5, 1783: [ref. 134].
MESSICK, Jacob - North Carolina land grant: [ref. 135].
MILLER, Isaac - 1787 Davidson Co. tax roll with 1 taxable:
[ref. 136].
MILLER, William - purchased land of William Purnell: [ref.
137].
MILLIKEN (variously, MILIKEN, MILLIGAN), Joseph - was the
first victim of the Indians, who killed him in 1780, on
Richland Creek, cutting his head off and carrying it away:
[ref. 138a]. Listed in the North Carolina Preemption Act
of 1784, as one of the settlers who had died in defense
of the Settlements, whose heirs were entitled to 640 acres
without any price to be paid to the public: [ref. 138b].
MILLS, Joel - killed in the spring of 1783 or 1788 at Dunham's
Station: [ref. 139].
MILTON, John - (heirs of) purchased land on the east fork
of Turnbull's Creek in 1788; and sold the land in 1788:
[ref. 140].
MINES (variously, MINER), George - signer of the Cumberland
Compact, May, 1780: [ref. 141].
MITCHELL, Aaron - son of Margaret Mitchell (see hereafter).
MITCHELL, David - signer of the Cumberland Compact, May,
1780: [ref. 142].
MITCHELL, Elizabeth - married Simon Rogers in Davidson Co.,
March 7, 1789: [ref. 143].

MITCHELL, Margaret - in her will, proven in Davidson Co., July 8, 1788, she bequeathed land left in her husband's will in "Guilford Co.." to grandson Robert Mitchell, son Aaron Mitchell, granddaughter Margaret Ross, and daughter Mary Ross. James Ross was executor: [ref. 144].

MITCHELL, Robert - son of Margaret Mitchell (see above), married Drusilla Everett in Davidson Co., June 1, 1789: [ref. 145].

MITCHELL, William - 1787 Davidson Co. tax roll with 2 taxables: [ref. 146a]. North Carolina land grant: [ref. 146b].

MOBLEY, William - purchased land in 1789, on Barton's Creek (Sumner Co. at the time; then Wilson Co.): [ref. 147].

MOLLOY, Thomas - signer of the Cumberland Compact, May, 1780: [ref. 148a]. Member of the Committee of the Cumberland Association, Jan., 1783: [ref. 148b]. See his interesting letter to the Virginia agent in Illinois and the Spanish Government in the Minutes of the Cumberland Association, May 6, 1783: [ref. 148c]. Member of the first Inferior Court of Pleas and Quarter Sessions, Oct. 6, 1783: [ref. 148d]. Purchased land of the Trustees of Nashville, July 26, 1784: [ref. 148e]. North Carolina land grants: [ref. 148f]. Purchased land of Thos. Callander, and of R. Nelson: [ref. 148g]. 1787 Davidson Co. tax roll with 3 taxables: [ref. 148h].

MONTFLORENCE, James Cole - North Carolina land grants: [ref. 149a]. Numerous land purchases: [ref. 149b]. One source reports he was a French spy, who covered his operations by association with important personages in the settlements: [ref. 149c].

MONTGOMERY, Col. John - D.A.R. membership on this line. Came to the Cumberland area to hunt with Mansker in 1771: [ref. 150a]. Later returned with the Donelson flotilla, April 24, 1780: [ref. 150b]. Signer of the Cumberland Compact, May, 1780: [ref. 150c]. Listed in the North Carolina Preemption Act of 1784, as one of the settlers on the Cumberland in 1780, who stayed and defended the Settlements, and entitled to 640 acres without any price to be paid to the public: [ref. 150d]. Plaintiff in lawsuit before the Superior Court of Law and Equity in 1790: [ref. 150e]. Killed by Indians at Clarksville: [ref. 150f]. Child: Katherine Montgomery: [ref. 150g]. See Sumner Co. section of this work for other Montgomery names.

MONTGOMERY, Rebecca - testified in case (Humphrey Hogan vs. Stephen Ray) before the Committee of the Cumberland Association, May 6, 1783: [ref. 151].

MONTGOMERY, Robert - North Carolina land grant: [ref. 152].

MOONSHAW, Joseph - was wounded by Indians at the Battle of the Bluffs, April 2, 1781: [ref. 153].

MOORE, Alexander - 1787 Davidson Co. tax roll with 1 taxable: [ref. 154].
MOORE, Dempsey - signer of the Cumberland Compact, May, 1780: [ref. 155].
MOORE, Edward - signer of the Cumberland Compact, May 1780: [ref. 156].
MOORE, Elijah - signer of the Cumberland Compact, May, 1780: [ref. 157].
MOORE, Isaac - North Carolina land grant: [ref. 158].
MOORE, James - signer of the Cumberland Compact, May, 1780: [ref. 159a]. Purchased land of John Craddock, 1788: [ref. 159b]. He died ca. 1788, and his partner John Rice, took over his affairs: [ref. 159c]. See power of attorney to Daniel Williams from Moses Moore of Jefferson Co., Kentucky, regarding the estate of James Moore, deceased, filed in Davidson Co., July 27, 1796: [ref. 159d].
MOORE, John - signer of the Cumberland Compact, May, 1780: [ref. 160].
MOORE, Mathews - purchased land of Thomas Isbell: [ref. 161].
MOORE, Richard - signer of the Cumberland Compact, May, 1780: [ref. 162].
MOORE, Robert - North Carolina land grant: [ref. 163].
MOORE, Samuel - signer of the Cumberland Compact, May, 1780: [ref. 164a]. North Carolina land grants [ref. 164b].
MOORE, William - 1787 Davidson Co. tax roll with 1 taxable: [ref. 165a]. Purchased land of the Trustees of Nashville in 1789: [ref. 165b].
MOORE, William H. - signer of the Cumberland Compact, May, 1780: [ref. 166].
MORE, William - signer of the Cumberland Compact, May, 1780: [ref. 167].
MORGAN, Griffith -(heirs of) sold land in 1789, on Sycamore Creek (Tennessee Co. at the time; then Robertson Co.): [ref. 168].
MORGAN, Isaac - married Judith Smith in Davidson Co., July 29, 1789: [ref. 169].
MORGAN, John - was appointed by the court with Edward Jennings, to inquire of damages sustained by plaintiff in lawsuit in Nov., 1790: [ref. 170].
MORRIS, William - signer of the Cumberland Compact, May, 1780: [ref. 171].
MORRELL, John - plaintiff in lawsuit before the Superior Court of Law and Equity, May, 1790: [ref. 172].
MORROW, Samuel - listed in the North Carolina Preemption Act of 1784, as one of the settlers who had died in defense of the settlements, whose heirs were entitled to 640 acres without any price to be paid to the public: [ref. 173].

MORROW, Thomas - purchased land on the north side of the Cumberland River, June 14, 1791: [ref. 174a]. His heirs sold land in 1790, on White's Creek: [ref. 174b].

MORTON, Joseph - signer of the Cumberland Compact, May, 1780: [ref. 175].

MOSELY, Joseph - signer of the Cumberland Compact, May, 1780: [ref. 176].

MOSELY, Thomas - while living at Freeland's Station, he was given power of attorney by Philip Alston in 1784: [ref. 177].

MOTHERALL, John - 1787 Davidson Co. tax roll with 1 taxable: [ref. 178a]. Purchased land on the south side of the Cumberland River in 1790: [ref. 178b].

MULHERRIN (variously, MULHEREN, MULHERIN), James - traveled with the Buchanan party from South Carolina to the Cumberland Settlements: [ref. 179a]. He recorded his stock mark in the Minutes of the Committee of the Cumberland Association, Mar. 4, 1783, thus: "A crop off the left ear, and an under kell in the right.": [ref. 179b]. Served on the first grand jury, Oct. 6, 1783: [ref. 179c]. Listed in the North Carolina Preemption Act of 1784, as one of the settlers on the Cumberland in 1780, who stayed and defended the Settlements, and entitled to 640 acres without any price to be paid to the public: [ref. 179d]. North Carolina land grant: [ref. 179e]. Purchased land in 1788, on Caney Fork River (Sumner Co. at the time; then Smith Co.): [ref. 179f]. Helped defend Buchanan's Station during the Indian attack of Sept. 30., 1792: [ref. 179g].

MULHERRIN, Jane - married Cornelius Riddle at Fort Nashboro: [ref. 180].

MULHERRIN, John - traveled with the Buchanan party from South Carolina to the Cumberland Settlements: [ref. 181a]. Listed in the North Carolina Preemption Act of 1784, as one of the settlers on the Cumberland in 1780, who had stayed and defended the Settlements, and entitled to 640 acres without any price to be paid to the public: [ref. 181b]. North Carolina land grants: [ref. 181c].

MULHERRIN, William - purchased land of the Trustees of Nashville: [ref. 182].

MULHERRIN, William - killed by Indians at Buchanan's Station in 1783: [ref. 183].

MULLEN, Malone - North Carolina land grant: [ref. 184].

MUNGLE, Daniel - signer of the Cumberland Compact, May, 1780: [ref. 185a]. He escaped an Indian ambush on Barren River: [ref. 185b].

MURDOCH (variously, MURDOCK), Allen - (heirs of) sold land in 1790: [ref. 186].

MURDOCH, John - 1787 Davidson Co. tax roll with 1 taxable: [ref. 187].
MURFREE, Fanny - daughter of Hardy Murfree (see hereafter).
MURFREE, Lt. Col. Hardy - D.A.R. membership on this line. Born June 15, 1752, in Hertford Co., NC; married Feb. 17, 1780, to Sallie Brickel, who was born July 29, 1757. Resided in Hertford Co., NC during the Revolution: [ref. 188a]. Defendant in lawsuit before the Superior Court of Law and Equity, Nov., 1790: [ref. 188b]. He died in Williamson Co., TN, April 6, 1809. Children: William, b. Sept. 2, 1781; Fanny, b. Aug. 23, 1783; Mary, b. March 9, 1786; Mathias, b. March 26, 1788; Rachel, b. Oct. 5, 1790; and several other children born after 1790: [ref. 188c].
MURFREE, Mary - daughter of Hardy Murfree (see above).
MURFREE, Mathias - son of Hardy Murfree (see above).
MURFREE, Rachel - daughter of Hardy Murfree (see above).
MURFREE, William - son of Hardy Murfree (see above).
MURRAY, Titus - signer of the Cumberland Compact, May, 1780: [ref. 189].
MURREY, Thomas - married Hannah Bushart in Davidson Co., Oct. 12, 1790: [ref. 190].
MURRY, Samuel - killed by Indians while gathering cymlings with Solomon Philips in what was later called Cross's Old Field in 1780: [ref. 191].
MURRY, Thomas - 1787 Davidson Co. tax roll with 1 taxable: [ref. 192].
MURRY, William - married Margaret Boyd in Davidson Co., March 31, 1790: [ref. 193a]. North Carolina land grants: [ref. 193b].
MYERS, Jacob - North Carolina land grant: [ref. 194].
MYHART, William - (heirs of) sold land in 1790, on Blooming Grove Creek (Tennessee Co. at the time; then Montgomery Co.): [ref. 195].

N

NAINE, _____ - son of Mrs. Naine, was captured by Creek Indians on White's Creek: [ref. 1].
NASH, William - 1787 Davidson Co. tax roll with 1 taxable: [ref. 2a]. Purchased land on the east fork of Stone's River in 1788: [ref. 2b]. Served on jury duty on the Superior Court of Law and Equity, Nov. 1788: [ref. 2c]. Married Polly Evans in Davidson Co., June 5, 1790: [ref. 2d].

NEAL, Thomas - 1787 Davidson County tax roll with 1 taxable:
[ref. 3].
NEELEY, (variously, NEALEY, NEALLY, NEELY), Alexander -
summoned from Sumner Co. for jury duty on the Superior
Court of Law and Equity meeting in Nashville, Nov. 1788:
[ref. 4a]. Killed by Indians near Greenfield Fort in 1790:
[ref. 4b].
NEELEY, Elizabeth - daughter of William Neeley (see hereafter).
NEELEY, Gean - daughter of William Neeley (see hereafter).
NEELEY, Isaac - son of William Neeley (see hereafter).
NEELEY, Isaac - arrived at the French Lick with his family
aboard the Donelson flotilla, April 24, 1780: [ref. 5a].
Gave deposition before the Committee of the Cumberland
Association, Jan. 18, 1783, and April 1, 1783: [ref. 5b].
1787 Davidson Co. tax roll with 2 taxables: [ref. 5c].
NEELEY, Jane - daughter of William Neeley (see hereafter).
NEELEY, John - son of William Neeley (see hereafter).
NEELEY, Margaret - daughter of William Neeley (see hereafter).
NEELEY, Margaret Patterson - wife of William Neeley (see
hereafter); was killed by Indians in Neeley's Bend in 1787:
[ref. 6].
NEELEY, Martha - daughter of William Neeley (see hereafter).
NEELEY, Mary - daughter of William Neeley (see hereafter);
was captured in the fall of 1780, by Indians who killed
her father. She was carried away by her captors to Michigan.
There she made her escape after two years and made her
way to New York state and eventually returned home. She
married in Kentucky: [ref. 7].
NEELEY, Samuel - son of William Neeley (see hereafter).
NEELEY, William - son of William Neeley (see hereafter).
NEELEY, William - D.A.R. membership on this line. Born ca.
1730, probably in SC. Married ca. 1754, to Margaret
Patterson: [ref. 8a]. Came to the Cumberland with the
Robertson party. He helped build Mansker's Station in
1779: [ref.8b]. He stayed and planted corn in 1779, and
settled at Neeley's Lick in the Neeley's Bend of Cumberland
River. He was killed there by Indians in 1780: [ref. 8c].
Listed in the North Carolina Preemption Act of 1784, as
one of the settlers who had died in the defense of the
Cumberland Settlements, whose heirs were entitled to 640
acres without any price to be paid to the public: [ref.
8d]. Children: Gean, b. July 7, 1755, m. Jacob Spears;
Elizabeth, b. Mar. 8, 1757; Isaac, b. Mar. 24, 1759, killed
by Indians; Mary, b. Aug. 20, 1761, m. Lt. George Spears
on Feb. 24, 1785; Martha, b. Apr. 25, 1764; William, Jr.,
b. Dec. 12, 1766; Jane, b. Dec. 31, 1767, m. Thomas Buchanan;
Samuel, b. May 30, 1769, m. Mary Watkins, d. ca. 1810;
Margaret, b. Dec. 20,1772; and John, b. May 16, 1774: [ref.
8e].

NEGRO - there were 105 blacks between the ages of 12 and 60 years in Davidson County in 1787, according to the tax roll for that year: [ref. 9].
NEGRO - slave of George Freeland was subject of a lawsuit (Freeland vs. Deson) before the Committee of the Cumberland Association, July 1, 1783: [ref. 10]. Witnesses testified that Samuel Deson had whipped the negro after the negro threw a clod at and struck Deson's little daughter. The negro was also accused of using abusive language to Sara Lucas and Jenny Tucker.
NEGRO - boy, slave of Capt. Robertson was killed during an Indian attack on Freeland's Station: [ref. 11].
NEGRO - man, killed in the Indian attack on Freeland's Station: [ref. 12].
NEGRO - slave of Capt. Thomas Hutchins, died of frostbite during the Donelson flotilla voyage to the French Lick: [ref. 13].
NEGRO Adam - slave of Robert Boyd: [ref. 14].
NEGRO Cumbo - slave of Daniel Williams, Sr.: [ref. 15].
NEGRO Dave - slave of Robert Boyd: [ref. 16].
NEGRO Febbee - slave of Robert Boyd: [ref. 17].
NEGRO Fib - slave of Robert Boyd: [ref. 18].
NEGRO George - slave of John Boyd, mentioned in lawsuit, Nov. 1790: [ref. 19].
NEGRO Jim - left at Clover Bottom by Col. Henderson, was killed there by Indians in 1780: [ref. 20].
NEGRO Milla - slave of Jonathan Jennings: [ref. 21].
NEGRO Patsy - a cook, the slave of John Donelson, came to the Cumberland on the Donelson flotilla, April 24, 1780: [ref. 22].
NELSON, John - North Carolina land grants: [ref. 23].
NELSON, Robert - purchased land in 1788, above the mouth of Red River (Tennessee Co.): [ref. 24a]. Summoned for Davidson Co. jury duty in Nov., 1788, on the Superior Court of Law and Equity: [ref. 24b]. He married Elizabeth Bell in Davidson Co., Sept. 1, 1789: [ref. 24c]. Summoned from Tennessee County for jury duty, May, 1790, on the Superior Court of Law and Equity: [ref. 24d]. Purchased land of Polk Montgomery and Crutcher: [ref. 24e].
NESSET, Grizzel - married James Hoggatt in Davidson Co., Sept. 8, 1790: [ref. 25].
NEVILLE (variously, NEVILLES), George - an attorney, who purchased land of the Trustees of Nashville: [ref. 26a]. 1787 Davidson Co. tax roll with 4 taxables: [ref. 26b].
NEVILLE, John - summoned for Davidson Co. jury duty, Nov. 1788, on the Superior Court of Law and Equity: [ref. 27].
NEWELL, George - North Carolina land grant: [ref. 28].

NEWELL, John - summoned for Davidson Co. jury duty, May, 1789, on the Superior Court of Law and Equity: [ref. 29].
NEWELL, Samuel - signer of the Cumberland Compact, May, 1780: [ref. 30].
NEWELL, William - North Carolina land grant: [ref. 31].
NEWHAM, Francis - (heirs of) sold land in 1790, on White's Creek: [ref. 32].
NEWTON, Edmund - signer of the Cumberland Compact, May, 1780: [ref. 33].
NEWSOM (variously, NEWSOME, NUSAM), Jonas - 1787 Davidson Co. tax roll with 2 taxables: [ref. 34].
NICELY, William - listed in the North Carolina Preemption Act of 1784, as one of the settlers who died in the defense of the Cumberland Settlements, whose heirs were entitled to 640 acres without any price to be paid to the public: [ref. 35].
NICKERSON, John - killed by Indians on May 27, 1791, at Smith's Fork (Sumner Co. at the time; then Smith Co.): [ref. 36].
NOBLE (variously, NOBLES), Mark - arrived with the Donelson flotilla, April 24, 1780: [ref. 37a]. He was sued by Solomon White for breach of contract, Mar. 5, 1783, before the Committee of the Cumberland Association: [ref. 37b]. Listed in the North Carolina Preemption Act of 1784, as one of the settlers on the Cumberland too young to receive land under the Preemption Act of 1782, but who was now entitled to 640 acres: [ref. 37c]. North Carolina land grant: [ref. 37d].
NOLAND, ____ - son of Thomas Noland, was killed in what is now Sumner Co. in 1783: [ref. 38].
NOLAND, Joseph - killed by Indians ca. 1783, within sight of Armstrong's Fort: [ref. 39].
NOLAND, Thomas - was killed by Indians near Armstrong's Fort in the fall of 1783: [ref. 40].
NOLANS, Thomas - killed by Indians in either Davidson or Sumner Co. after Jan. 1, 1787: [ref. 41].
NORRINGTON, Joshua or Joseph - was killed by Indians in the summer of 1783, or 1788, near the place where Joseph Irwin's house later stood on Richland Creek: [ref. 42].
NORRIS, Ezekial - signer of the Cumberland Compact, May, 1780: [ref. 43].
NORRIS, John - summoned from Sumner Co. for jury duty on the Superior Court of Law and Equity, meeting in Nashville in 1788: [ref. 44].

O

O'BRYAN, Lawrence - purchased land in May, 1790, on the Dry Fork of West Fork of Red River (Tennessee Co. at the time; then Montgomery Co.): [ref. 1].

O'BRYAN, Tido - (heirs of) sold land in 1790, on Barton's Creek (Sumner Co. at the time; then Wilson Co.): [ref. 2].

O'CONNER, James - called "Jemmy," was born in Ireland. He helped defend Buchanan's Station during the Indian attack of Sept. 30, 1792: [ref. 3].

O'NEAL (variously, O'NEALL), Jonathan - 1787 Davidson Co. tax roll with 2 taxables: [ref. 4].

O'NEAL, Mitchell - married Delilah Martin in Davidson Co., Mar. 5, 1790: [ref. 5a]. He was appointed Constable to the Grand Jury in May, 1790: [ref. 5b].

O'NEAL, William - purchased land in 1790, on the East Fork of Round Lick Creek (Sumner Co. at the time; then Smith Co.): [ref. 6].

OGLESBY, Daniel - mentioned as being "of Davidson Co.," and son of Elisha Oglesby of 96 District, SC, in Davidson Co. probate records, Jan. 6, 1783: [ref. 7].

OGLESBY, John - 1787 Davidson Co. tax roll with 1 taxable: [ref. 8].

ORE, William - summoned from Sumner Co. for jury duty on the Superior Court of Law and Equity meeting in Nashville, Nov. 1790: [ref. 9].

OSTIN, William - (heirs of) sold land in 1790, on Payton's Creek (Sumner Co. at the time; then Smith Co.): [ref. 10].

OVERALL, Nathaniel - listed with William Overall in the 1787 Davidson Co. tax roll with 2 taxables: [ref. 11].

OVERALL, Susannah - wife of William Overall (see hereafter).

OVERALL, William - (the records on William Overall suggests we have records on two individuals of the same name). He was with the Robertson party in early 1779, at the French Lick, and stayed to plant corn and to keep the buffaloes out of the corn: [ref. 12a]. He recorded his stock mark in the Minutes of the Committee of the Cumberland Association on March 5, 1783, thus: "A crop and a slit in the right ear, and a drop off the left.": [ref. 12b]. Appointed administrator of the estate of Patrick Quigley, deceased, by the Cumberland Association, April 1, 1783: [ref. 12c]. Security for Sheriff Williams on Oct. 6, 1783: [ref. 12d]. Listed in the North Carolina Preemption Act of 1784, as one of the settlers on the Cumberland in 1780, who stayed

(continued next page)

OVERALL, William - (continued)

and defended the settlements, and entitled to 640 acres without any price to be paid to the public: [ref. 12e]. North Carolina land grants: [ref. 12f]. Listed with Nathaniel Overall in the 1787 Davidson Co. tax roll: [ref. 12g]. One source states he was killed by Indians while going from the Bluff to Kentucky in 1783: [ref. 12h]. His estate inventory was filed in Davidson Co. in January, 1795, by Susannah Overall, administrix: [ref. 12i].

OVERTON, John - purchased land in 1790, on Yellow Creek: [ref. 13a]. He was admitted to practice law in May, 1790: [ref. 13b].

OWENS, Arthur - listed with Charles Owens on the 1787 Davidson Co. tax roll with 2 taxables: [ref. 14].

OWENS, Charles - listed with Arthur Owens on the 1787 Davidson Co. tax roll: [ref. 15].

OWENS, John - signer of the Cumberland Compact, May, 1780: [ref. 16].

OYER, Milcher (variously, Melcher) - summoned from Tennessee Co. for jury duty on the Superior Court of Law and Equity meeting in Nashville, May, 1789: [ref. 17].

P

PADDLER, Thomas - (heirs of) sold land in 1790, on the west side of Red River (Tennesee Co. at the time; then probably, Montgomery Co.): [ref. 1].

PAINE (variously, PAIN - see also, PAYNE), ____ - killed by Indians near Asher's Station: [ref. 2].

PAINE, John - William Paine, his heir, sold land in 1789, on Round Lick Creek (Sumner Co. at the time; then Smith Co.): [ref. 3a]. His heir sold land on Mill creek in 1790: [ref. 3b].

PAINE, William - heir of John Paine (see beforementioned).

PALMER, Elisha - (heirs of) sold land in 1790, on Yellow Creek: [ref. 4].

PARKER, Isom - (heirs of) sold land in Sumner Co. in 1790: [ref. 5].

PATRICK, James - signer of the Cumberland Compact, May, 1780: [ref. 6].

PATTERSON, John - (heirs of) sold land in 1789, on the east fork of Stone's River: [ref. 7].

PAYNE (see also, PAINE), ____ - young man by this name, was
with Blackmore's party on the Donelson flotilla, and was
killed March 8, 1780: [ref. 8].
PAYNE, George - listed with Josiah and Matthew Payne on the
1787 Davidson Co. tax roll with 3 taxables: [ref. 9].
PAYNE, Josiah - listed with George and Matthew Payne on the
1787 Davidson Co. tax roll: [10a]. He was married to Mary
Barnett in Davidson Co., May 4, 1789: [ref. 10b].
PAYNE, Matthew - married Mary Green, daughter of Lewis Green:
[ref. 11a]. North Carolina land grant: [ref. 11b]. Listed
with George and Josiah Payne on the 1787 Davidsun Co. tax
roll: [ref. 11c].
PAYTON - see PEYTON.
PEARSON, James - land purchased in 1788, on the east fork
of Stone's River: [ref. 12].
PENNINGTON, Isaac - North Carolina land grant: [ref. 13a].
1787 Davidson Co. tax roll with 3 taxables: [ref. 13b].
Killed by Indians July 15, 1792, at Dripping Spring: [ref.
13c].
PENNINGTON, Jacob - 1787 Davidson Co. tax roll with 4 taxables:
[ref. 14].
PERRAULT, Mr. - carried messages from James Robertson to
the Cherokees in July, 1787: [ref. 15].
PETERSON, Elliott - listed on a North Carolina land grant
with Isaac Peterson: [ref. 16].
PETERSON, Isaac - listed with Elliott Peterson in a North
Carolina land grant: [ref. 17a]. 1787 Davidson Co. tax
roll with 1 taxable: [ref. 17b].
PETTIT, Benjamin - purchased land of the Trustees of Nashville:
[ref. 18].
PEYTON (variously, PAYTON), Thomas - purchased land in 1788;
and purchased land in 1790, on Dickson (sic) Creek (Sumner
Co.; then Smith Co.): [ref. 19].
PHARR (variously, PHAR), Ephriam - purchased land in 1788,
in Sumner Co.: [ref. 20].
PHARRIS, Samuel - signer of the Cumberland Compact, May 1780:
[ref. 21].
PHEOBE - a woman living at Buchanan's Station at the time
of the Indian attack on Sept. 30, 1792. She had several
children. During the attack, she tried to surrender herself
and her children, but was stopped by Sally Buchanan: [ref.
22].
PHELPS - (often confused in the record with PHILIPS, PHILLIPS.)
PHELPS, John - signer of the Cumberland Compact, May 1780:
[ref. 23].
PHELPS, Solomon.- listed in the North Carolina Preemption Act of
1784, as one of the settlers who had died in defense

PHELPS, Solomon - (continued)

of the Cumberland Settlements, whose heirs were entitled
to 640 acres without any price to be paid to the public:
[ref. 24]. (see Solomon Phillips).
PHILIPS (variously, PHILLIPS; see also, PHELPS), ____ - was
wounded by Indians at Asher's Station in the latter part
of 1780: [ref. 25]
PHILIPS, David - North Carolina land grant: [ref. 26].
PHILIPS, Eleonor - daughter of Philip Philips (see hereafter).
PHILIPS, Elizabeth - daughter of Philip Philips (see
hereafter).
PHILIPS, John - son of Philip Philips (see hereafter).
PHILIPS, John - signer of the Cumberland Compact, May, 1780:
[ref. 27a]. 1787 Davidson Co. tax roll: [ref. 27b].
PHILIPS, Joseph - son of Philip Philips (see hereafter).
PHILIPS, Mann - purchased land in 1788, on Red River (Tennessee
Co. at the time; then Montgomery or Robertson Co.): [ref.
28].
PHILIPS, Mary - daughter of Philip Philips (see hereafter).
PHILIPS, Nancy - daughter of Philip Philips (see hereafter).
PHILIPS, Philip - purchased land on Stone's River and Barton's
Creek in 1790: [ref. 29a]. His will was proven in Davidson
Co., Nov. 27, 1797. It mentions his wife Susannah; and
children: John, James, Eleonor, Joseph, Elizabeth, Mary,
Nancy, and William. The will also records a bequest to
"Sarah James raised by wife's sister, Elizabeth..": [ref.
29b].
PHILIPS, Solomon - went from Fort Nashboro to a place nearby
called Cross's old field for cymlings. The Indians ambushed
him and mortally wounded him, but he made it back to the
fort before dying: [ref. 30].
PHILIPS, Susannah - wife of Philip Philips (see above).
PHILLIPS, William - son of Philip Philips (above).
PILLOW, William - participated in Capt. Shannon's attack
on an Indian raiding party in 1787; and afterward, he was
a Col. of Maury Co.: [ref. 31].
PIRTLE, George - 1787 Davidson Co. tax roll with 1 taxable:
[ref. 32].
PLEAK, John - signer of the Cumberland Compact, May, 1780:
[ref. 33].
POE, William - "of Baltimore Town County, Baltimore, Maryland;
a hatter," purchased land of Andrew Breaky: [ref. 34a].
North Carolina land grant: [ref. 34b].
POITEVENT, Peter - North Carolina land grant: [ref. 35].
POLK, William - came to the Cumberland Settlements in 1783:
[ref. 36].
POLLOCK, B. William - purchased land of E. Titus, Oct. 5,
1785: [ref. 37a]. Purchased land on Big Harpeth River
in 1789: [ref. 37b]. (see William Barkley Pollock)

POLLOCK, William Barkley - 1787 Davidson Co. tax roll with
1 taxable: [ref. 38a]. Served as Clerk of Tennessee County,
Nov. 1788: [ref. 38b].
POPE, Willis - signer of the Cumberland Compact, May, 1780:
[ref. 39].
PORTER, Benjamin - arrived with his family at the French
Lick, April 24, 1780, aboard the Donelson flotilla: [ref.
40a]. Listed in the North Carolina Preemption Act of 1784,
as one of the settlers, who had died in the defense of
the Cumberland Settlements, whose heirs were entitled to
640 acres without any price to be paid to the public: [ref.
40b].
PORTER, David - listed in the North Carolina Preemption Act
of 1784, as one of the settlers who had died in the defense
of the Cumberland Settlements, whose heirs were entitled
to 640 acres without any price to be paid to the public:
[ref. 41].
PORTER, Hannah- daughter of John Porter (see hereafter).
PORTER, John - son of John Porter (see hereafter).
PORTER, John - D.A.R. membership on this line. Born ca.
1750 in Lancaster, PA or Orange Co., NC. Married Hannah
Hamilton, Mar. 23, 1773, in Guilford Co., NC: [ref. 42a].
He was killed by Indians in the cedars within view of
Heaton's Station in 1780: [ref. 42b]. His estate inventory
was filed in Davidson Co. in 1784: [ref. 42c]. Children:
Mary, b. Feb. 25, 1774, m. Wm. McKay; Hannah, b. 1776;
Thomas, b. 1778; and John, b. 1780: [ref 42d].
PORTER, Mary - daughter of John Porter (see above).
PORTER, Rus - summoned for Davidson Co. jury duty, Nov. 1788:
[ref. 43].
PORTER, Samuel - (heirs of) sold land in 1790, on Yellow
Creek: [ref. 44].
PORTER, Thomas - son of John Porter (see above).
PORTERFIELD, James - purchased land in 1788, on Nelson's
Creek: [ref. 45].
POTTER, John - North Carolina land grant: [ref. 46].
POTTER, Rice - purchased land of John Forde: [ref. 47].
POWELL, Clayton - sent on a scout from Buchanan's Station
with Jonathan Gee on Sept. 29, 1792, and was killed along
with Gee by the Indians: [ref. 48].
POWER, George - signer of the Cumberland Compact, May, 1780:
[ref. 49].
PRATT, Ephriam - arrived with the Donelson flotilla, April
24, 1780: [ref. 50a]. Listed in the North Carolina
Preemption Act of 1784, as one of the settlers on the
Cumberland in 1780, who stayed and defended the Settlements,
and entitled to 640 acres without any price to be paid
to the public: [ref. 50b]. He married Sarah Buchanan in
Davidson Co., June 28, 1790: [ref. 50c].

PREVIEW, James - his heir, John Preview, sold land in 1790: [ref. 51].

PREVIEW, John - heir of James Preview (see above).

PRICE, Elisha - summoned for Davidson Co. jury duty, Nov. 1790: [ref. 52].

PRICE, Jonathan - summoned from Tennessee Co. for jury duty on the Superior Court of Law and Equity, May, 1789; and again in Nov., 1790: [ref. 53].

PRICE, William - signer of the Cumberland Compact, May, 1780: [ref. 54a]. He lived with his family at Hendrick's Station on Station Camp Creek when attacked by Indians in 1787. He and his wife were killed and their children "chopped" and wounded: [ref. 54b].

PRINCE, Francis - elected Captain of militia at Mauldings Station in 1783: [ref. 55a]. Was a member of the first Inferior Court of Pleas and Quarter Sessions, Oct. 6, 1783: [ref. 55b]. Purchased land of the Trustees of Nashville: [ref. 55c]. 1787 Davidson Co. tax roll with 10 taxables: [ref. 55d]. Summoned from Tennessee Co. for jury duty on the Superior Court of Law and Equity, May, 1790: [ref. 55e]. (See D.A.R. information on William Prince for possible connection.)

PRINCE, Robert - summoned from Tennessee County for jury duty on the Superior Court of Law and Equity, May, 1790: [ref. 56].

PRINCE, William - summoned from Tennessee Co. for jury duty on the Superior Court of Law and Equity, Nov. 1790: [ref. 57].

PROCHMAN, Phil - 1787 Davidson Co. tax roll with 1 taxable: [ref. 58].

PROTZMAN, Lawrence - purchased land, July 19, 1788, on Jones' Creek of Harpeth River; [ref. 59].

PRUETT, Capt. William - elected Captain of militia at Nashborough Station in Mar. 1783: [ref. 60a]. Raised 20 men to pursue an Indian raiding party to the Richland Creek of Elk River in 1783, and he was killed by Indians near camp on Duck River: [ref. 60b].

PUGH, Thomas - was killed by Indians on March 2, 1786, while on a surveying trip with John and Ephraim Peyton and John Frazier on Defeated Creek in what is now Sumner Co.: [ref. 61].

PURNELL, Mary - wife of John Donelson, Jr. (see beforementioned).

PURNELL, William - signer of the Cumberland Compact, May, 1780: [ref. 62a]. North Carolina land grant: [ref. 62b].

PURSLEY, John - (heirs of) sold land in 1790, on Mill Creek: [ref. 63].

PURVELL, Barnett - (heirs of) sold land in 1790: [ref. 64].

Q

QUIGLEY, Patrick - signer of the Cumberland Compact, May, 1780: [ref. 1a]. He was killed by Indians at Mansker's Station in 1781. He was sleeping late the morning the station was broken up and was shot in bed by Indians shooting through the portholes in the fort: [ref. 1b]. Listed in the North Carolina Preemption Act of 1784, as one of the settlers on the Cumberland, who had died in defense of the Settlements, and whose heirs were entitled to 640 acres without any price to be paid to the public: [ref. 1c]. His estate was administered by William Overall before the Committee of the Cumberland Association, April 1, 1793: [ref. 1d].

QUILLON, Daniel - his heir, Thomas Quillon, sold land in 1789: [ref. 2].

QUILLON, Thomas - heir of Daniel Quillon (see above).

R

RAGSDALE (variously, RAGSDELL, RAGSDIL), Daniel - signer of the Cumberland Compact, May, 1780: [ref. 1].

RAGSDALE, Daniel - signer of the Cumberland Compact, May, 1780: [ref. 2].

RAINS, Barbara - daughter of Capt. John Rains, Sr. (see hereafter).

RAINS, Christina - daughter of Capt. John Rains, Sr. (hereafter).

RAINS, Elizabeth - daughter of Capt. John Rains, Sr. (see hereafter).

RAINS, Capt. John, Sr. - was in a company of 20 adventurers from North Carolina, Rockbridge in Virginia, and New River, who hunted in the Cumberland area in 1769: [ref. 3a]. After returning to his home, he set out from New River to go to Kentucky. Enroute he met James Robertson who persuaded him to come to the Cumberland in Oct. 1779, bringing his family and livestock: [ref. 3b]. He was sued by Solomon White, Mar. 4, 1783, before the Committee of the Cumberland Association: [ref. 3c].

RAINS, John, Jr. - son of Capt. John Rains, Sr., made a prisoner of an Indian in Sept. 1787, and brought him back to Nashville: [ref. 4].

RAINS, Martha - daughter of Capt. John Rains, Sr. (see above).

RAINS, Mary - daughter of Capt. John Rains, Sr. (see above).

RAINS, Mereday - signer of the Cumberland Compact, May, 1780: [ref. 5].

RAINS, Nancy - daughter of Capt. John Rains, Sr. (see above).

RAINS, Patsy - was riding horseback with Betsy Williams when Betsy was killed by Indians: [ref. 6].

RAINS, Peter - (heirs of) sold land in 1790: [ref. 7].

RAINS, Sarah - daughter of Capt. John Rains, Sr. (see abovementioned).

RAINS, William - son of Capt. John Rains, Sr. (see above).

RALSTON, David - 1787 Davidson Co. tax roll with 1 taxable: [ref. 8].

RAMSEY, ____ - married Amos Heaton: [ref. 9].

RAMSEY, ____ - married Col. John Montgomery: [ref. 10].

RAMSEY, Henry - arrived with the Donelson flotilla, April 24, 1780: [ref. 11a]. He brought Mrs. Jones to safety after the Battle Creek Massacre: [ref. 11b]. He was ordered by the Committee of the Cumberland Association, April 1, 1783, to help lay off a road from Heatonsburg (Heaton's Station) to Mansker's Station: [ref. 11c]. Listed in the North Carolina Preemption Act of 1784, as one of the settlers on the Cumberland in 1780, who had stayed and defended the settlements and entitled to 640 acres without any price to be paid to the public: [11d]. He was shot through the body by Indians near Bledsoe's Creek between Greenfield and Morgan's Station, 3/4 mile from Bledsoe's Lick in the fall of 1788: [ref. 11e]. His heirs sold land in 1789, on Round Lick Creek (Sumner Co. at the time; then possibly Smith Co.): [ref. 11f].

RAMSEY, Josiah - son of Josiah Ramsey of Reidy Creek in Wythe Co., VA, and brother of Mrs. Eaton and Thomas Ramsey. He came with his brother to the Cumberland Settlements in 1780: [ref. 12a]. Elected Captain of militia at Heatonsburg (Heaton's Station) in 1783: [ref. 12b]. North Carolina land grants: [ref. 12c]. 1787 Davidson Co. tax roll with 2 taxables: [ref. 12d]. Summoned from Tennessee Co. for jury duty on the Superior Court of Law and Equity, May, 1790: [ref. 12e].

RAMSEY, Solomon - (heirs of) sold land in 1790, on Blooming Grove Creek (Tennessee Co. at the time; then Montgomery Co.): [ref. 13].

RAMSEY, Thomas - son of Josiah Ramsey, and brother of Josiah Ramsey (see beforementioned).

RAMSEY, William - settled in the Cumberland Settlements with his family from western Virginia in the fall of 1781: [ref. 14a]. 1787 Davidson Co. tax roll with 1 taxable: [ref. 14b]. He was killed by Indians: [ref. 14c].
RATER, Thomas - received 640 acres under the 1784 Noirth Carolina Preemption Act: [ref. 15].
RATLETF (variously, RATLIFF, possibly, RATCLIFF), Daniel - signer of the Cumberland Compact, May, 1780: [ref. 16].
RAY, James, Jr. - signer of the Cumberland Compact, May, 1780: [ref. 17].
RAY, James, Sr. - signer of the Cumberland Compact, May, 1780: [ref. 18a]. North Carolina land grant: [ref. 18b].
RAY, Stephen - bondsman for Daniel Hogan, the administrator of the estate of James Harrod, before the Committee of the Cumberland Association, Mar. 4, 1783; and he was bondsman for William Overall, April 1, 1783: [ref. 19a]. Elected first Constable at Heaton's Station, Oct. 7, 1783: [ref. 19b]. Listed in the North Carolina Preemption Act of 1784, as one of the settlers on the Cumberland in 1780, who stayed and defended the Settlements, and entitled to 640 acres without any price to be paid to the public: [ref. 19c]. 1787 Davidson Co. tax roll with 1 taxable: [ref. 19d].
RAY, William - signer of the Cumberland Compact, May, 1780: [ref. 20].
RECKNER, Coonrod - 1787 Davidson Co. tax roll with 1 taxable: [ref. 21].
REED (see also, REID), Alexander - 1787 Davidson Co. tax roll: [ref. 22].
REED, Elizabeth - wife of Jesse Reed (see hereafter).
REED, Jesse - North Carolina land grants: [ref. 23a]. His will proven in Davidson Co., July, 1797, mentions his wife Elizabeth and "children": [ref. 23b].
REED, Major John - made a motion to the Committee of the Cumberland Association on June 3, 1783, to assemble all the Southern Tribes of Indians at the French Lick to discuss a treaty: [ref. 24a]. He was candidate for the first Entry Taker and lost election: [ref. 24b].
REEVES, Charlotte - wife of James Robertson (see hereafter).
REEVES, William - arrived with the Donelson flotilla, April 24, 1780: [ref. 25].
REID, Alexander - purchased land in 1790, on White's Creek: [ref. 26].
REID, John - signer of the Cumberland Compact, May, 1780: [ref. 27].
REID, Joseph - signer of the Cumberland Compact, May, 1780: [ref. 28].
RENFROE (variously, RENFRO, RENTFRO) - family of, were on the Donelson flotilla and left the flotilla, April 24, 1780, at Red River. They built a fort near the mouth of Red River, and afterwards, moved from Red River to the French Lick: [ref. 29].

RENFROE, Bartlette - was killed by Indians near the French Lick near a mound on the south side of the spot "where the steam mill is now." John Maxwell and John Kendrick were taken prisoner at the same time: [ref. 30].

RENFROE, Isaac - signer of the Cumberland Compact, May, 1780: [ref. 31].

RENFROE, James - mentioned in a lawsuit (Olive Shaw vs. Frederick Stump) regarding Renfroe's sale of land near Heatonsburg to Shaw, heard before the Committee of the Cumberland Association, April 1, 1783: [ref. 32].

RENFROE, Joseph - killed by Indians at Battle Creek in 1780: [ref. 33a]. Listed in the North Carolina Preemption Act of 1784, as one of the settlers who had died in defense of the settlements, whose heirs were entitled to 640 acres without any price to be paid to the public: [ref. 33b].

RENFROE, Josiah - shot through the head and killed instantly in 1787, during an Indian ambush on his party going by boat on the punitive expedition to the Indian town of Coldwater near Muscle Shoals: [ref. 34].

RENFROE, Moses - traveled with this family in the Donelson flotilla as far at the Red River: [ref. 35].

RENFROE, Peter - was referred to as "old" when he was killed in the summer of 1781, between Freeland's Station and the French Lick: [ref. 36].

RHYMES, Jesse - purchased land on the north side of Cumberland River in 1789: [ref. 37].

RICE, Elisha - son of John Rice and brother of Joel, Nathan, and William H. Rice, according to power of attorney recorded in Davidson Co., July, 1794: [ref. 38a]. Defendant in court case, Nov. 1790: [ref. 38b].

RICE, Joel - son of John Rice, and brother of Elisha, Nathan, and William H. Rice, purchased land of the Sheriff: [ref. 39a]. Summoned for Davidson Co. jury duty on the Superior Court of Law and Equity, Nov. 1788: [ref. 39b]. He executed power of attorney to his brother Elisha for matters regarding their inheritance: [ref. 39c].

RICE, John - defendant in a lawsuit brought by John Montgomery for slander which was dismissed by plaintiff before the Committee of the Cumberland Association, July 1783: [ref. 40a]. He was a merchant. Defendant in a court case before the Superior Court of Law and Equity, Nov., 1790: [ref. 40b]. He was killed by Indians Jan. 7, 1791/92, at Red River: [ref. 40c]. His son Joel Rice executed a power of attorney to his brother Elisha Rice in July, 1794, "for the conveyance of land inherited from father, John Rice." Other heirs mentioned in the power of attorney were Nathan and William H. Rice: [ref. 40d].

RICE, William H. - son of John Rice (see beforementioned).

RIDDLE, Cornelius - was married to Miss Jane Mulherrin at Fort Nashboro by Trustee James Shaw: [ref. 41a]. Listed in the North Carolina Preemption Act of 1784, as one of the settlers on the Cumberland in 1780, who stayed and defended the Settlements, and entitled to 640 acres without any price to be paid to the public: [ref. 41b]. He was killed by Indians near Buchanan's Station on a small path leading to Stone's River according to the historian, Haywood, who gives his date of death as 1784, and again after Jan. 1, 1787: [ref. 41c].

RIDLEY, Abigail - daughter of George Ridley (see hereafter).

RIDLEY, Betsy - daughter of George Ridley (see hereafter).

RIDLEY, Beverly - son of George Ridley (see hereafter). He was killed by Indians during an expedition against the Indians under Capt. Rains in Sept. 1787: [ref. 42].

RIDLEY, Col. Daniel - was born in 1737, in Tidewater, Williamsburg, VA. He was a Revolutionary soldier. He settled in 1779, in Holston country and removed to the Cumberland Settlements in 1790, and built a fort in that year about two miles from Buchanan's Station on Mill Creek: [ref. 43].

RIDLEY, George - son of George Ridley (see hereafter).

RIDLEY, George - D.A.R. membership on this line. Born Jan. 11, 1737, in Isle of Wight Co., VA. Married (1st) Elizabeth Weatherford on Sept. 20, 1761, who died in 1766. He married (2nd) in 1777, to Sarah Vincent, who was born 1754, and died 1836, in Williamson Co., TN: [ref. 44a]. Summoned for jury duty on the Superior Court of Law and Equity, Nov., 1790: [ref. 44b]. Children: (by 1st wife) Beverly, b. July 3, 1762, m. (1st) Ann Williams, m. (2nd) Elizabeth Gooch; George, b. Jan. 11, 1764; John, b. June 5, 1765, m. a German lady; William, b. Feb. 2, 1767; Patsy, b. Mar. 13, 1770, m. James Wright; Betsy, b. Feb. 13, 1772, m. (1st) Wm. M. Smith, m. (2nd) ____ McMinn; Sally, b. Nov. 28, 1773, m. Maj. John Buchanan; Lettie, b. Nov. 24, 1776, m. James Roberts. Children: (by second wife) Capt. V., b. June 26, 1778, m. Lydia Everett; Thomas, b. Feb. 16, 1780, m. Margaret Harwood; Moses, b. June 6, 1782, m. Kate Howard; James, b. May 21, 1784, m. Amy Hamilton; Abigail, b. Apr. 26, 1786, m. Dr. Charles Mulherrin; Wimford, b. Feb. 7, 1789; Samuel, b. Oct. 1, 1791; and Henry, b. May 29, 1794: [ref. 44c].

RIDLEY, Henry - son of George Ridley (see beforementioned).

RIDLEY, Henry - son of George Ridley (see beforementioned).

RIDLEY, John - son of George Ridley (see beforementioned).

RIDLEY, Littie - daughter of George Ridley (see beforementioned).

RIDLEY, Moses - son of George Ridley (see beforementioned).
RIDLEY, Patsy - daughter of George Ridley (see beforementioned).
RIDLEY, Sally - daughter of George Ridley (see beforementioned).
RIDLEY, Samuel - son of George Ridley (see beforementioned).
RIDLEY, Thomas - son of George Ridley (see beforementioned).
RIDLEY, Capt. V. - son of George Ridley (see beforementioned).
RIDLEY, William - son of George Ridley (see beforementioned). While in the Company of men commanded by Capt. William Martin in pursuit of Indians who had attacked the settlements on Bledsoe's Creek in 1787, he was accidently killed when his camp was fired upon by members of George Winchester's Company who were also in pursuit of the Indians: [ref. 45].
RIDLEY, Wimford - child of George Ridley (see beforementioned).
RIED, John - signer of the Cumberland Compact, May, 1780: [ref. 46].
RIGHT, see WRIGHT.
RISTON, Abraham - defendant in a court case in Nov. 1790: [ref. 47].
ROBERTS, Isaac - 1787 Davidson Co. tax roll with 1 taxable: [ref. 48a]. Summoned for Davidson Co. jury duty, Nov. 1788: [ref. 48b].
ROBERTS, Jesse - North Carolina land grant: [ref. 49].
ROBERTS, Lewis - purchased land of William Mabane: [ref. 50].
ROBERTS, Obed - North Carolina land grant: [ref. 51].
ROBERTSON, Alexander (variously, Alex) - North Carolina land grant: [ref. 52a]. 1787 Davidson Co. tax roll with 2 taxables: [ref. 52b].
ROBERTSON, Ann - see Ann Robertson Johnson Cockrill.
ROBERTSON, Charles - arrived with the Donelson flotilla, April 24, 1780: [ref. 53].
ROBERTSON, Charlotte - daughter of James Robertson (see hereafter).
ROBERTSON, Charlotte - daughter of James Robertson (see hereafter).
ROBERTSON, Delilah - daughter of James Robertson (see hereafter).
ROBERTSON, Eldridge - son of James Robertson (see hereafter).
ROBERTSON, Capt. Elijah - D.A.R. membership on this line. Born April 4, 1744, in Brunswick Co., VA. Married Sarah Maclin, 1780, in Brunswick Co.: [ref. 54a]. Order by Col. James Robertson to pursue the Indians who had attacked his Station and wounded him in the foot: [ref. 54b]. 1787 Davidson Co. tax roll with 6 taxables: [ref. 54c]. He

(continued next page)

ROBERTSON, Capt. Elijah - (continued)

died in Nashville in 1794, and his will, which was proven in Davidson Co. in 1797, mentions his wife "Sally" and children: Elizabeth, Patsy, Sterling, Eldridge, and James: [ref. 54d]. Another source lists the following children: Elizabeth, b. Mar. 12, 1783, m. John Childress; Matilda, b. 1784, m. Washington L. Hannum; Sterling, b. Oct. 2, 1785; Eldridge, b. 1786; and James: [ref. 54e].

ROBERTSON, Elizabeth - daughter of Elijah Robertson (see above).

ROBERTSON, Elizah - purchased land of T. Mollow in 1784: [ref. 55].

ROBERTSON, Dr. Felix - son of James Robertson, was the first child born in Nashville: [ref. 56].

ROBERTSON, Felix - listed with Jackson Robertson on a North Carolina land grant: [ref. 57].

ROBERTSON, Henry - (heirs of) sold land in 1790, on Dry Fork of West Fork of Red River (Tennessee Co. at the time; then Montgomery Co.): [ref. 57b].

ROBERTSON, Jackson - listed on a North Carolina land grant with Felix Robertson: [ref. 58].

ROBERTSON, James - D.A.R. membership on this line. Born June, 1742, in Brunswick Co., VA. Married Charlotte Reeves, Jan. 21, 1768, who was born Jan. 2, 1751, in Wake Co., NC. He started overland with settlers to the Cumberland area in Oct. 1779: [ref. 59a]. Signer of the Cumberland Compact, May, 1780: [ref. 59b]. Listed in the North Carolina Preemption Act of 1784, as one of the settlers on the Cumberland in 1780, who stayed and defended the settlements, and entitled to 640 acres without any price to be paid to the public: [ref. 59c]. 1787 Davidson Co. tax roll with 8 taxables: [ref. 59d]. Purchased land of the Trustees of Nashville: [ref. 59e]. Wounded by Indians at his own plantation, May 24, 1792: [ref. 59f]. Died Sept. 1, 1814, at the Chickasaw Agency, and Charlotte died in 1845: [ref. 59g]. He was brother to Mark, John, and Ann Robertson: [ref. 59h]. Children: Jonathan, b. June 13, 1769, m. Kiddy (Ciddy) Davis, Dec. 17, 1791; James Randolph, b. Dec. 11, 1771, killed by Indians; Delilah, b. Nov. 30, 1773, m. John Beasly, Aug. 12, 1789; Peyton, b. July 11, 1775, killed by Indians; Charlotte, b. July 11, 1778, died in infancy; Felix, b. Jan. 11, 1781, m. Lydia Waters, Oct. 9, 1808; Charlotte (2nd), b. Mar. 11, 1783, m. Richard Napier in 1798; William b. 1785; Peyton (2nd), b. Dec. 11, 1787; Rachel, b. Feb. 23, 1790; and John, b. Apr. 26, 1792: [ref. 59i]. James Robertson is called the founder of Nashville.

ROBERTSON, James - son of Elijah Robertson (see previously).

ROBERTSON, James Randolph - son of James Robertson, was 9 years old in 1779/80. He was killed by Indians with Abel Gower, Jr., in a boat on the Cumberland River near Clover Bottom: [ref: 60]. Note: The historian Haywood refers to him as "John."

ROBERTSON, John - son of James Robertson (see beforementioned).

ROBERTSON, John - listed in the North Carolina Preemption Act of 1784, as one of the settlers who had died in the defense of the Cumberland Settlements, whose heirs were entitled to 640 acres without any price to be paid to the public: [ref. 61].

ROBERTSON, John - son of James Robertson (see beforementioned).

ROBERTSON, Jonathan (F.) - son of James Robertson (see beforementioned). Wounded by Indians at his plantation, May 24, 1792. He died in 1814, and was buried on the bank of the Cumberland River beside his daughter, Susanna, and infant son, Peter H. A headstone placed at the grave. His headstone was inscribed; "J. F. Robertson." The headstone was discovered in 1921, and memorial services were held at Nashville City Cemetery, and his remains reinterred on the Robertson plot: [ref 62a]. His will was proved in Davidson Co., July 15, 1816: [ref. 62b].

ROBERTSON, Lavinia - daughter of James Robertson (see beforementioned).

ROBERTSON, James Randel - son of Gen. Robertson, was killed on the waters of Caney Fork River in 1793, where he and John Grimes had gone to trap beavers: [ref. 63].

ROBERTSON, M. - listed with Mark Robertson on the 1787 Davidson Co. tax roll with 2 taxables: [ref. 64].

ROBERTSON, Mark - brother of James, John, and Ann Robertson, was with his brother, James, on his trip to the French Lick in 1779: [ref. 65a]. He also accompanied his brother to the Illinois Country: [ref. 65b]. Signer of the Cumberland Compact, May, 1780: [ref. 65c]. He recorded his stock mark in the Minutes of the Committee of the Cumberland Association, Feb. 11, 1783, thus: "A swallow fork and an upper kell in each ear.": [ref. 65d]. Listed in the North Carolina Preemption Act of 1784, as one of the settlers on the Cumberland in 1780, who had stayed and defended the Settlements, and entitled to 640 acres without any price to be paid to the public: [ref. 65e]. He was killed by Indians in May, 1787: [ref. 65f]. His will, proven in Davidson Co., mentioned his wife Mary; his sister Ann Cockrill's three daughters, Mary, Elizabeth, and Charity; and his brother, James Robertson: [ref. 65g].

ROBERTSON, Matilda - daughter of Elijah Robertson (see beforementioned).

ROBERTSON, Mary - wife of Mark Robertson (see beforementioned).

ROBERTSON, Patsy - daughter of Elijah Robertson (see beforementioned).
ROBERTSON, Peyton - son of James Robertson (see beforemention-
ed), was killed by Indians in March, 1787, at the age of
12. He was buried at the spring near the banks of Richland
Creek about 100 yards from the Robertson brick home: [ref.
66].
ROBERTSON, Peyton - son of James Robertson (see previously).
ROBERTSON, Rachel - daughter of James Robertson (see beforemen-
tioned).
ROBERTSON, Richard - 1787 Davidson Co. tax roll with 1 taxable:
[ref. 67a]. Killed by Indians in 1793: [ref. 67b].
ROBERTSON, Sally - wife of Elijah Robertson (see previously).
ROBERTSON, Sterling - son of Elijah Robertson (see previously).
ROBERTSON, William - son of James Robertson (see previously).
ROBIDEAUX, Joseph - sued Joshua Baker in the Superior Court
of Law and Equity, Oct. 28, 1788: [ref. 68].
ROCHESTER, Nicholas - (heirs of) sold land in 1790, on Duck
River: [ref. 69].
ROGERS, John - a Chickasaw informant for Capt. James Robertson:
[ref. 70].
ROGERS, (Mram?) - purchased land in 1790, on Caney Fork River
(Sumner Co. at the time; then Smith Co.): [ref. 71].
ROGERS, Simon - married Elizabeth Mitchell in Davidson Co.,
Mar. 7, 1789: [ref. 72].
ROQUERING, Hugh - was shot through the body during an Indian
ambush in 1787, of his Company going by boat on the punitive
expedition to the Indian town of Coldwater near Muscle
Shoals: [ref. 73].
RORDINE, Francis - married Rebecca Cashaw in Davidson Co.,
Mar. 9, 1790: [ref. 74].
ROSEBERRY, Robert - his preemption boundaries mentioned in
a deed of Richard Flowron: [ref. 75].
ROSS, Henry - purchased land: [ref. 76].
ROSS, James - North Carolina land grant, Sept. 6, 1787: [ref.
77a]. 1787 Davidson Co. tax roll with 1 taxable: [ref.77b].
Purchased land of Jno. Campbell: [ref. 77c].
ROSS, James - is mentioned along with his wife Mary, and
child Margaret, in the will of Margaret Mitchell: [ref.
78].
ROSS, John - (heirs of) sold land in 1788, on Cripple Creek
of Stone's River: [ref. 79].
ROSS, Margaret - wife of James Ross (see previously).
ROSS, Samuel - (heirs of) sold land in 1789: [ref. 80].
ROSS, William - North Carolina land grants: [ref. 81].
ROUNSEVAL (variously, ROUNSAVALL, ROUNCEVALL), David - signer
of the Cumberland Compact, May, 1780: [ref. 82a]. Listed
in the North Carolina Preemption Act of 1784, as one of

(continued next page)

ROUNSEVAL, David - (continued)

the settlers on the Cumberland in 1780, who stayed and defended the Settlements, and entitled to 640 acres without any price to be paid to the public: [ref. 82b]. Listed with Isaac and Josiah Rounseval on the 1787 Davidson Co. tax roll with 3 taxables: [ref. 82c]. Summoned for Davidson Co. jury duty, May, 1790: [ref. 82d]. North Carolina land grant: [ref. 82e].

ROUNSEVAL, Isaac - was one of those arriving by land, who settled at Heaton's Station: [ref. 83a]. Signer of the Cumberland Compact, May, 1780: [ref. 83b]. Listed in the North Carolina Preemption Act of 1784, as one of the settlers on the Cumberland too young for a grant under the 1782 Preemption Act, but now entitled to 640 acres: [ref. 83c]. Listed with David and Josiah Rounseval on the 1787 Davidson Co. tax roll: [ref. 83d].

ROUNSEVAL, Josiah - listed with David and Isaac Rounseval on the 1787 Davidson Co. tax roll: [ref. 84].

ROUNSIFER, ____ - "old man and his family" arrived with the Donelson flotilla, April 24, 1780: [ref. 85].

ROWAN, Daniel - fined for failing to appear for jury duty on the Superior Court of Law and Equity, Oct. 1788: [ref. 86].

ROWLER, Martin - purchased land in 1788, on Marrowbone Creek: [ref. 87].

RULAND, James - 1787 Davidson Co. tax roll with 1 taxable: [ref. 88].

RUSE, James - summoned from Sumner Co. for jury duty on the Superior Court of Law and Equity, May, 1790: [ref. 89].

RUSSELL, ____ - who was "almost blind," came with his son to the Cumberland area to hunt in 1771: [ref. 90].

RUSSELL, James - purchased land from Jonathan Drake: [ref. 91].

RUSSELL, Robert - "of Spotswood," received a North Carolina land grant: [ref. 92].

RUSSELL, Thomas - married Engley Gower in Davidson Co., Nov. 13, 1790: [ref. 93].

RUSSELL, W., Jr. - signer of the Cumberland Compact, May, 1780: [ref. 94].

RUSSELL, William - signer of the Cumberland Compact, May, 1780: [ref. 95a]. Purchased land in 1788: [ref. 95b].

RUTH, Elijah - sued John Rains in Nov., 1788, before the Superior Court of Law and Equity: [ref. 96].

S

SADLER, John - defendant in lawsuit brought by John Thomas before the Committee of the Cumberland Association, Jan. 7, 1783. Kasper Mansker was garnishee of Sadler: [ref. 1].

SAMPSON, David - (heirs of) sold land in 1789, on the south side of the Cumberland River: [ref. 2].

SANDERETH, Abraham - summoned from Sumner Co. for jury duty on the Superior Court of Law and Equity, Nov., 1790: [ref. 3].

SANDERS, Abraham - summoned from Sumner Co. for jury duty on the Superior Court of Law and Equity, Nov., 1790: [ref. 4].

SANDERS, James - purchased land of the Trustees of Nashville in 1789: [ref. 5].

SANDERS, Julius - lost a lawsuit against James Thomson over contract concerning a "piece of cleared grounds," before the Committee of the Cumberland Association, May 6, 1783: [ref. 6a]. Purchased land of the Trustees of the town of Nashville: [ref. 6b]. Wounded by Indians in 1794: [ref. 6c].

SAUNDERS, John - said to be the first white child born in the settlements ca. 1780. He became Sheriff of Montgomery Co. He was killed by Indians on Red River: [ref. 7].

SANDFORD, Julianna - the heir of John Patterson, purchased land on the east fork of Stone's River in 1789: [ref. 8].

SAPPINGTON, Eleanor - daughter of Mark B. Sappington (see hereafter).

SAPPINGTON, Francis Brown - daughter of Mark B. Sappington (see hereafter).

SAPPINGTON, John - son of Mark B. Sappington (see hereafter). Purchased land of James Robertson: [ref. 9].

SAPPINGTON, Mark B. - purchased land of Thomas Molloy: [ref. 10a]. Summoned for Davidson Co. jury duty on the Superior Court of Law and Equity, May, 1790: [ref. 10b]. Bill of Sale to his children, Aug. 14, 1795; mentions them by name: Francis Brown Sappington, John, Eleanor T., Thomas, and Rebecca Sappington: [ref. 10c].

SAPPINGTON, Rebecca - daughter of Mark B. Sappington (see above).

SAPPINGTON, Thomas - son of Mark B. Sappington (see above).

SAWYER, Thomas - North Carolina land grant: [ref. 11].

SAWYER, Sampson - signer of the Cumberland Compact, May, 1780: [ref. 12].

SCOTT, James - 1787 Davidson Co. tax roll with 1 taxable: [ref. 13a]. North Carolina land grant: [ref. 13b].

SCOTT, John - purchased land in 1788: [ref. 14a]. Purchased
   land of Margaret Allen: [ref. 14b].
SCOTT, Marmaduke - North Carolina land grant: [ref. 15].
SCOTT, Samuel - listed in the North Carolina Preemption Act
   of 1784, as one of the settlers who died in defense of the
   Cumberland Settlements, whose heirs were entitled to 640
   acres without any price to be paid to the public: [ref.
   16].
SEARCY (variously, SEARCEY), Bennett - purchased land in 1790,
   on Yellow Creek: [ref. 17].
SEARCY, John - listed in the North Carolina Preemption Act
   of 1784, as one of the settlers who had died in the Cumberland
   Settlements, whose heirs were entitled to 640 acres without
   any price to be paid to the public: [ref. 18].
SELGRAVES, Joseph Arnold - appointed Clerk of the Court of
   Equity, Nov. 1790: [ref. 19].
SETGRAVES, John - North Carolina land grant: [ref. 20].
SEXTON, William - North Carolina land grant: [ref. 21].
SHACKLER, Philip - purchased land in 1788, on Round Lick Creek
   (Sumner Co. at the time): [ref. 22a]. James Hays was charged
   with stealing his horse before the Superior Court of Law
   and Equity, May 1789: [ref. 22b]. Purchased land on Red
   River (Tennessee Co.; then Robertson Co.): [ref. 22c].
SHAFFER, Richard - married Elizabeth Gambal (sic) in Davidson
   Co., Oct. 21, 1789: [ref. 23a]. Summoned for Davidson Co.
   jury duty on the Superior Court of Law and Equity, Nov.
   1788: [ref. 23b]. Killed by Indians in 1793: [ref. 23c].
SHANE (variously, SHAIN, SHEAN, SHINE, SKEAN), Morris - was
   wounded by Indians on the north side of Duck River, while
   returning with Capt. Wm. Pruett's Company from a punitive
   expedition against the Indians in 1783: [ref. 24a]. Listed
   in the North Carolina Preemption Act of 1784, as one of
   the settlers on the Cumberland in 1780, who stayed and
   defended the settlements, and entitled to 640 acres: [ref.
   24b]. North Carolina land grant: [ref. 24c]. Helped defend
   Buchanan's Station during the Indian attack of Sept. 30,
   1792: [ref. 24d].
SHANKIN, James - listed in the North Carolina Preemption Act
   of 1784, as one of the settlers who died in the defense
   of the Cumberland Settlements, whose heirs were entitled
   to 640 acres without any price to be paid to the public:
   [ref. 25].
SHANNON, Capt. - pursued party of Indians under the leadership
   of Big Foot; killing him and 5 of his followers in 1787:
   [ref. 26].

SHANNON, David - signer of the Cumberland Compact, May, 1780:
[ref. 27a]. North Carolina land grant in 1787: [ref. 27b].
Listed with David and William Shannon on the 1787 Davidson
Co. tax roll with 3 taxables: [ref. 27c]. North Carolina
land grant: [ref. 27d].
SHANNON, James - sold land to Samuel Shannon: [ref. 28].
SHANNON, John - signer of the Cumberland Compact, May, 1780:
[ref. 29a]. 1787 Davidson Co. tax roll with 1 taxable:
[ref. 29b]. Purchased land of Morris Shain and wife; [ref.
29c].
SHANNON, Samuel - North Carolina land grant, 1787: [ref.30a].
Listed with David and William Shannon on the 1787 Davidson
Co. tax roll: [ref. 30b]. Purchased land of James Shannon:
[ref. 30c]. Purchased land on White's Creek in 1789: [ref.
30d]. Coroner of Davidson Co, May, 1790: [ref. 30e].
SHANNON, Thomas - signer of the Cumberland Compact, May,
1780: [ref. 31].
SHANNON, William - listed with David and Samuel Shannon on
the 1787 Davidson Co. tax roll: [ref. 32].
SHARON, John - summoned for Davidson Co. jury duty on the
Superior Court of Law and Equity, May, 1789: [ref. 33].
SHARP, Anthony - North Carolina land grant: [ref. 34a].
Summoned from Tennessee Co. for jury duty on the Superior
Court of Law and Equity in 1790: [ref. 34b].
SHARP, Thomas - came to the Cumberland area with Spencer
and others in 1776 to hunt: [ref. 35a]. Purchased land
in 1788, on Big Harpeth River: [ref. 35b].
SHAVER, Michael - signer of the Cumberland Compact, May,
1780: [ref. 36a]. He recorded his stock mark in the Minutes
of the Committee of the Cumberland Association, April 2,
1783, thus: "A crop off the right ear, and a halfpenny
out of the upper side of the left ear, and brands thus
- MS.": [ref. 36b]. Witness in a lawsuit (Wm. Mitchell
vs. Geo. Mansker), Apr. 1, 1783, before the Cumberland
Association: [ref. 36c]. He was killed by Indians, June
26, 1792, at Zeigler's Station: [ref. 36d].
SHAWS - sold preemptions and removed to lands between Walnut
Hill and Natchez: [ref. 37].
SHAW, Annor - wife of James Shaw, charged Simon Suggs with
assault and battery, before the Superior Court of Law and
Equity, Nov., 1790: [ref. 38].
SHAW, James - signer of the Cumberland Compact, May, 1780:
[ref. 39a]. Member of the Committee of the Cumberland
Association, Feb. 5, 1783: [ref. 39b]. He performed several
of the first marriages at Fort Nashboro: [ref. 39c]. Over-
seer of the laying off of a road from Mansker's Station
to Buchanan's spring: [ref. 39d]. Listed in the North

(continued next page)

SHAW, James - (continued)

   Carolina Preemption Act of 1784, as one of the settlers
   on the Cumberland in 1780, who had stayed and defended
   the Settlements, and entitled to 640 acres without any
   price to be paid to the public: [ref. 39e]. Listed with
   Joseph and William Shaw on the 1787 Davidson Co. tax roll
   with 3 taxables: [ref. 39f].
SHAW, Joseph - listed with James and William Shaw on the
   1787 Davidson Co. tax roll: [ref. 40].
SHAW, Olive - plaintiff in lawsuit against Frederick Stump
   for trespass, heard before the Committee of the Cumberland
   Association, Mar. 4, 1783: [ref. 41a]. The suit involved
   land cleared at Heaton's Station by William Renfroe, and
   sold to her by him. Stump was living on the land and failed
   to pay rent, claiming he purchased the property. The committee ordered that the matter be settled between the parties,
   and Stump agreed to pay 30 bushels of Indian corn as rent
   the following autumn: [ref. 41b]. She purchased land of
   Lardner Clark [ref. 41c].
SHAW, Robert - summoned from Sumner Co. for jury duty on
   the Superior Court of Law and Equity, meeting in Nashville,
   Nov. 1790: [ref. 42].
SHAW, William - listed with James and Joseph Shaw on the
   1787 Davidson Co. tax roll: [ref. 43a]. Purchased land
   of Absalom Hooper and wife: [ref. 43b]. Witness in court
   case (Territory vs. Simon Suggs) for assault and battery
   upon Annor Shaw, Nov. 1791: [ref. 43c].
SHELBY, Anthony - son of David Shelby (see hereafter).
SHELBY, Evan - son of Gen'l. Evan Shelby (see D.A.R. membership
   information on this line). 1787 Davidson Co. tax roll
   with 4 taxables: [ref. 44a]. Summoned from Tennessee County
   for jury duty on the Superior Court of Law and Equity,
   Nov., 1790: [ref. 44b]. North Carolina land grant: [ref.
   44c]. He was killed by Indians in 1789, while hunting
   with Abednego Lewellen: [ref. 44d].
SHELBY, Isaac - purchased land of L. Thompson: [ref. 45].
SHELBY, John - son of David Shelby (see previously).
SHELBY, John, Jr. - North Carolina land grant: [ref. 46].
SHELBY, Moses - was in the Company going by boat on the punitive expedition to the Indian town of Coldwater, which
   was ambushed by Indians on the Cumberland River at the
   mouth of the Harpeth: [ref. 47a]. North Carolina land
   grant: [ref. 47b]. Summoned from Tennessee Co. for jury
   duty on the Superior Court of Law and Equity, May, 1789;
   and subsequently, May and Nov., 1790: [ref. 47c].
SHELTON, David - signer of the Cumberland Compact, May, 1780:
   [ref. 48].

SHELTON, Samuel - signer of the Cumberland Compact, May 1780: [ref. 49].
SHEPPART, Col. John - purchased land in 1788, on Caney Fork River (Sumner Co.; then Smith Co.)
SHOAT, Isaac - 1787 Davidson Co. tax roll with 1 taxable: [ref. 49b].
SHOCKLEY (variously, SHOCTLY), John - killed by Indians at Mansker's Lick in 1780: [ref. 51a]. Listed in the North Carolina Preemption Act of 1784, as one of the settlers, who had died in defense of the Cumberland Settlements, whose heirs were entitled to 640 acres without any price to be paid to the public: [ref. 51b].
SIDES, Peter - witness for the plaintiff in lawsuit (Freeland vs. Deson) before the Committee of the Cumberland Association, July 1, 1783: [ref. 52a]. 1787 Davidson Co. tax roll with 2 taxables: [ref. 52b].
SIMMONS, Felix - purchased land in 1788, on Little Harpeth River: [ref. 53].
SIMMONS, Jesse - killed by Indians in 1782, at Kilgore's Station: [ref. 54].
SIMMONS, Joshua - (heirs of) sold land in 1789: [ref. 55].
SIMPSON, Elizabeth - daughter of William Simpson (see hereafter).
SIMPSON, Gabriel - son of William Simpson (see hereafter).
SIMPSON, Hugh - signer of the Cumberland Compact, May 1780: [ref. 56].
SIMPSON, Mary - daughter of William Simpson (see hereafter).
SIMPSON, Sarah - daughter of William Simpson (see hereafter).
SIMPSON, Thomas - purchased land in 1790: [ref. 57a]. Summoned from Sumner Co. for jury duty on the Superior Court of Law and Equity in 1790: [ref. 57b].
SIMPSON, William - North Carolina land grants: [ref. 58a]. His wife presented his nuncupative will in court, Oct. 7, 1788. She was pregnant at the time, and the couple's children were: Gabriel, William, Sarah, Mary, and Elizabeth: [ref. 58b]. His estate inventory was delivered to court, January 1797, by John Kennedy, administrator, "in right of his wife.": [ref. 58c].
SIMS, Bartlett - purchased land of E. Robertson: [ref. 59].
SIMS, Matthew - purchased land of E. Robertson: [ref. 60].
SIMS, Richard - signed the Cumberland Compact, May 1780: [ref. 61].
SINGLETARY, Jno. - purchased land of James Donnally: [ref. 62].
SINGLETARY, John Stern - was fined for failing to appear for jury duty, Oct. 1788: [ref. 63a]. His wife was the former Catherine Thompson, daughter of James Thompson. Child: John Singletary: [ref. 63b].

SINGLETON, St. John - 1787 Davidson Co. tax roll with 1 taxable: [ref. 64].

SLAYTON, Edward - married Nancy Williams in Davidson Co., July 8, 1789: [ref. 65].

SLEADHAM, Tobias - (heirs of) sold land in 1789: [ref. 66].

SLOSS, John - purchased land in 1788, on Caney Fork River (Sumner Co. at the time; then Smith Co.): [ref. 67].

SMILIN, Jonathan - (heirs of) sold land in 1790, on Dry Fork of West Fork of Red River (Tennessee Co. at the time; then Montgomery Co.): [ref. 68].

SMITH, Black, Jr. - "of Davidson County;" a yeoman, mentioned in court case before the Superior Court of Law and Equity, Nov. 1788: [ref. 69].

SMITH, Daniel - member of the first Inferior Court of Pleas and Quarter Sessions, Oct. 6, 1783: [ref. 70].

SMITH, Ezekiel - listed with Jesse Smith on the 1787 Davidson Co. tax roll with 2 taxables: [ref. 71a]. North Carolina land grant, April 17, 1788: [ref. 71b]. Purchased land of Jno. Drake: [ref. 71c].

SMITH, Henry - came to the Cumberland area to hunt in 1769, with 20 adventurers from North Carolina, Rockbridge in Virginia, and New River: [ref. 72].

SMITH, Israel (variously, Ezeral) - summoned for Davidson Co. jury duty on the Superior Court of Law and Equity, Nov. 1790: [ref. 73].

SMITH, Jesse - listed with Ezekiel Smith on the 1787 Davidson Co. tax roll: [ref. 74].

SMITH, John - purchased land, Dec. 25, 1789: [ref. 75].

SMITH, Mary - married Joshua Harlin in Davidson Co., Nov. 17, 1789: [ref. 76].

SMITH, Thomas - "a hatter;" was summoned for Davidson Co. jury duty on the Superior Court of Law and Equity, May, 1790: [ref. 77].

SMITH, William Bailey - signer of the Cumberland Compact, May, 1780: [ref. 78].

SMOTHERS, A. - 1787 Davidson Co. tax roll with 1 taxable: [ref. 79].

SMOTHERS, William - killed by Indians in either Davidson or Sumner Co., after Jan. 1, 1787: [ref. 80].

SNODDY (variously, SNODY), William - summoned from Sumner Co. for jury duty on the Superior Court of Law and Equity, May, 1790: [ref. 81].

SNYDER, Charles - married Elizabeth Sevier in Davidson Co. in 1790: [ref. 82a]. Purchased land in 1789, on White's Creek: [ref. 82b].

SOMMERVILLE, James - recorded his stock mark in the Minutes of the Committee of the Cumberland Association, Feb. 11, 1783, thus: "A crop off the right ear, and a slit in the left, but not extending to the end, and an upper kell.": [ref. 83].

SPENCER, Thomas - came to the Cumberland from Kentucky in 1776: [ref. 84a]. Plaintiff in lawsuit against James Todd to recover a debt, heard before the Committee of the Cumberland Association, May 6, 1783: [ref. 84b]. Listed in the North Carolina Preemption Act of 1784, as one of the settlers on the Cumberland in 1780, who stayed and defended the Settlements, and entitled to 640 acres without any price to be paid to the public: [ref. 84c].

SPENCER, Thomas Sharpe - early hunter to the Cumberland area, was with a hunting party including Espey, Andrew Lucas, and Johnston, on the head waters of Drake's Creek, when attacked by Indians. Spencer escaped: [ref. 85a]. North Carolina land grant: [ref. 85b]. See the many references to him in Haywood's work: [ref. 85c].

SPILES, W. - 1787 Davidson Co. tax roll with 1 taxable: [ref. 86].

STAFFORD, Cuthbert - purchased land in 1789, on the West Fork of Red River (Tennessee Co. at the time; then Montgomery Co.): [ref. 87].

STALL, Jacob - listed in the North Carolina Preemption Act of 1784, as one of the settlers who had died in the defense of the Cumberland Settlements, whose heirs were entitled to 640 acres without any price to be paid to the public: [ref. 88].

STANAFAND(?), Benjamin - purchased land on the south fork of Harpeth River: [ref. 89].

STANDLEY, Abraham - purchased land in 1789, on Sulphur Fork of Red River (Tennessee Co. at the time; then Robertson Co.): [ref. 90].

STANDLEY, David - listed with Joseph and John Standley on the 1787 Davidson Co. tax roll with 3 taxables: [ref. 91].

STANDLEY, John - listed with David and Joseph Standley on the 1787 Davidson Co. tax roll: [ref. 92].

STANDLEY, Joseph - listed with David and John Standley on the 1787 Davidson Co. tax roll: [ref. 93].

STANLEY, ___ - killed by Indians in May, 1789, near the Clinch River, while accompanying Judge McNairy making his rounds of the settlements: [ref. 94].

STANLEY, John - summoned from Tennessee County for jury duty on the Superior Court of Law and Equity in 1790: [ref. 95].

STANTON, Richard - signer of the Cumberland Compact, May, 1780: [ref. 96a]. An account against the estate of Richard Stanton, "deceased," was proved by James Maulding, Mar. 4, 1783, before the Committee of the Cumberland Association: [ref. 96b].

STATEN, Mr. - was killed by Indians in either Davidson or Sumner Co., after Jan. 1, 1787: [ref. 97].

STEAD, James - North Carolina land grant: [ref. 98].
STEEL, Andrew - 1787 Davidson Co. tax roll with 1 taxable: [ref. 99].
STEELE, David - killed by Indians on the waters of Blooming Grove (below the present site of Clarksville) in 1786 (Tennessee Co.; then Montgomery Co.): [ref. 100].
STEELE, William - was in the Company commanded by Capt. Rains in pursuit of the Indians toward Coldwater, the Indian town near Muscle Shoals, following their attack on the settlements in 1787: [ref. 101].
STERN, William - North Carolina land grant: [ref. 102].
STEWART, John - North Carolina land grant: [ref. 103].
STEWART, Robert - purchased land in 1789, on Spring Creek (Sumner Co. at the time; then Wilson Co.): [ref. 104].
STEWART, William - appeared before the Committee of the Cumberland Association, Jan. 18, 1783, and proved an account against the estate of James Lumsday, deceased, of 22 pounds and 9 shillings: [ref. 105a]. Listed in the North Carolina Preemption Act of 1784, as one of the settlers on the Cumberland in 1780, who stayed and defended the Settlements, and entitled to 640 acres without any price to be paid to the public: [ref. 105b]. He was killed by Indians Oct. 8, 1792, near Nashville: [ref. 105c]. (See also, William Stuart.)
STONE, Euriah - first came to the Cumberland area on what is now Stone's River in 1767, to trap with a Frenchman. He later returned to the Cumberland area with the Mansker party in 1769/70: [ref. 106].
STONE, Joel - (heirs of) sold land in 1790, on Mill Creek: [ref. 107].
STONE, Littleberry - (heirs of) sold land in 1789, on Clay Lick Branch of Sulphur Fork River (Tennessee Co. at the time): [ref. 108].
STOPH, Christopher - came to the Cumberland area to hunt in 1771, with Mansker, and was captured by the Indians: [ref. 109].
STONER, Michael - first came to the Cumberland area from Illinois to hunt with Harrod in 1767. He discovered Stoner's Lick in 1780: [ref. 110a]. Signer of the Cumberland Compact, May, 1780: [ref. 110b].
STOVALL (variously, STOWBALL), _____ - killed by Indians during their attack on Brown's Station: [ref. 111].
STUART - family and friends, twenty-eight people in all, were killed during the Donelson voyage: [ref. 112].
STUART, William - arrived with the Donelson flotilla, April 24, 1780: [ref. 113a]. According to one source, he lived on the forks of Mill Creek in 1785, where Haywood late:

(continued next page)

STUART, William - (continued)

    lived: [ref. 113b]. Davidson Co. Court Minutes indicate
he lived on White's Creek: [ref. 113c]. 1787 Davidson
Co. tax roll with 1 taxable: [ref. 113d]. Summoned for
Davidson Co. jury duty in May, 1789: [ref. 113e]. (See
also, William Stewart)
STULL, Jacob - listed in the North Carolina Preemption Act
of 1784, as one of the settlers, who died in defense of
the Cumberland Settlements, whose heirs were entitled to
640 acres without any price to be paid to the public: [ref.
114].
STULL, Zacheriah - 1787 Davidson Co. tax roll with 1 taxable:
[ref. 115a]. North Carolina land grant: [ref. 115b].
STUMP, Frederick - was a Pennsylvanian, of German origins,
came with the Heaton party to settle on White's Creek near
the ford of the trace to Clarksville: [ref. 116a]. Signer
of the Cumberland Compact, May, 1780: [ref. 116b]. Listed
in the North Carolina Preemption Act of 1784, as one of
the settlers who stayed and defended the Cumberland
Settlements, and entitled to 640 acres without any price
to be paid to the public: [ref. 116c]. 1787 Davidson Co.
tax roll with 1 taxable: [ref. 116d]. North Carolina land
grant: [ref. 116e]. See also various references to him
by the historian Haywood: [ref. 116f].
STUMP, Frederick, Jr. - signer of the Cumberland Compact,
May, 1780: [ref. 117a]. 1787 Davidson Co. tax roll with
1 taxable: [ref. 117b].
STUMP, Jacob - signer of the Cumberland Compact, May, 1780:
[ref. 118a]. He was killed by Indians at Heaton's Station
in November or December, 1780: [ref. 118b]. Listed in
the North Carolina Preemption Act of 1784, as one of the
settlers on the Cumberland who had died in defense of the
Settlements, whose heirs were entitled to 640 acres without
any price to be paid to the public: [ref. 118c].
SUGG, Abegail - widow of Aequilla Sugg of Edgecombe Co.,
NC, delivered his will to Court in Davidson Co. in July,
1789. The will, written Feb. 7, 1785, mentioned 2 sons,
William and Nash (sic) Sugg: [ref. 119a]. She purchased
land in 1790, on Barton's Creek (Sumner Co. at the time;
then Wilson Co.): [ref. 119b].
SUGG, George A. - summoned for Davidson Co. jury duty in
1788: [ref. 120a]. Purchased land in 1789, on Spencer's
Creek (Sumner Co. at the time; then Wilson Co.): [ref.
120b].
SUGG, Henry - came to the Cumberland area to hunt in 1777
with Mansker: [ref. 121].

SUGG, Simon - appointed Constable for the Grand Jury, Nov. 1790: [ref. 122a]. Charged with assault and battery on Annor Shaw, wife of James Shaw in Nov., 1792: [ref. 122b].

SULLIVAN, James - (heirs of) sold land in 1790: [ref. 123].

SUMMERS (variously, SUMERS), Jesse - sued William Leaton for debt before the Committee of the Cumberland Association, Mar. 4, 1783: [ref. 124].

SUMMERS, William - signer of the Cumberland Compact, May, 1780: [ref. 125].

SUTTON, John - purchased land in 1788: [ref. 126].

SUTTON, Malichiah - 1787 Davidson Co. tax roll with 1 taxable: [ref. 127a]. His estate inventory was filed in Davidson Co., Aug. 22, 1794: [ref. 127b].

SWANSON, Edward - D.A.R. membership on this line. Born Dec. 28, 1759, in NC: [ref. 128a]. He was with the Robertson party at the French Lick, who stayed and planted corn and kept the buffaloes out of the corn in 1779: [ref. 128b]. He married (1st) at Fort Nashborough in 1780, the widow, Mary Luny Carvin: [ref. 128c]. Elected Constable at Freeland's Station, Oct. 7, 1783: [ref. 128d]. Listed in the North Carolina Preemption Act of 1784, as one of the settlers on the Cumberland in 1780, who stayed and defended the Settlements, and entitled to 640 acres without any price to be paid to the public: [ref. 128e]. Children: Peter, and Richard Swanson, b. Dec. 8, 1790 (others were born after 1790): [ref. 128f].

SWANSON, Ned - was clubbed down by Indians during the Battle of the Bluffs, April 2, 1781, but was saved by old Mr. Buchanan: [ref. 129].

SWANSON, Peter - son of Edward Swanson (see above).

SWANSON, Richard - son of Edward Swanson (see above).

T

TAITLE, William - North Carolina land grant: [ref. 1].

TAIT (variously, TAITT), Robert - plaintiff in a lawsuit before the Superior Court of Law and Equity, Nov., 1790: [rer. 2].

TAIT, William - 1787 Davidson Co. tax roll with 1 taxable: [ref. 3a]. Summoned for Davidson Co. jury duty on the Superior Court of Law and Equity, Nov., 1788: [ref. 3b].

TALBOT, Matthew - elected first clerk of Davidson Co., Oct. 6, 1783. He resigned soon thereafter for lack of security or bondsman: [ref. 4].

TALBOT (variously, TALBOTT), Thomas - summoned for Davidson Co. jury duty on the Superior Court of Law and Equity, Nov., 1790: [ref. 5].

TARDIVEAU, B. - purchased land with Peter Tardiveau from Lardner Clark: [ref. 6].

TARDIVEAU, Peter - purchased land with B. Tardiveau of Lardner Clark (see above). See the interesting case of robbery involving swivel guns stolen from Peter on Dec. 29, 1784, on the Mississippi River, in the Court Minutes of the Superior Court of Law and Equity: [ref. 7].

TART, _____ - purchased with Edgar, land of Sanders: [ref. 8].

TATOM (variously, TATUM), Absalom - signer of the Cumberland Compact, May, 1780: [ref. 9a]. His slave was taken prisoner by the Indians during their attack at Clover Bottom in 1780: [ref. 9b].

TATOM, Howell - was admitted to the Bar as an attorney in Nashville, Nov., 1790: [ref. 10a]. Purchased land in 1791: [ref. 10b].

TATOM, William - purchased land of Robert Nelson: [ref. 11].

TAYLOR, Thomas - North Carolina land grant: [ref. 12a]. 1787 Davidson Co. tax roll with 1 taxable: [ref. 12b].

TERRILL (variously, TEREL), Obadiah - came to the Cumberland area in 1769, to hunt with a company of 20 adventurers from North Carolina, Rockbridge in Virginia, and New River: [ref. 13a]. He recorded his stock mark in the Minutes of the Committee of the Cumberland Association, April 23, 1783, thus: "A crop and under kell in the right ear, and a nick under and over the left, and brands thus - T.": [ref. 13b]. Defendant in a lawsuit brought by Daniel Hogan to recover a debt, heard before the Cumberland Committee, May 6, 1783: [ref. 13c].

TERRILL, Timothy - signer of the Cumberland Compact, May, 1780: [ref. 14a]. "From North Carolina," he was killed by Indians in the fall of 1781: [ref. 14b]. Listed in the North Carolina Preemption Act of 1784, as one of the settlers who had died in the defense of the Cumberland Settlements, whose heirs were entitled to 640 acres without any price to be paid to the public: [ref. 14c].

THACKSON, James - North Carolina land grant: [ref. 15].

THOMAS, Eneas - arrived with the Donelson flotilla, April 24, 1780: [ref. 16a]. He and Joshua Thomas were charged with threatening the life of James Hollis, Sr., before the Committee of the Cumberland Association, Jan. 7, 1783: [ref. 16b]. Listed in the North Carolina Preemption Act of 1784, as one of the settlers on the Cumberland too young at the time of the 1782 Preemption Act to receive a grant, but who was now entitled to 640 acres: [ref. 16c]. He was killed by Indians after Jan. 1, 1787: [ref. 16d].

THOMAS, Isaac - purchased land of Thos. Mollow: [ref. 18a]. 1787 Davidson Co. tax roll: [ref. 18b].

THOMAS, James - killed by Indians after Jan. 1, 1787: [ref. 19].

THOMAS, Jesse - North Carolina land grant: [ref. 20].

THOMAS, John, Sr. - member of the first Grand Jury, Oct. 7, 1783: [ref. 21a]. Listed in the North Carolina Preemption Act of 1784, as one of the settlers on the Cumberland in 1780, who stayed and defended the Settlements, and entitled to 640 acres without any price to be paid to the public: [ref. 21b]. Listed with John, Isaac, and William Thomas on the 1787 Davidson Co. tax roll with 4 taxables: [ref. 21c]. North Carolina land grant: [ref. 21d]. Summoned for Davidson Co. jury duty, March, 1789: [ref. 21e]. (See also, John Sadler).

THOMAS, John - listed with John, Isaac, and William Thomas on the 1787 Davidson Co. tax roll: [ref. 22].

THOMAS, John - son of Joshua Thomas (see hereafter).

THOMAS, Joshua - signer of the Cumberland Compact, May, 1780: [ref. 23a]. Elected Ensign of Militia at Heatonsburg (Heaton's Station) in 1783: [ref. 23b]. Charged, along with Eneas Thomas, with threatening the life of James Hollis, Sr., Jan. 7, 1783, before the Committee of the Cumberland Association: [ref. 23c]. Listed in the North Carolina Preemption Act of 1784, as one of the settlers on the Cumberland at the time of the 1782 Preemption Act, too young to receive a grant, but were now entitled to 640 acres: [ref. 23d]. He was mortally wounded by Indians: [ref. 23e]. His will, probated in Davidson Co., Aug. 29, 1794, names his wife Nancy, and mentions two "daughters," and his son John: [ref. 23f].

THOMAS, Micajah - land purchase in 1789, on Marrowbone Creek: [ref. 24].

THOMAS, Nancy - wife of Joshua Thomas (see above).

THOMAS, Philemon - "of County Fayette, Virginia," recorded North Carolina land grant, June 9, 1787: [ref. 25a]. Purchased land of Richard Thomas: [ref. 25b].

THOMAS, Richard - "of Orange County, North Carolina," recorded land grant, Feb. 1, 1787: [ref. 26a]. Purchased land of James Glasgow: [ref. 26b].

THOMAS, Robert - summoned for Davidson Co. jury duty, Nov., 1788: [ref. 27].

THOMAS, William - listed with Isaac, John, and John Thomas on the 1787 Davidson Co. tax roll: [ref. 28].

THOMELU, Edward - signer of the Cumberland Compact, May, 1780: [ref. 29].

THOMPSON - see also, THOMSON.
THOMPSON, Alexander - listed in the North Carolina Preemption
Act of 1784, as one of the settlers who had died in the
defense of the Cumberland Settlements, whose heir were
entitled to 640 acres without any price to be paid to the
public: [ref. 30].
THOMPSON, Alice - daughter of James Thompson (see hereafter);
was taken prisoner by Indians, Feb. 25, 1792, four miles
from Nashville; [ref. 31a]. Following her release from
captivity, she married Edmond Collinsworth: [ref. 31b].
THOMPSON, Andrew - listed in the North Carolina Preemption
Act of 1784, as one of the settlers on the Cumberland in
1780, who had stayed and defended the Settlements, and
entitled to 640 acres without any price to be paid to the
public: [ref. 32a]. North Carolina land grant: [ref. 32b].
Listed with Laurence and Thomas Thompson on the 1787 Davidson
Co. tax roll with 3 taxables: [ref. 32c].
THOMPSON, Azariah - 1787 Davidson Co. tax roll with 4 taxables:
[ref. 33].
THOMPSON, Catherine - daughter of James Thompson (see below).
THOMPSON, Charles - signer of the Cumberland Compact, May,
1780: [ref. 34a]. North Carolina land grant: [ref. 34b].
Listed with James and Robert Thompson on the 1787 Davidson
Co. tax roll with 3 taxables: [ref. 34c].
THOMPSON, Elijah - signer of the Cumberland Compact, May,
1780: [ref. 35].
THOMPSON, Elizabeth - daughter of James Thompson (see below).
THOMPSON, Jacob - son of James Thompson (see hereafter).
THOMPSON, James - D.A.R. membership on this line. Born ca.
1735, in Scotland or Ireland. Married Elizabeth Stump
in 1760: [ref. 36a]. Signer of the Cumberland Compact,
May, 1780: [ref. 36b]. Listed in the North Carolina Preemption Act of 1784, as one of the settlers on the Cumberland
in 1780, who stayed and defended the Settlements, and entitled to 640 acres without any price to be paid to the public:
[ref. 36c]. Purchased land of the Trustees of Nashville:
[ref. 36d]. Listed with Charles and Robert Thompson on
the 1787 Davidson Co. tax roll: [ref. 36e]. He and his
wife were killed by Indians in 1792: [ref. 36f]. Another
source records four Thompson individuals being killed by
Indians, four miles from Nashville, on February 25, 1792:
[ref. 36g]. Children: Robert, b. June 30, 1763 , m. (1st)
Sarah Robertson; John, killed by Indians in 1792; Catherine,
m. John Singletary; Elizabeth, killed by Indians in 1792;
Alice, captured by Indians, m. Edmond Collinsworth; and
Jacob: [ref. 36h].

THOMPSON, Jason - purchased land on the Little Harpeth River
and Mill Creek in 1788: [ref. 37a]. North Carolina land
grant: [ref. 37b]. Wounded by Indians on the Cumberland
Trace in 1792: [ref. 37c].
THOMPSON, John - son of James Thompson (see previously).
THOMPSON, Laurence (variously, Lawrence) - purchased land
of Bushnell and Dobbins: [ref. 38a]. Listed with Andrew
and Thomas Thompson on the 1787 Davidson Co. tax roll:
[ref. 38b]. Summoned from Sumner Co. for jury duty on
the Superior Court of Law and Equity, May, 1790: [ref.
38c].
THOMPSON, Robert - son of James Thompson (see previously).
THOMPSON, Robert - signer of the Cumberland Compact, May,
1780: [ref. 39a]. Listed in the North Carolina Preemption
Act of 1784, as one of the settlers on the Cumberland at
the time of the 1782 Preemption Act, too young to receive
and grant, but who were now entitled to receive 640 acres:
[ref. 39b]. He was married to Sarah Castleman in Nashville,
11 April, 1785: [ref. 39c]. Listed with Charles and James
Thompson on the 1787 Davidson Co. tax roll: [ref. 39d].
He deeded 740 acres on Mill Creek to his sisters, "Alsee
and Elizabeth Thompson.": [ref. 39e].
THOMPSON, Robin - helped defend Buchanan's Station during
the Indian attack of Sept. 30, 1792: [ref. 40].
THOMPSON, Thomas - listed with Andrew and Laurence Thompson
on the 1787 Davidson Co. tax roll: [ref. 41].
THOMPSON, Thomas - travelled with the Buchanan group from
South Carolina to the Cumberland Settlements: [ref. 42a].
He left his family in Danville, while he proceeded to the
French Lick to build a cabin: [ref. 42b]. North Carolina
land grant: [ref. 42c].
THOMPSON, William - North Carolina land grant: [ref. 43].
THOMSON, Abselom (variously, Absolom) - signer of the Cumber-
land Compact, May, 1780: [ref. 44].
THOMSON, Andrew - signer of the Cumberland Compact, May,
1780: [ref. 45].
THOMSON, Charles - signer of the Cumberland Compact, May,
1780: [ref. 46a]. Member of the first Grand Jury, Oct.
7, 1783: [ref. 46b].
THOMSON, Elijah - signer of the Cumberland Compact, May,
1780: [ref. 47].
THOMSON, James - signer of the Cumberland Compact, May, 1780:
[ref. 48a]. Defendant in lawsuit brought by Julius Sanders,
heard before the Committee of the Cumberland Association,
May 6, 1783, in which the Committee found for the defendant:
[ref. 48b].

THOMSON, Robert - signer of the Cumberland Compact, May, 1780: [ref. 49a]. Witness for the plaintiff (Sanders vs. James Thompson) heard before the Committee of the Cumberland Association, May 6, 1783: [ref. 49b].
TILLSFORTH, Isaac - 1787 Davidson Co. tax roll with 3 taxables: [ref. 50]. (See Isaac Titsorth).
TILMAN, Thomas - purchased land in 1789: [ref. 51].
TINNEN (variously, TINNEN, TENEN, TENNIN), Col. Hugh - listed with James Tinnen on the 1787 Davidson Co. tax roll with 2 taxables: [ref. 52a]. Purchased land in 1788, on Red River (Tennessee Co.; then Robertson Co.): [ref. 52b]. Ambushed by Indians while hunting in 1789, but he escaped. He was later killed with Grimes and Brown in Holly Tree Gap in what is now Williamson Co.: [ref. 52c].
TITUS, Ebenezer - signer of the Cumberland Compact, May, 1780: [ref. 53a]. Member of the Committee of the Cumberland Association, Jan., 1783: [ref. 53b]. Recorded his stock mark in the Minutes of the Committee of the Cumberland Association, Mar. 4, 1783, thus: "A slope under the left ear and an under kell in the right, and a slit in the dewlap, and brands thus - ET": [ref. 53c]. Member of the first Grand Jury, Oct. 7, 1783: [ref. 53d]. North Carolina land grants: [ref. 53e]. 1787 Davidson Co. tax roll with 1 taxable: [ref. 53f].
TITSWORTH, Isaac - summoned from Tennessee Co. for jury duty on the Superior Court of Law and Equity in 1790: [ref. 54a]. While moving near the mouth of Sulphur Fork of Red River with his family and the family of John Titsworth, the group were attacked by Indians and all killed including the wives and children: [ref. 54b].
TITSWORTH, John - summoned from Tennessee Co. for jury duty on the Superior Court of Law and Equity in 1790: [ref. 55]. He was killed by Indians at the same time as Isaac Titsworth (see above).
TISON, A. - (heirs of) sold land in 1789, on Spring Creek (Sumner Co. at the time; then Wilson Co.): [ref. 56].
TODD, James - 1787 Davidson Co. tax roll with 1 taxable: [ref. 57a]. North Carolina land grant: [ref. 57b]. Purchased land in 1788, on Hickman Creek (Sumner Co.; then Smith Co.): [ref. 56c]. He was fined for failing to appear for jury duty on the Superior Court of Law and Equity, Nov., 1788: [ref. 57d].
TODD, Isreal - was with Peter Tardivo when robbed on the Mississippi River. See Court case filed in Davidson Co., Nov. 1788, regarding this robbery: [ref. 58].
TOP, Roger - one of the guards who came with the Commissioners; was killed by Indians in 1783: [ref. 59].

TOPP, Jno. - purchased land of Robert Nelson: [ref. 60a].
He was with the party who went by boat on the punitive
expedition mounted against the Indian town Coldwater in
the year 1787. The flotilla was ambushed by Indians on
the Cumberland River at the mouth of the Harpeth River,
and he was shot through the body: [ref. 60b].

TOPP, Ruth - married Enoch Heaton in Davidson Co., Oct. 20,
1789: [ref. 61].

TOTWINE, William - purchased land in 1789, on Big Cedar Creek:
[ref. 62].

TRAMMELL (variously, TRAMEL, TRAMMEL), Nicholas - had been
a member of Capt. Benjamin Logan's Company in Kentucky
in 1779: [ref. 63a]. Signer of the Cumberland Compact,
May, 1780: [ref. 63b]. Listed in the North Carolina Preemption Act of 1784, as one of the settlers who had died in
defense of the Settlements, whose heirs were entitled to
640 acres without any price to be paid to the public: [ref.
63c].

TRAMMELL, Noal (variously, Noah) - killed by Indians on Goose
Creek in 1780: [ref. 64].

TRAMMELL, Philip - came from Kentucky to the Cumberland.
He was called as a witness in the case of Humphrey Hogan
vs. Brown and Mayfield, heard before the Committee of the
Cumberland Association, April 1, 1783: [ref. 65a]. Defendant
in Court, May, 1790, before the Superior Court of Law and
Equity: [ref. 65b]. He was killed by Indians in early
1784: [ref. 65c].

TROUBLEFIELD, Benjamin - (heirs of) sold land in 1790, on
Dry Fork of West Fork of Red River (Tennessee Co. at the
time; then Montgomery Co.): [ref. 66].

TROUSDALE, Agnes - daughter of James Trousdale (see hereafter).

TROUSDALE, Alexander - son of James Trousdale (see hereafter).

TROUSDALE, Ann - daughter of James Trousdale (see hereafter).

TROUSDALE, Bryson - son of James Trousdale (see hereafter).

TROUSDALE, Catron - son of James Trousdale (see hereafter).

TROUSDALE, Elizabeth - daughter of James Trousdale (see below).

TROUSDALE, James - son of James Trousdale (see hereafter).

TROUSDALE, Capt. James - D.A.R. membership on this line.
Born Dec. 16, ca. 1736, in Scotland. Married (1st) Elizabeth
Ferguson. Married (2nd) Elizabeth Dobbins, in 1775, who
was born Mar. 10, 1753. Resided in Orange Co., NC during
the Revolution: [ref. 67a]. North Carolina land grant,
Dec. 4, 1782: [ref. 67b]. He died Dec. 24, 1818 in Gallatin,
Sumner Co., TN: [ref. 67c]. Though he received a land
grant in 1782, we find no records presently which indicate
he was actually in the Cumberland Settlements during the
period of this census. Children: (by first wife) John,b. Oct.

(continued next page)

TROUSDALE, Capt. James - (continued)

3, 1762, m. Elizabeth Stoddard; Alexander, b. May 26, 1765, m. Nancy Emily Allen; Ann, b. Nov. 27, 1768; Mary, b. Apr. 1, 1770; Elizabeth, b. Aug. 25, 1772. Children: (by second wife) James, b. Dec. 16, 1775; Robert, b. Dec. 12, 1777; Jonathan, b. Apr. 7, 1780; Catron, b. Dec. 19, 1782; Agnes, b. Aug. 26, 1785; Sarah, b. Apr. 25, 1788; William, b. Sept. 23, 1790; and Bryson, b. Dec. 19, 1793: [ref. 67d].

TROUSDALE, John - son of James Trousdale (see above); purchased land in 1790, on Blooming Grove Creek (Tennessee Co. at the time; then Montgomery Co.): [ref. 68].

TROUSDALE, Jonathan - son of James Trousdale (see above).

TROUSDALE, Mary - daughter of James Trousdale (see above).

TROUSDALE, Robert - son of James Trousdale (see above).

TROUSDALE, Sarah - daughter of James Trousdale (see above).

TROUSDALE, William - son of James Trousdale (see above).

TRUELOCK, Bryan - heir of George D. Truelock (see hereafter).

TRUELOCK, George D - his heir, Bryan Truelock, sold land in 1790, on Cedar Creek (Sumner Co. at the time; then Wilson Co.): [ref. 69].

TRYALE, Christoper - (heirs of) sold land in 1789, on Lick Creek on the south side of the Cumberland River: [ref. 70].

TUCKER, Jenny - defense witness in Court case (Freeman vs. Deson), before the Committee of the Cumberland Association, July 1, 1783: [ref. 71].

TUCKER, John - signer of the Cumberland Compact, May, 1780: [ref. 72a]. He as married to Miss Jenny Herod by Trustee James Shaw, at Fort Nashborough, in 1780: [ref. 72b]. Wounded by Indians, who shot him, breaking his arm, at the Battle of the Bluffs, April 2, 1781: [ref. 72c]. Another source states that he was wounded and his arm broken during an Indian ambush while returning from Freeland's Station to the Bluffs in Feb. 1782: [ref. 72d]. See **Appendix**.

TURNBULL, John - was a trader from Natchez, who came to the Cumberland Settlements in the latter part of 1783, with horses and skins he bought from the Chickasaw Nation: [ref. 73].

TURNBULL, Robin - helped defend Buchanan's Station during the Indian attack of Sept. 30, 1792: [ref. 74].

TURNBULL, William - North Carolina land grants: [ref 75a]. Purchased land in 1791: [ref. 75b].

TURNER, Daniel - signer of the Cumberland Compact, May, 1780: [ref. 76].

TURNER, John - signer of the Cumberland Compact, May, 1780: [ref. 77a]. The administration of his estate was given John Marney by the Committee of the Cumberland Association, Feb. 5, 1783: [ref. 77b]. Subsequently, Elizabeth Marney, wife of John Marney, was named administratrix of the estate of John Turner on behalf of Turner's children: [ref. 77c].

TURNER, William - (heirs of) sold land in 1790, on Blooming Grove Creek (Tennessee Co. at the time; then Montgomery Co.): [ref. 78].

TURNEY, Charlotte - daughter of Peter Turney (see below).

TURNEY, Elizabeth - daughter of Peter Turney (see below).

TURNEY, Henry (variously, Hy) - listed in the North Carolina Preemption Act of 1784, as one of the settlers on the Cumberland in 1780, who stayed and defended the Settlements, and entitled to 640 acres without any price to be paid to the public: [ref. 79a]. He married Martha Lancaster in Davidson Co., Dec. 13, 1788: [ref. 79b]

TURNEY, Hopkins - son of Peter Turney (see hereafter).

TURNEY, James - son of Peter Turney (see hereafter).

TURNEY, Peter - D.A.R. membership on this line. Born ca. 1734, probably in Holland: [ref. 80a]. North Carolina land grant: [ref. 80b]. Children: James, Samuel, Elizabeth, Polly, Charlotte, Susannah, and Hopkins: [ref. 80c].

TURNEY, Polly - daughter of Peter Turney (see above).

TURNEY, Samuel - son of Peter Turney (see above).

TURNEY, Susannah - daughter of Peter Turney (see above).

TURPIN - family of, sold preemptions and removed to lands between Walnut Hills and Natchez: [ref. 81].

TURPIN, James - listed in the North Carolina Preemption Act of 1784, as one of the settlers who had died in defense of the Cumberland Settlements, whose heirs were entitled to 640 acres without any price to be paid to the public: [ref. 82].

TURPIN, Nathan - killed by Indians at Red River Station: [ref. 83a]. Listed in the North Carolina Preemption Act of 1784, as one of the settlers who died in defense of the Cumberland Settlements, whose heirs were entitled to 640 acres without any price to be paid to the public: [ref. 83b].

TURPIN, Solomon - arrived with the Donelson flotilla in 1780, and was one of those to settle on Red River: [ref. 84a]. Signer of the Cumberland Compact, May, 1780: [ref. 84b].

TUTON, William - purchased land in 1788, on Mulherrin Branch of Caney Fork River (Sumner Co. at the time; the Smith Co.): [ref. 85].

U

UNDERWOOD, James - (heirs of) sold land in 1790: [ref. 1].

V

VALENTINE, Silas - (heirs of) sold land in 1790, on Yellow Creek: [ref. 1].
VANCE, John - North Carolina land grant: [ref. 2].
VERNER, Samuel - killed by Indians: [ref. 3].
VERNON, Samuel - North Carolina land grant: [ref. 4].

W

WALKER, George - purchased land in 1788: [ref. 1a]. Married Rachel Caffrey in Davidson Co. on Aug. 9, 1790: [ref. 1b].
WALKER, John - listed with Phil and Samuel Walker on the 1787 Davidson Co. tax roll with 3 taxables: [ref. 2].
WALKER, John (Sr.) - 1787 Davidson Co. tax roll with 2 taxables: [ref. 3a]. Summoned for Davidson Co. jury duty on the Superior Court of Law and Equity, Nov., 1788: [ref. 3b]. North Carolina land grant: [ref. 3c]. Summoned for Davidson Co. jury duty, May, 1789: [ref. 3d].
WALKER, Philip (variously, Phil) - listed with John and Samuel Walker on the 1787 Davidson Co. tax roll: [ref. 4a]. North Carolina land grant: [ref. 4b].
WALKER, Richard - summoned from Sumner Co. for jury duty on the Superior Court of Law and Equity in 1790: [ref. 5].
WALKER, Samuel - defendant in lawsuit brought by Samuel Martin, April 1, 1783, before the Committee of the Cumberland Association, which found for the plaintiff for his debt of 5 dollars and costs: [ref. 6a]. Listed in the North Carolina Preemption Act of 1784, as one of the settlers on the Cumberland in 1780, who stayed and defended the settlements, and entitled to 640 acres without any price to be paid to the public: [ref. 6b]. Listed with John and Phil Walker on the 1787 Davidson Co. tax roll: [ref. 6c]. North Carolina land grant: [ref. 6d].
WALKER, Dr. Thomas - Virginia Commissioner for running boundary between Virginia and North Carolina, arrived at the Bluff in 1780: [ref. 7].
WALLACE, Joseph - summoned from Sumner Co. for jury duty on the Superior Court of Law and Equity, Nov. 1790: [ref. 8].
WALLACE, Samuel - 1787 Davidson Co. tax roll with 1 taxable: [ref. 9].

WALLS, Mr. - killed by Indians after Jan. 1, 1787: [ref. 10].

WALTON, Isaac - summoned from Sumner Co. for jury duty on the Superior Court of Law and Equity, Nov. 1788: [ref. 11].

WALTERS, ____ - killed by Indians near Winchester Mills: [ref. 12].

WARD, Elijah - (heirs of) sold land in 1790, on Shackler's Creek on the north side of the Cumberland River: [ref. 13].

WATERS, ____ - killed by Indians near Winchester's Mill in 1788: [ref. 14].

WEAKLEY, Col. - was in the company of Edmund Hickman when killed by Indians on Piney River: [ref. 15].

WEAKLEY, Robert - D.A.R. membership on this line. Born July 2, 1764, in Halifax Co., VA. Married Jane Lock, Aug. 11, 1791. She was born July 11, 1769: [ref. 16a]. Summoned for Davidson Co. jury duty in Nov., 1788: [ref. 16b]. Purchased land on Stone's River in 1789: [ref. 16c]. First appeared as a Davidson Co. taxpayer in 1789: [ref. 16d]. North Carolina land grants: [ref. 16e]. The couple had several children after the year 1790.

WEATHERFORD, Martin - plaintiff in lawsuit before the Superior Court of Law and Equity, Nov., 1790: [ref. 17].

WEATHERLY, Isaac - (heirs of) sold land in 1789, on Murfree's Fork: [ref. 18].

WEBB, Moses - signer of the Cumberland Compact, May, 1780: [ref. 19].

WEBB, Hugh - killed by Indians in 1789, on the Kentucky Trace near Barren River, as he and others were bringing salt from Kentucky to the Cumberland Settlements: [ref. 20].

WEBBER, William - bond made to him by John Brand and Samuel Barton in the matter of an attachment against Webber's estate, before the Committee of the Cumberland Settlements, June 7, 1783: [ref. 21].

WELLS, Anna - second white child born in the Cumberland Settlements: [ref. 22a]. Later lived in Montgomery Co.: [ref. 22b].

WELLS, Heydon (variously, Aydon, Headon) - came overland with the Heaton party arriving at the French Lick, Dec. 24, 1779: [ref. 23a]. Signer of the Cumberland Compact, May, 1780: [ref. 23b]. Helped build Heaton's Station, completed in the spring of 1782: [ref. 23c]. Member of the Committee of the Cumberland Association, Jan., 1783: [ref. 23d]. Served on the first Grand Jury, Oct. 7, 1783: ref. 23e]. Listed in the North Carolina Preemption Act

(continued next page)

WELLS, Heydon - (continued)
of 1784, as one of the settlers on the Cumberland in 1780,
who stayed and defended the Settlements, and entitled to
640 acres without any price to be paid to the public: [ref.
23f]. He was a one-eyed man: [ref. 23g]. 1787 Davidson
Co. tax roll with 1 taxable: [ref. 23h]. Summoned for
Davidson Co. jury duty on the Superior Court of Law and
Equity, May, 1789: [ref. 23i]. North Carolina land grants:
[ref. 23j].
WHITAKER, John - purchased land in 1788, on Stone's River:
[ref. 24].
WHITE, Burgess - signer of the Cumberland Compact, May, 1780:
[ref. 25].
WHITE, Dr. James - came to the Cumberland Settlements in
1784, and purchased service rights on the bluff on the
Cumberland River in 1797, and the right to use the log
cabin in which to practice medicine: [ref. 26].
WHITE, John - witness for the plaintiff in a lawsuit (Andrew
Keller vs. Samuel Martin), heard before the Committee of
the Cumberland Association, May 6, 1783: [ref. 27a]. Listed
in the North Carolina Preemption Act of 1784, as one of
the settlers on the Cumberland in 1780, who stayed and
defended the settlements, and entitled to 640 acres without
any price to be paid to the public: [ref. 27b]. Killed
by Indians, July 15, 1791, in the Cumberland Mountains:
[ref. 27c].
WHITE, Robert - married Nancy Hayes in Davidson Co., Jan.
7, 1789: [ref. 28].
WHITE, Samuel - signer of the Cumberland Compact, May, 1780:
[ref. 29].
WHITE, Capt. Solomon - plaintiff in lawsuit (White vs. John
Rains & Mark Noble), for breach of contract concerning
delivery of Indian corn, heard before the Committee of
the Cumberland Association, Mar. 4, 1783: [ref. 30a]. Member
of the first Grand Jury, Oct. 7, 1783: [ref. 30b]. On
June 13, 1786, one Solomon White hit John Harris on the
head with a cutting pole inflicting a mortal wound "depth
of ¼ inch, from which Harris died instantly." He was found
guilty of manslaughter, Nov., 1788. He was ordered to
"be continued at the Bar of the court and there be branded
on the braun of the left thumb with the letter 'M' and
that the iron be kept there on until the said Solomon White
expressed the words, "God save the State.": [ref. 30c].
1787 Davidson County tax roll with 1 taxable: [ref. 30d].
WHITE, Thomas - purchased land in 1788: [ref. 31a]. Purchased
land of Samuel Barton: [ref. 31b].

WHITE, Zachariah – came to the French Lick with the Robertson
    party in early 1779, and remained with part of that party
    to plant corn and help build forts at the French Lick,
    while Robertson went to the Illinois territory in 1779:
    [ref. 32a].   Signer of the Cumberland Compact, May 1780:
    [ref. 32b].   He was a teacher in the fort schools.   He
    died during the night from wounds received at the Battle
    of the Bluffs, April 2, 1781: [ref. 32c].   Listed in the
    North Carolina Preemption Act of 1784, as one of the settlers
    who died in defense of the Cumberland Settlements, whose
    heirs were entitled to 640 acres without any price to be
    paid to the public: [ref. 32d].   His heirs sold his land
    in 1791: [ref. 32e].
WHITESIDE, John – summoned from Sumner Co. for jury duty
    on the Superior Court of Law and Equity, May, 1790: [ref.
    33].
WHITNELL, Blount – North Carolina land grant: [ref. 34].
WILCOX (variously, WILCOCKS), Samuel – 1787 Davidson Co.
    tax roll with 6 taxables: [ref. 35].
WILCOX, Thomas – helped defend Buchanan's Station during
    the Indian attack of Sept. 30, 1792: [ref. 36].
WICUFF & CLARK – North Carolina land grants: [ref. 37].
WICUFF, William, Jr. – purchased land of Robert Nelson: [ref.
    38].
WILDER, Randal – (heirs of) sold land in 1790, on Yellow
    Creek: [ref. 39].
WILFORD, John – signer of the Cumberland Compact, May, 1780:
    [ref. 40].
WILHEIM, Mary – married Joshua Hollis in Davidson Co., Aug.
    19, 1789: [ref. 41].
WILLIAMS – wife and child of Benjamin Williams were killed
    by Indians in their own house, May 8, 1792: [ref. 42].
WILLIAMS, Amos – son of Daniel Williams, Sr. (see previously).
WILLIAMS, Benjamin – one source states he was killed by Indians
    May 8, 1792, at his own house: [ref. 43a].   Another source
    states he was killed in 1787, near the head of Station
    Camp Creek: [ref. 43b].
WILLIAMS, Betsy – killed by Indians: [ref. 44].
WILLIAMS, Curtis – North Carolina land grant: [ref. 45a].
    He was killed by Indians near the mouth of the Harpeth
    River in 1787: [ref. 45b].
WILLIAMS, Daniel, Jr. – son of Daniel Williams, Sr., was
    listed on the 1787 Davidson Co. tax roll with his father
    and two taxables: [ref. 46].
WILLIAMS, Daniel, Sr. – travelled with the Buchanan party
    from South Carolina to the Cumberland Settlements, leaving

(continued next page)

WILLIAMS, Daniel, Sr. - (continued)

his family at Danville in 1779-80, while he proceeded to
the French Lick to build cabins: [ref. 47a]. Signer of
the Cumberland Compact, May, 1780: [ref. 47b]. Ordered
by the Committee of the Cumberland Association to help
lay off a road from Nashborough toward Mansker's Station,
April 1, 1783: [ref. 47c]. He was sheriff and served on
the first Grand Jury, Oct. 7, 1783: [ref. 47d]. North
Carolina land grant: [ref. 47e]. Summoned for Davidson
Co. jury duty, Nov. 1788: [ref. 47f]. He was a Revolutionary
soldier. His will was proven in Davidson Co., Jan., 1794,
and listed the following children: Sampson; Eunice Carmick;
Wright; Amos (incapable of getting his living); and Nimrod:
[ref. 47g]. Other sources list other children: Daniel,
Jr.; Oliver; and Turner Williams: [ref. 47h].
WILLIAMS, Elizabeth - daughter of Nimrod Williams (see before).
WILLIAMS, Eunice - daughter of Daniel Williams (see hereafter).
WILLIAMS, Eunice - daughter of Nimrod Williams (see hereafter).
WILLIAMS, John - North Carolina land grant: [ref. 48].
WILLIAMS, Joseph - (heirs of) sold land in 1789, on the north
side of the Cumberland River: [ref. 49].
WILLIAMS, Mary - daughter of Nimrod Williams (see hereafter).
WILLIAMS, Nancy - married Edward Slayton in Davidson Co.,
July 8, 1789: [ref. 50].
WILLIAMS, Nathaniel - purchased land in 1788: [ref. 51].
WILLIAMS, Nimrod - was born 1750, in Laurens Dist., SC.
Married Christiana Griffin in 1775. She was born in 1758.
She died in 1811; and he died Feb., 1820, in Davidson Co.,
TN. Children: Mary, b. Jan. 20, 1776, m. Anthony Hampton;
Elizabeth, b. Aug. 2, 1787, m. Joseph Garner; Eunice, m.
_____ Estes; and Turner, b. Sept. 25, 1796, m. Ann Currin:
[ref. 52].
WILLIAMS, Oliver - son of Daniel Williams, Sr., was wounded
by Indians on the Cumberland Trace in 1793: [ref. 53].
WILLIAMS, Capt. Sampson - son of Daniel Williams, Sr., left
his family at Danville, while he proceeded to the French
Lick to help build cabins with the other men of the family:
[ref. 54a]. Signer of the Cumberland Compact, May, 1780:
[ref. 54b]. Listed in the North Carolina Preemption Act
of 1784, as one of the settlers too young to receive a
grant under the 1782 Preemption Act, but now entitled to
recieve 640 acres: [ref. 54c]. 1787 Davidson Co. tax roll
with 1 taxable: [ref. 54d]. Purchased land on the west
fork of West Harpeth River in 1788: [ref. 54e]. He was
ordered to aid Col. Elijah Robertson in the pursuit of
the Indian raiding party which had attacked Robertson's
Station in 1789: [ref. 54f]. Helped defend Buchanan's
Station during the Indian attack of Sept. 30, 1792: [ref.
54g].

WILLIAMS, Shaderick - summoned for Davidson Co. jury duty, Nov. 1790: [ref. 55a]. He was killed by Indians near Cotteral's on Sept. 6, 1792: [ref. 55b].

WILLIAMS, Thomas - sold land in 1790, on the west fork of Red River (Tennessee Co. at the time; then Robertson Co.): [ref. 56].

WILLIAMS, Turner - son of Daniel Williams, Sr. (see beforementioned). North Carolina land grant: [ref. 57].

WILLIAMS, Turner - son of Nimrod Williams (see beforementioned).

WILLIAMS, William - 1787 Davidson Co. tax roll with 2 taxables: [ref. 58].

WILLIAMS, Wright - son of Daniel Williams, Sr. (see beforementioned).

WILLIAMSON, Hugh - purchased land in 1788, on Deer River: [ref. 59].

WILLIAMSON, James - 1787 Davidson Co. tax roll with 3 taxables: [ref. 60].

WILLIS, James - 1787 Davidson Co. tax roll with 1 taxable: [ref. 61].

WILSON, Capt. David - D.A.R. membership on this line. Born 1752 in Cumberland Co., PA. Married prior to 1773, to Jane ____. He resided in Mecklenburg Co., NC during the Revolution: [ref. 62a]. North Carolina land grant: [ref. 62b]. Purchased land in 1790, on Flynn's Creek: [ref. 62c]. He built Wilson's Station, and it was there that Robert Jones was killed by Indians in 1787: [ref. 62d]. Summoned from Sumner Co. for jury duty on the Superior Court of Law and Equity, Oct., 1788: [ref. 62e]. Children: Elizabeth, m. Zacheus Wilson; James; (daughter), m. Wm. Street; William; Mary, m. Mark Dodd; and David: [ref. 62f].

WILSON, David - son of Capt. David Wilson (see previously).

WILSON, Eleanor - was taken prisoner by the Indians, who attacked Zeigler's Station, June 26, 1792: [ref. 63].

WILSON, Elizabeth - daughter of Capt. David Wilson (see previously).

WILSON, George - killed by Indians, May 25, 1791, near Station Camp Creek [ref. 64a]. His heirs sold his land in 1789, on Spencer's Creek (Sumner Co. at the time; then Wilson Co.): [ref. 64b].

WILSON, James - son of Capt. David Wilson (see previously). Purchased land in 1788, at Station Camp Creek north of the Cumberland River (Sumner Co.): [ref. 65a]. Fined for failure to appear for jury duty, Nov., 1788: [ref. 65b]. Summoned from Sumner Co. for jury duty on the Superior Court of Law and Equity, May, 1790: [ref. 65c].

WILSON, James - son of Capt. David Wilson (see previously).

WILSON, John - signer of the Cumberland Compact, May, 1780: [ref. 66a]. North Carolina land grant: [ref. 66b]. Summoned from Sumner Co. for jury duty on the Superior Court of Law and Equity, Nov., 1788: [ref. 66c]. Summoned from Tennessee County for jury duty on the Superior Court of Law and Equity, Nov., 1790: [ref. 66d].
WILSON, Ralph - signer of the Cumberland Compact, May, 1780: [ref. 67].
WILSON, Samuel - signer of the Cumberland Compact, May, 1780: [ref. 68a]. North Carolina land grant: [ref. 68b]. Summoned from Tennessee Co. for jury duty on the Superior Court of Law and Equity, May 1790: [ref. 68c].
WILSON, William - son of Capt. David Wilson (see previously).
WINCHESTER, David - purchased land between Stone's River and the Cumberland River in 1790: [ref. 69].
WINCHESTER, George - commanded a company of settlers pursuing the Indians who had attacked the settlements on Bledsoe's Lick in 1787: [ref. 70].
WINCHESTER, Gen'l James - D.A.R. membership on this line. Born Feb. 6, 1752, in Westminister, Maryland: [ref. 71a]. Summoned from Sumner Co. for jury duty on the Superior Court of Law and Equity, Nov., 1788: [ref. 71b]. Purchased land in Sumner Co. in 1789: [ref. 71c]. Married Susan Black in Davidson Co., 1792: [ref. 71d].
WINCHESTER, John - purchased land in Sumner Co. in 1789: [ref. 72].
WINNEHAM, Thomas - purchased land in 1788, on Red River (Tennessee Co.; then Robertson Co.): [ref. 73].
WINSTEELE, Thomas - (heirs of) sold land in 1789, on Stone's River: [ref. 74].
WINTERS, Aaron - son of Moses Winters (see hereafter).
WINTERS, Amy - daughter of Moses Winters (see hereafter).
WINTERS, Caleb - listed in the North Carolina Preemption Act of 1784, as one of the settlers on the Cumberland at the time of the 1782 Preemption Act, too young to receive a grant, but who was now entitled to 640 acres: [ref. 75a]. Listed as C. Winters with M(oses) Winters on the 1787 Davidson Co. tax roll with 2 taxables: [ref. 75b].
WINTERS, Catherine - daughter of Moses Winters (see hereafter).
WINTERS, Elizabeth - daughter of Moses Winters (see hereafter).
WINTERS, Mary - daughter of Moses Winters (see hereafter).
WINTERS, Moses - D.A.R. membership on this line. Married Elizabeth Head: [ref. 76a]. Settled at Heaton's Station: [ref. 76b]. Listed in the North Carolina Preemption Act of 1784, as one of the settlers on the Cumberland in 1780, who stayed and defended the settlements, and entitled to 640 acres without any price to be paid to the public: [ref.

(continued next page)

WINTERS, Moses - (continued)
    76c]. Summoned from Tennessee Co. for jury duty on the
    Superior Court of Law and Equity, May, 1789:   [ref.
    76d]. Children: Elizabeth, m. ___ McNeely; Mary, m. ___
    Smothers; Amy; Nancy, m. ____ Cocks; Catherine; Caleb,
    b. ca. 1765, m. (1st) Sarah Harris, (2nd) Mary Duncan;
    Moses, who was a minor in 1798; and Aaron, who was a minor
    in 1798: [ref. 76e].
WINTERS, Nancy - daughter of Moses Winters (see above).
WINTERS, Pheobe - daughter of Moses Winters (see above).
WINTERS, Sarah - daughter of Moses Winters (see above).
WITHS, Richard - killed by Indians Jan. 16, 1791, at Papon's
    Creek: [ref. 77].
WOOD, Thomas - (heirs of) sold land in 1788, on Caney Fork
    River (Sumner Co.; then Smith Co.): [ref. 78].
WOODS, John - administrator and plaintiff vs. Elijah Robertson,
    Oct. 28, 1788, before the Superior Court of Law and Equity:
    [ref. 79].
WOODS, William - signer of the Cumberland Compact, May, 1780:
    [ref. 80].
WOODWARD, Noah - North Carolina land grant: [ref. 81].
WOODWARD, Thomas - North Carolina land grant: [ref. 82].
WOOLARD, Isaac - 1787 Davidson Co. tax roll with 1 taxable:
    [ref. 83].
WRIGHT (variously, RIGHT), Jacob - land purchase on the West
    Fork of Harpeth River, 1788: [ref. 84].
WRIGHT, Johnny - Englishman, who built a distillery on White's
    Creek: [ref. 85]. Because no further record was found
    on this individual during preparation of this work, he
    may not belong to this enumeration.
WYATTE, Ephriam - his heir, Thomas Wyatte, sold land in 1788,
    on Cedar Lick Creek (Sumner Co.; then Wilson Co.): [ref.
    86].
WYATTE, Thomas - heir of Ephriam White (see above).

Y

YATES, James - summoned from Sumner Co. for jury duty on
    the Superior Court of Law and Equity, Nov., 1790: [ref.
    1].
YOCUM, Mathias - "of the County of Mercer, Kentucky," purchased
    land of Thomas Denton and Wife: [ref. 2].
YOUNG, Adam - purchased land on Sycamore Creek (Tennessee
    Co.; then Robertson Co.): [ref. 3].
YOUNG, Margaret - married Robert Barnett in Davidson Co.,
    July 31, 1789: [ref. 4].

Z

ZAMBERT, Aron - purchased land in 1789, on Sycamore Creek (Tennessee Co.; then Robertson Co.): [ref. 1].
ZARLETT, James - (heirs of) sold land in 1789, on Sulphur Fork of Red River (Tennessee Co.; the Robertson Co.): [ref. 2].

Part Two

THE INHABITANTS OF RECORD, BETWEEN THE YEARS 1786 AND 1790, IN SUMNER COUNTY, NORTH CAROLINA, WHICH HAD BEEN FORMED OUT OF DAVIDSON COUNTY, NORTH CAROLINA BY ACT OF THE GENERAL ASSEMBLY OF NORTH CAROLINA ON NOVEMBER 17, 1786

A

AGNEW (variously, EGNEW), Thomas - 1787 Sumner Co. tax roll with 1 taxable and 640 acres: [ref. 1a]. Juror on the Sumner Co. Court, Apr. 15, 1788, and on Oct. 6, 1790: [ref. 1b].

ALEXANDER, James - juror on the Sumner Co. Court, April Session, 1788: [ref. 2].

ALEXANDER, Matthew - juror for April Session, 1789, on the Sumner Co. Court: [ref. 3].

ALEXANDER, Richard - an early settler in Smith Co., which was established in 1799, from a part of Sumner Co.: [ref. 4].

ALFRED, John - sold land (see p. 1, Davidson Co. section).

ALLEN, Theophilas - land purchase in Sumner Co.: [ref. 5].

ALLEN, Walter - of Craven Co., NC, purchased land in Sumner Co., 1791: [ref. 6].

ALLEY, Thomas - juror, July Session, 1788, on the Sumner Co. Court: [ref. 7].

ANDERSON, Daniel - purchased land in 1789 (see p. 2, Davidson Co. section).

ANDERSON, Matthew - (see p. 2, Davidson Co. section); 1787 Sumner Co. tax roll with 2 taxables and 640 acres: [ref. 8a]. Recorded his stock mark in Minutes of the County Court, July, 1787: [ref. 8b].

ANDERSON, Stephen - bondsman for the marriage of William Anderson and Betsey Jones in Sumner Co., Nov. 23, 1791: [ref. 9].

ANDERSON, Uriah - juror on the Sumner Co. Court in 1787: [ref. 10].

ANDERSON, William - married Betsey Jones in Sumner Co., Nov. 23, 1791: [ref. 11]. (See also, p. 2 Davidson Co. section.)

ARMSTRONG, Martin - land purchase recorded in Davidson Co. (see p. 3).

ARRINGTON, Charles - grand juror on the Sumner Co. Court, 1787: [ref. 12]. Land purchase recorded in Davidson Co. (see p. 3).

ARRINGTON, Susannah - married Thomas Hampton in Sumner Co., June 19, 1787: [ref. 13].

ASHE, Samuel - NC land grant, Mar. 14, 1788, for 2563 acres on Wolf Creek, which was recorded in Davidson Co. though at the time, the land was in Sumner Co. (afterwards, Smith Co.): [ref. 14]. (See also, p. 3).

ASHER, _____ - built a fort called Asher's Station about 2½ miles south of the place where Gallatin now stands and near the Buffalo path from Mansker's Lick to Bledsoe's Lick, about the same time as Mansker's Station was constructed: [ref. 15].

ATKINS, John - land sale by his heirs recorded in Davidson Co. (see p. 4).

B

BADSBY, John - (see p. 4, Davidson Co. section).

BAILEY, Ethelred - (see p. 4, Davidson Co. section).

BAIRD, (boy) - killed by Indians on Station Camp Creek in 1787: [ref. 1].

BAKER, Capt. John - (see p. 4, Davidson Co. section).

BALDWIN, Joshua - grand jury presentment against Joshua Baldwin for altering his name to Joshua Campbell: [ref. 2a]. Estate administration filed in Sumner Co., Jan. 23, 1790: [ref. 2b].

BALDWIN, William - 1787 Sumner Co. tax roll with 1 poll and no land: [ref. 3a]. Witness to nuncupative will of Abner Bush, proven in Court of Pleas and Quarter Sessions, Oct. 1787: [ref. 3b]. Overseer of road from the dividing ridge between McKain's Creek and Ben Creek to Maj. Wilson's: [ref. 3c].

BALENDER, Jethro - (see p. 5, Davidson Co. section).

BALESTINE, Jessie - killed by Indians at Mansker's Lick late in 1780: [ref. 4].

BALLEW, Page - Bill of Sale, Sept. 26, 1791, for negroes to Peter Lum and John Pullen: [ref. 5]. (See also, BELLEW, BILLEIU)

BARNES, Frederick - juror on Sumner Co. Court, Oct. 6, 1790, for lawsuit (NC vs. Phebe McNeely): [ref. 6].

BARTLETT, John - juror for Oct. 13, 1789 term of Court: [ref. 7].

BARTLETT, William - killed by Indians on the road to Big Barrens, June 4, 1793: [ref. 8].

BARTLEY, James - D.A.R. membership on this line. Born in Anson Co., NC, Oct. 3, 1746; died 1783, Davidson Co. Wife, Polly Redford. Children: John, b. 1767, killed by Indians

(continued next page)

BARTLEY, James - (continued).
near Greenfield Fort; James, b. 1768; Mary, b. 1770; and
Richard, b. 1774, killed by Indians near Greenfield Fort.
James Bartley died 1783, in Davidson Co.: [ref. 9].
BARTLEY, James - son of James Bartley (see beforementioned).
BARTLEY, John - son of James Bartley (see beforementioned).
Ordered by the Co. Court to work on road: [ref. 10].
BARTLEY, Mary - daughter of James Bartley (beforementioned).
BARTLEY, Richard - son of James Bartley (see beforementioned).
Killed by Indians near "Walnut-field Fort,": [ref. 11].
BARTON, Samuel - land purchase recorded in Davidson Co. (see
p. 5).
BAY, Sgt. Andrew - land purchase recorded in Davidson Co.
(see p. 5).
BEARD, David - 1787 Sumner Co. tax roll with 1 poll & 320
acres: [ref. 12a]. Juror on County Court, Jan. 1788: [ref.
12b]. Overseer of road cleared from Kasper Creek to Drake's
Creek: [ref. 12c]. (See also, p. 6.)
BEARD, John - killed by Indians in 1786/87 near the head
of Big Station Camp Creek: [ref. 13].
BELL, Robert - 1787 Sumner Co. tax roll with 1 poll & 1990
acres: [ref. 14a]. Juror during 1787 term of Court: [ref.
14b]. Overseer of road from Kasper Creek to Drake's Creek:
[ref. 14c]. (See Robert Bell, p. 6).
BELLEW, Thomas - 1787 Sumner Co. tax roll with 2 polls &
374 acres: [ref. 15a]. Recorded his stock mark in the
Co. Court Minutes, 1787: [ref. 15b]. (See also, BALLEW,
BELLEW, BELEW, BILLEIU.)
BENNETT, Peter - killed by Indians in either Davidson or
Sumner Co. in the latter part of 1787: [ref. 16].
BERRY, Redmond D. - mentioned as early settler of Sumner
Co., who introduced Kentucky bluegrass and brought his
blooded horse, Gray Metley, from North Carolina: [ref.
17].
BERRY, Thomas - land grant recorded in Davidson Co. (see
p. 6).
BETTIS, Jno. - land sale recorded in Davidson Co. (see p.
6).
BILLEIU, Thomas - 1787 Sumner Co. tax roll with 2 polls &
394 acres: [ref. 18]. (See also, BALLEW, BELLEW).
BIRD, Abraham - juror on Co. Court, Apr. 1790: [ref. 19].
BIRD, William - jury duty recorded in Davidson Co. (see p.
7).
BISWELL, James - killed by Indians in either Davidson or
Sumner Co. after Jan. 1, 1787 : [ref. 20].
BITER, Betsy - married Charles Myars, 1791 (see hereafter).
BLACK, Gabriel - wounded during the Indian attack on Zeigler's
Station, June 26, 1792: [ref. 21].
BLACK, Michael - mentioned in deed as being "of Sumner Co."
[ref. 22].

BLACK, William - land purchase recorded in Davidson Co. (see
p. 7).
BLACKEMORE (variously, BLACKAMORE, BLACKMORE), Elizabeth
- daughter of George Dawson Blackemore (see hereafter).
BLACKEMORE, Elizabeth Neeley Montgomery - wife of George
Dawson Blackemore (see hereafter).
BLACKEMORE, George - 1787 Sumner Co. tax roll with 1 poll
& 976 acres: [ref. 23a]. Juror on Co. Court, July, 1788:
[ref. 23b]. Married Sallie Thompson in Sumner Co., Sept.
12, 1787. George Dawson Blackemore was bondsman: [ref.
23c]. (See the BLACKEMORE family in Part 1, Davidson Co.)
BLACKEMORE, George Dawson - D.A.R. lineage on this line.
Born 1762, in Hagerstown, MD. Married Elizabeth Neeley
Montgomery in 1786: [ref. 24a]. Listed on 1787 Sumner
Co. tax roll with 1 poll & 976 acres: [ref. 24b]. Bondsman
for marriage of George Blackemore in 1787: [ref. 24c].
Recorded his stock mark in Co. Court Minutes, 1788: [ref.
24d]. Children: Polly, Margaret, Elizabeth, Rachel, Kather-
ine, William, James, and George: [ref. 24e].
BLACKEMORE, Katherine - daughter of George Dawson Blackemore
(see beforementioned).
BLACKEMORE, Margaret - daughter of George Dawson Blackemore
(see beforementioned).
BLACKEMORE, Polly - daughter of George Dawson Blackemore
(see beforementioned).
BLACKEMORE, Rachel - daughter of George Dawson Blackemore
(see beforementioned).
BLACKEMORE, George - witnessed deed of James Bosley, Mar.
17, 1789: [ref. 25]. (See also, p. 7.)
BLEDSOE, Abraham - son of Anthony Bledsoe (see hereafter).
Came to the Cumberland area in 1769, with 20 adventurers
from N.C., Rockbridge in VA, and New River: [ref. 26].
BLEDSOE, Anthony (Jr.) - son of Anthony Bledsoe (hereafter).
BLEDSOE, Anthony - son of Isaac Bledsoe (see hereafter).
D.A.R. membership on this line. Born 1733, in Culpepper
Co., VA; married Mary Ramsey in Augusta Co., VA: [ref.
27a]. Built a fort in 1784, at Greenfield, 2½ miles north
of Bledsoe's Lick: [ref. 27b]. Listed in the 1787 Sumner
Co. tax roll with 10 polls & 11,120 acres, and listed in
the 1788 tax roll with 4 polls & 390 acres: [ref. 27c].
Took oath as Lt. Colonel Commandant of Militia in 1787:
[ref. 27d]. Recorded stock mark in the County Court Minutes,
1787: [ref. 27e]. Appointed by County Court, April 1788,
to divide estate of Jourdan Gibson, deceased: [ref. 27f].
Bondsman for marriage of Thomas Hampton and Susannah Arrington, June 19, 1787: [ref. 27g]. He and his son, Thomas,
were killed by Indians about July 20, 1788, at the fort
at Bledsoe's Lick: [ref. 27h]. His will, dated July 20,

(continued next page)

BLEDSOE, Anthony - (continued)
1788, proved Oct. 18, 1788, mentions land in Kentucky and
land on the Holston to be sold; children to be equally edu-
cated; lands to be divided equally between children; and
appoints his wife Mary, and his brother Issac Bledsoe, executrix and executor with Col. Daniel Smith: [ref. 27i]. Mary
Bledsoe was appointed guardian to Thomas, Anthony, Isaac,
Polly, Abraham, Henry, and Prudence Bledsoe, his orphans,
in July 1789: [ref. 27j]. Mentioned in the will of his
father, 1791: [ref. 27k]. Children: Abraham, b. 1762;
m. Amelia Weathred; Sarah, b. 1763-70, m. David Shelby;
Betsy, b. 1768, m. James Clendening; Thomas, b. 1774; Anthony;
Isaac, m. Margaret Neeley; Henry, m. Nancy Gillespie; Rachel,
m. Wm. Neeley; Polly, b. 1780, m. Wearred (James?); Prudence,
m. Joseph Sewell; and Susan, m. William Penny: [ref. 27l].
BLEDSOE, Elizabeth "Betsy" - daughter of Isaac Bledsoe (see
hereafter).
BLEDSOE, Henry - son of Anthony Bledsoe (beforementioned).
BLEDSOE, Isaac - son of Anthony Bledsoe (beforementioned).
BLEDSOE, Isaac - son of Isaac Bledsoe (see hereafter).
BLEDSOE, Maj. Isaac - came to the Cumberland area with Mansker
in 1771: [ref. 28a]. Member of the Committee of the Cumberland Association, qualified Jan. 18, 1783; and elected Captain
of defense at Mansker's Station in 1783: [ref. 28b]. He
built a fort at Bledsoe's Lick in 1784: [ref. 28c]. Listed
on the 1787 Sumner Co. tax roll with 5 polls & 3190 acres:
[ref. 28d]. Member of the County Court, 1787: [ref. 28e].
Helped lay off road from his fort to the State line in 1787:
[ref. 28f]. Took oath as 1st Major of Militia, 1787: [ref.
28g]. Recorded his stock mark in the County Court Minutes,
1787: [ref. 28h]. Appointed one of the administrators of
the estate of William Hall, deceased, 1787: [ref. 28i].
Appointed with others to divide estate of Jourdan Gibson,
dec'd, 1788: [ref. 28j]. Mentioned in Court Mins., 1788:
[ref. 28k]. Appointed executor of his brother Anthony Bledsoe's will in 1788: [ref. 28l]. Purchased land of John
Weathers, 1790: [ref. 28m]. Took oath required by Congress
for the support of the Constitution of the U.S., April,
1790: [ref. 28n]. "Added to the bench" in 1787: [ref. 28o].
One source states he was killed by Indians at Bledsoe's
Lick Fort in 1788, however, his will was dated 1791. In
it are mentioned his wife Katy, and children: Peggy, Sally,
Polly, Anthony, Isaac, and William Lytle Bledsoe: [ref.
28p].
BLEDSOE, Katy - wife of Isaac Bledsoe (beforementioned).
BLEDSOE, Mary - wife of Anthony Bledsoe (beforementioned).
Married Nathaniel Parker in Sumner Co., Dec. 4, 1791: [ref.
29a]. She was almost killed by Indians, but they were kept
at bay by Thomas Spencer while she made her escape: [ref.
29b].

BLEDSOE, Peggy - daughter of Isaac Bledsoe (beforementioned).
BLEDSOE, Polly - daughter of Anthony Bledsoe (beforementioned).
BLEDSOE, Polly - daughter of Isaac Bledsoe (beforementioned).
BLEDSOE, Prudence - daughter of Anthony Bledsoe (see beforementioned).
BLEDSOE, Prudy - daughter of Isaac Bledsoe (beforementioned).
BLEDSOE, Rachel - daughter of Isaac Bledsoe (beforementioned).
BLEDSOE, Sally - daughter of Anthony Bledsoe (beforementioned).
BLEDSOE, Sally - sister of Isaac Bledsoe (see beforementioned).
BLEDSOE, Sarah - daughter of Anthony Bledsoe (beforementioned).
BLEDSOE, Susannah - daughter of Isaac Bledsoe (see beforementioned).
BLEDSOE, Thomas - son of Anthony Bledsoe (see beforementioned);
   killed by Indians at the fort at Bledsoe's Lick (the house
   of his late uncle, Col. Isaac Bledsoe) on 20 Oct. 1794:
   [ref. 30].
BLEDSOE, William Lytle - son of Isaac Bledsoe (see beforementioned).
BOLES, John - fined for swearing and breaking the Sabbath,
   April, 1788: [ref. 31].
BONE, James - juror on County Court, July and Oct. Sessions,
   1788: [ref. 32a]. Appointed constable, Jan. 1790: [ref.
   32b]. Witnessed Bill of Sale for Lawrence Thompson, Dec.,
   1790: [ref. 32c]. See also, James BONN, p. 8.
BOWEN, William - 1787 Sumner Co. tax roll with 1 poll & 4032
   acres: [ref. 33a]. Juror on County Court, Jan. & Apr.
   Sessions, 1788: [ref. 33b]. Grantee of Deed from Nicholas
   Long, 1788: [ref. 33c]. Juror on Superior Court, Apr.
   15, 1788: [ref. 33d]. (See also, William BOIN, p. 8, &
   William BOWEN, p. 9.)
BOWEN, William - listed on the 1787 Sumner Co. tax roll with
   1 poll & 4032 acres: [ref. 34].
BOWMAN, Mr. - (see p. 10, Davidson Co. section).
BOWMAN, W. - 1787 Sumner Co. tax roll with 1 poll and 4032
   acres: [ref. 35a]. Delinquent 1787 taxes: [ref. 35b].
   Juror on County Court, 1787: [ref. 35c]. (See also, p.
   10.)
BOYD, Robert - (see p. 10, Davidson Co. section.)
BRATTON, William - killed by Indians near White's Station
   within sight of the fort in 1786 or 1787: [ref. 36].
BREHON, James G. - land purchase recorded in Davidson Co.
   (see p. 11).
BRIGANCE, John - juror on Co. Court, 1787: [ref. 37]. Land
   purchase recorded in Davidson Co. (see p. 11).
BRIGANCE, Robert - juror on County Court, 1787: [ref. 38].
BRIGHAM, David - 1787 Sumner Co. tax roll with 1 poll & 320
   acres: [ref. 39a]. Delinquent tax, 1787: [ref. 39b].
   Appointed Constable, 1787: [ref. 39c].
BRIGHAM, John - 1787 Sumner Co. tax roll with 1 poll: [ref.
   40a]. Delinquent taxes, 1787: [ref. 40b]. Grand juror
   in 1787: [ref. 40c]. Juror on Co. Court, Jan. & July Sessions, 1788: [ref. 40d].

BRIGHAM, Robert - mentioned as an early settler in Sumner
    Co.: [ref. 41a]. Juror on County Court, July Session,
    1788: [ref. 41b]. Killed by Indians in 1786 or 1787, near
    White's Station on the waters of Desha's Creek, a fork
    of Bledsoe's Creek: [ref. 41c].
BRIGHAM, William - juror during July 1788, Session of Court:
    [ref. 42].
BRISTON, James - land purchase recorded in Davidson Co. (see
    p. 11).
BROWN, James - land sale by his heirs recorded in Davidson
    Co. (see p. 12).
BUCK, Elender - married John Gatlin in Sumner Co., Mar. 26,
    1791: [ref. 43].
BUSH, Abner - appointed with others to view and mark road
    from Maj. Bledsoe's to the State Line in 1787: [ref. 44a].
    Produced commission and took oath as Militia officer in
    1787: [ref. 44b]. His nuncupative will proved by Uriah
    Anderson and others and his wife Eleanor appointed executrix,
    1787: [ref. 44c].
BUSH, Eleanor - wife of Abner Bush (see above).
BUSH?, William - nominated one of the executors of Simpson
    Hart's will, Feb. 1790: [ref. 45].
BUSHNELL, Eurebius - sold land with William Dobbins to William
    Frazier in 1790: [ref. 46]. (See also, p. 15).
BYRNS, John - mentioned as an early settler: [ref. 47].
BYRNS, Joseph - mentioned as an early settler: [ref. 48].

                                C

CAGE, Albert - son of Maj. William Cage (see hereafter).
CAGE, Edward - son of Maj. William Cage (see hereafter).
CAGE, Elizabeth - daughter of Maj. William Cage (hereafter).
CAGE, Harry - son of Maj. William Cage (see hereafter).
CAGE, James - son of Maj. William Cage (see hereafter).
CAGE, Jessie - child of Maj. William Cage (see hereafter).
CAGE, John - son of Maj. William Cage (see hereafter).
CAGE, Loftain - son of Maj. William Cage (see hereafter).
CAGE, Patsy - daughter of Maj. William Cage (see hereafter).
CAGE, Reuben - son of Maj. William Cage (see hereafter).
CAGE, Richard - son of Maj. William Cage (see hereafter).
CAGE, Richard - son of Maj. William Cage (see hereafter).
CAGE, Robert - son of Maj. William Cage (see hereafter).
CAGE, Sally - daughter of Maj. William Cage (see hereafter);
    married John Carr in Sumner Co., Nov. 22, 1791: [ref. 1].

CAGE, Maj. William - D.A.R. membership on this line. Born in VA 1745/46; married (1st) Elizabeth Douglas in Fauquier Co., VA in 1768; married (2nd) Ann Morgan in Sumner Co., TN, 1796: [ref. 2a]. Appointed sheriff of Sumner Co. in 1790: [ref. 2b]. He died in Sumner Co., March 12, 1811. Children: (by 1st wife) Priscilla; Wilson, b. 1775; Reuben; William, Jr.; Sally; James; Edward; John, b. 13 Feb. 1780; Loftain; and Jessie. Children: (by 2nd wife) Richard; Harry; Albert; Robert; Elizabeth; and Patsy: [ref. 2c]. (See also, p. 15.)

CAGE, William (Jr.) - son of Maj. William Cage (see abovementioned).

CAGE, Wilson - son of Maj. William Cage (beforementioned); married Rachel Cooper in Sumner Co., Dec. 31, 1795. William Parmer was bondsman: [ref. 3].

CAMBLER, R. 1787 Sumner Co. tax roll with 1 poll & 50 acres, and was delinquent taxpayer that year: [ref. 4].

CAMPBELL, ____ - an Irishman, who had been a servant of George and James Winchester, was killed by Indians at Bledsoe's Lick about July 20, 1788: [ref. 5].

CAMPBELL, Joshua - listed on the 1787 Sumner Co. tax roll with 1 poll & 150 acres: [ref. 6a]. Defendant in lawsuit with Samuel Campbell brought by David Shelby in 1787: [ref. 6b]. Appointed Constable in 1787: [ref. 6c]. Grand jury presentment accused Joshua Baldwin of using name of Joshua Campbell: [ref. 6d]. Plaintiff vs. William McNeely in 1788: [ref. 6e]. Defendant in lawsuit brought by Ephraim Payton for slander in 1788: [ref. 6f].

CAMPBELL, Michael - land purchase recorded in Davidson Co. (see p. 16).

CAMPBELL, Philip - land purchase recorded in Davidson Co. (see p. 16).

CAMPBELL, Robert - married Martha Hamilton in Sumner Co., Mar. 29, 1793. John Hamilton was bondsman: [ref. 7].

CAMPBELL, Sarah - married David Hainey in Sumner Co., Oct. 19, 1791: [ref. 8].

CANTRELL, Alfred - son of Stephen Cantrell (see hereafter).

CANTRELL, Ota - child of Stephen Cantrell (see below).

CANTRELL, Stephen (Jr.) - son of Stephen Cantrell (see hereafter).

CANTRELL, Stephen - D.A.R. membership on this line. Born July 28, 1758, near Abington, VA. Married Mary S. Blakemore at Ft. Blount in 1782: [ref. 9a]. Assignee of a North Carolina land grant, Sept. 15, 1787, for 640 acres on Red River: [ref. 9b]. Summoned from Sumner Co. for jury duty on the Superior Court of Law and Equity, Nov. 1790: [ref. 9c]. North Carolina land grant, Oct. 8, 1797, for 640 acres on Stuart's Creek: [ref. 9d]. Children: Stephen, b. March 10, 1783; Sarah, b. Feb. 14, 1785; Ota; Alfred, died in infancy; and William, b. Jan. 22, 1792: [ref. 9e].

CANTRELL, William - son of Stephen Cantrell (see beforementioned).

CARR, John - married Sallie Cage in Sumner Co., Nov. 22,
1791. James Frazier and King Carr were bondsmen: [ref.
10]. (See also, p. 17.)

CARR, King - juror during the April 1790, Session of Court:
[ref. 11a]. Bondsman for the marriage of John Carr & Sally
Cage, 1791: [ref. 11b].

CARR, Richard - listed on the 1787 Sumner Co. tax roll with
1 poll: [ref. 12a]. Juror during 1787,1788, & 1790 Sessions
of Court: [ref. 12b].

CARSON, James - married Nancy Stuart in Sumner Co., Dec.
19, 1791. Joseph Waller was bondsman: [ref. 13].

CARTER, Charles - with James McCain, James Franklin, and
Elmore Douglass, he made a settlement in the fall of 1783,
on the west side of Big Station Camp Creek where the upper
Nashville Road crossed: [ref. 14a]. Listed on the 1787
Sumner Co. tax roll with 3 polls and 320 acres: [ref. 14b].
Recorded his stock mark in the County Court Minutes in
1787: [ref. 14c]. Juror during Oct. 1787, and Jan. 1788,
Sessions of Court: [ref. 14d]. Bondsman in 1789, for James
Douglas's appointment as Sheriff: [ref. 14e]. Witnessed
Bill of Sale for Thomas Kenney, 1787: [ref. 14f].

CARTWRIGHT, James - mentioned as an early settler of Sumner
Co.: [ref. 15]. (See also, p. 17.)

CATRON, Francis - listed on the 1787 Sumner Co. tax roll
with 1 poll & 460 acres: [ref. 16a]. Juror during the
1787 and april 1789, Sessions of Court: [ref. 16b]. Mentioned in the will of John Shavin, 1791: [ref. 16c]. (See
also, p. 19.)

CAVITT (variously, CAVEAT, CAVERT, CAVIOT, CAVIT), Michael
- listed on the 1787 Sumner Co. tax roll with 1 poll and
100 acres: [ref. 17a]. Juror for April Session, 1788,
of Superior Court: [ref. 17b]. Ordered by the County Court
in 1788, to view land claimed and cabins built by Jethro
Sumner, and to make further inquiries: [ref. 17c]. Appointed
overseer of part of the road being constructed from Col.
Mansker's to the Virginia line in 1789: [ref. 17d]. Replaced
as road overseer by Christopher Funkhouser in 1790: [ref.
17e].

CHOAT, Valentine - juror during April 1790, Session of Court:
[ref. 18]. (See also, p. 20).

CHRISTMAN, Thomas - witnessed Bill of Sale for John Dawson,
Dec. 17, 1790: [ref. 19].

CLACY, William - juror during Jan. 1788 Session of Court:
[ref. 20].

CLARK, Sgt. William - land purchase recorded in Davidson
Co. (see p. 20).

CLARY, Elisha - juror, Jan. 1788 Session of Court: [ref.
21].

CLARY, William - arrest warrant issued for his living with Nancy Hicks "in an unlawful way" in 1788: [ref. 22].

CLAY, Elisha - juror, July Session, 1788: [ref. 23].

CLAY, William - juror, Oct. 1787, Session of Court: [ref. 24].

CLERY, William - married Lilly Hays in Sumner Co., Oct. 3, 1794. Peter Luna (Looney) was bondsman: [ref. 25].

CLENDENNING, James - juror, April Session, 1788: [ref. 26a]. Juror on Superior Court, April 1788: [ref. 26b]. Witnessed will of Anthony Bledsoe, July 20, 1788: [ref. 26c].

CLYERS, James - land sale recorded in Davidson Co. (see p. 20).

CLYERS, John - land sale by his heirs recorded in Davidson Co. (see p. 20).

CONYERS (variously, CONGER), Thomas - listed on 1787 Sumner Co. tax roll with 1 poll & 100 acres: [ref. 27a]. Overseer of road built from Kasper's Creek to dividing ridge between Drake's Creek & Station Camp Creek, 1790: [ref. 27b]. Married Jane Wills in Sumner Co., Sept. 16, 1787. James Frazier was bondsman: [ref. 27c].

COOPER, William - his land was the subject of a lawsuit brought by Robert Espey, July, 1789, - "Tract of land formerly entered for said William Cooper on the north side of the Cumberland on the second branch above the mouth of Kasper's Lick Creek about 2 miles up said branch including a spring, there marked R E entry no. 27 - Dec. 29, 1783." [ref. 28].

CRADY, David - listed on the 1787 Sumner Co. tax roll with 1 poll: [ref. 29].

CRAFFORD - see CRAWFORD.

CRAFT Mill - mentioned in Court Minutes ordering road to be cleared "sufficient for wagons to pass from Craft Mills to Courthouse," in 1788: [ref. 30].

CRANE, Lewis - listed on the 1787 Sumner Co. tax roll with 1 poll & 640 acres: [ref. 31a]. Juror during Jan. 1788, and Oct. 1789 Sessions of Court: [ref. 31b].

CRAVINS, John - listed on the 1787 Sumner Co. tax roll with 1 poll & 300 acres: [ref. 32a]. Juror during Jan. & July 1788 Sessions of Court: [ref. 32b]. Witnessed the will of Henry Ruyle, Feb. 16, 1790: [ref. 32c].

CRAWFORD (variously, CRAFFERD, CRAFFORD), Hugh - listed in the 1787 Sumner Co. tax roll with 1 poll and 560 acres: [ref. 33a]. Juror during Jan. & Oct. 1788 Sessions of Court: [ref. 33b]. Juror on the Superior Court, Nov. 1790: [ref. 33c]. (See also, p. 24.)

CRIBBINS, Thomas - juror, April, 1790: [ref. 34].

CROMWELL, Alexander - sold negroes to Joseph Desha, Jan. 1, 1791: [ref. 35].

CROSS, Zachariah - listed on the 1787 Sumner Co. tax roll with 1 poll, and delinquent in taxes the same year: [ref. 36].

D

DANIEL, Edmund - his deposition taken for the court case, Payton vs. Martin, 1788: [ref. 1].

DAVIS, Andrew - plaintiff vs. Edmund Jennings, Jan. 1789: [ref. 2].

DAVIS, Moses - land sale by his heirs recorded in Davidson Co. (see p. 27).

DAWSON, John - sold negroes to Elmon Douglass, Dec. 1790: [ref. 3a]. Bondsman for the marriage of Bazel Fry and Jane Mansker, March 1791: [ref. 3b]. (see also, p. 27.)

DELANEY, James - land purchase recorded in Davidson Co. (see p. 27).

DELOACH, John - witnessed the will of Joseph Barnes, Dec. 1794: [ref. 4].

DELOACH, Ruffin - sold negroes to Michael Shavin, Aug. 1791: [ref. 5].

DESHA, Benjamin - son of Robert Desha (see hereafter), was killed by Indians between White's Station and Col. Saunders' Fort on the waters of Desha's Creek, in 1786 or 1787: [ref. 6].

DESHA, John - appointed to view and mark road from Capt. Keykendall's to Capt. Winchester's Mill in 1787: [ref. 7a]. Witnessed will of Isaac Bledsoe in 1791: [ref. 7b].

DESHA, Joseph - purchased negroes from Alexander Cromwell, Jan. 1791: [ref. 8].

DESHA, Robert - listed on 1787 Sumner Co. tax roll with 4 polls and 540 acres: [ref. 9a]. Appointed overseer of road being cleared from Maj. Bledsoe's to the State line in 1787: [ref. 9b]. Juror for Jan. Session of Court, 1788: [ref. 9c]. Appointed appraiser of the estate of William Hall, deceased, in 1788: [ref. 9d]. Deed to Joseph Dixon in 1788, and Bill of Sale from William Harrison, Jan. 1788, both recorded in Court Minutes: [ref. 9e]. Juror on the Superior Court, Apr. 1788: [ref. 9f]. Purchased negro of Abraham Sanders in 1789: [ref. 9g]. Road laid off and cleared by people at Desha's Station from Maj. Wilson's to the Courthouse in 1788: [ref. 9h].

DESHA, Robert - son of Robert Desha (see above), was killed by Indians on Desha's Creek near White's Station: [ref. 10].

DEVER, Alan - juror during 1787 Session of Court: [ref. 11].

DEVER, Alex - juror during 1787 Session of Court: [ref. 12].

DICKERSON, John - juror during Oct. 1788, Session of Court: [ref. 13]. (See also, p. 28.)

DICKERSON, Joseph - juror during Oct. 1788, Session of Court: [ref. 14].

DICKINSON, Henry - land sale by his heir, Mason Dickinson, recorded in Davidson Co. (see p. 28).

DICKINSON, James - killed by Indians in 1786 or 1787, between White's Station and Col. Saunders' Fort: [ref. 15].

DICKINSON, Mason - heir of Henry Dickinson (see p. 28).

DICKSON (variously, DIXON), Joseph - listed in the 1787 Sumner Co. tax roll with 1 poll and 200 acres: [ref. 16a]. Juror during 1787 Session of Court: [ref. 16b]. Deed from Robert Desha recorded April, 1788: [ref. 16c]. Killed by Indians near White Station in 1788: [ref. 16d].

DIXON, Tilman - mentioned as an early settler of Smith Co. which was formed in 1799 from Sumner Co. (Moore, I, 874).

DOBBINS, William - deed to William Frazier recorded Jan. 1790: [ref. 17].

DONALSON (variously, DONELSON, DONALDSON), Robert - witnessed Bill of Sale for L. Thompson Dec. 13, 1790: [ref. 18].

DONELSON, Stokely - witnessed deed of James Bosley, Mar. 17, 1789: [ref. 19].

DONOHO (variously, DUNIHOO, DUNNEHOE, DUNNIHOU), John - listed on the 1787 Sumner Co. tax roll with 1 poll and 1280 acres: [ref. 20a]. Juror during the Jan. 1788, and April 1790 Sessions of Court: [ref. 20b].

DOUGLAS, Col. Edward - D.A.R. membership on this line. Born Oct. 13, 1713, in Fauquier Co., VA; married Sarah George in 1740. Resided in Chatham Co., NC during the Revolution. Died Feb. 2, 1795, in Sumner Co., and his wife Sarah died Jan. 2, 1797. Children: John, b. 1741; William, b. 1742, m. Peggy Stroud; Elizabeth, b. 1754, m. William Cage; Elmore, b. Jan. 1, 1753, m. Betsy Blackemore; Ezekiel, m. May Gibson; Sally, m. Thomas Blackemore; Edward, b. 1745, m. Elizabeth Howard; Reuben, m. Elizabeth Edwards; James, b. 1763, m. Catherine Collier: [ref. 21].

DOUGLAS, Edward - son of Col. Edward Douglas (see beforementioned). Led a party with General Winchester in pursuit of Indians who had attacked Zeigler's Fort and captured several persons. See interesting account of the pursuit in Carr's book: [ref. 22a]. Listed on the 1787 Sumner Co. tax roll with 1 poll & 640 acres: [ref. 22b]. Took oath as Sheriff of Sumner Co., April 1790: [ref. 22c]. Bondsman with others for James Douglas, who was appointed Sheriff in 1789: [ref. 22d]. Witnessed Bill of Sale for John & Benjamin Williams, 1790: [ref. 22e]. Witnessed Deed & Power of Attorney in 1790, for Nathaniel Parker: [ref. 22f]. Witnessed Bill of Sale for John Dawson, Dec. 1790: [ref. 22g]. Bondsman for marriage of Reuben Douglas & Betsy Edwards, Jan. 23, 1791: [ref. 22h].

DOUGLAS, Edward - son of Edward Douglas (see beforementioned).

DOUGLAS, Elmon - (could this be Edward?) Bondsman for James Douglas who was appointed Sheriff of Sumner Co., 1789: [ref. 23].

DOUGLAS, Elizabeth - daughter of Edward Douglas (see above).

DOUGLAS, Capt. Elmore - son of Col. Edward Douglas (see beforementioned). Listed on the 1787 Sumner Co. tax roll with
1 poll and 640 acres: [ref. 24a]. Appointed with others
to view and lay off road from Maj. Bledsoe's to the State
line in 1787: [ref. 24b]. Grand juror, 1787: [ref. 24c].
Took Oath as Capt. of Militia, 1787: [ref. 24d]. Mentioned
in Minutes of the County Court regarding tax collection
in 1787: [ref. 24e]. Juror during 1787 and 1788 Sessions
of Court: [ref. 24f]. Road ordered cut from Capt. Douglas's
to Maj. Wilson's in 1788: [ref. 24g]. The Sumner County
Court met at the house of Elmore Douglas in July, 1789:
[ref. 24h]. James McKain was appointed road overseer in
place of Capt. Douglas in 1789: [ref. 24i]. The Sumner
County Court met again in the house of Elmore Douglas in
Jan. and April, 1790: [ref. 24j].
DOUGLAS, Ezekiel - son of Col. Edward Douglas (see beforementioned). Listed on the 1787 Sumner Co. tax roll with 1
poll and 320 acres: [ref. 25a]. Recorded his stock mark
in the Minutes of the County Court in 1787: [ref. 25b].
Juror during Jan. and April Sessions of Court, 1788: [ref.
25c].
DOUGLAS, James - son of Edward Douglas (see beforementioned).
Listed on the 1787 Sumner Co. tax roll with 1 poll: [ref.
26a]. Appointed to take a list of all inhabitants within
Capt. Elmore Douglas' district: [ref. 26b]. Juror during
1787 and 1788 Sessions of Court: [ref. 26c]. Appointed
Sheriff of Sumner Co. in 1789: [ref. 26d]. Bondsman for
marriage of Nathaniel Parker and Mary Bledsoe, Dec. 5, 1791:
[ref. 26e].
DOUGLAS, John - son of Col. Edward Douglas (beforementioned).
DOUGLAS, Reuben - son of Col. Edward Douglas (see beforemen-
tioned). Listed on the 1787 Sumner Co. tax roll with 1
poll and 140 acres: [ref. 27a]. Juror during 1787 and July
1788 Sessions of Court: [ref. 27b]. Witnessed Deed of William
Edwards, Nov. 1789: [ref. 27c]. Married Elizabeth "Betsy"
Edwards in Sumner Co., Jan. 23, 1791: [ref. 27d].
DOUGLAS, Sally - daughter of Col. Edward Douglas (see beforementioned).
DOUGLAS, William - son of Col. Edward Douglas (see beforementioned). (See also, p. 30).
DOWER, Alan - juror during Jan. 1788 Session of Court: [ref.
28].
DREW, John - land purchase recorded in Davidson Co. (see p.
30).
DUNN (variously, DUN), Alexander - appointed Joseph McKelworth,
attorney to adjust and settle accounts, to recover "a legacy"
which fell to him "by heirship of my mother's death..."
1790: [ref. 29].
DYAL, Jenny - fined, Jan. 1790, for committing adultry with
Alexander Montgomery: [ref. 30].

E

ECCLES, Joe - wounded by Indians near Zeigler's Station in June 1792: [ref. 1].

EDWARDS, Betsy - married Reuben Douglas (beforementioned).

EDWARDS, Darkus - married Edw. Williams Dec. 12? 1791: [ref. 2].

EDWARDS, John - an early settler of Sumner Co., was killed by Indians in 1790, about 4 miles north-west of the present site of Gallatin, near the later site of Salem Church: [ref. 3].

EDWARDS, William - juror during April 1790 Session of Court: [ref. 4a]. Sold negroes to Elmon Douglas, 1789: [ref. 4b].

EGNEW, Thomas - see Thomas AGNEW.

ELLIOTT, Zebpa? - land purchase recorded in Davidson Co. (see p. 33).

ELLIS, Joel - wounded by Indians, June 26, 1792, at Zeigler's Station: [ref. 5].

ENGLISH, Joshua - land sale by heirs recorded in Davidson Co. (see p. 33).

ENGLISH, Thomas - his deposition taken in Court case: Payton vs. Martin, 1788: [ref. 6].

ESPEY, John - listed on the 1787 Sumner Co. tax roll with 1 poll and 1920 acres: [ref. 7]. (See also, p. 34.)

ESPEY, Robert - listed on the 1787 Sumner Co. tax roll with 1 poll and 1920 acres: [ref. 8a]. Plaintiff in suit brought against William Cooper, July 1789, for attachment on a "tract of land" formerly entered for said Cooper on the north side of the Cumberland on the second branch above the mouth of Kasper Lick Creek about 2 miles up said branch including a spring there marked R. E. entry no. 27 - Dec. 29, 1783: [ref. 8b]. (See also, p. 34.)

ESPEY, Thomas - listed on the 1787 Sumner Co. tax roll with 1 poll and 640 acres: [ref. 9].

F

FARR, James - juror during Oct. 1788 Session of Court: [ref. 1].

FARR, Samuel - killed by Indians near Walnut-field Fort in 1786 or 1787, according to John Carr, who also wrote that Farr was killed about 1790, near the Cumberland River, below Cairo: [ref. 2].

FERGUSON, Joshua - mentioned in Sumner Co. Court Minutes as living in Nelson Co., Kentucky: [ref. 3].

FERGUSON (variously, FORGUSSON), Nancy - married John Roberts
in Sumner Co., Oct. 19, 1791: [ref. 4].
FINEKHEVEDER, Christopher - see Christopher FUNKHOUSER.
FISHER, Archibald - juror during April 1789 Session of Court:
[ref. 5].
FISHER, William - married Faithy Hix in Sumner Co., May 17,
1791. Robert Locney was bondsman: [ref. 6].
FORD, John - land purchase recorded in Davidson Co. (see
p. 37).
FORT, Elias - land purchase recorded in Davidson Co. (see
p. 38).
FRANKLIN, James - helped view and mark a road from Maj. Bledsoe's to the State line in 1787: [ref. 7a]. Grand juror,
1787: [ref. 7b]. Juror during Jan. & Apr. 1788 Sessions
of Court: [ref. 7c]. Witnessed Bill of Sale for Page Ballew,
Sept. 1791: [ref. 7d]. (See also, p. 39.)
FRAZIER, Capt. Thomas - listed on the 1787 Sumner Co. tax
roll with 1 poll and 300 acres: [ref. 8a]. Took oath as
Lieutenant of Militia in 1787: [ref. 8b]. Juror during
1788 Session of Court: [ref. 8c]. Bondsman for marriage
of Thomas Conier and Jane Wills, Sept. 1787: [ref. 8d].
Bondsman with King Carr for marriage of John Carr and Sally
Cage, Nov. 1791: [ref. 8e]. (See also, p. 39.)
FRAZIER, John - wounded by Indians in 1786, on Defeated Creek
- see interesting account of the battle in Carr's history:
[ref. 9]. (See also, p. 39.)
FRAZIER, William - listed on the 1787 Sumner Co. tax roll
with 1 poll and 320 acres: [ref. 10a]. Juror during Jan.
1788 Session of Court: [ref. 10b]. Grantee of deed from
Bushnell & Dobbins in 1790: [ref. 10c]. Witnessed Bill
of Sale for John & Benj. Williams in 1790: [ref. 10d].
Mentioned as an early settler of Sumner Co.: [ref. 10e].
FRY, Basil - fined for swearing and breaking the Sabbath
in 1788: [ref. 11a]. Ordered to answer to the Grand Jury
for living in an unlawful manner with Jane Mansker: [ref.
11b]. Married Jane Mansker (alias Meseker) in Sumner Co.,
Mar. 8, 1791. John Dawson was bondsman: [ref. 11c].
FUNKHOUSER (variously, FINEKHEVEDER), Christopher - juror
during April and July 1790 Sessions of Court: [ref. 12a].
Appointed overseer of road in place of Richard Cavert:
[ref. 12b].

G

GALBRAITH, Arthur - executed Power of Attorney to Thomas
Sharp in Jan. 1790: [ref. 1].
GAMBILL, Henry - 1787 Sumner Co. tax roll with 1 poll: [ref.
2a]. Juror during Oct. 1789 Session of Court: [ref. 2b].
GATLIN, John - married Elender Buck in Sumner Co., Mar. 26,
1791. John Payton was bondsman: [ref. 3].

GEE, Capt. John - land purchased recorded in Davidson Co. (see p. 41).

GERRARD, Charles - land purchased recorded in Davidson Co. (see p. 42).

GIBSON, "Old man" - killed by Indians in 1786/87: [ref. 4].

GIBSON, Jordan (variously, Jourdan) - purchased a bed from Jas. McCane (sic), according to a deposition taken before the Committee of the Cumberland Association, Jan. 18, 1783: [ref. 5a]. 1787 Sumner Co. tax roll with 2 polls & 320 acres: [ref. 5b]. On the motion of James Harrison, James Odom, & George Gibson, the Sumner Co. Court in 1788, ordered Anthony and Isaac Bledsoe and George Winchester to "divide the personal estate of the late Jourdan Gibson and divide it into four equal parts: [ref. 5c]. (See also, p. 42.)

GIBSON, Roger - juror during the Oct. 1789 Session of Court: [ref. 6a]. Bondsman for marriage of John Neiley and Mary Harrison, Apr. 1791: [ref. 6b].

GIBSON, W. - early settler at Bledsoe's Lick (see p. 43).

GILBERT, Alia - was married in Sumner Co., Nov. 16, 1791, to Thomas Payton: [ref. 7].

GILBERT, Samuel - bondsman for marriage of Alia Gilbert to Thomas Payton: [ref. 8].

GILBREATH, Arthur - of Hawkins Co., North Carolina, executed Power of Attorney, Nov. 18, 1789, to Thomas Sharp to recover notes from James McKain: [ref. 9].

GILLESPIE (variously, GILLESPY), George - land purchase recorded in Davidson Co. (see p. 43).

GLASGOW, Cornelius - was listed on the 1787 Sumner Co. tax roll with 1 poll: [ref. 10].

GLASGOW, James - land purchase recorded in Davidson Co. (see p. 43).

GODFREY, William - land purchase recorded in Davidson Co. (see p. 44).

GOODWIN, Nathan - land purchase recorded in Davidson Co. (see p. 44).

GRACE, James - land sale by his heirs recorded in Davidson Co. (see p. 45).

GRAGG (variously, GREGG), Samuel - juror during 1788, April & Oct. 1789 Sessions of Court: [ref. 11].

GRAVES, Anthony - juror during April 1790 Session of Court: [ref. 12].

GRAVES, Dennis - juror on the Superior Court, Oct. 1792: [ref. 13].

GRAY, James - heir of John Gray (see p. 45).

GRAY, John - land sale by his heirs, James and Joseph Gray, recorded in Davidson Co. (see p. 45).

GRAY, Joseph - heir of John Gray (see beforementioned).

GREEN, William - juror during Oct. 1789 Session of Court: [ref. 14].

GREEN, Zachariah - listed on the 1787 Sumner Co. tax roll
with 2 polls: [ref. 15a]. Listed on the 1788 tax roll
with 1 poll and 100 acres: [ref. 15b]. Grand juror, 1787:
[ref. 15c]. Took oath as Ensign of Militia in 1787: [ref.
15d]. Juror for April 1788, and Oct. 1789 Sessions of
Court: [ref. 15e]. Purchased household furniture from
Thcmas Kenny, Oct. 12, 1789: [ref. 15f].
GRIGG, Samuel - jury duty recorded in Davidson Co. (see p.
46).
GWYNS, Edward - land purchase recorded in Davidson Co. (see
p. 46).

H

HACKELL (variously, HASKELL), William - listed on the 1787
Sumner Co. tax roll with 1 poll and 100 acres: [ref. 1].
HACKER (variously, HACHN?), Elizabeth - beneficiary in will
of John Shavin to receive 100 acres on Drake's Creek, and
to receive "all papers, etc." from Frances Catron: [ref.
2].
HACKER, John - listed in the 1787 Sumner Co. tax roll with
1 poll and 200? acres: [ref. 3].
HACKER, William - ordered by the Sumner Co. Court in 1787,
to help clear road: [ref. 4a]. Grand juror, 1787: [ref.
4b]. Recorded his stock mark in the Minutes of the County
Court, 1787: [ref. 4c].
HADLEY, Joshua - D.A.R. lineage on this line. Juror during
April 1790 Session of Court: [ref. 5a]. Bondsman with
others for James Douglas' appointment as Sheriff of Sumner
Co. in 1789: [ref. 5b]. Capt. Joshua Hadley commanded
a company of soldiers in Evans' battalion sent to the Cumber-
land for the protection of the settlements: [ref. 5c].
(See also, pp. 46,47).
HAGAN, Edward - see Edward HOGAN.
HAINEY, (variously, HEANY), David - juror during April 1788
Session of Court: [ref. 6a]. Married Sarah Campbell in
Sumner Co., Oct. 19, 1791. John Roberts was bondsman:
[ref. 6b]. Bondsman for marriage of John Roberts and Nancy
Forgusson (sic), 1791: [ref. 6c].
HAINEY, Francis (variously, Frank) - listed in the 1787 Sumner
Co. tax roll with 1 poll: [ref. 7a]. Plaintiff in suit
by attachment brought against Thomas Spencer, July 1787:
[ref. 7b]. Juror during April 1790 Session of Court: [ref.
7c]. Wounded by Indians in 1789, on Smith's Fork, while
with a scouting party under Gen'l Winchester: [ref. 7d].

HALL, General - mentioned as the brother-in-law of James Hall, who was killed by Indians: [ref. 8a]. Mentioned as brother-in-law of Charles Morgan, who was killed by Indians: [ref. 8b].

HALL, "Old Mrs." - escaped an Indian massacre with Gen. Hall, his brother, John, and sister, Prudence: [ref. 9].

HALL, James - grandson of Maj. William Hall, was killed by Indians near the residence of his brother, Gen'l. Hall in 1786 or 1787: [ref. 10].

HALL, John - escaped an Indian massacre with Gen'l. Hall and other members of the family: [ref. 11a]. Mentioned as an early settler in Sumner Co.: [ref. 11b].

HALL, Prudence - daughter of Gen'l Hall and sister of John Hall, escaped an Indian massacre in 1786 or 1787: [ref. 12].

HALL, Richard - brother of Maj. William Hall, was killed by Indians in 1786 or 1787: [ref. 13].

HALL, Thankful - administratrix of the estate of William Hall, deceased: [ref. 14a]. Recorded her stock mark in the Minutes of the Sumner Co. Court in 1789: [ref. 14b]. Sold a negro to Isaac Bledsoe, Sept. 1790: [ref. 14c]. Married George Ridley in Sumner Co., Oct. 10, 1787: [ref. 14d].

HALL, Maj. William - took oath as Magistrate of Sumner Co. in 1787: [ref. 15a]. Listed in the 1787 Sumner Co. tax roll with 2 polls and 640 acres: [ref. 15b]. Killed by Indians in 1786 or 1787: [ref. 15c]. Thankful Hall was appointed the administratrix of his estate (see beforementioned). A negro from his estate was sold by Thankful Hall in 1790: [ref. 15d]. (See also, p. 47.)

HALL, (heirs of William) - listed on the 1787 Sumner Co. tax roll with 2 polls and 640 acres: [ref. 16].

HAMBLETON, John - (see John HAMILTON). Listed in the 1787 Sumner Co. tax roll with 560 acres: [ref. 17].

HAMBLETON, Robert - juror during the Oct. 1789 Session of Court: [ref. 18].

HAMBLETON, Thomas - land purchase recorded in Davidson Co. (see p. 47).

HAMILTON, George - witnessed Bill of Sale for Joseph Wallace, Aug. 1789: [ref. 19]. He was wounded by Indians (see p. 47).

HAMILTON, James - listed on the 1787 Sumner Co. tax roll with 1 poll and 471 acres: [ref. 20a]. Juror during April 1788 Session of Court: [ref. 20b]. Overseer in 1789, of road from the ridge between Cumberland River and the waters of Red River to Arrington Creek: [ref. 20c].

HAMILTON (variously, HAMBLETON), John - listed on the 1787 Sumner Co. tax roll with 560 acres: [ref. 21a]. The Court of Pleas & Quarter Sessions was held at his home, Oct.

(continued next page)

HAMILTON, John - (continued)
1787: [ref. 21b]. Juror during 1787 Session of Court:
[ref. 21c]. Security for Eleanor Bush, executrix of the
estate of her husband, Abner Bush in 1787: [ref. 21d].
Overseer of road from Simon Keykendall's to the Courthouse
in 1788: [ref. 21e]. (See also, p. 48.)

HAMILTON, Thomas - appointed with others to view and mark
a road from Capt. Keykendall's to the head of Desha's Fork
of Bledsoe's Creek in 1787: [ref. 22a]. Juror during the
Oct. 1789 Session of Court: [ref. 22b]. (See also, p.
48.)

HAMILTON, Thomas Sr. - juror during April 1789 Session of
Court: [ref. 23].

HAMMAN, Charles - witnessed deed for Hugh McGary of Mercer
Co., KY in 1789: [ref. 24].

HAMPTON, Michael - killed by Indians either at the head of
Red River or on the waters of Drake's Creek in 1786 or
1787: [ref. 25].

HAMPTON, Thomas - listed on the 1787 Sumner Co. tax roll
with 1 poll: [ref. 26a]. Juror during 1787 Session of
Court: [ref. 26b]. Married Susannah Arington (sic) in
Sumner Co., June 19, 1787. Anthony Bledsoe was bondsman:
[ref. 26c].

HANCOCK, Isham - land purchase recorded in Davidson Co. (see
p. 48).

HANNA, Eneas - his deed from Philip Trammell recorded in
Sumner Co. Court Minutes, July, 1789: [ref. 27].

HANNAH, James - listed in the 1787 Sumner Co. tax roll with
1 poll & 200 acres: [ref. 28a]. Witness to the nuncupative
will of Abner Bush in 1787: [ref. 28b].

HANNAH, John Duke (variously, Doak, Doke) - listed in the
1787 Sumner Co. tax roll with 2 polls and 420 acres: [ref.
29a]. Recorded his stock mark in the Minutes of the County
Court in 1787: [ref. 29b]. Juror during the April 1788
and 1789, Sessions of Court: [ref. 29c]. Sold negroes
to Isaac Bledsoe, Aug. 14, 1790: [ref. 29d]. (See also,
p. 48.)

HARDIN, John - listed on the 1787 Sumner Co. tax roll with
2 polls and 228 acres: [ref. 30a]. Member of the Sumner
Co. Court, July Term, 1787: [ref. 30b]. Returned the estate
inventory of William Price, deceased, to Court in 1787:
[ref. 30c]. Administrator of the estate of Jos. McElurath,
deceased, Oct. 1787: [ref. 30d]. Juror on Superior Court
of Law & Equity, April 1788: [ref. 30e]. (See also, p.
49.)

HARDIN, John Jr. - appointed Sheriff of Sumner Co. in 1787:
[ref. 31a]. Fined for swearing and breaking the Sabbath
in 1788: [ref. 31b].

HARDIN, Robert - killed by Indians on the Cumberland River
while hunting: [ref. 32].

HARDIN, Sarah - married Jacob Sanders in Sumner Co., May 31, 1791: [ref. 33].

HARKER (variously, HACKN, HACKER), Elizabeth - (see Elizabeth HACKER). Beneficiary in the will of John Shavin to receive 100 acres on Drake's Creek and to receive "all papers, etc." from Frances Catron in 1791: [ref. 34].

HARKER (variously, HACKER, HACKED), Isom - listed on the 1787 Sumner Co. tax roll with 1 poll: [ref. 35].

HARLEY, Joseph - land purchase recorded in Davidson Co. (see p. 49).

HARMON, ____ - Grand juror, 1787: [ref. 36].

HARNEY, Francis - witnessed a Bill of Sale for Page Ballew, Sept. 1791: [ref. 37].

HARPOCL (variously, HARPOLE, HARTPOOL), John - ordered in 1789, to help lay off road from Maddison's Lick to Major Wilson's or into the road from Red River to the Courthouse, and to serve as overseer: [ref. 38a]. Juror during April 1790, Session of Court: [ref. 38b]. One of the spies attached to Gen'l Winchester's & Col. Douglas' party in pursuit of Indians who had attacked the settlements in 1792 (see interesting account in John Carr's book): [ref. 38c]. Called a "Dutchman" and brother of Martin Harpool. While under fire from Indians in 1789, he told his brother Martin to "run down and drive them up, while (I) kill one!" Called a fine soldier by Carr in his book: [ref. 38d].

HARPOLE, Martin - brother of John Harpool (see beforementioned). Called by the Indians the "fool warrior" after a fight with the Indians in which he "raised a great whoop at the top of his voice, and made the cane crack," causing the Indians to break and run: [ref. 39a]. Married Betsy Rule in Sumner Co., Aug. 16, 1791. William Reed was bondsman: [ref. 39b]. Bondsman for the marriage of William Reed and Peggy Rule in 1791: [ref. 39c].

HARRINGTON, Chas. - (see also, HERRINGTON). Listed on the 1787 Sumner Co. tax roll with 5 polls and 960 acres: [ref. 40a]. Juror during the Oct. 1788 Session of Court: [ref. 40b]. Appointed overseer of road from Wm. Maxwell's on Red River to the dividing ridge between McKain Creek and Ben Creek, in 1788: [ref. 40c].

HARRISON, James - listed on the 1787 Sumner Co. tax roll with 3 polls and 577 acres: [ref. 41a]. Ordered with others to view and mark a road from Maj. Bledsoe's to the State line in 1787: [ref. 41b]. Juror during the 1787, and Jan. 1788 Session of Court: [ref. 41c]. Entered motion in 1788, to the Court regarding the estate division of Jourdan Gibson, deceased: [ref. 41d]. Juror during the July 1788 Session of Court: [ref. 41e]. (See also, p. 50.)

HARRISON, Mary - married John Neiley (sic) in Sumner Co., Apr. 6, 1791: [ref. 42].

HARRISON, Polly - married Cornelius Herndon in Sumner Co., Sept. 27, 1791: [ref. 43].

HARRISON, William - his Bill of Sale to Robert Desha proved in Court by Thomas Jimason, Jan. 1788 : [ref. 44].

HARRY, ___ - killed by Indians (see p. 51, Davidson Co. Section).

HART, China - sister of Simpson Hart, was a minor mentioned in his will dated Feb. 1790 (see hereafter).

HART, Cumberland - brother of Simpson Hart, was a minor mentioned in his will dated Feb. 1790 (see hereafter).

HART, Green - brother of Simpson Hart, was a minor mentioned in his will dated Feb. 1790 (see hereafter).

HART, Kiziah - sister of Simpson Hart, married Lawrence Thompson, brother of Richard Lawrence, Sarah Fanny, Nathaniel Hart, China Burton, and Azaniah Thompson, all of whom are mentioned in Simpson Hart's will (see hereafter).

HART, Mary - sister of Simpson Hart, was a minor mentioned in his will dated Feb. 1790 (see hereafter).

HART, Richard - brother of Simpson Hart, was a minor mentioned in his will dated Feb. 1790 (see hereafter).

HART, Simpson - son of Nathaniel Hart, inherited lands from his father in Virginia, North Carolina, and Kentucky, and mentioned in Simpson's will, dated Feb. 23, 1790, in which he left his estate to his brothers & sisters: [ref. 45a]. His will was proven, Oct. 1790: [ref. 45b].

HART, Thomas - brother of Simpson Hart, was a minor mentioned in his will dated Feb. 1790 (see beforementioned).

HAWKINS (variously, HAKINS), Frances - listed on the 1787 Sumner Co. tax roll with 1 poll and 460 acres: [ref. 46].

HAYCRAFT, Joshua - his deposition taken at the house of Joshua Ferguson in Nelson Co., KY, for the court case (Wynn vs. Mason) in 1789: [ref. 47].

HAYES (variously, HAYS), James - (see James Hays). Listed on the 1787 Sumner Co. tax roll with 1 poll and 315 acres: [ref. 48a]. Juror during Oct. 1788 Session of Court: [ref. 48b]. Overseer of road from Simon Keykendall's to the Courthouse in 1789: [ref. 48c]. Mentioned as an early settler in Sumner Co.: [ref. 48d]. (see also, p. 52, Davidson Co. Section.)

HAYES, William - killed by Indians (see p. 52, Davidson Co. Section).

HAYS, James - appointed with others to view and lay off a road from Major Bledsoe's to the State line in 1787: [ref. 49a]. Juror during Jan. & Apr. 1788 Sessions of Court: [ref. 49b]. Killed one of the Indians who had attacked the settlers in 1786 or 1787: [ref. 49c].

HAYS, Lillie - married William Clery in Sumner Co., Oct. 9, 1787: [ref. 50].

HAYS, Samuel - juror during Oct. 1789 Session of Court: [ref.
    51]. (See also, p. 52.)
HEANY, Frank - see Francis HAINEY.
HENDRICKS, Thomas - listed on the 1787 Sumner Co. tax roll
    with 1 poll and 320 acres: [ref. 52].
HERN, Drewry (variously, Drury) - land sale by his heir,
    George Hern, recorded in Davidson Co. (see p. 54).
HERN, George - heir of Drewry (Drury) Hern (see p. 54).
HERNDON, Cornelius - married Polley Harrison in Sumner Co.,
    Sept. 27, 1791. James Odam was bondsman: [ref. 53].
HERNDON, Elias - juror during Jan. 1789 Session of Court:
    [ref. 54].
HERNDON, Frances - married Amos West in Sumner Co., April
    7, 1791: [ref. 55].
HERRINGTON, Elisa - land purchase recorded in Davidson Co.
    (see p. 54).
HEYKENOL, Benjamin - killed by Indians (see p. 54, Davidson
    Co. Section). Could this be KEYKENDAL?
HICKERSON, ___ - young man killed by Indians in 1786 or
    1787, while moving with others from where Gen'l Hall lived
    to the Fort at the Lick: [ref. 56].
HICKERSON (variously, HICKISON, HICKSON), Capt. John - took
    oath as Ensign of Militia in 1787: [ref. 57a]. Listed
    on the 1787 Sumner Co. tax roll with 2 polls and 540 acres:
    [ref. 57b]. Juror during Oct. 1788, and April 1789, Sessions
    of Court: [ref. 57c]. Killed by Indians on Smith's Fork,
    "now in Dekalb Co.," ca. 1787: [ref. 57d].
HICKMAN, Edwin - his deed to William Minor recorded in Court
    Minutes, July 1789: [ref. 58].
HICKS, John - listed on 1789 Sumner Co. tax roll with 1 poll:
    [ref. 59a]. Appointed with others to lay off road from
    Capt. Keykendall's to the head of Desha's fork of Bledsoe's
    Creek in 1787: [ref. 59b]. Juror during 1787, and Jan.
    1788, Sessions of Court: [ref. 59c].
HICKS, Nancy - subject of Grand Jury deliberations in April
    1788, considering the evidence against William Clay (Clary)
    for keeping Nancy Hicks unlawfully: [ref. 60a]. A Capeas
    was issued against William Clary and Nancy Hicks was cited
    before the Court: [ref. 60b].
HIX, Faithy - married William Fisher in Sumner Co., May 17,
    1791: [ref. 61].
HOGAN (variously, HOGIN), Edward - listed on the 1787 Sumner
    Co. tax roll with 1 poll and 320 acres: [ref. 62a]. Juror
    during Jan. 1788, Session of Court: [ref. 62b]. Appointed
    Constable of Sumner Co. in 1788: [ref. 62c]. Witnessed
    Bill of Sale of Silas McBee, Oct. 2, 1790: [ref. 62d].
HOGAN, Richard - listed on the 1787 Sumner Co. tax roll with
    2 polls and 440 acres: [ref. 63a]. Proved, with others,
    the nuncupative will of Abner Bush, Oct. 1787: [ref. 63b].

(continued next page)

HOGAN, Richard - (continued)
Juror during Jan. & July 1788, Sessions of Court: [ref. 63c]. Bondsman for the marriage of William Smith and Elsy McDonald, and Amos West and Frances Herndon, in 1791: [ref. 63d]. (See also, p. 54.)

HOUDESHALL (variously, HOWDISHALL), Henry - listed on the 1787 Sumner Co. tax roll with 1 poll and 640 acres: [ref. 64a]. Acknowledged indebtedness to State, Oct. 1788: [ref. 64b]. Juror during Oct. 1788 Session of Court: [ref. 64c]. Assisted in working on road in 1789: [ref. 64d]. Married Isabel Snoddy in Sumner Co., Oct. 9, 1787: [ref. 64e]. Killed by Indians in 1786 or 1787 near the Walnut-field Fort, according one source: [ref. 64f]. The same source states he was killed in 1790, with Samuel Farr near the Cumberland River, below Cairo: [ref. 64g]. (See Henry Howdishall, p. 58, Davidson Co. Section.)

HUBBARD, Zebulon - helped clear road from Capt. Keykendall's to Capt. Winchester's Mill in 1787: [ref. 65a]. Juror during 1787 and Jan. 1788, Sessions of Court: [ref. 65b]. (See also, p. 58.)

HUGHES, David - listed on the 1787 Sumner Co. tax roll with 1 poll and 100 acres: [ref. 66a]. Juror during Oct. 1789, Session of Court: [ref. 66b].

HUGHES, Jesse - listed on the 1787 Sumner Co. tax roll with 1 poll: [ref. 67a]. Witnessed the will of Isaac Bledsoe in 1791: [ref. 67d].

HUGHES, John - listed on the 1787 Sumner Co. tax roll with 1 poll: [ref. 68a]. Juror during April 1790, Session of Court: [ref. 68b].

HUGHES, Peter - listed on the 1787 Sumner Co. tax roll with 1 poll: [ref. 69].

HUMPHRIES, David - land purchase recorded in Davidson Co. (see p. 59).

HUNTER, Mary - her deed to Isaac Pendleton recorded in the Sumner Co. Court Minutes, July, 1789: [ref. 70].

HUSTON, Chamberlain - land purchase recorded in Davidson Co. (see p. 59).

HUTCHINSON, James - land purchase recorded in Davidson Co. (see p. 59).

HUTCHISON, John - witnessed will of John Shavin in 1791: [ref. 71].

HYMAN, Jno. - witnessed Bill of Sale for John Dawson, Dec. 1790: [ref. 72].

HYNES (sic), Betsy - married John Lawrence in Sumner Co. on Feb. 4, 1791: [ref. 73].

HYNNIMAN, Lloyd - killed by Indians in Feb. 1791, at the Sugar Camp near Bledsoe's Lick: [ref. 74].

J

JACKSON, Andrew (variously, Andy) - produced his license to practice as an attorney at law and took oath, Jan. 1789: [ref. 1a]. Witnessed deed of Hugh McGary of Mercer Co., KY, Sept. 1789: [ref. 1b].

JAMES, John - land sale by his heirs recorded in Davidson Co. (see p. 60).

JAMISON (variously, JIMASON, JIMESON), Thomas - listed on the 1787 Sumner Co. tax roll with 2 polls: [ref. 2a]. Witnessed Bill of Sale between Wm. Harrison and Robert Desha, Jan. 1788: [ref. 2b]. Juror during Oct. 1788, and Jan. 1789 Sessions of Court: [ref. 2c].

JENNINGS, Edmund - defendant in lawsuit brought by Andrew Davis, Jan. 14, 1789: [ref. 3].

JONEER, Stephen - land sale by his heirs recorded in Davidson Co. (see p. 63).

JONES, Betsy - married William Anderson in Sumner Co., Nov. 23, 1791: [ref. 4].

JONES, Edward - witnessed will of Henry Ruhyl (sic), Feb. 16, 1790: [ref. 5].

JONES, John - juror during April 1790, Session of Court: [ref. 6a]. Witnessed Bill of Sale for Silas McBee, Oct. 2, 1790: [ref. 6b].

JONES, Mollie - taken prisoner by Indians during their attack on Zeigler's Station, 26 June 1792: [ref. 7].

JONES, Richard - juror during April 1790, Session of Court: [ref. 8].

JONES, Robert - killed by Indians about 2 miles east of the present site of Gallatin in 1786 or 1787: [ref. 9].

JONES, Thomas - listed on the 1787 Sumner Co. tax roll with 1 poll and 50 acres: [ref. 10a]. Juror during April 1788, Session of Court: [ref. 10b].

K

KAIN, James W. - grand juror in 1787: [ref. 1].

KEDAR, Capt. Ballard - land purchase recorded in Davidson Co. (see p. 64).

KEEFE, Thomas - wounded by Indians during their attack on Zeigler's Station, June 26, 1792: [ref. 1b].

KEINDEN, Cornelius - wounded by Indians (see p. 64).

KEITH, James - his deposition taken in court case (Payton vs. Martin) in 1788: [ref. 2].

KEITH, Reuben - his deposition taken in court case (Payton vs. Martin) in 1788: [ref. 3].

KENDRICK, Jane - fined 25 shillings in 1788, for having a base born child: [ref. 4a]. In 1788, she made oath before the Court that she had a bastard child, and that George Winchester was the father: [ref. 4b]. (See also, p. 64.)

KENNY, Thomas - sold to Zachariah Green for 16 pounds Virginia money, household furniture on Oct. 12, 1789: [ref. 5].

KEYKENDALL (see KUYKENDALL)

KILGORE, Thomas - listed on the 1787 Sumner Co. tax roll with 1 poll and 2058 acres, and in 1788, with 2130 acres: [ref. 6a]. Appointed with others to lay off road in 1787, from Capt. Keykendall's to the head of Desha's Fork of Bledsoe's Creek: [ref. 6b]. Juror during 1787, Session of Court: [ref. 6c]. Appointed overseer of road in 1787: [ref. 6d]. Juror during Jan. & April 1788, Sessions of Court: [ref. 6e]. (See also, p. 66, Davidson Co. Section.)

KNELL, William B. - see William B. NEEL.

KUYKENDALL (variously, KEYKENDALL) Station - mentioned in Court Minutes in 1788: [ref. 7].

KUYKENDALL, Adam - juror during April 1790, Session of Court: [ref. 8].

KUYKENDALL, Benjamin - listed on the 1787 Sumner Co. tax roll with 2 polls and 640 acres: [ref. 9a]. Grand juror in 1787: [ref. 9b]. Juror during the April 1788, Session of Court: [ref. 9c]. Killed by Indians in 1786 or 1787, on Desha's Creek between White's Station and Col. Saunder's Fort: [ref. 9d]. (See also, p. 65.)

KUYKENDALL, James - appointed with others to view and mark road in 1787: [ref. 10].

KUYKENDALL, John - listed on the 1787 Sumner Co. tax roll with 2 polls and 100 acres: [ref. 11a]. Juror during Jan. 1788, Session of Court: [ref. 11b]. Ordered with others to view and lay off road from Col. Mansker's to the Virginia line in 1789: [ref. 11c].

KUYKENDALL, Capt. Joseph - a list of the inhabitants within Capt. Keykendale's (sic) Company was taken by Ezekiel Norris in 1787: [ref. 12a]. Road ordered to be cleared from Capt. Keykendall's (sic) to Capt. Winchester's Mill: [ref. 12b]. Listed on the 1787 Sumner Co. tax roll with 2 polls and 420 acres: [ref. 12c]. Member of the County Court, July Term, 1787: [ref. 12d]. Took oath as Captain of Militia in 1787: [ref. 12e]. Appointed to take list of taxables in his district in 1787: [ref. 12f]. Juror on the Superior Court, April 12, 1788: [ref. 12g]. Appointed with others to view and lay off a road in 1789: [ref. 12h]. The men in his Company worked clearing a road from Col. Mansker's to the Virginia line in 1789: [ref. 12i]. Summoned from Sumner Co. for jury duty on the Superior Court of Law and Equity (see p. 66).

KUYKENDALL, Mathew - listed on the 1787 Sumner Co. tax roll with 2 polls and 200 acres: [ref. 13a]. Juror during 1787, April 1788, and Oct. 1789, Sessions of Court: [ref. 13b].
KUYKENDALL, Peter - listed on the 1787 Sumner Co. tax roll with 1 poll and 100 acres: [ref. 14a]. Juror during April 1788, Session of Court: [ref. 14b].
KUYKENDALL, Simeon - listed in the 1787 Sumner Co. tax roll with 3 polls and 540 acres: [ref. 15a]. Referred to as Capt. Keykendall in Sumner Co. Court Minutes for 1787: [ref. 15b]. Juror during April 1788, Session of Court: [ref. 15c]. County Court met at Simon Keykendall's (sic) "Station" in Oct. 1788: [ref. 15d]. Road cleared in 1788, from Simon Keykendale's (sic) to the Courthouse: [ref. 15e]. (See also, p. 66.)

L

LACEY, Hopkins - given license to practice law and took oath, July, 1790: [ref. 1a]. Appointed Solicitor for Sumner Co., Oct. 1790: [ref. 1b].
LANDERS (variously, LAUDERS), Jacob - juror during Jan. 1789, Session of Court: [ref. 2].
LANIER, James - land sale by his heirs recorded in Davidson Co. (see p. 67).
LANNER (variously LANIER?), Thomas - witnessed the will of John Shavin, June 9, 1791: [ref. 3].
LATHAN, John - his power of attorney to Isaac Bledsoe recorded July, 1788: [ref. 4a]. His deed to John Provine recorded, July, 1788, in the County Court Minutes: [ref. 4b].
LATIMER (variously, LATIMORE), Charles - son of Jonathan Latimer (see hereafter).
LATIMER, Daniel - son of Jonathan Latimer (see hereafter).
LATIMER, George - son of Jonathan Latimer (see hereafter).
LATIMER, Griswood - son of Jonathan Latimer (see hereafter).
LATIMER, Hannah - son of Jonathan Latimer (see hereafter).
LATIMER, Jonathan (Jr.) - son of Jonathan Latimer (see hereafter).
LATIMER, Jonathan - D.A.R. membership on this line. Born May 27, 1724; married Lucretia Griswood, Jan. 28, 1749, who was born May 26, 1731. Jonathan died in Sumner Co. in 1794. Children: George; Jonathan; Wetherel, b. 1757; m. (1st) Abby Fitch, (2nd) Margaret Anderson; Charles; Robert; Nicholas; Griswood; Josephine; Nathan; Daniel; Hannah: [ref. 5].
LATIMER, Nathan - son of Jonathan Latimer (see abovementioned). Killed by Indians near Rock Island on the Caney Fork River during the battle in which Lt. Snoddy defeated the Indians, ca. 1786: [ref. 6].

LATIMER, Nicholas - son of Jonathan Latimer (beformentioned).
LATIMER, Robert - son of Jonathan Latimer (beforementioned).
LATIMER, Wetherel - son of Jonathan Latimer (beforementioned).
Land purchase recorded in Davidson Co. (see p. 68).
LAWRENCE, Adam - jury duty recorded in Davidson Co. (see
p. 68).
LAWRENCE, John - married Betsy Hynes in Sumner Co., Feb.
4, 1791. William Lawrence was bondsman: [ref. 7].
LAWRENCE, John - killed by Indians in 1786 or 1787, on the
northside of the Ridge, either at the head of Red River
or on the waters of Drake's Creek: [ref. 8].
LAWRENCE, William - bondsman for marriage of John Lawrence
(see above).
LEIR, James - land sale by his heirs recorded in Davidson
Co. (see p. 69).
LEMAN (variously, LEMAR), Gallant - listed on 1787 Sumner
Co. tax roll with 1 poll: [ref. 9].
LEMAN (variously, LEMAR), William - listed on 1787 Sumner
Co. tax roll with 1 poll and 100 acres, and delinquent
taxes in 1787: [ref. 10].
LEVI, Matthew - land sale by his heirs recorded in Davidson
Co. (see p. 69).
LINDSEY, Mr. - mentioned in 1788, as living adjacent to Col.
Smith's Station and appointed to help lay road from Drake's
Creek to George Mansker's house: [ref. 11].
LINDSEY, Isaac - listed on 1787 Sumner Co. tax roll with
1 poll and 640 acres: [ref. 12a]. Member of the County
Court, July term, 1787: [ref. 12b]. Took oath required
by Congress for the support of the Constitution of the
United States, April, 1790: [ref. 12c].
LINTON, Capt. Isreal - his deposition taken for lawsuit (Payton
vs. Martin) in 1788: [ref. 13].
LONG, Nicholas - his deed to William Bowen recorded in the
Sumner Co. Court Minutes in 1788: [ref. 14].
LOONEY, David - mentioned as one of the early settlers in
Sumner Co.: [ref. 15a]. In 1793, while a resident of Sulli-
van Co., he executed power of attorney to Edward Douglass
of Sumner Co. to convey tract of land between Lindsey's
Bluff and Hogan's Pond: [ref. 15b].
LOONEY, Peter - grand juror in 1787: [ref. 16a]. Recorded
his stock mark in the Sumner Co. Court Minutes in 1787:
[ref. 16b]. Juror during April 1788, Session of Court:
[ref. 16c]. Witnessed the deed of John D. Hannah, Aug.
1790: [ref. 16d]. (This may be one of the two individuals
by the name of Peter Looney listed hereafter.)
LOONEY, Peter H. - 1787 Sumner Co. tax roll with 1 poll &
640 acres: [ref. 17a]. Recorded his stock mark in the
Minutes of the County Court in 1787: [ref. 17b]. Bondsman
for Thomas Martin, who was appointed Sheriff & Collector
of Sumner Co. in 1787: [ref. 17c]. (See also, p. 71.)

LOONEY, Peter P. - listed on the 1787 Sumner Co. tax roll
with 1 poll and 440 acres: [ref. 18].
LOONEY, Robert - juror during Jan. & April 1788, Session
of Court: [ref. 19a]. Bondsman for marriage of William
Fisher and Faithy Hix, May 17, 1791: [ref. 19b]. Mentioned
as one of the early settlers of Sumner Co. [ref. 19c].
(See also, p. 71.)
LOVING, Henry -listed on the 1788 Sumner Co. tax roll with
540 acres: [ref. 20a]. Mentioned as one of the early
settlers of Sumner Co.: [ref. 20b].
LUM, Peter - purchased negroes from Page Ballew, Sept. 26,
1791: [ref. 21].
LUNN, James - witnessed the will of Isaac Bledsoe in 1791:
[ref. 22].
LYNN (variously, LYNNE), Capt. Charles Morgan - was appointed
by the Court in 1787, to take a list of all inhabitants
in Capt. Lynn's District: [ref. 23a]. The inhabitants
of Capt. Lynne's (sic) company were appointed to work on
road from Maj. Bledsoe's to the State line: [ref. 23b].
George Winchester appointed to make a list of taxables
in Capt. Lynn's District in 1788: [ref. 23c].
LYNN, James - listed on the 1787 Sumner Co. tax roll with
1 poll and 540 acres: [ref. 24a]. Delinquent taxes in
1787: [ref. 24b]. Ordered with others to view and mark
road from Maj. Bledsoe's to the State line: [ref. 24c].
Elected Capt. of Militia and produced commission and took
oath before the County Court in 1787: [ref. 24d]. Juror
during the July and Oct. 1789, Sessions of Court: [ref.
24e].
LYTLE, Archibald - land purchase recorded in Davidson Co.
(see p. 73).

Mc

McBEE, Silas - sold negroes to Thomas Hendricks, Oct. 2,
1790: [ref. 1a]. Juror in court case (NC vs. Phebe McNeely),
Nov. 1790: [ref. 1b].
McCAIN, James - mentioned as an early settler of Sumner Co.:
[ref. 2]. See James McCann. (See also, p. 74, Davidson
Co. Section.)
McCANN, Capt. James - killed a celebrated Indian Chief called
"Moon": [ref. 3a]. Mentioned as an early settler of Sumner
Co.: [ref. 3b].
McCAULISTON, James - appointed one of the executors of the
will of Alexander Robinson, July 28, 1791: [ref. 4].
McCOWAN, Alexander - his deposition taken at the house of
Joshua Ferguson in Nelson Co., KY, in 1789: [ref. 5].

McCULLOUCH, Benjamin - land purchase recorded in Davidson Co. (see p. 76).

McDONALD (variously, McDANOLD), Elsy - married William Smith in Sumner Co., Mar. 25, 1791: [ref. 6].

McELWRATH, Joseph - jury duty recorded in Davidson Co. (see p. 76).

McGOODEN, Daniel - appointed by the County Court to assist John Hamilton in working road in 1789: [ref. 7].

McGUFFEE, Henry - his deposition taken for court case (Payton vs. Martin) in 1788: [ref. 8].

McIDUM, James - listed on the 1787 Sumner Co. tax roll with 2 polls and 120 acres: [ref. 9].

McKAIN, ____ - road cleared from McKain's down McKain's Creek in 1788: [ref. 10].

McKAIN (variously, McKEEN, McKEIN), James - listed on the 1787 Sumner Co. tax roll with 2 polls and 120 acres: [ref. 11a]. Appointed with others to view and mark a road from Maj. Bledsoe's to the State line: [ref. 11b]. Recorded his stock mark in the Minutes of the County Court in 1787: [ref. 11c]. Juror during April 1788, Session of Court: [ref. 11d]. Erected a mill in 1789, on the Middle Fork of Red River within 300 yards of the place where Philip Trammel lived: [ref. 11e]. Appointed overseer of road in place of Capt. Douglas: [ref. 11f]. Mentioned in Arthur Gilbreath's deed (from Hawkins Co.) as having notes due Gilbreath, dated Dec. 26, 1782, and Sept. 28, 1782: [ref. 11g].

McKAIN (variously, McKEEN), James, Jr. - listed on the 1787 Sumner Co. tax roll with 1 poll and 320 acres: [ref. 12a]. Juror for 1787, and Oct. 1788, Sessions of Court: [ref. 12b]. Juror for Superior Court, Nov. 1790: [ref. 12c]. Witnessed Bill of Sale for Thomas Kenny, 1789: [ref. 12d]. (See also, McKEEN.)

McKAIN, James, Sr. - juror during Oct. 1788, Session of Court: [ref. 13].

McKELSWORTH, Joseph - given power of attorney by Alexander Dun(n) in 1790, to adjust and settle accounts & to recover legacy left by Dunn's mother: [ref. 14]. (See also, Joseph McELURATH.)

McELURATH (variously, MCKILWRATH, McELWORTH), James - juror during July 1788, Session of Court: [ref. 15].

McELURATH, John - listed on the 1787 Sumner Co. tax roll with 1 poll & 200 acres: [ref. 16].

McELURATH, Maj. Joseph - listed on the 1787 Sumner Co. tax roll with 1 poll and 200 acres: [ref. 17a]. Elected Ensign of Militia and produced commission and took oath in 1787: [ref. 17b]. Replaced as administrator of John Hardin in 1787: [ref. 17c]. Deed from William Snoddy to McElurath recorded in 1788: [ref. 17d]. Purchased negroes from John Sadler in 1791: [ref. 17e]. Escaped being killed by Indians in ambush in 1789, on Smith's Fork: [ref. 17f].

McMURRAY, William - killed by Indians at Winchester Mill
on Bledsoe's Creek in 1780: [ref. 18].
McNAIRY, John - deed from Elijah Robinson recorded in 1789:
[ref. 19].
McNEELY, Pheobe - defendant in a suit brought by North Carolina
in 1790: [ref. 20].
McNEELY, William - listed on the 1787 Sumner Co. tax roll
with 1 poll & 640 acres: [ref. 21a]. Defendant in lawsuit
brought by Joshua Campbell, July 15, 1788: [ref. 21b].
Juror during April 1790, Session of Court: [ref. 21c].
McWHIRTER, George - witnessed deed of Abraham Sanders in
1789: [ref. 22].

M

M____, Jesse - listed on the 1787 Sumner Co. tax roll, the
last name not being legible except that it began with M.
M____, William - listed on the 1787 Sumner Co. tax roll,
the last name not being legible except that it began with
M.
MALONE, Isom - listed on the 1789 Sumner Co. tax roll with
1 poll and 160 acres: [ref. 1].
MANSKER (variously, MESEKER, MANSCO), Col. - road laid off
between Col. Mansker's and the Virginia line: [ref. 2].
MANSKER, George - helped view and mark off road from Maj.
Bledsoe's to the State line in 1787: [ref. 3a]. Grand
juror in 1787: [ref. 3b]. Elected Lt. of Militia and took
oath in 1787: [ref. 3c]. Juror during July 1788, Session
of Court: [ref. 3d]. Overseer of road being cut from Drake's
Creek to Mansker's house in 1788: [ref. 3e].
MANSKER, Jane - Basil Fry was ordered in 1788, to answer
to the Grand Jury for living in an unlawful manner with
Jane Mansker: [ref. 4a]. Jane Mansker (alias, Meseker)
married Basil Fry in Sumner Co., Mar. 8, 1791: [ref. 4b].
MANSKER, Kasper - listed on the 1787 Sumner Co. tax roll
with 3 taxables and 1280 acres: [ref. 5a]. Elected Major
of Militia and took oath in 1787: [ref. 5b]. Recorded
his stock mark in the Minutes of the County Court in 1787:
[ref. 5c]. Juror during the April 1788, Session of Court:
[ref. 5d]. Juror on the Superior Court, April 15, 1788:
[ref. 5e]. Purchased negroes from Hugh McCrary of Mercer
Co., KY, in Sept. 1789: [ref. 5f]. (See also, p. 80.)
MARTIN, George - listed on the 1787 Sumner Co. tax roll with
1 poll and 320 acres: [ref. 6a]. Delinquent taxes in 1787:
[ref. 6b]. Juror during the July 1788, Session of Court:
[ref. 6c]. (See also, p. 81.)

MARTIN (variously, MASTEN), Thomas - listed on the 1787 Sumner
Co. tax roll with 1 poll and 200 acres: [ref. 8a]. Delinquent taxes in 1787: [ref. 8b]. Nominated and appointed
Sheriff of Sumner Co. in 1787: [ref. 8c]. Defendant in
lawsuit brought by Ephraim Payton: [ref. 8d]. Appointed
Sheriff & Collector of Sumner Co., 1788: [ref. 8e]. (See
also p. 82, Davidson County Section.)

MARTIN, Col. William - Capt. afterwards Col. Martin, who
died in Smith County, commanded a Company in Evan's battalion
in 1787, sent by North Carolina to protect the Cumberland
Settlements, and was to receive bounty land for service:
[ref. 9]. (See also, p. 82.)

MASON, Michael Siffer? - juror during Oct. 1788, Session
of Court: [ref. 10].

MASON, Samuel - defendant in lawsuit brought by James Wynn
in 1789: [ref. 11].

MASTEN - see Thomas MARTIN, above.

MAXEY, Jesse - listed in the 1787 Sumner Co. delinquent tax
roll with 1 poll and 100 acres: [ref. 12].

MAXWELL, James - juror during Jan. 1789, Session of Court:
[ref. 13].

MAXWELL, William - listed on the 1787 Sumner Co. tax roll
with 1 poll and 320 acres: [ref. 14a]. Overseer of road
laid off from Capt. Keykendall's to the head of Desha's
Fork in 1787: [ref. 14b]. Grand juror, 1787: [ref. 14c].
Thomas Kilgore was named overseer of William Maxwell's
road in 1787: [ref. 14d]. Juror during the April 1788,
Session of Court: [ref. 14e]. Ordered in 1788, to view,
with others, the cabins built by Jethro Sumner on the plantation of the late William Starr, and to make inquiry as
to the trouble Sumner had in tending Starr in his illness:
[ref. 14f]. Road laid in 1788, from William Maxwell's
on Red River to the dividing ridge between McKain and Ben
Creek: [ref. 14g]. (See also, p. 83.)

MEMURY, ____ - killed by Indians in 1782 or 1783, while trailing the buffalo path from Bledsoe's Lick to Mansker's Lick:
[ref. 15].

MILBURN, David - listed on the 1787 Sumner Co. tax roll with
1 poll. Delinquent 1787 taxes: [ref. 16].

MINOR, John - juror during April 1788, Session of Court:
[ref. 17a]. Juror on Superior Court, April 1788: [ref.
17b].

MINOR, William - deed from Edwin Hickman recorded in the
County Court Minutes, July 1789: [ref. 18].

MOBLEY, William - land purchase recorded in Davidson Co.
(see p. 86).

MONTGOMERY, Alex - 1787 Sumner Co. tax roll with 1 poll &
150 acres: [ref. 19a]. Juror during Oct. 1787, & July
1788, Sessions of Court: [ref. 19b]. Jenny Dyal was fined
for committing adultry with Alexander Montgomery, Jan.
1790: [ref. 19c].

MONTGOMERY, John - son of William Montgomery, was killed as
were his brothers, Robert & Thomas, by Indians 2½ miles
below Shackle Island on Drake's Creek in the spring of 1788:
[ref. 20].

MONTGOMERY, Robert - bondsman for James Douglas who was appointed Sheriff in 1789: [ref. 21]. (See also, p. 86, Davidson
Co. Section).

MONTGOMERY, Robert - son of William, was killed by Indians
in 1788, as were his brothers, John and Thomas (see John
Montgomery).

MONTGOMERY, Thomas - son of William, was killed by Indians
in 1788, as were his brothers John and Robert (see beforementioned).

MORGAN, "Old Man" - father of Esq. John Morgan, was killed
by Indians ca. 1787, near his fort between White's Station
and Col. Saunders' Fort: [ref. 22]. (See Charles Morgan,
hereafter, whose death date matches this death date.)

MORGAN, Armstead - delinquent taxpayer in Sumner Co., 1787,
with 1 poll: [ref. 23a]. Killed by Indians ca. 1787, while
guiding through Capt. Handley and a company of men from
"Southwest Point" for the protection of the Cumberland Settlements. He was a brother of Capt. Charles Morgan: [ref.
23b].

MORGAN, Benjamin - delinquent taxpayer in Sumner Co., 1787,
with 1 poll: [ref. 24].

MORGAN, Capt. Charles - came to the Cumberland Settlements
in 1786, and settled at Morgan's Station on the west side
of Bledsoe's Creek some 4 or 5 miles from the Lick: [ref.
25a]. Listed on the 1787 Sumner Co. tax roll with 1 poll:
[ref. 25b]. Appointed to take list of all inhabitants within
Capt. Lynn's district in 1787: [ref. 25c]. Appointed with
others to view and mark road from Major Bledsoe's to the
State Line: [ref. 25d]. Recorded his stock mark in Minutes
of the County Court in 1787: [ref. 25e]. Juror during the
April 1788, Session of Court: [ref. 25f]. Killed by Indians
near Bledsoe's Lick ca. 1787. He was a brother of Armistead
Morgan and son-in-law of Gen'l Hall (see beforementioned):
[ref. 25g].

MORGAN, Isaac - listed on the 1787 Sumner Co. tax roll with
1 poll: [ref. 26a]. Proved will of Charles Morgan, April
1788: [ref. 26b].

MORGAN, John - listed on the 1787 Sumner Co. tax roll with
1 poll: [ref. 27a]. Ordered to help view and mark road
in 1787, from Capt. Keykendall's to the head of Desha's
Fork: [ref. 27b]. Juror during Oct. 1788, Session of Court:
[ref. 27c]. Mentioned as a son of Old Mr. Morgan (Charles),
killed by Indians ca. 1787: [ref. 27d].

MORGAN, Joseph - listed on the 1787 Sumner Co. tax roll with 1 poll: [ref. 28a]. Juror during the Jan. 1788, and April 1789, Sessions of Court: [ref. 28b]. Appointed Constable in 1789: [ref. 28c].

MORRISON, John - juror during Oct. 1790, Session of Court: [ref. 29].

MORRISON, William - mentioned as one of the early settlers in Sumner Co.: [ref. 30].

MOTHERALL, Joseph - witnessed deed from William Sanders to Robert Motherall, Jan. 1790: [ref. 31].

MOTHERALL, Robert - deed from William Sanders recorded Jan. 1790: [ref. 32].

MONTFLORENCE, James Cole - licensed to practice law and took oath, Jan. 1790: [ref. 33]. (See also, p. 86.)

MULHERRIN, James - land purchase recorded in Davidson Co. (see p. 88).

MURRY, Thomas - witnessed the will of Anthony Bledsoe, July 10, 1788: [ref. 34].

MYARS, Charles - married Betsey Biter in Sumner Co., May 23, 1791. Bondsman: Jacob _?_ : [ref. 35].

N

NEEL (perhaps NEAL), Charles - his deposition ordered to be taken, July 15, 1788, in court case (Payton vs. Martin): [ref. 1].

NEEL, William - his deposition ordered to be taken, July 15, 1788, in court case (Payton vs. Martin): [ref. 2].

NEEL, William B. - see William B. KNELL.

NEELEY (variously, NEELY, NEILEY), Capt. Alexander - listed on the 1787 Sumner Co. tax roll with 1 poll and 940 acres: [ref. 3a]. Appraiser of the estate of William Hall, dec'd, 1788: [ref. 3b]. Juror on the Superior Court, April 1788: [ref. 3c]. Juror during Oct. 1788, Session of Court: [ref. 3d]. Recorded his stock mark in the Minutes of the County Court, Jan. 1789: [ref. 3e]. Juror during April 1790, Session of Court: [ref. 3f]. Carr, in his history, states that Alexander Neeley and two sons were killed by Indians about a mile from Bledsoe's Lick in 1788, however, in Chapter III of Carr's book, he states only that two sons of Capt. Alexander Neely were killed: [ref. 3g]. (See also, p. 90.)

NEELEY, (2 sons of Alexander) - killed by Indians ca. 1788 (see Alexander Neeley, beforementioned).

NEELEY, John - witnessed deed for William Edwards, Sept. 1790: [ref. 4].

NEELEY, William - bondsman for marriage of Nathaniel Parker and Sally Ramsey, Dec. 1794: [ref. 5a]. Fought off an Indian attack upon a party of settlers who were plowing fields near Greenfield Station ca. 1787. His father and two brothers were killed by Indians: [ref. 5b].

NEGRO - killed by Indians, June 26, 1792, at Zeigler's Station:
  [ref. 7].
NEGRO man - killed by Indians ca. 1787, while plowing near
  Greenfield Fort: [ref. 8].
NEGRO - named Arthur, sold by John and Benjamin Williams to
  Elmon Douglas, July 13, 1790: [ref. 9].
NEGRO - named Benjamin, sold by John & Benjamin Williams
  to Elmon Douglas, July 13, 1790: [ref. 10].
NEWTON, William - witnessed the will of Edward Tinnon, Nov.
  5, 1790: [ref. 11].
NICK - a mulatto boy, sold by James Bosley of Davidson Co.
  to David Shelby of Sumner Co., Mar. 17, 1789: [ref. 12].
NICKERSON, John - killed by Indians (see p. 92).
NOLAND, ____ - killed by Indians (see p. 92).
NOLAND, Joseph - killed by Indians (see p. 92).
NOLAND, Thomas - killed by Indians (see p. 92).
NORRIS, Ezekiel - delinquent 1787 taxes, and listed on the
  1788 Sumner Co. tax roll with 1 poll and 100 acres: [ref.
  13a]. Appointed by the Court to list all the inhabitants
  of Capt. Keykendall's District in 1787: [ref. 13b]. Helped
  clear road from Capt. Keykendall's to Capt. Winchester's
  Mill in 1787: [ref. 13c]. Juror during 1787, and Jan.
  1788, Sessions of Court: [ref. 13d]. Juror on Superior
  Court, April 1788: [ref. 13e]. Appointed by the Court
  to view land claimed and cabins built by Jethro Sumner
  on the late William Starr's plantation and make inquiry
  as to what trouble Sumner had taking care of Starr in his
  illness: [ref. 13f]. Helped view and lay off road in 1789,
  from Col. Mansker's to the Virginia line: [ref. 13g].
NORRIS, John - listed on the 1787 Sumner Co. tax roll with
  1 poll & 100 acres: [ref. 14a]. Grand juror in 1787: [ref.
  14b]. Juror during April 1788, Session of Court: [ref.
  14c]. Overseer of road from George Mansker's to east of
  Station in 1788: [ref. 14d]. Juror during April 1790,
  Session of Court: [ref. 14e]. (See also, p. 92.)

O

O'BRYAN, Tido - land sale by his heirs recorded in Davidson
  Co. (see p. 93).
O'NEAL, William - land purchase recorded in Davidson Co.
  (see p. 93).
OAR (variously, ORE), William - juror on Superior Court,
  Nov. 1790: [ref. 1]. (See also, William ORE, p. 93.)

ODAM (variously, ODOM, ODOMS), James - entered motion to the
    Court, April 1788, requiring the division of the personal
    estate of Jourdan Gibson, deceased: [ref. 2a]. Juror during
    Oct. 1788, Session of Court: [ref. 2b]. Recorded his stock
    mark in the Minutes of the County Court, Jan. 1789: [ref.
    2c]. Bondsman for marriage of Cornelius Herndon and Polley
    Harrison, Sept. 1791: [ref. 2d]. Appointed by John Odum
    of the Government of Natchez, Aug. 1794, to handle collection
    for supplies: [ref. 2e].
OGLESBY, Daniel - listed on the 1789 Sumner Co. tax roll with
    1 poll: [ref. 3].
OGLESBY, Elijah - listed on the 1787 & 1788 Sumner Co. tax
    rolls with 1 poll and 100 acres: [ref. 4].
OGLESBY, Elisha - listed on the 1789 Sumner Co. tax roll with
    1 poll and 100 acres: [ref. 5a]. Juror during April 1788,
    Session of Court: [ref. 5b]. Helped lay off road from
    Maddison's Lick to Major Wilson's in 1789: [ref. 5c].
OLDHAM, Jesse - named one of the executors of the will of
    Simpson Hart, Feb. 1790: [ref. 6].
ORE, William - see William OAR.
OSTIN, William - land sale by his heirs recorded in Davidson
    Co. (see p. 93).
OVERTON, John - licensed to practice law and took oath, April
    1790: [ref. 7].

P

PAINE (variously, PAYNE), John - land sale by his heir, William
    Paine, recorded in Davidson Co. (see p. 94).
PAINE, William - heir of John Paine (see above).
PARKER, Mrs. Mary? - the former Mrs. Anthony Bledsoe, was
    nearly killed by Indians, but saved by Thomas Spencer, ca.
    1787: [ref. 1].
PARKER, Isom - land sale by his heirs recorded in Davidson
    Co. (see p. 94).
PARKER, Nathaniel - of Hampshire Co., VA, appointed Elmon
    Douglas of Sumner Co. attorney to act for him in sale and
    all matters in his interest, Sept. 30, 1790: [ref. 2a].
    Married Mary Bledsoe in Sumner Co., Dec. 4, 1791. James
    Douglas was bondsman: [ref. 2b]. Nathaniel Parker married
    Sally Ramsey in Sumner Co., Dec. 1794. William Neely was
    bondsman: [ref. 2c].
PATTON, Thomas - listed on the 1787 Sumner Co. tax roll with
    1 poll & 200 acres: [ref. 3a]. Overseer of road cleared
    in 1787, from Desha's Fork to Winchester's Mill: [ref. 3b].
PEAL (variously, PEEL), Thomas - listed on the 1787 Sumner
    Co. tax roll with 1 poll: [ref. 4a]. Witnessed will of
    Isaac Bledsoe in 1791: [ref. 4b].

PENDLETON, Isaac - deed from Mary Hunter recorded July 1789: [ref. 5].
PENNY, William - juror on the Superior Court, Oct. 1790: [ref. 6].
PERRY, Leon - juror during April 1789, Session of Court: [ref. 7].
PERRY, Scion - witnessed deed of William Edwards, Nov. 1789: [ref. 8a]. Bondsman for marriage of Reuben Martin and Jenney Kuykendal: [ref. 8b].
PERVINE, John - killed by Indians in 1786 or 1787 about 2 miles east of the present site of Gallatin: [ref. 9].
PEYTON (variously, PAYTON), "Old Mr." - grandfather of Hon. Baylie Peyton, was killed by Indians at Bledsoe's Lick in 1788: [ref. 10].
PEYTON, Hon. Baily - mentioned as son of John Peyton, who had a twin brother, Ephriam, and another brother, Thomas Peyton: [ref. 11].
PEYTON, Ephraim - twin brother of John Peyton (see Bailey Peyton, above). Listed on the 1787 Sumner Co. tax roll with 1 poll & 900 acres: [ref. 12a]. Helped view and mark road from Maj. Bledsoe's to the State line in 1787: [ref. 12b]. Juror during 1788, Session of Court: [ref. 12c]. Acknowledged Security in bond for John Hardin as Administrator in Oct. 1787: [ref. 12d]. Fined for swearing and breaking the Sabbath in 1788: [ref. 12e]. Plaintiff in lawsuit brought against Joshua Campbell for slander: [ref. 12f]. Plaintiff in lawsuit brought against Thomas Martin in 1788: [ref. 12g]. Was in a party of 5 men hunting and surveying in the winter of 1786, when attacked by Indians. He was the only one not wounded. See Carr's interesting account of this battle: [ref. 12h]. (See also, p. 95.)
PEYTON, John - juror during Jan. 1788, Session of Court: [ref. 13a]. Bondsman for the marriage of John Gatlin and Elender Buck, Mar. 26, 1791: [ref. 13b]. Twin brother of Ephraim & brother of Thomas Peyton. Was in the party including his brothers, Ephriam and Thomas, during an Indian attack in 1786, in which he had his arm broken in two places by musket balls fired by the Indians: [ref. 13c].
PEYTON, Thomas - married Alia Gilbert in Sumner Co., Nov. 16, 1791. Samuel Gilbert was bondsman: [ref. 14]. Was in the party with Ephriam and John Peyton, his brothers, during an Indian attack in 1786, in which he was shot through the shoulder (see Ephraim Peyton, beforementioned).
PHARR, Ephraim - land purchase recorded in Davidson Co. (see p. 95).
PHILIPS, N. - witnessed will of Simpson Hart, Feb. 23, 1790, and witnessed will of Henry Ruyle (Rule), Feb. 19, 1790: [ref. 15].

PORTER, Benjamin - mentioned as one of the early settlers of Sumner Co.: [ref. 16].

PRICE, Mr. & Mrs. - killed by Indians in 1786 or 1787, down Station Camp Creek just below the present site of Gallatin: [ref. 17].

PRICE, William - orphan of William Price, for whom John Wilson was appointed guardian, April 1789: [ref. 18].

PRICE, William - estate inventory of, returned by John Hardin in 1787: [ref. 19a]. Father of William Price: [ref. 19b]. (See also, p.98.)

PROVINE, John - deed from John Latham recorded July 1788: [ref. 20a]. According to the Power of Attorney executed Jan. 1788, by John (Tathum or Luthin?) of Washington Co., VA, Isaac Bledsoe was to act in his behalf to transact with John Provine of Sullivan Co. buying land in Sumner Co. on Station Camp Creek, containing 640 acres: [ref. 20b].

PRYOR, Joseph - witnessed will of John Shavin, June 9, 1791: [ref. 21].

PULLEN, John - purchased negroes with Peter Lum from Page Ballew, Sept. 26, 1791: [ref. 22].

PURVIANCE, John - killed by Indians, May 7, 1792, near Sumner Court House: [ref. 23].

R

RAMSEY, Helty - appointed administrator of Henry Ramsey, deceased, June 1790: [ref. 1].

RAMSEY, Henry - listed on the 1787 Sumner Co. tax roll with 1 poll & 960 acres: [ref. 2a]. Juror during Jan. 1788, Session of Court: [ref. 2b]. Killed by Indians between Greenfield and Bledsoe's Lick in 1786 or 1787: [ref. 2c]. Helty Ramsey was named administrator of his estate, July 6, 1790: [ref. 2d].

RAMSEY, Mary - (see Anthony Bledsoe).

RAMSEY, Thomas - listed on the 1787 delinquent tax rolls of Sumner Co. with 200 acres: [ref. 3].

RAMSEY, William - killed by Indians ca. 1787, at the mouth of the lane leading from Bledsoe's Lick Fort to Bledsoe's Creek: [ref. 4].

REESE, James - juror during Oct. 1789, Session of Court: [ref. 5].

REID, Capt. William - was wounded by Indians in 1792, while on a scouting party on Caney Fork River: [ref. 6].

RHODES, Anthony - listed on the 1787 delinquent Sumner Co. tax roll with 10 polls and 11,120 acres: [ref. 7].

RICE, James - witnessed the will of Michael Shavin, Feb. 11, 1789: [ref. 8].

RIDLEY, George - listed on the delinquent 1787 Sumner Co. tax roll with 1 poll: [ref. 9a]. Juror during the 1787, and Oct. 1788, Sessions of Court: [ref. 9b]. Recorded his stock mark in the Minutes of the County Court, Jan. 1789: [ref. 9c]. Married Thankful Hall in Sumner Co., Oct. 10, 1787: [ref. 9d].
ROAN, William - licensed to practice law, Jan. 1790: [ref. 10].
ROBERTS, John - juror during the 1787, July 1788, and April 1790, Sessions of Court: [ref. 11a]. Bondsman for marriage of David Hainey and Sarah Campbell , Oct. 19, 1791: [ref. 11b]. Married Nancy Forgusson (sic) in Sumner Co., Oct. 19, 1791. David Hainey as bondsman: [ref. 11c].
ROBERTSON, Alexander - juror on the Superior Court, Nov. 1790: [ref. 12]. (See also, p. 104.)
ROBERTSON, Henry - juror during lawsuit (North Carolina vs. Phebe McNeely) in 1790: [ref. 13]. (See also, p. 105.)
ROBERTSON, Col. James - his deposition taken in 1788, for the court case (Payton vs. Martin): [ref. 14]. (See also, p. 105.)
ROBINSON, Elijah - his deed to John McNary recorded July 1789: [ref. 15]. (See also, Elijah ROBERTSON, p. 104.)
ROBINSON, John - was indicted and fined by the Court for fornification with Margery Robinson, Jan. 1789: [ref. 16].
ROBINSON, Margery - see John Robinson, above.
ROGAN, Mr. - father of Hugh Rogan mentioned in Carr's book: [ref. 17].
ROGAN, Hugh - planted corn in the Clover Bottom with Col. John Donelson and helped him build a fort: [ref. 18a]. He was a signer of the Cumberland Compact, May, 1780. After the Indian atrocities, he took charge of the widow Neeley and her family and conducted them to safety in Kentucky in 1780/81. He moved to Mansker's Station when Donelson went to Kentucky: [ref. 18b]. Hugh came from Ireland in 1775. He was 32 years old when he started for the Cumberland Settlements. Four years previous he had come with his brothers-in-law to upper Yadkin County to trade. His wife and child were left in Northern Ireland, and it was about 20 years before he could return again. His brother-in-law remarried. Hugh returned for his wife in 1794, and settled on a land grant in Sumner Co.: [ref. 18c]. Listed on the 1787 Sumner Co. tax roll with 1 poll and 320 acres: [ref. 18d]. Witnessed will of Anthony Bledsoe, July 201 1788: [ref. 18e]. Witnessed the deed of Isaac Bledsoe, Sept. 1790: [ref. 18f]. Wounded by Indians while on a punitive expedition under Capt. Shelby, against the Indians about 1786. The party were ascending the Tennessee River at the

(continued next page)

ROGAN, Hugh - (continued)
mouth of the Duck River when attacked. He was called a
"brave Irishman." He helped defend Col. Bledsoe's Fort
when attacked by Indians, and he was along with Gen'l Smith
about the year 1782 or 1783, before Bledsoe's Lick was
settled, and was fired upon by Indians while trailing the
buffalo path from Bledsoe's Lick to Mansker's Lick: [ref.
18b].
ROGERS, (Mram?) - land purchase recorded in Davidson Co.
(see p. 107).
RULE (variously, RUYLE), Aaron - son of Henry Rule, was mentioned in his father's will, Feb. 16, 1790: [ref. 19].
RULE, Andrew - son of Henry Rule, was mentioned in his father's
will, dated Feb. 16, 1790: [ref. 20].
RULE, Betsy - married Martin Harpool in Sumner Co., Aug.
16, 1791: [ref. 21].
RULE, Catherine - wife of Henry Rule, was the executrix of
his will, July 1790: [ref. 22].
RULE, Delia - daughter of Henry Rule, was mentioned in her
father's will as "Delia Cotes," Feb. 1790: [ref. 23].
RULE, Elizabeth - daughter of Henry Rule, was mentioned in
her father's will, dated Feb. 1790: [ref. 24].
RULE, Henry - listed on the 1787 Sumner Co. tax roll with
1 poll and 640 acres: [ref. 25a]. Juror during Jan. &
July 1788, Sessions of Court: [ref. 25b]. His will, dated
Feb. 16, 1790, bequeaths the plantation, etc. to his wife
Catherine to raise his young children. His eldest son
Henry and his son, Andrew, were left 5 shillings, having
been previously provided for. His sons John, Solomon,
Moses, Aaron, and Peter Rule were to receive the plantation
after the remarriage or death of his widow. His son Peter,
mentioned above, "being the youngest" could have the cleared
land. Daughters Mary Cravins, Magdalon Jones, Margaret,
Elizabeth, and Delia Rule receive 5 shillings having been
previously provided for. His wife Catherine and son John
were named executrix and executor. The will was witnessed
by N. Philips, Jno. Cravins, and Edward Jones, and proved
July, 1790: [ref. 25c].
RULE, Henry (Jr.) - eldest son of Henry Rule (see beforemen-
tioned).
RULE, John - son of Henry Rule (see beforementioned).
RULE, Magdalon - daughter of Henry Rule, was mentioned in
her father's will as "Magdalon Jones," (see beforementioned).
RULE, Margaret - daughter of Henry Rule (beforementioned).
RULE, Mary - daughter of Henry Rule, was mentioned in her
father's will as "Mary Cravins," (see beforementioned).
RULE, Moses - son of Henry Rule (see beforementioned).
RULE, Peggy - daughter of Henry Rule (see beforementioned).
RULE, Peter - son of Henry Rule (see beforementioned).
RUSE, James - jury duty recorded in Davidson Co. (see p.
108).

S

SADLER, John - sold negroes to J. McElworth in 1791: [ref. 1].

SANDERETH, Abraham - jury duty recorded in Davidson Co. (see p. 109).

SANDERS (variously, SAUNDERS), Col. - 2 sons of, killed by Indians near Col. Saunder's (sic) Fort ca. 1787: [ref. 2a]. Mentioned as having built a fort in Sumner Co.: [ref. 2b].

SANDERS, Abraham - juror during April 1789, Session of Court: [ref. 3a]. Sold a negro to Robert Desha in 1789: [ref. 3b]. (See also, p. 109).

SANDERS, Jacob - married Sarah Hardin, May 31, 1791, in Sumner Co. Richard Hogan was bondsman: [ref. 4].

SANDERS, William - his deed to Robert Motherall recorded in the County Court Minutes, Jan. 1790: [ref. 5].

SANDERSON, Jacob - juror during April 1790, Session of Court: [ref. 6].

SAWYER, John - mentioned as an early settler of Sumner Co.: [ref. 7].

SCOBY, David - killed by Indians in 1792, near Rock Island on Caney Fork, while scouting with Lt. Snoddy: [ref. 8].

SEARCY, Bennet (variously, Benount) - witnessed deed and power of attorney of Alexander Dun(n), May 1790: [ref. 9].

SETGRAVE, Joseph Arnold - licensed to practice law and took oath, Jan. 1790: [ref. 10].

SEVIER, Michael - killed by Indians while working the fields near Zeigler's Station, June 26, 1792: [ref. 11].

SHACKLER (variously, SHOCKLER), Philip - listed on the 1787 Sumner Co. delinquent tax roll with 3893 acres and with 1 poll and 6073 acres: [ref. 11b]. (See also, p. 110.)

SHARP, Anthony - juror during Oct. 1789, Session of Court: [ref. 12].

SHARP, Thomas - was given Power of Attorney by Arthur Galbraith, Jan. 1790: [ref. 13].

SHAVER (variously, SHAFFER, SHAVEN, SHAVIN, SHAVOM, SHAVROM), John - will dated June 9, 1791, mentions Elizabeth Hacker (sic) and Peter Shavin (sic): [ref. 14a]. According to the will of his brother, Michael, his eldest son's name was John: [ref. 14b].

SHAVER, John - son of John Shaver (see beforementioned).

SHAVER, Michael (variously, Michail) - listed on the 1787 Sumner Co. tax roll with 1 poll and 1268 acres [ref. 15a]. Killed by Indians in June 1792, near Zeigler's Station, while he was working in the field. He was killed in the first part of the day, and the neighbors having collected

(continued next page)

SHAVER, Michael - (continued)
   together to bring the body from the field into the fort,
   were ambushed by the Indians and retreated to the fort.
   Towards night, the men in the fort went out and brought
   the body in.   Later that night the Indians set fire to
   the fort and took it, killing or capturing all its inhabitants: [ref. 15b].   His will dated, Feb. 11, 1789, proved
   Jan. 1793, mentions his wife Catherine and brother John
   Shavin's (sic) eldest son, John, to whom he left all his
   real and personal property: [ref. 15c].
SHAVER, Peter - mentioned in the will of John Shavin (sic),
   dated June 1791: [ref. 16].
SHAW, Robert - juror during the Oct. 1789, Session of Court:
   [ref. 17a].   Juror on the Superior Court, Nov. 1790: [ref.
   17b].   (See also, p. 112.)
SHELBY, David - appointed clerk of Sumner Co. Court, and
   office which he held during his life: [ref. 18a].   Listed
   on the 1787 Sumner Co. tax roll with 1 poll and 1280 acres:
   [ref. 18b].   Brought lawsuit against John & Samuel Campbell
   in 1787: [ref. 18c].   Recorded his stock mark in the Minutes
   of the County Court in 1787: [ref. 18d].   Took oath required
   by Congress for the support of the Constitution, April,
   1790: [ref. 18e].   Witness to the making of a bond in 1788,
   for Thomas Martin's appointment as Sheriff of Sumner Co.:
   [ref. 18f].   Purchased for 20 pounds, a mulatto boy named
   Nick, from James Bosley, Mar. 17, 1789: [ref. 18g].
SHEPPARD, Benjamin - mentioned as one of the early settlers
   of Sumner Co. [ref. 19].
SHEPPARD, James - listed on the 1787 Sumner Co. tax roll
   with 1 poll: [ref. 21].
SHEPPARD (variously, SHEPPART), Col. John - land purchase
   recorded in Davidson Co. (see p. 113).
SHOAT, Coletine - juror during April, 1790, Session of Court:
   [ref. 22].
SIMPSON, Thomas - listed on the 1787 Sumner Co. tax roll
   with 2 polls: [ref. 23a].   Juror during Oct. 1789, Session
   of Court: [ref. 23b].   (See also, p. 113.)
SLOSS, John - land purchase recorded in Davidson Co. (see
   p. 114).
SMITH, Col. Daniel - listed on the 1787 Sumner Co. tax roll
   with 7 polls and 4,494 acres: [ref. 24a].   Recorded his
   stock mark in the Minutes of the County Court in 1787:
   [ref. 24b].   Appointed to take list of taxables in Simon
   Keykendall's District in 1787: [ref. 24c].   The people
   at his station were appointed to help lay off a road from
   Drake's Creek to Geo. Mansker's house in 1788: [ref. 24d].
   As Esquire (Justice) of Sumner Co., he took oath required
   by Congress for the support of the Constitution in April,
   1790: [ref. 24e].   Co-executor of the will of Anthony Bledsoe, dated July 20, 1788; proved Oct. 1788: [ref. 24f].
   Executor of the will of Isaac Bledsoe, 1791: [ref. 24g].

SMITH, William - married Elsy McDanold (sic) in Sumner Co.,
Mar. 25, 1791. Richard Hogan was bondsman [ref. 25].
SMOTHERS, William - killed by Indian (see p. 114).
SNODDY, Lt. - led a force of settlers in battle with the
Indians near the Rock Island on Caney Fork, in which he
defeated them and returned home with great honor: [ref.
26].
SNODDY, Isabell - married Henry Houdeshell in Sumner Co.,
Oct. 9, 1787: [ref. 27].
SNODDY, William - listed on the 1787 Sumner Co. tax roll
with 1 poll and 440 acres: [ref. 28a]. Grand juror in
1787: [ref. 28b]. His deed to Joseph McElurath recorded
in the Co. Court Minutes, April 1788: [ref. 28c]. Juror
during Oct. 1788, Session of Court: [ref. 28d]. Helped
lay off a road in 1789, from Maddison's Lick to Maj. Wil-
son's: [ref. 28e]. (See also, p. 114.)
SPARLOCK - see SPURLOCK.
SPENCER, Thomas - listed on the 1789 Sumner Co. tax roll
with 1 poll & 3148 acres with the notation "2280 acres
in this county": [ref. 29a]. Held off Indians while Mrs.
Parker, the former Mrs. Anthony Bledsoe, made her escape.
He was called "the bravest of the brave." [ref. 29b].
He was killed by Indians between Carthage and "South-west
Point" about 1787, at a place afterwards called Spencer's
Hill: [ref. 29c].
SPURLOCK (variously, SPARLOCK), John - his deposition taken
July 1788, in lawsuit (Payton vs. Martin): [ref. 30].
SPURLOCK, William - his deposition taken July 1788, in lawsuit
(Payton vs. Martin): [ref. 31].
STANDARD, William - inventory of his estate rendered into
Court in April 1788: [ref. 32].
STARR, William - listed on the 1787 Sumner Co. tax roll with
1 poll & 320 acres: [ref. 33a]. Jesse Summers was appointed
the administrator of his estate in Oct. 1787: [ref. 33b].
Commissioners were appointed by the Court in 1788, to go
to the plantation of the late William Starr, and to view
the land claimed and cabins built by Jethro Sumner, and
to make inquiry what trouble the said Sumner had in taking
care of and tending Starr in his illness: [ref. 33c]. Jethro
Sumner was allowed 129 pounds from the estate of the late
William Starr: [ref. 33d]. In Oct. 1789, the Court ordered
the preemption of the heirs of William Starr, deceased,
be exposed to sale: [ref. 33e].
STATEN, Mr. - killed by Indians (see p. 115).
STEEL, Andrew - juror during Oct. 1789, Session of Court:
[ref. 34a]. Wounded in 1792, while in the party of Lt.
Snoddy in battle with Indians near Rock Island on the Caney
Fork River: [ref. 34b].
STEEL, Elizabeth - daughter of James Steel, was killed by
Indians ca. 1787, while passing from Greenfield to Morgan
Station. She was a "grown young lady": [ref. 35].

STEEL, James - killed by Indians as was his daughter Elizabeth, while passing from Greenfield to Morgan's Station ca. 1787: [ref. 36].

STEEL, John - Grand juror in 1787: [ref. 37a]. Juror during July 1788, Session of Court: [ref. 37b].

STEEL, Robert - listed on the 1787 Sumner Co. delinquent tax roll with 1 poll and 320 acres: [ref. 38a]. Mentioned as one of the early settlers of Sumner Co.: [ref. 38b].

STEWART, Robert - land purchase recorded in Davidson Co. (see p. 116).

STUART, Nancy - married James Carson in Sumner Co., Dec. 19, 1791. Joseph Waller was bondsman: [ref. 39].

STUT, Robert - listed on the 1787 Sumner Co. tax roll with 1 poll and 320 acres: [ref. 40].

SUGG, Abegail - land purchase recorded in Davidson Co. (see p. 117).

SUGG, George A. - land purchase recorded in Davidson Co. (see p. 117).

SUMNER (variously, SUMMERS), Jethro (variously, Jesse) - listed on the 1787 Sumner Co. tax roll with 1 poll: [ref. 41a]. Helped clear road in 1787, from Capt. Keykendall's to Capt. Winchester's Mill: [ref. 41b]. He cleared lands and built cabins on the plantation of William Starr and took care of Starr in his illness before Starr's death ca. 1788. He was allowed 129 pounds from the estate of Starr in Jan. 1789: [ref. 41c]. Appointed administrator in Jan. 1788, of the estate of William Starr, deceased: [ref. 41d].

SUTTON, John - listed on the 1787 Sumner Co. tax roll with 2 polls and 1238 acres: [ref. 42a]. Helped clear road from Capt. Keykendall's to Capt. Winchester's Mill in 1787: [ref. 42b]. Juror during Jan. 1788, Term of Court: [ref. 42c].

T

TATE, James - juror on the Superior Court, Nov. 1790: [ref. 1].

TATE, William - juror during Jan. 1788, Session of Court: [ref. 2].

TATUM (variously, TATHUM), Howell - produced license to practice as an attorney and took oath, July 1789: [ref. 3].

TATUM, John - "of Washington Co., VA," appointed Isaac Bledsoe his lawful attorney to sell land in Sumner Co. on Station Camp Creek containing 640 acres to John Provine, Jan. 1788: [ref. 4].

TENNEN, Hugh - see Hugh TINNON.

TENNEN, Thomas - see Thomas TINNON.

TERRELL, Obediah - listed on the 1787 Sumner Co. tax roll with 1 poll and 200 acres: [ref. 5a]. Helped clear road from Maj. Bledsoe's to the State Line in 1787: [ref. 5b].

TERRELL, Obediah - (continued)
Overseer of road from Indian Creek to Bledsoe's Lick in 1788: [ref. 5c]. Witnessed Bill of Sale for Silas McBee, Oct. 12, 1790: [ref. 5d].
THOMPSON, Azaniah - mentioned in the will of Simpson Hart, dated Feb. 23, 1790, as child of Kiziah Thompson, wife of Lawrence Thompson, who was a brother-in-law to Simpson Hart. Azaniah was to inherit land in NC and VA: [ref. 6a]. With John Whitsell, he purchased a horse, colt, negroes, and household goods from Lawrence Thompson, Dec. 13, 1790: [ref. 6b]. Appointed co-executor of the will of Alexander Robinson, dated July 28, 1791: [ref. 6c].
THOMPSON, China Burton - mentioned in the will of Simpson Hart as daughter of Lawrence and Kiziah Thompson (see hereafter).
THOMPSON, Joseph - listed on the 1787 Sumner Co. tax roll with 1 poll and 100 acres: [ref. 7a]. Juror during the April 1788, Session of Court: [ref. 7b].
THOMPSON, Kiziah - see Kiziah HART.
THOMPSON, Lawrence (variously, Laurence) - listed on the 1787 Sumner Co. delinquent tax roll with 2 polls and 200 acres: [ref. 8a]. Juror during the April 1790, Session of Court: [ref. 8b]. Married Kiziah Hart, sister of Simpson Hart (son of Nathaniel Hart), whose will, dated Feb. 23, 1790, mentions Lawrence and Kiziah and gives bequest of land in NC and VA to Kiziah's children: Richard Lawrence Thompson; Sarah Fanny Thompson; Nathaniel Hart Thompson; China Burton Thompson; and Azaniah Thompson Thompson: [ref. 8c]. (See also, p. 122.)
THOMPSON, Nathaniel Hart - son of Lawrence & Kiziah (Hart) Thompson (see beforementioned).
THOMPSON, Richard Lawrence - son of Lawrence & Kiziah (Hart) Thompson (see beforementioned).
THOMPSON, Sarah Fanny - daughter of Lawrence & Kiziah (Hart) Thompson (see beforementioned).
THOMPSON, Sally - married George Blackemore in Sumner Co., Sept. 12, 1787: [ref. 9].
THOMPSON, Thomas - listed on the 1787 Sumner Co. tax roll with 1 poll & 490 acres: [ref. 10a]. Juror during Jan. 1788, Session of Court: [ref. 10b].
THOMPSON, William - juror during 1787 Session of Court: [ref. 11a]. His deposition taken for court case (Payton vs. Martin) in July 1788: [ref. 11b].
TINNON (variously, TINNEN, TENNEN), Edward - will dated Nov. 5, 1790, proved Jan. 13, 1791, mentioned his wife Elizabeth and daughter Patty. Other children were not called by name: [ref. 12].
TINNON, Elizabeth - wife of Edward Tinnon (beforementioned).

TINNON, Hugh - witnessed will of Simpson Hart, Feb. 23, 1790: [ref. 13]. (See also, p. 123.)

TINNON, Patty - daughter of Edward Tinnon (beforementioned).

TINNON, Thomas - witnessed will of Alexander Robinson, July 28, 1791: [ref. 14].

TISON, A. - land sale by his heirs recorded in Davidson Co. (see p. 123).

TODD, James - land purchase recorded in Davidson Co. (see p. 123).

TOWEL, Isaac - listed in the 1787 Sumner Co. tax roll with 1 poll: [ref. 15a]. Juror during Jan. 1788, Session of Court: [ref. 15b].

TRAMMELL, Phillip - listed on the 1787 Sumner Co. tax roll with 1 poll and 1168 acres: [ref. 16a]. Helped clear road from Capt. Keykendall's to Capt. Winchester's Mill in 1787: [ref. 16b]. Appointed Constable in 1787 and 1788: [ref. 16c]. His deed to Eneas Hannah recorded in the County Court Minutes, July 1789: [ref. 16d]. Granted permission by the Court in July 1789, to erect a mill on the middle fork of Red River with 300 yards of the place where he lived: [ref. 16e].

TROUSDALE, James - mentioned as an early settler of Sumner Co.: [ref. 17].

TRUELOCK, Bryan - heir of George D. Truelock (see hereafter).

TRUELOCK, George D. - land sale by his heir, Bryan Truelock, recorded in Davidson Co. (see p. 125).

TURNEY, Peter - juror during the July 1790, Session of Court: [ref. 18].

TUTON, William - land purchase recorded in Davidson Co. (see p. 126).

V

VININGHAM, Thomas - juror during April 1790, Session of Court: [ref. 1].

W

WALKER, Richard - jury duty recorded in Davidson Co. (see p, 127),

WALL, Pierce - juror during the April 1790, Session of Court: [ref. 1a]. Sold negroes to Isaac Bledsoe, Jan. 1, 1791: [ref. 1b]. Witnessed Bills of Sale for Ruffin Deloach and Richard Strother, Aug. 11, 1791: [ref. 1c].

WALLACE, Joseph - juror during April 1790, Session of Court: [ref. 3a]. Sold negro woman, Aug. 1789: [ref. 3b]. Deed of Edward & Joseph Wallace to James Wilson recorded April 1790: [ref. 3c]. Juror on Superior Court, Nov. 1790: [ref. 3d].

WALLER, Joseph - juror during April 1790, Session of Court: [ref. 4a]. Bondsman for marriage of James Carson and Nancy Stuart, Dec. 1791: [ref. 4b]. (See also, p. 127.)

WALTERS, ____ - killed by Indians (see p. 128).

WALTON, Isaac - listed on the 1787 Sumner Co. tax roll with 3 polls and 165 acres: [ref. 5a]. Juror during Jan. 1788, Session of Court: [ref. 5b]. Juror on the Superior Court, April 1788: [ref. 5c]. Overseer of part of the road construction from Col. Mansker's to the Virginia line in 1789: [ref. 5d]. (See also, p. 128.)

WALTON, Capt. William - listed on the 1787 Sumner Co. tax roll with 2 polls and 9040 acres: [ref. 6a]. Appointed in 1787, to take a list of the inhabitants in Capt. Keykendall's Company: [ref. 6b]. Appointed Coroner of Sumner Co., Oct. 1787: [ref. 6c].

WATERS, ____ - killed by Indians on Bledsoe's Creek ca. 1787: [ref. 7]. (See also, p. 128.)

WEALS?, George - listed on the 1787 delinquent Sumner Co. tax roll with 2 polls and 428 acres: [ref. 8].

WEATHERS, John - his deed to Isaac Bledsoe recorded in the County Court Minutes, Jan. 1790: [ref. 9].

WEST, Amos - married Frances Herndon in Sumner Co., April 7, 1791. Richard Hogan was bondsman: [ref. 10].

WHITESIDE, John - jury duty recorded in Davidson Co. (see p. 130).

WHITSETT, James - witnessed the will of Simpson Hart, Feb. 23, 1790: [ref. 11a]. Witnessed will of Alexander Robinson, July 28, 1791: [ref. 11b].

WHITSETT, John - purchased with Azaniah Thompson, a horse, colt, negroes, and household goods from Lawrence Thompson, Dec. 13, 1790: [ref. 12a]. Witnessed the will of Simpson Hart, Feb. 2, 1790: [ref. 12b].

WILLIAMS, Benjamin - appointed Constable, Oct. 5, 1790: [ref. 13a]. On July 13, 1790, he and John Williams sold to Elmon Douglas for 200 pounds Virginia currency, 2 negro boys, Arthur and Benjamin: [ref. 13b]. Named executor of the will of Edward Tinnon, dated Nov. 5, 1790: [ref. 13c]. Settled in the year 1790, about $2\frac{1}{2}$ miles north of the present site of Gallatin. The Indians came in the night and killed him, his wife, and one or two negroes: [ref. 13d]. (See also, p. 130.)

WILLIAMS, Edward - listed on the 1787 Sumner Co. tax roll with 1 poll: [ref. 14a]. Married Darkuss Edwards in Sumner Co., Dec. (12?), 1791: [ref. 14b]. Bondsman for the marriage of Thomas Edwards and Elizabeth Turner, Feb. 1792: [ref. 14c].

WILLIAMS, John - and Benjamin Williams, sold two negro boys named Arthur and Benjamin to Elmon Douglas, July 13, 1790: [ref. 15].

WILLS, Jane - married Thomas Collier in Sumner Co., Sept. 16, 1787: [ref. 16].

WILSON, ____ - helped mark road from Maj. Bledsoe's to the State line in 1787: [ref. 17].

WILSON, Archy - described as "a fine young man," who had volunteered his services to protect the people at Zeigler's Fort on the night it was attacked and destroyed by the Indians. He fought bravely, but was wounded, and retreating from the fort, he was brought to bay about 100 yards from the fort. John Carr, who visited the site the next day, wrote, "the ground was beaten all around, showing the desperate defence Wilson had made. The Indians had broken the breech of a gun over his head in the fight, and had he not been badly wounded, there is little doubt he would have gotten off. It was an awful sight." [ref. 18].

WILSON, Maj. David - listed in the 1787 and 1788 Sumner Co. tax roll with 2 polls and 3640 acres: [ref. 19a]. Bondsman in 1787, for Thankful Hall to serve as administratrix of the estate of William Hall, deceased: [ref. 19b]. Recorded his stock mark in the Minutes of the County Court, 1788: [ref. 19c]. Road ordered cleared by the people of his station in 1788: [ref. 19d]. Road ordered cleared from McKains Creek dividing ridge to his station in 1788, and from Middle Fork to his station in the same year: [ref. 19e]. Road ordered to be cleared from Maddison's Lick to his station in 1789: [ref. 19f]. Took oath as County Esquire (magistrate or justice) to support the Constitution, April 1790: [ref. 19g]. Witnessed the deed of Abraham Sanders in 1789, and a Bill of Sale for Ruffin Deloach, Aug. 11, 1791: [ref. 19h]. Executor of the will of Michael Shavin (sic), dated Feb. 11, 1789, proved in Sumner Co. Jan. 1793: [ref. 19i]. He had settled about 2 miles east of the present site of Gallatin: [re. 19j].

WILSON, George - killed by Indians (see p. 132).

WILSON, James - listed on the 1787 and 1788 Sumner Co. tax rolls with 1 poll and 200 acres: [ref. 20a]. Helped mark road from Maj. Bledsoe's to the State line in 1787: [ref. 20b]. Juror during the 1787, Session of Court: [ref. 20c]. Overseer of road from East Fork of Station Camp to Indian Creek in 1788: [ref. 20d]. Juror during Oct. 1789, Session of Court: [ref. 20e]. Deed from Edward & Joseph Wallace to him recorded in the Minutes of the County Court, April 1790: [ref. 20f]. Appointed Deputy Ranger in 1790: [ref. 20g]. Witnessed Bill of Sale for Joseph Wallace, Aug. 1789: [ref. 20h]. Married Rachel Harrington in Sumner Co., Mar. 10, 1794. Charles Harrington was bondsman: [ref. 20i]. (See also, p. 132.)

WILSON, James (Jr.) - juror during Jan. 1788, Session of Court: [ref. 21].

WILSON, John - listed on the 1787 and 1788 Sumner Co. tax rolls with 2 polls and 200 acres: [ref. 22a]. Juror on the Superior Court, April 1788: [ref. 22b]. Appointed Guardian for William Price, orphan of William Price, deceased, in April 1789: [ref. 22c]. Executor of the will of Michael Shavin (sic), dated Feb. 11, 1789, proved Jan. 1793: [ref. 22d]. Bondsman for marriage of James Wilson and Mary Wilson, Sept. 17, 1787: [ref. 22e]. (See also, p. 133.)

WILSON, Joseph - and his wife and 7 children were in Zeigler's Fort in June, 1792, when it was destroyed by Indians. He was wounded but escaped with his son, 12 years of age. His wife and 6 children were taken into captivity to the Cherokee nation. See John Carr's interesting account of the settlers' pursuit of the raiding party and their captives: [ref. 23].

WILSON, Mary - married James Wilson in Sumner Co., Sept. 17, 1787: [ref. 24].

WILSON, Samuel - mentioned as an early settler in Sumner Co.: [ref. 25].

WILSON, Sarah - one of the 6 children of Joseph Wilson, who was captured by Indians at Zeigler's Station in 1792 (see Joseph Wilson, beforementioned).

WILSON, William - listed on the 1787 Sumner Co. tax roll with 1 poll: [ref. 26a]. Juror during the 1787, and Jan. 1788, Sessions of Court: [ref. 26b]. Witnessed the will of Edward Tinnon, Nov. 5, 1790, and witnessed the will of Michael Shavin (sic), 1791: [ref. 26c]. Fought Indians at Greenfield Fort 1787: [ref. 26d].

WILSON, Zacheus - one of the 6 children of Joseph Wilson captured by Indians at Zeigler's Fort in 1792. He was taken by the Indian named "Little Owl" (see Joseph Wilson beforementioned).

WINCHESTER, (Capt./Major) George - took oath as County Magistrate in April 1787: [ref. 27a]. Listed with James Winchester ("J. & G. Winchester") on the 1787 Sumner Co. tax roll with 3 polls and 428 acres: [ref. 27b]. Member of the first County Court in 1787: [ref. 27c]. Helped clear road from Maj. Bledsoe's to the State line: [ref. 27d]. Appointed to take list of taxables in Capt. Lynn's District: [ref. 27e]. Bondsman for Thankful Hall in 1787, as administratrix of the estate of William Hall, deceased: [ref. 27f]. Appointed Sumner Co. Registrar, Oct. 9, 1787: [ref. 27g]. Appointed one of the commissioners to divide the estate of Jourdan Gibson, deceased, into four equal parts: [ref. 27h]. Jane Kendrick made oath in 1788, to the Court that

(continued next page)

WINCHESTER, George - (continued)
George Winchester was the father of her bastard child:
[ref. 27i]. Witnessed Bill of Sale for Pierce Wall, Jan.
1, 1791: [ref. 27j]. Witnessed will of Isaac Bledsoe in
1791: [ref. 27k]. Killed by Indians near the present site
of Gallatin in 1793. He was the brother of Gen'l Winchester:
[ref. 27l]. (See also, p. 133.)

WINCHESTER, James - listed with George Winchester on the
1787 Sumner Co. tax roll (see beforementioned). Appointed
County Trustee, April 1789: [ref. 28a]. Witnessed Bill
of Sale for Pierce Wall, Jan. 1, 1791: [ref. 28b]. (See
also, p. 133.)

WINCHESTER, John - land purchase recorded in Davidson Co.
(see p. 133).

WITHERS, John - mentioned as early settler in Sumner Co.
in one source, however, we find no early public record
as yet on this individual: [ref. 29].

WOOD, Thomas - land sale by his heirs recorded in Davidson
Co. (see p. 134).

WYATT, Ephraim - sale of his land by Thomas Wyatt, his heir,
recorded in Davidson Co. (see p. 134).

WYATT, Thomas - heir of Ephraim Wyatt (see above).

WYER, William - juror during the April 1790, Session of Court:
[ref. 30].

WYNN, James - plaintiff in lawsuit brought against Samuel
Mason in 1789: [ref. 31].

Y

YATES, James - 1787 Sumner Co. tax roll with 1 poll & 640
acres: [ref. 1a]. Juror during July 1788, and Oct. 1789,
Sessions of Court: [ref. 1b]. (See also, p. 135.)

YEIGER, Jacob - listed on the 1787 Sumner Co. tax roll with
1 poll & 640 acres: [ref. 2].

YOUNG, John - juror during April 1790, Session of Court:
[ref. 3].

Z

ZEIGLER, Elizabeth - taken prisoner June 26, 1792, by Indians
at Zeigler's Station. Was purchased by traders from the
Shawnees for $58.00: [ref. 1].

ZEIGLER, Hannah - taken prisoner June 26, 1792, by Indians
at Zeigler's Station. Was purchased by traders from the
Shawnees for $58.00: [ref. 2].

ZEIGLER, Jacob - missing June 26, 1792, at Zeigler's Station.
Supposed to be burned in his house by Indians: [ref. 3].

ZEIGLER, Mary - taken prisoner June 26, 1792, at Zeigler's
Station by Indians. Was purchased by traders from the
Shawnees for $58.00: [ref. 4].

185

Part Three

THE INHABITANTS OF RECORD,
IN THAT AREA OF DAVIDSON COUNTY, NORTH CAROLINA
KNOWN AFTER NOVEMBER, 1788, AS
TENNESSEE COUNTY, NORTH CAROLINA,
THE ORGANIZATION OF WHICH WAS NOT COMPLETED
UNTIL JANUARY, 1791

A

ANDERSON, Daniel - land purchased recorded in Davidson Co.
(see p. 2).
ARMSTRONG, Martin - with John Montgomery, laid off the land
and made the plan of a town (Clarksville) on the north
bank of the Cumberland River just above the mouth of Red
River an entered the land in 1784: [ref. 1]. (See also,
pp. 3 & 136.)
ARMSWORTH, Thomas - sale of his land by his heirs recorded
in Davidson Co. (see p. 3).
ARRINGTON, Charles - land purchase and jury duty recorded
in Davidson & Sumner Cos., respectively, (see pp. 3 & 136).

B

BALLARD, Burnell - sale of his land by his heirs recorded
in Davidson Co. (see p. 5).
BARKER, Samuel - sale of his land by heirs recorded in Davidson
Co. (see p. 5).
BARNETT, Peter - killed by Indians (see p. 5).
BELL, George - mentioned as one of the earliest inhabitants
of Clarksville, who had come from South Carolina, and was
an early settler in that area of Tennessee County from
which Montgomery Co. was formed in 1796: [ref. 1]. Land
grant recorded in Davidson Co. (see p. 6).
BIRD, Amos - mentioned as one of the earliest inhabitants
of Clarksville: [ref. 2].
BLOUNT, John Gray - land purchase recorded in Davidson Co.
(see p. 8).
BOONE, James - land purchase recorded in Davidson Co. (see
p. 9).
BOREN, Bazel - jury duty recorded in Davidson Co. (see p.
9).
BORIN, Stephen - jury duty recorded in Davidson Co. (see
p. 9).

BOURLAND, John - land purchase recorded in Davidson Co. (see
p. 9).
BOWAN, William - (see p. 9).
BOYD, ____ - killed by Indians, Jan. 14, 1791, at Clarksville:
[ref. 3].
BREAKY, Andrew - assignee of land grant recorded in Davidson
Co. (see p. 11).
BROCK, Joseph - land grant recorded in Davidson Co. (see
p. 12).
BROWN, Dr. Morgan - was an early settler from North Carolina
in that area of Tennessee County from which Montgomery
Co. was formed in 1796: [ref. 4].

C

CANNON, James - land purchase recorded in Davidson Co. (see
p. 16).
CANTRELL, Stephen - assignee of land grant recorded in Davidson
Co. (see p. 17).
COBB, William - land sale recorded in Davidson Co. (see p.
21).
COLCHESTER, John - land sale by heirs recorded in Davidson
Co. (see p. 22).
COMSTOCK, Thomas - land purchase recorded in Davidson Co.
(see p. 22).
COUTS, Chrisley - jury duty recorded in Davidson Co. (see
p. 24).
CROCKETT, Samuel - jury duty recorded in Davidson Co. (see
p. 25).
CRUTCHER, Anthony - mentioned with William Crutcher as having
come from North Carolina and one of the earliest settlers
in the Town of Clarksville in that area of Tennessee Co.
from which Montgomery Co. was formed in 1796: [ref. 1].
(See also, p. 25.)
CRUTCHER, William - see Anthony CRUTCHER, above. (See also,
p. 25).

D

DAW, Jeffery - land sale by his heirs recorded in Davidson
Co. (see p. 27).
DENNING, Robert - lot purchase in Clarksville recorded in
Davidson Co. (see p. 27).
DUNBAR, Thomas - jury duty recorded in Davidson Co. (see
p. 31).

DUNCAN, Martin - jury duty recorded in Davidson Co. (see p. 31).
DUNCAN, William - jury duty recorded in Davidson Co. (see p. 31).
DUNNING, Robert - jury duty recorded in Davidson Co. (see p. 32).

E

ELDER, James - mentioned as coming from Pennsylvania, and one of the earliest settlers in Montgomery Co. which was formed from Tennessee Co. in 1796: [ref. 1].
ELLIOTT, Tilpa? - land purchase recorded in Davidson Co. (see p. 33).
ESEINS, Thomas - land sale by his heirs recorded in Davidson Co. (see p. 33).

F

FORD, Col. James - mentioned as having come from South Carolina and an early settler in Montgomery Co. which was formed out of Tennessee Co. in 1796: [ref. 1].
FORT, ____ - mentioned as one of the leading families of Tennessee County: [ref. 2].
FRAZIER, George - land purchase recorded in Davidson Co. (see p. 39).

G

GAMBLE, Edward - land purchase recorded in Davidson Co. (see p. 41).
GIBSON, Gadi - jury duty recorded in Davidson Co. (see p. 42).
GIBSON, John - land sale by his heirs and jury duty recorded in Davidson Co. (see p. 42).
GILBERT, John - land purchase recorded in Davidson Co. (see p. 43).
GLOSTER, Thomas - land purchase recorded in Davidson Co. (see p. 43).
GRANTHAM, ____ - killed by Indians, Nov. 5, 1791, at Red River, "northwards": [ref. 1].
GRAY, Randal - land sale by his heirs recorded in Davidson Co. (see p. 45).
GREEN, William - land purchase recorded in Davidson Co. (see p. 46).

GRIMBS (GRIMES?), William - the 3rd session of the Montgomery Court of Pleas and Quarter Sessions was held at his house: [ref. 2].

H

HAGGARD, John - jury duty recorded in Davidson Co. (see p. 47).

HARRELL, Peter - land purchase recorded in Davidson Co. (see p. 50).

HARRY, ____ - killed by Indians June 29, 1791, on Red River: [rer. 1].

HENNIS, Benbury - land sale by his heirs recorded in Davidson Co. (see p. 53).

HENRY, ____ - jury duty recorded in Davidson Co. (see p. 53).

HOGAN, Daniel - land purchase recorded in Davidson Co. (see p. 55).

HOGAN, Humphrey - land sale by his heirs recorded in Davidson Co. (see p. 56).

HOLLEY, Nathaniel - land purchase recorded in Davidson Co. (see p. 56).

HOLLIS, James - one of the company with Moses Renfroe, who left the Donelson flotilla and ascended Red River to the mouth of Person's Creek, where they built Renfroe's Station: [ref. 2].

HOSKINS (variously, HAUSKINS), Josiah (variously, Joseph) - killed by Indians at Kilgore's Station: [ref. 3].

J

JENKINS, Josiah - land sale by his heirs recorded in Davidson Co. (see p. 61).

JONES, James - one of the men in Moses Renfroe's company, who left the Donelson flotilla and ascended the Red River to the mouth of Person's Creek, where he helped build Renfroe's Station: [ref. 1].

JOHNSON, Andrew - land sale by his heirs recorded in Davidson Co. (see p. 61).

JOHNSON, Archibald - land sale by his heirs recorded in Davidson Co. (see p. 61).

JOHNSON, Cave - son of Gen'l Thomas Johnson (see hereafter).

JOHNSON, Lancelot - land purchase recorded in Davidson Co. (see p. 62).

JOHNSON, Gen'l Thomas - called one of the leading men in early Tennessee County, and the father of Hon. Cave Johnson: [ref. 2].

JOHNSON, William - jury duty recorded in Davidson Co. (see p. 62).
JOHNSTON, Thomas - jury duty recorded in Davidson Co. (see p. 63).
JONES, "widow" - was one of the Renfroe party who left the Donelson flotilla and ascended the Red River to the mouth of Person's Creek, where Renfroe's Station was subsequently built: [ref. 3].

K

KING, Ann - killed by Indians at Valentine Sevier's Station: [ref. 1].
KING, James - son of Ann King (see above), was killed by Indians at Valentine Sevier's Station.

L

LAMBERT, Aaron - land purchase recorded in Davidson Co. (see p. 67).
LEE, Timothy - land sale by his heirs recorded in Davidson Co. (see p. 68).
LUSK, William - jury duty recorded in Davidson Co. (see p. 73).

Mc

McALLISTER, Aeneas - mentioned as one of the earliest inhabitants of Clarksville: [ref. 1].
McCARTY, Jacob - jury duty recorded in Davidson Co. (see p. 75).
McDANIEL, John - land sale by his heirs recorded in Davidson Co. (see p. 76).
McNEES, Benjamin - land purchase recorded in Davidson Co. (see p. 79).

M

MAHON, Archibald - land purchase and jury duty recorded in Davidson Co. (see p. 80).
MARTIN, Joseph - Tennessee County Coroner (see p. 81).

MASON - two young men by that name, killed by Indians and scalped as they went from Kilgore's Station to a clay lick to look for deer: [ref. 1].

MASON, John - land sale by his heirs recorded in Davidson Co. (see p. 82).

MASON, Philip - killed by Indians (see p. 82).

MASON, Samuel - helped build Kilgore's Station (see p. 82).

MAULDING, Ambrose - helped build Kilgore's Station (see p. 82).

MAULDING, Moses - helped build Kilgore's Station (see p. 82).

MAYFIELD, Isaac - one of those in Moses Renfroe's company, who left the Donelson flotilla and ascended the Red River to the mouth of Person's Creek, where he helped build Renfroe's Station: [ref. 2].

MEDILL, George - came from South Carolina with Joseph B. Medill, and built a fort on Red River between Prince's Station and Clarksville: [ref. 3].

MEDILL, Joseph B. - came from South Carolina with George Medill (see above).

MONTGOMERY, John - mentioned as having come from Virginia, via Watauga, and was an early settler in Montgomery Co. which was formed from Tennessee County in 1796: [ref. 4]. See also, p. 86)

MORGAN, Griffith - land sale by his heirs recorded in Davidson Co. (see p. 87).

MYHART, William - land sale by his heirs recorded in Davidson Co. (see p.89).

N

NELSON, Robert - mentioned as having come from North Carolina and one of the settlers of Montgomery Co., which was formed from Tennessee County in 1796: [ref. 1]. Land purchase recorded in Davidson Co. (see p. 91).

NEVILL, George - mentioned as having come from North Carolina and an early settler in Montgomery Co. which was formed out of Tennessee Co. in 1796: [ref. 2].

NEVILL, Joseph B. - mentioned as having been born in North Carolina, and an early settler in Montgomery Co. which was formed from Tennessee Co. in 1796: [ref. 3].

NORRIS, Elizabeth - killed by Indians, Aug. 6, 1792, at the Sulphur Fork: [ref. 4].

O

O'BRYAN, Lawrence - land purchase recorded in Davidson Co. (see p. 93).

OYER, Milcher - jury duty recorded in Davidson Co. (see p. 94).

P

PADDLER, Thomas - land sale by his heirs recorded in Davidson Co. (see p. 94).

PARKS, ____ - killed by Indians, June 22, 1792, at Sycamore: [ref. 1].

PALMER, Elisha - land sale by his heirs recorded in Davidson Co. (see p. 94).

PASKLEY, Mrs. & daughter - taken prisoner and killed by Indians, Feb. 17, 1792, at Big Barren: [ref. 2].

PHILIPS, Mann - land purchase recorded in Davidson Co. (see p. 96).

POLLOCK, William Barkley - Clerk of Tennessee County (see p. 97).

PORTER, Samuel - land sale by his heirs recorded in Davidson Co. (see p. 97).

POSTON, John H. - mentioned as having come from Virginia, via Watauga, and one of the early settlers in Montgomery County which was formed from Tennessee Co. in 1796: [ref. 3].

PRICE, Jonathan - jury duty recorded in Davidson Co. (see p. 98).

PRINCE, Francis - mentioned as having come from South Carolina with William Prince, and one of the early settlers in Montgomery Co. which was formed from Tennessee County in 1796: [ref. 4].

PRINCE, Robin - jury duty recorded in Davidson Co. (see p. 98).

PRINCE, William - (see Francis Prince, above.) See also, p. 98.

R

RAMSEY, Josiah - jury duty recorded in Davidson Co. (see p. 100).

RAMSEY, Solomon - land sale by his heirs recorded in Davidson Co. (see p. 100).

RENFROE (variously, RENTFROE, RENTFROE), Isaac - member of the Renfroe family including Moses, Joseph, and James Renfroe, who left the Donelson flotilla and ascended the Red River to the mouth of Person's Creek, and there built Renfroe's Station: [ref. 1]. (See also, p. 102.)

RENFROE, James - see Isaac Renfroe, above. (See also, p. 102).

RENFROE, Joseph - see Isaac Renfroe, above. (See also, p. 102.)

RENFROE, Moses - led the company which left the Donelson
flotilla to settle on Red River at the mouth of Person's
Creek and build Renfroe's Station (see Isaac Renfroe,
beforementioned). See also, p. 102.
RICE, John - killed by Indians: [ref. 2].
ROBERTSON, Henry - land sale by his heirs recorded in Davidson
Co. (see p. 105).

S

SAUNDERS, John - see p. 109.
SEVIER, John - brother of Valentine Sevier: [ref. 1a]. Killed
by Indians during their attack on Valentine Sevier's Station:
[ref. 1b].
SEVIER, Joseph - killed by Indians during their attack on
Valentine Sevier's Station: [ref. 2].
SEVIER, Valentine - mentioned as having come from Virginia,
via Watauga, and an early settler in Montgomery Co. which
was formed from Tennessee County in 1796. He was a brother
of John Sevier. Three of his sons were killed by Indians:
[ref. 3].
SHARP, Anthony - jury duty recorded in Davidson Co. (see
p. 11).
SHELBY, Evan - mentioned as having come from Virginia, via
Watauga, with Moses Shelby, and an early settler in
Montgomery Co. which was formed from Tennessee County in
1796: [ref. 4]. (See also, p. 112.)
SHELBY, Moses - see Evan Shelby, above. (See also, p. 112.)
SIMMONS, Jesse - killed by Indians (see p. 113).
SMILIN, Jonathan - land sale by his heirs recorded in Davidson
Co. (see p. 114).
SNYDER, Mr. & Mrs. - killed by Indians during their attack
on Valentine Sevier's Station. They had a son, John, also
killed: [ref. 5].
SNYDER, John - killed by Indians (see Mr. & Mrs. Snyder,
above.)
STAFFORD, Cuthbert - land purchase recorded in Davidson Co.
(see p. 115).
STANDLEY, Abraham - land purchase recorded in Davidson Co.
(p. 115).
STANLEY, John - jury duty recorded in Davidson Co. (see p.
115).
STEELE, David - killed by Indians (see p. 116).
STEWART, Charles - mentioned as having come from North Carolina
with Duncan and James Stewart, all of whom were early
settlers in Montgomery Co., which was formed from Tennessee
County in 1796: [ref. 6].

STEWART, Duncan - see Charles Stewart, beforementioned.
STEWART, James - see Charles Stewart, beforementioned.
STONE, Littleberry - land sale by his heirs recorded in Davidson Co. (see p. 116).

T

TITSWORTH, Isaac - the first and second sessions of the Court of Pleas and Quarter Sessions for Tennessee Co. in 1788, held in his house: [ref. 1]. (See also, p. 123.)
TITSWORTH, John - jury duty recorded in Davidson Co. (see p. 123).
TROUBLEFIELD, Benjamin - land sale by his heirs recorded in Davidson Co. (see p. 124).
TROUSDALE, John - land purchase recorded in Davidson Co. (see p. 125).
TURNER, William - land sale by his heirs recorded in Davidson Co. (see p. 126).
TURPIN, Nathan - with Solomon Turpin, he was one of the company of Moses Renfroe, who left the Donelson flotilla and ascended the Red River to the mouth of Person's Creek, and helped build Renfroe's Station: [ref. 2a]. Killed by Indians at Red River Station: [ref.2b]. (See also, p. 126.)
TURPIN, Solomon - see Nathan Turpin, above. (See also, p. 126.)

V

VALENTINE, Silas - land sale by his heirs recorded in Davidson Co. (see p. 127).

W

WALKER, Richard - jury duty recorded in Davidson Co. (see p. 127).
WELLS, Anna - lived in Montgomery Co. which was formed from Tennessee Co. in 1796 (see p. 128).
WELLS, Haydon - mentioned as having come from North Carolina, and one of the early settlers in Montgomery Co. which was formed from Tennessee Co. in 1796: [ref. 1]. (See also, p. 128.)
WILDER, Randall - land sale by his heirs recorded in Davidson Co. (see p. 130).
WILLIAMS, Thomas - land sale recorded in Davidson Co. (see p. 132).

WILSON, John - jury duty recorded in Davidson Co. (see p. 133).
WILSON, Samuel - jury duty recorded in Davidson Co. (see p. 133).
WINNEHAM, Thomas - land purchase recorded in Davidson Co. (see p. 133).
WINTERS, Moses - jury duty recorded in Davidson Co. (see p. 133).

Y

YOUNG, Adam - land purchase recorded in Davidson Co. (see p. 135).

Z

ZAMBERT, Aron - land purchase recorded in Davidson Co. (see p. 135).
ZARLETT, James - land sale by his heirs recorded in Davidson Co. (see p. 135).

- - - -

REFERENCES

Part One

DAVIDSON COUNTY

(see bibliography following)

A

[1] Deed Book A, 212. [2] A. W. Putnam, History Of Middle Tennessee (Nashville: Southern Methodist Publishing House, 1859) p. 297 (afterward referred to as Putnam); also, J.G.M. Ramsey, Annals Of Tennessee To The End Of The 18th Century (Charleston: J. Russell Company, 1853) p. 483 (afterward referred to as Ramsey); also, John Haywood, Civil And Political History Of The State Of Tennessee (Nashville: Methodist Episcopal Church South Publishing House, 1823) p. 249 (afterward referred to as Haywood). [3] County Court Minutes, A, (W.P.A.), pp. 41-42 (afterwards referred to as Co. Court Minutes, A). [4] Co. Court Minutes, A, 27. [5] Land Records, 1788-1793, p. 27. [6] Ibid. [7] The Tax Roll. [8] Joseph C. Guild, Old Times In Tennessee (Nashville: Tavel, Eastman & Howell, 1878) p. 93 (afterwards referred to as Guild). [9] Co. Court Minutes, A, 31-32. [10] Haywood, p. 91. [11] State Records of North Carolina, XXIV, 629-30 (afterward referred to as State Records of NC). [12a] Haywood, p. 194. [12b] Co. Court Minutes, A, 7; see also, File #T100, Tennessee Historical Society. [13] Deed Book, A, 193. [14] Cumberland Compact, File T44, Tennessee Historical Society. [15a] Putnam, p. 229. [15b] Haywood, p. 143. [15c] Putnam, p. 229. [15d] Wills & Inventories, I, p. 1. [16] Mss T44, TN Hist. Soc. [17] Putnam, p. 161. [18a] Land Records, 1788-1793, pp. 3,16,24. [18b] Ibid., p. 16. [19] The Tax Roll. [20] The Document, File #T44, TN. Hist. Soc. [21] Haywood, pp. 237, 409. [22] The Document, File #T44, TN. Hist. Soc. [23] Co. Court Minutes, A, 17. [24] Land Records, 1788-1793, p. 5. [25a] Haywood, pp. 107, 218. [25b] Minutes, Committee of the Cumberland Association, file #T44, TN Hist. Soc. [25c] State Record of NC, XXIV, 629-30. [25d] Deed Book A, 161. [25e] Haywood, p. 340. [26] Haywood, p. 326. [27] Haywood, p. 3. [28a] Haywood, pp. 4,8. [28b] Deed Book, A, 261. [28c] Land Records, 1788-1793, p. 23. [28d] Kentucky Gazette, June 6, 1789; see also, Will Book, I, 287-90; and, Lyman Draper MSS #335, pp. 59-60, Historical Society of Wisconsin (afterwards referred to as Draper). [29] Deed Book, A, 325. [30a] Deed Book, A, 63. [30b] Co. Court Minutes, A, 1. [30c] See Tennessee D.A.R. Roster. [31] Land Records, 1788-1793, p. 22. [31b] Deed Book, A, 319. [32] Deed Book, A, pp. 190, 336; see also, TN D.A.R. Roster. [33] Deed Book, A, 189. [34] State Record of NC, XXIV, 629-30. [35a] Putnam, p. 295. [35b] Haywood, p. 245. [36] Haywood, p. 143. [37] Land Records, 1788-1793, p. 23. [38] Co. Court Minutes, A, 29.

DAVIDSON COUNTY

B

(see bibliography following)

[1] Deed Book A, p. 189. [2] Land Records, 1788-1793, p. 25.
[3] Land Records, 1788-1793, p. 5. [4] The Tax Roll. [5a]
Co. Court Minutes, A, 27. [5b] Will Book, II, 47. [6] Land
Records, 178-1793, p. 23. [7] John Haywood, Civil And Political
History Of The State Of Tennessee (Nashville: Methodist Episcopal
Church South Publishing House, 1823), pp. 88-91 (afterward
referred to as Haywood). [8a] Co. Court Minutes, A, 9-10.
[8b] See TN D.A.R. Roster. [9a] The Tax Roll. [9b] Will Book,
II, 19. [10] Land Records, 1788-1793, p. 3. [11] The Tax
Roll. [12] Will Book, II, 19. [13] Co. Court Minutes, A,
20. [14] Land Records, 1788-1793, p. 25. [15] Haywood, p.
125. [16] State Records of NC, XXIV, 629-630. [17] Land Record,
1788-1793, p. 22. [18] Land Records, 1788-1793, p. 15. [19]
Haywood, p. 142. [20] Haywood, p. 227. [21] Marriage Book,
1, p. 4. [22] Deed Book, A, 303. [23] The Document, file
#T44, TN Hist. Soc. [24] State Record of NC, XXIV, 629-630.
[25a] The Document, file T44, TN Hist. Soc. [25b] State Record
of NC, XXIV, 629-630. [25c] Haywood, pp. 133,285. [25d] Land
Record, 1788-1793, p. 19. [26] Ibid., p. 10. [27] Co. Court
Minutes, A, pp. 3,17,29. [28] Deed Book, A, 207. [29] Co.
Court Minutes, A, 27. [30] Deed Book, A, 172. [31a] See TN
D.A.R. Roster. [31b] Haywood, pp. 255,257. [31c] Deed Book,
A, 315. [32] Draper MSS, 305, pp. 81,242. [33] Deed Book
A, 102. [34] Land Records, 1788-1793, p. 1. [35] Ibid., p.
25. [36a] Haywood, p. 125. [36b] State Records of NC, XXIV,
629-630. [37] Deed Book, A, 198. [38] Land Records, 1788-1793,
p. 16. [38b] The Document, file T44, TN Hist. Soc. [39] Co.
Court Minutes, A, 28. [40] Haywood, p. 243. [41] Deed Book,
A, 227. [42] Land Records, 1788-1793, p. 5. [43] Haywood,
p. 257. [44] The Tax Roll. [45a] Deed Book, A, 211. [45b]
The Tax Roll. [46] The Document, file T44, TN Hist. Soc. [47a]
Haywood, pp. 101,107. [47b] The Document, file T44, TN Hist.
Soc. [47c] Ibid. [47d] State Records of NC, XXIV, 629-630.
[48a] The Tax Roll. [48b] Deed Book, A, 179. [48c] Co. Court
Minutes, A, 7. [49a] The Tax Roll. [49b] Deed Book, A, 257.
[50] Co. Court Minutes, A, 17. [51] Land Records, 1788-1793,
p. 28. [52a] J. C. Guild, Old Times In Tennessee (Nashville:
Tavel, Eastman & Howell, 1878) p. 307 (afterward referred to
as Guild). [52b] Haywood, p. 386. [53] The Tax Roll. [54]
Land Records, 1788-1793, p. 13. [55a] Deed Book, A, 190. [55b]
Deed Book, A, 190. [55c] Land Records, 1788-1793, p. 23. [55d]
A. B. Keith, ed., The John Gray Blount Papers, I, (Raleigh:
State Dept. of Archives & History, 1952). [56] Deed Book,
A, 191; and Land Records, 1788-1793, p. 6. [57] Deed Book,
A, 192. [58a] The Tax Roll. [58b] Marriage Book, 1, p. 2.

DAVIDSON COUNTY

B

(see bibliography following)

[59] Co. Court Minutes, A, pp. 2-3. [60] Co. Court Mins., A, 36. [61] Land Records, 1788-1793, p. 3. [62] Land Records, 1788-1793, p. 22. [63] Land Records, 1788-1793, p. 6. [64] State Records of NC, XXIV, 629-30. [65] Land Records, 1788-1793, p. 5. [66a] The Tax Roll. [66b] Co. Court Minutes, A, 29. [67] The Tax Roll. [68] Co. Court Minutes, A, 29. [69] The Tax Roll. [70] Deed Book, A, 324. [71a] Family tradition, compiler's collection. [71b] Deed Book, A, 17. [71c] The Tax Roll. [71d] Deed Book, A, 33. [72] Co. Court Minutes, A, 17. [73] Land Records, 1788-1793, p. 24. [74] Family tradition, compiler's files. [75] Land Records, 1788-1793, p. 13. [76] Deed Book, A, 312. [77] The Tax Roll. [78] Haywood, p. 94. [79a] Deed Book, A, 312. [79b] Family tradition, compiler's files. [80] Haywood, p. 243. [81a] Deed Book, A, 209. [81b] Co. Court Minutes, pt. 1, pp. 3,9,17. [82] Land Record, 1788-1793, p. 3. [83] The Tax Roll. [84a] See TN D.A.R. Roster. [84b] Haywood, p. 107. [84c] The Document, file T44, TN Hist. Soc. [84d] Minutes, Committee of the Cumberland Association. [84e] Deed Book, A, 29. [84f] The Tax Roll. [84g] Draper MSS, 30S, 252-53. [85a] Marriage Book, 1, 6. [85b] The Tax Roll. [86] Marriage Book, 1, 4. [87a] Co. Court Minutes, A, 27. [87b] Will Book, I, 300. [88] The Tax Roll. [89] The Tax Roll. [90] The Tax Roll. [91] The Document, file T44, TN Hist. Soc. [92] The Document, file T44, TN Hist. Soc. [93] Deed Book, A, 333. [94] The Document, file T44, TN Hist. Soc. [95a] The Tax Roll. [95b] Deed Book, A, 245. [96] Land Records, 1788-1793, p. 25. [97] State Record of NC, XXIV, 629-30. [98] Deed Book, A, 153. [99] Haywood, p. 92. [100] Deed Book, A, 80. [101] The Document, file T44, TN Hist. Soc. [102] State Record of NC, XXIV, 629-30. [103] Land Records, 1788-1793, p. 5. [104] Land Records, 1788-1793, p. 27. [105] Land Records, 1788-1793, p. 11. [106] Land Records, 1788-1793, p. 4. [107] Haywood, p. 126. [108a] Deed Book, A, 276. [108b] Land Records, 1788-1793, p. 3. [109] Haywood, p. 89. [110] Haywood, pp. 345,414,480. [111] A. W. Putnam, History Of Middle Tennessee (Nashville: Southern Methodist Publishing House, 1859) p. 296; also, Haywood, p. 249. [112] Will Book, II, 24. [113a] Land Record, 1788-1793, p. 19. [113b] Will Book, II, 91. [114] J.G.M. Ramsey, Annals Of Tennessee, pp. 516-17; 608-11. [115a] The Document, file T44, TN Hist. Soc. [115b] Deed Book, A, 144. [115c] Haywood, p. 249. [115d] Haywood, p. 416. [115e] American State Papers, I, 555-56. [118] Haywood, p. 143. [119a] The Tax Roll. [119b] Will Book, II, 24. [120a] The Tax Roll. [120b] Haywood, p. 256. [121] Land Records, 1788-1793, p. 25. [122a] Deed Book, A, 116. [122b] Co. Court Minutes, A, 1. [123] Land Records, 1788-1793, p. 21.

DAVIDSON COUNTY

B

(see bibliography following)

[**124a**] Co. Court Minutes, A, 1. [124b] J. C. Guild, <u>Old Times In Tennessee</u> (Nashville: Tavel, Eastman & Howell, 1878) p. 307. [**125a**] John Carr, <u>Early Times In Middle Tennessee</u> (Nashville: E. Stevenson & F. A. Owen, 1857), p. 14; also Draper MSS 32s, p. 314. [125b] State Records of NC, XXIV, 629-30. [**126a**] See TN DAR Roster. [126b] The Tax Roll. [126c] TN D.A.R. Roster. [126d] Will Book, 3, 120. [**127**] The Document, file T44, TN Hist. Soc. [**128**] The Document, file T44, TN Hist. Soc. [**129a**] See TN D.A.R. Roster. [129b] The Document, file T44, TN Hist. Soc. [129c] Land Records, 1788-1793, p. 5. [129d] Co. Court Minutes, A, 1. [**130**] State Record of NC, XXIV, 629-30. [**131a**] See TN D.A.R. Roster; Haywood (p. 98) stated he was from South Carolina, and there is evidence available that several of his party were indeed from SC. [131b] Haywood, p. 98. [131c] Guild, p. 209; and, Haywood, p. 243; see also, Will Book, I, 7,59. [131d] See TN D.A.R. Roster. [**132**] See TN D.A.R. Roster. [**133**] Marriage Book, I, 3. [**134a**] Haywood, p. 241. [134b] Will Book, II, 56. [**135**] Marriage Book, I, 6. [**136**] Land Records, 1788-1793, p. 28. [**137**] Deed Book, A, 248. [**138**] The Document, file T44, TN Hist. Soc. [**139**] The Document, file T44, TN Hist. Soc. [**140**] Land Records, 1788-1793, p. 15. [**141**] Deed Book, A, 276. [**142**] Deed Book, A, 262. [**143**] Marriage Book, I, 26. [**144a**] Deed Book, A, 44. [144b] The Tax Roll. [144c] Will Book, I, 120. [**145**] The Document, file T44, TN Hist. Soc. [**146**] The Tax Roll. [**147**] Deed Book, A, 251. [**148**] Deed Book, A, 77. [**149**] Deed Book, A, 168.

C

[**1a**] John Haywood, <u>Civil And Political History Of Tennessee</u> (Nashville: Methodist Episcopal Church South Publishing House, 1823), pp. 100,101,104,107,128,129. [1b] The Document, file T44, TN Hist. Soc. [1c] Haywood, pp. 128-29. [**2a**] Deed Book, A, 35. [2b] <u>American State Papers</u>, Indian Affairs, I, 322. [**3**] Marriage Book, I, 2. [**4**] Deed Book, A, 25. [**5a**] Haywood, p. 107. [5b] The Document, file T44, TN Hist. Soc. [**6**] The Tax Roll. [**7**] The Document, file T44, TN Hist. Soc. [**8a**] Deed Book, A, 68. [8b] Deed Book, A, 249. [**9**] The Document, file T44, TN Hist. Soc. [**10**] The Document, file T44, TN Hist. Soc. [**11**] Co. Court Minutes, A, 27. [**12**] The Document, file T44, TN Hist. Soc. [**13a**] Deed Book, A, 76. [13b] Deed Book, A, 182. [**14**] Co. Court Minutes, A, 26. [**15**] Land Records, 1788-1793, p. 21. [**16**] Land Records, 1788-1793, p. 21.

DAVIDSON COUNTY

C

(see bibliography following)

[17] Land Records, 1788-1793, p. 2. [18] Land Records, 1788-1793, p. 5. [20] The Tax Roll. [21] Land Records, 1788-1793, p. 3. [22a] The Tax Roll. [22b] Co. Court Minutes, A, 27. [23] Lyman Draper MSS 30s, pp. 294-296, Wisconsin Historical Society. [24] The Tax Roll. [25] Draper, 30s, pp. 294-296. [26] Will Book, 1, p. 7. [27] Land Records, 1788-1793, p. 9. [28] The Tax Roll. [29] Deed Book, A, 266. [30] Co. Court Minutes, A, 2. [31a] See Tennessee D.A.R. Roster. [31b] Haywood, pp. 101,107. [31c] The Document, file T44, TN Hist. Soc. [31d] State Record of NC, XVI, 1025; also, XX, 241,352. [31e] Deed Book, A, 187. [31f] TN D.A.R. Roster. [32a] John Carr, Early Times In Middle Tennessee (Nashville: E. Stevenson & F. A. Owen, 1857), p. 13. [32b] Ibid. [33] State Record of NC, XXIV, 629-630. [34a] Haywood, p. 125. [34b] Haywood, p. 219. [35] Haywood, p. 139. [36] Haywood, p. 219. [37] Deed Book, A, 160. [38] Marriage Book, 1, p. 4. [39a] The Document, file T44, TN Hist. Soc. [39b] State Records of NC, XXIV, 629-30. [40] State Records of NC, XXIV, 629-630. [41] The Tax Roll. [42a] The Tax Roll. [42b] Haywood, p. 232. [43a] The Document, file T44, TN Hist. Soc. [43b] The Tax Roll. [43c] Deed Book, A, 211. [43d] Co. Court Minutes, A, 5. [44a] Haywood, p. 133. [44b] The Tax roll. [44c] John C. Guild, Old Times In Tennessee (Nashville: Tavel, Eastman & Howell, 1878), p. 307. [45] Haywood, p. 133. [46] Haywood, p. 133. [47] Guild, p. 307. [48] Deed Book, A, 312. [49] Minutes, Committee of the Cumberland Association, file T44, TN Hist. Soc. [50] Ibid. [51a] Minutes, Committee of the Cumberland Association, file T44, TN Hist. Soc. [51b] Deed Book, A, 224. [52a] The Document, file T44, TN Hist. Soc. [52b] Haywood, p. 128. [52c] Deed Book, A, 161. [53] TN Historical Commission Marker #3a-31, Nashville. [54] Deed Book, A, 236. [55] Deed Book, A, 59. [56] Co. Court Minutes, A, 27. [57] Land Records, 1788-1793, p. 23. [58] The Document, file T44, TN Hist. Soc. [59] Haywood, pp. 120,128. [60] Haywood, pp. 120,128. [61] American State Papers, Indian Affairs, I, 324; see also, Haywood, p. 276. [62a] The Tax Roll. [62b] Co. Court Minutes, A, 1. [63] Deed Book, A, 332. [64] Land Records, 1788-1793, p. 6. [65] Land Records, 1788-1793, p. 11. [66] Guild, p. 205. [67] American State Papers, Indian Affairs, I, 324. [68] Guild, p. 205; also, Haywood, pp. 369,371. [69] Land Records, 1788-1793, p. 6. [70] Land Records, 1788-1793, p. 16. [71] Co. Court Minutes, A, 25. [72] Land Records, 1788-1793, p. 26. [73] The Tax Roll. [74] Land Records, 1788-1793, p. 22. [75] Co. Court Minutes, A, 8. [76] Family file, compiler's collection. [77a] See TN D.A.R. Roster; see also, family bible in collection of the

DAVIDSON COUNTY

C

(see bibliography following)

TN Hist. Soc. [77b] Draper, 6XX(50), pp. 6-8. [77c] Family papers, compiler's file. [77d] State Record of NC, XXIV, 629-30. [78a] Haywood, p. 107. [78b] The Document, file T44, TN Hist. Soc. [78c] State Record of NC, XXIV, 629-630. [78d] Deed Book, A, 129. [78e] The Tax Roll. [78f] Haywood, p. 256. [79] Land Records, 1788-1793, p. 4. [80] Haywood, p. 143. [81] The Document, file T44, TN Hist. Soc. [82a] Family data, compiler's files. [82b] State Record of NC, XXIV, 629-630. [83] American State Papers, Indian Affairs, I, 324. [84] American State Papers, Indian Affairs, I, 324. [85] Will Book II, 34. [86] American State Papers, Indian Affairs, I, 324. [87] Will Book, II, 34. [88a] Deed Book, A, 132. [88b] Will Book, II, 34. [89] Haywood, p. 243. [90a] Deed Book, A, 314. [90b] Land Records, 1788-1793, p. 2. [91a] Family data, compiler's files. [91b] State Record of NC, XXIV, 629-630. [92] The Document, file T44, TN Hist. Soc. [93] The Tax Roll. [94a] Collins, Kentucky (1882), p. 12. [94b] Haywood, p. 129. [94c] State Record of NC, XXIV, 629-630. [95] The Document, file T44, TN Hist. Soc. [96] The Tax Roll. [97] The Document, file T44, TN Hist. Soc. [98] State Record of NC, XXIV, 629-630. [99a] Co. Court Minutes, A, 7. [99b] Ibid., p. 7. [100] Marriage Book, 1, p. 32. [101a] The Document, file T44, TN Hist. Soc. [101b] The Tax Roll. [101c] Deed Book, A, 234. [102] The Tax Roll. [103] State Record of NC, XXIV, 629-630. [104] Land Records, 1788-1793, p. 23. [105a] John Donelson's, "Journal of a voyage.." [105b] Co. Court Minutes, A, 37. [106] Marriage Book, 1, p. 1. [107] Co. Court Minutes, A, 8. [108] The Document, file T44, TN Hist. Soc. [109a] Haywood, p. 88. [109b] John Carr, Early Times In Middle Tennessee (Nashville: E. Stevenson & F. A. Owen, 1857), p. 12. [110] Deed Book, A, 111. [111] The Tax Roll. [112a] Minutes, Committee of the Cumberland Association, file T44, TN Hist. Soc. [112b] The Tax Roll. [113a] The Document, file T44, TN Hist. Soc. [113b] The Tax Roll. [114a] Deed Book, A, 215. [114b] Land Records, 1788-1793, p. 8. [115a] The Tax Roll. [115b] Deed Book, A, 311. [116] The Tax Roll. [117a] Carr, p. 7. [117b] State Record of NC, XXIV, 629-630. [118] The Tax Roll. [119] Co. Court Minutes, A, 28. [120] Deed Book, A, 70. [121a] See TN D.A.R. Roster. [121b] Deed Book, A, 214. [121c] TN D.A.R. Roster. [122a] The Document, file T44, TN Hist. Soc. [122b] Deed Book, A, 214. [123] Deed Book, A, 215. [124] Haywood, p.89. [125] Co. Court Minutes, A, 28-29. [126] The Tax Roll. [127a] The Document, file T44, TN Hist. Soc. [127b] Deed Book, A, 125. [128] Deed Book, A, 23. [129] Co. Court Minutes, A, 1. [130a] The Tax Roll. [130b] Co. Court Minutes, A, 1. [131a] Deed Book, A, 4. [131b] The Tax Roll. [131c] The Tax Roll.

DAVIDSON COUNTY

C

(see bibliography following)

[131d] Land Records, 1788-1793, p. 22. [132] State Record of NC, XXIV, 629-630. [133] Haywood, p. 107. [134] Minutes, Committee of the Cumberland Association, file T44, TN Hist. Soc. [135] American State Papers, I, 322. [136] Co. Court Minutes, A, 7. [137a] Co. Court Minutes, A, 8. [137b] American State Papers, I, 322.

D

(see bibliography following)

[1] Co. Court Minutes, A, 1. [2] Land Records, 1788-1793, p. 19. [3] The Document, file T44, TN Hist. Soc. [4] Ibid. [5] The Document, file T44, TN Hist. Soc. [6] Deed Book, A, 187. [7] Marriage Book, 1, p. 31. [8] Deed Book, A, 277. [9a] See TN DAR Roster. [9b] Deed Book, A, 266. [9c] Co. Court Minutes, A, 29. [9d] TN DAR Roster. [10] Land Records, 1788-1793, p. 19. [11] Land Records, 1788-1793, p. 16. [12] Co. Court Minutes, A, 29. [13] Co. Court Minutes, A, 37. [14] Land Records, 1788-1793, p. 21. [15a] The Document, file T44, TN Hist. Soc. [15b] Minutes, Committee of the Cumberland Association, file T44, TN Hist. Soc. [15c] Ibid. [15d] Deed Book, A, 286. [16a] The Roll. [16b] Land Records, 1788-1793, p. 4. [17a] See TN DAR Roster. [17b] Co. Court Minutes, A, 10-11. [18a] Deed Book, A, 235. [18b] The Roll. [18c] The Document, file T44, TN Hist. Soc. [19] Haywood, p. 249. [20] Haywood, p. 232. [21] The Document, file T44, TN Hist. Soc. [22] Co. Court Minutes, A, 3,9. [23] Co. Court Minutes, A, 41-42. [24] Land Records, 1788- 1793, p. 23. [25] Land Records, 1788-1793, p. 19. [26] Land Records, 1788-1793, pp. 23 & 27, respectively. [27] Land Records, 17881793, p. 28. [28a] Deed Book, A, 103. [28b] Land Records, 1788-1793, p. 10. [29] The Document, file T44, TN Hist. Soc. [30] Co. Court Minutes, A, 10-11. [31] The Roll. [32a] Haywood, p. 143. [32b] The Roll. [32c] Co. Court Minutes, A, 5. [32d] Will Book, II, 45. [33a] See TN DAR Roster. [33b] Ibid., see also, Haywood, pp. 30,98-100,104-107, 128,172,288,375,380,414. [33c] The Document, file T44, TN Hist. Soc. [33d] Draper, 32s, 310-311; and 30s, 504-509. [33e] TN DAR Roster. [34a] Haywood, pp. 100,104,107. [34b] The Roll. [34c] Deed Book, A, 103. [35a] The Roll. [35b] Deed Book, A, 143. [35c] Co. Court Minutes, A, 7. [35d] Deed Book, A, 186. [36a] Deed Book, A, 108. [36b] Land Records, 1788-1793, p. 24. [37] Land Records, 1788-1793, p. 6. [38] Deed Book, A, 3. [39] Land Records, 1788-1793, p. 2.

DAVIDSON COUNTY

D

(see bibliography following)

[40a] Family data, compiler's files. [40b] The Document, file T44, TN Hist. Soc. [40c] First Records of Davidson Co., TN Hist. Soc. [40d] The Roll [40e] Haywood, p. 253. [40f] Deed Book, A, 116. [41a] The Roll. [41b] Co. Court Minutes, A, 17. [42] Deed Book, A, 186. [43] The Document, file T44, TN Hist. Soc. [44a] The Document, file T44, TN Hist. Soc. [44b] The Roll. [44c] Deed Book, A, 186. [45a] See TN DAR Roster. [45b] Deed Book, A, 20. [45c] Deed Book, A, 184. [45d] TN DAR Roster. [46] Haywood, pp. 88,91,92. [47] Nell McNish Gambill, The Kith And Kin Of Captain James Leeper And Susan Drake, His Wife (n.p., n.d. 1946) p. 13. [48] Deed Book, A, 184. [49a] Land Records, 1788-1793, p. 11. [49b] Deed Book, A, 332. [50] Haywood, p. 143. [51] Co. Court Minutes, A, 37. [52] Co. Court Minutes, A, 27. [53] The Document, file T44, TN Hist. Soc. [54] Co. Court Minutes, A, 22. [55] Co. Court Minutes, A, 29. [56] The Roll. [57] The Roll. [58] Haywood, p. 94. [59] The Roll. [60a] The Roll. [60b] Haywood, p. 232. [60c] Co. Court Minutes, A, 17,29. [61] The Roll. [62a] The Roll. [62b] Co. Court Minutes, A, 29. [63a] Minutes, Committee of the Cumberland Association, file T44, TN Hist. Soc. [63b] Putnam, p. 295; also, Haywood, 142. See also Haywood, pp. 243,245,256. [64] Deed Book, A, 118. [65a] Family data, compiler's files. [65b] The Document, file T44, TN Hist. Soc. [65c] Minutes, Committee of the Cumberland Association, file T44, TN Hist. Soc. [65d] Ibid. [65e] State Record of NC, XXIV, 629-630. [65f] Deed Book, A, 119. [66a] Haywood, p. 125. [66b] Haywood, p. 142. [67] Will Book, II, 24. [68a] Haywood, p. 125. [66b] Haywood, p. 142. [69] Marriage Book, 1, p. 4. [70] The Document, file T44, TN Hist. Soc. [71] Co. Court Minutes, A, 29. [72] Deed Book, A, 170. [73] Guild, p. 307; also, Territorial Papers Of The United States, IV, 196.

E

(see bibliography following)

[74] American State Papers, I, 324. [75] Deed Book, A, 73. [76a] The Roll. [76b] Co. Court Minutes, A, 1. [76c] Deed Book, A, 173. [77] Haywood, p. 245. [78] Co. Court Minutes, A, 1. [79a] The Document, file T44, TN Hist. Soc. [79b] Deed Book, A, 173. [80] The Roll. [81] The Roll. [82] The Roll. [83] Deed Book, A, 113. [84] Land Records, 1788-1793, p. 2. [85] Land Records, 1788-1793, p. 26. [86] American State Papers, I, 323. [87a] Family tradition. [87b] State Records of NC, XXIV, 629-630.

DAVIDSON COUNTY

E

(see bibliography following)

[87c] Co. Court Minutes, A, 37. [88] Land Records, 1788-1793, p. 15. [89a] Family data, compiler's files. [89b] State Records of NC, XXIV, 629-630. [90] Land Records, 1788-1793, p. 24. [91] Haywood, p. 233. [92] Haywood, p. 233. [93a] The Document, file T44, TN Hist. Soc. [93b] Haywood, p. 136. [93c] State Record of NC, XXIV, 629-630. [94a] The Document, file T44, TN Hist. Soc. [94b] Minutes, Committee of the Cumberland Association, file T44, TN Hist. Soc. [94c] State Records of NC, XXIV, 629-630. [94d] The Roll. [94e] Deed Book, A, 172. [95] Family data; compiler's file. [96a] Family data; compiler's files. [96b] The Document, file T44, TN Hist. Soc. [96c] First Records of Davidson Co., TN Hist. Soc. [96d] Ibid. [96e] Haywood, p. 127. [97] Land Records, 1788-1793, p. 19. [98] Land Records, 1788-1793, p. 28. [99] The Roll. [100] The Roll. [101] Haywood, p. 238; see also, pp. 205,320. [102] The Document, file T44, TN Hist. Soc. [103a] The Document, file T44, TN Hist. Soc. [103b] State Record of NC, XXIV, 629-630. [104] The Document, file T44, TN Hist. Soc. [105] Marriage Book, 1, 32. [106] Haywood, p. 240. [107] Deed Book, A, 248. [108] Marriage Book, 1, 4. [109] American State Papers, I, 323. [110] Guild, p. 318; see also, Haywood, p. 340. [111a] See TN DAR Roster. [111b] The Roll. [111c] TN DAR Roster. [112a] See TN DAR Roster. [112b] The Document, file T44, TN Hist. Soc. [112c] Minutes, Committee of the Cumberland Association, file T44, TN Hist. Soc. [112d] Deed Book, A, 27. [112e] The Roll. [112f] op. cit. Minutes, Committee of the Cumberland Association. [112g] TN DAR Roster. [112h] Will Book, Vol. 4-6, pp. 235-236. [112i] TN DAR Roster. [113] Deed Book, A, 320. [114] The Roll.

F

(see bibliography following)

[1] State Records of NC, XXIV, 629-630. [2] Deed Book, A, 323. [3] Land Records, 1788-1793, p. 9. [4] Ibid. [5a] Minutes, Committee of the Cumberland Association, file T44, TN Hist. Soc. [5b] Deed Book, A, 73. [6a] See TN DAR Roster. [6b] Land Records, 1788-1793, p. 5. [6c] Deed Book, A, pp. 135,251. [6d] TN DAR Roster. [7] TN DAR Roster. [8] Deed Book, A, 98. [9a] Haywood, pp. 94-95. [9b] Haywood, p. 317. [10a] Guild, p. 307. [10b] Territorial Papers, IV, 196. [11a] See TN DAR Roster. [11b] Land Records, 1788-1793, p. 28. [11c] TN DAR Roster. [12] Co. Court Minutes, A, 17. [13] The Roll.

DAVIDSON COUNTY

F

(see bibliography following)

[14] Deed Book, A, 122. [15] The Document, file T44, TN Hist. Soc. [16a] The Document, file T44, TN Hist. Soc. [16b] Minutes, Committee of the Cumberland Association, file T44, TN Hist. Soc. [16c] Ibid. [16d] Ibid. [16e] Haywood, p. 238. [16f] American State Papers, I, 322. [16g] Haywood, p. 238. [17a] Family tradition, compiler's files. [17b] State Record of NC, XXIV, 629-30. [18] Deed Book, A, 64. [19a] Minutes, Committee of the Cumberland Association, file T44, TN Hist. Soc. [19b] Deed Book, A, 33. [20] Land Record, 1788-1793, p. 3. [21] The Roll. [22a] Haywood, p. 230. [22b] Co. Court Minutes, A, 17,28. [22c] Co. Court Minutes, A, 38. [23a] The Roll. [23b] Deed Book, A, 51. [23c] Land Records, 1788-1793, p. 3. [23d] Ibid., p. 10; see also, p. 5, for land purchase on White's Creek, 1788. [24] The Roll. [25] Deed Book, A, 286. [26a] Deed Book, A, 49. [26b] Deed Book, A, 154,165. [27a] TN D.A.R. Roster. [27b] Land Records, 1788-1793, p. 2. [27c] TN D.A.R. Roster. [27d] Ibid. [28a] See TN D.A.R. Roster. [28b] Ibid. [28c] Land Records, 1788-1793, p.2. [28d] TN D.A.R. Roster. [29] Haywood, p. 256. [30a] Family Tradition, compiler's files. [30b] The Document, file T44, TN Hist. Soc. [30c] State Record of NC, XXIV, 629-30. [30d] The Roll. [30e] Deed Book, A, 249. [31] State Record of NC, XXIV, 629-30. [32] Deed Book, A, 154. [33a] See TN D.A.R. Roster. [33b] Carr, p. 19. [33c] State Record of NC, XXIV, 629-30. [33d] Co. Court Minutes, A, 9. [33e] TN D.A.R. Roster. [34a] Carr, p. 7. [34b] Deed Book, A, 124-25. [35a] Land Records, 1788-1793, p. 10. [35b] Co. Court Minutes, A, 8. [36a] Co. Court Minutes, A, 9. [36b] Ibid., p. 10. [37a] Haywood, p. 227. [37b] The Roll. [38] Putnam, p. 161. [39a] Haywood, p. 95. [39b] Family data, compiler's files. [39c] Minutes, Committee of the Cumberland Association, file T44, TN Hist. Soc. [39d] Ibid. [39e] State Record of NC, XXIV, 629-30. [39f] Deed Book, A, 183. [39g] Ibid., pp. 124-25. [40a] Family tradition, compiler's files. [40b] The Document, file T44, TN Hist. Soc. [41a] The Document, file T44, TN Hist. Soc. [41b] State Record of NC, XXIV, 629-30. [42a] Deed Book, A, 73. [42b] The Roll. [43] American State Papers, I, 322. [44] The Roll. [45] The Document, file T44, TN Hist. Soc.

G

(see bibliography following)

[1] State Record of NC, XXIV, 629-30. [2] State Record of NC, XXIV, 629-30. [3] State Record of NC, XXIV, 629-30. [4] The Roll. [5] State Record of NC, XXIV, 629-30.

DAVIDSON COUNTY

G

(see bibliography following)

[6] Co. Court Minutes, A, 1. [7] Land Records, 1788-1793, p. 18. [8] Co. Court Minutes, A, 22. [9] Land Records, 1788-1793, p. 16. [10] Marriage Book, 1, p. 6. [11a] The Document, file T44, TN Hist. Soc. [11b] Co. Court Minutes, A, 19. [12] State Record of NC, XXIV, 629-630. [13] State Record of NC, XXIV, 629-630. [14] Land Record, 1788-1793, p. 7. [15] American State Papers, I, 324; see also, Haywood, pp. 369-371. [16] The Document, file T44, TN Hist. Soc. [17] The Roll. [18] State Record of NC, XXIV, 629-630. [20a] Deed Book, A, 284. [20b] The Roll. [21a] Deed Book, A, 215. [21b] Land Records, 1788-1793, p. 5. [22] State Record of NC, XXIV, 629-630. [23] Co. Court Minutes, A, 18. [24a] Donelson's Journal. [24b] The Document, file T44, TN Hist. Soc. [24c] Minutes, Committee of the Cumberland Association, file T44, TN Hist. Soc. [24d] State Record of NC, XXIV, 629-630. [24e] The Roll. [24f] Co. Court Minutes, A, 8. [24h] American State Papers, I, 322; see also, Haywood, p. 341, which gives different date. [24i] Land Record, 17881793, p. 25. [25] Minutes, Committee of the Cumberland Association, file T44, TN Hist. Soc. [26] Haywood, p. 227. [27] Land Record, 1788-1793, p. 4. [28a] State Record of NC, XXIV, 629-630; also, Haywood, p.219. [28b] Will Book, II, 57. [29a] Haywood, p. 129. [29b] Ibid. [30] Haywood, p. 131. [31] Land Record, 1788-1793, p. 23. [32a] Co. Court Minutes, A, 1. [32b] Deed Book, A, 110,152. [33] The Roll. [34] Land Record, 1788-1793, p. 10. [35] The Document, file T44, TN Hist. Soc. [36] The Document, file T44, TN Hist. Soc. [37] Deed Book, A, 87. [38] Land Record, 1788-1793, p. 7. [39] Haywood, p. 141. [40] Co. Court Minutes, A, 1. [41a] The Roll. [41b] Co. Court Minutes, A, 3. [41c] Deed Book, A, 278. [42] Land Records, 1788-1793, p. 16. [43] Land Records, 1788-1793, p. 28. [44a] Haywood, pp. 125-130. [44b] Minutes, Committee of the Cumberland Association, file T44, TN Hist. Soc.; see also, Will Book, I, 296. [45] The Document, file T44, TN Hist. Soc. [46] Land Records, 1788-1793, p. 7. [47] The Roll. [48] Haywood, p. 89. [49a] The Document, T44, TN Hist. Soc. [49b] Minutes, Committee of the Cumberland Association, file T44, TN Hist. Soc. [49c] Ibid. [49d] Deed Book, A, 161. [50a] Haywood, p. 128. [50b] State Record of NC, XXIV, 629-630. [51] Haywood, p. 102. [52a] Marriage Book, 1, p. 32. [52b] Will Book, II, 34. [53] Marriage Book, 1, p. 47. [54] Haywood, p. 102. [55a] Haywood, p. 102. [55b] The Document, file T44, TN Hist. Soc. [55c] Minutes, Committee of the Cumberland Association, file T44, TN Hist. Soc. [55d] Deed Book, A, 33. [56] Land Records, 1788-1793, p. 25. [57] Land Records, 1788-1793, p. 17. [58a] Minutes, Committee of the Cumberland Association, file T44, TN Hist. Soc.

DAVIDSON COUNTY

G

(see bibliography following)

[58b] Deed Book, A, 165. [59] The Tax Roll. [60] The Tax Roll. [61a] Land Records, 1788-1793, p. 5. [61b] Ibid., p. 23. [62] Land Records, 1788-1793, p. 23. [63] The Document, file T44, TN Hist. Soc. [64] The Document, file T44, TN Hist. Soc. [65] The Document, file T44, TN Hist. Soc. [66] Wills & Inventories, I, 26. [67a] Co. Court Minutes, A, 1. [67b] Deed Book, A, 255. [68a] The Document, file T44, TN Hist. Soc. [68b] State Record of NC, XXIV, 629-30. [69] Land Records, 1788-1793, p. 16. [70] Deed Book, A, 354. [71] The Document, file T44, TN Hist. Soc. [72] Co. Court Minutes, A, 28. [73] The Document, file T44, TN Hist. Soc. [74] The Document, file T44, TN Hist. Soc. [75] Deed Book, A, 110,152. [76] The Tax Roll. [77] Marriage Book, 1, p. 5. [78a] See TN D.A.R. Roster. [78b] The Document, file T44, TN Hist. Soc. [78c] TN D.A.R. Roster. [79] Land Records, 1788-1793, p. 3. [80] Minutes, Committee of the Cumberland Association, file T44, TN Hist. Soc.

H

(see bibliography following)

[1] Land Records, 1788-1793, p. 20. [2] Haywood, p. 241. [3a] See TN D.A.R. Roster. [3b] Deed Book, A, 121. [4] Land Records, 1788-1793, p. 10. [5] Ramsey, p. 483; see also, Haywood, p. 249. [6] Co. Court Minutes, A, 28. [7a] Co. Court Minutes, A, 28. [7b] Will Book, II, 4. [8] Haywood, p. 340. [9] The Document, file T44, TN Hist. Soc. [10] The Document, file T44, TN Hist. Soc. [11] State Record of NC, XXIV, 629-30. [12] Land Records, 1788-1793, p. 5. [13a] The Tax Roll. [13b] Haywood, p. 243. [15] Haywood, pp. 230,243. [16] The Document, file T44, TN Hist. Soc. [17a] Haywood, p. 227. [17b] Haywood, pp. 230,243. [18] Land Records, 1788-1793, p. 13. [19] Deed Book, A, 182. [20] Haywood, p. 244. [21] The Document, file T44, TN Hist. Soc. [22a] Minutes, Committee of the Cumberland Association, file T44, TN Hist. Soc. [22b] Ibid. [22c] Co. Court Minutes, A, 10. [22d] Ibid., p. 9. [23a] Land Records, 1788-1793, p. 2. [23b] Co. Court Minutes, A, 9. [24] Deed Book, A, 280. [25] Deed Book, A, 280. [26a] The Tax Roll. [26b] Co. Court Minutes, A, 4. [26c] Deed Book, A, 149,168. [27a] Co. Court Minutes, A, 29. [27b] Co. Court Minutes, A, 30. [28] Land Records, 1788-1793, p. 4. [29] Deed Book, A, 226. [30a] The Tax Roll. [30b] Deed Book, A, 310. [31] Carr, p. 7. [32a] Haywood, p. 95. [32b] Ramsey, p. 194. [33] Land Records, 1788-1793, p. 28. [34] The Tax Roll. [35] Land Records, 1788-1793, p. 28. [36] The Tax Roll. [37a] See TN DAR Roster. [37b] Deed Book, A, 298. [37c] TN DAR Roster. [37d] Ibid. [38] The Roll. [39] The Document, file T44, TN Hist. Soc. [40a] The Document, file T44, TN Hist. Soc. [40b] The Tax Roll. [41a] Co. Court Minutes, A, 3. [41b] Ibid., p. 2. [41c] Ibid., p. 7.

DAVIDSON COUNTY

H

(see bibliography following)

[41d] Land Records, 1788-1793, p. 23. [42a] Land Records, 1788-1793, p. 1. [42b] Deed Book, A, 262. [43] Deed Book, A, 248. [44] Land Records, 1788-1793, p. 5. [45] Marriage Book, 1, p. 3. [46] The Document, file T44, TN Hist. Soc. [47] Minutes, Committee of the Cumberland Association, file T44, TN Hist. Soc. [48a] The Roll. [48b] Co. Court Minutes, A, 5. [49] State Record of NC, XXIV, 629-630. [50] Land Records, 1788-1793, p. 20. [51] Land Records, 1788-1793, p. 23. [52] Marriage Book, 1, p.4. [53a] Family tradition; compiler's file. [53b] Minutes, Committee of the Cumberland Association, file T44, TN Hist. Soc. [53c] State Records of NC, XXIV, 629-630. [53b] The Roll. [54a] Minutes, Committee of the Cumberland Association, file T44, TN Hist. Soc. [54b] Ibid. [54c] Ibid. [54d] Ibid. [54e] Co. Court Minutes, A, 23. [55] Haywood, p. 227. [56] Donelson's Journal; also, Haywood, p. 99. [57] Ibid. [58] Land Records, 1788-1793, p. 28. [59] The Roll. [60] Minutes, Committee of the Cumberland Association. [61a] Haywood, pp. 88,219. [61b] The Document, file T44, TN Hist. Soc. [61c] Minutes, Committee of the Cumberland Association, file T44, TN Hist. Soc. [62] The Roll. [63] American State Papers, I, 322. [64] Family notes, compiler's file. [65a] Land Records, 1788-1793, p. 26. [65b] Deed Book, A, 352-354. [65c] Will Book, II, 20. [66] Land Record, 1788-1793, p. 3. [67] The Document, file T44, TN Hist. Soc. [68] Carr, p. 16. [69] Deed Book, A, 162. [70] Land Records, 1788-1793, p. 10. [71] The Document, file T44, TN Hist. Soc. [72a] Haywood, p. 235. [72b] The Roll. [73a] Carr, p. 12; also, Haywood, p. 235. [73b] State Record of NC, XXIV, 629-630. [74] Deed Book, A, 335. [75] Co. Court Minutes, A, 14. [76] Marriage Book, 1, p. 32. [77] The Document, file T44, TN Hist. Soc. [78] The Document, file T44, TN Hist. Soc. [79] Deed Book, A, 335. [80] Co. Court Minutes, A, 29. [81a] See TN DAR Roster. [81b] Deed Book, A, 31. [81c] The Roll. [81d] Deed Book, A, pp. 206,308-309. [81e] Haywood, p. 230. [81f] Nashville Whig Newspaper, Sept. 18, 1819. [81g] TN DAR Roster. [82a] Haywood, p. 143. [82b] Deed Book, A, 210. [82c] Co. Court Minutes, A, 3. [82d] Ibid., p. 2. [82e] Will Book, II, 7. [82f] Ibid., p. 20. [83] Haywood, p. 243. [84a] Haywood, p. 98. [84b] State Record of NC, XXIV, 629-630. [84c] Deed Book,A,118. [84d] The Roll. [84e] Will Book,II,13. [85] Marriage Book, 1, p. 3. [86a] The Roll. [86b] Deed Book, A, 112. [87] Land Records, 1788-1793, p. 15. [88] Deed Book, A, 147,166. [89] The Document, file T44, TN Hist. Soc. [90] The Document, file T44, TN Hist. Soc. [91] The Document, file T44, TN Hist. Soc. [92a] Haywood, p. 133; also, Guild, p. 93.

DAVIDSON COUNTY

H

(see bibliography following)

[92b] Putnam, p. 157. [93a] The Document, file T44, TN Hist. Soc. [93b] Co. Court Minutes, A, 14. [94] Land Records, 1788-1793, p. 23. [95] Co. Court Minutes, A, 17. [96a] Donelson's Journal; also, Haywood, pp. 99,150. [96b] The Roll. [97] The Roll. [98] Haywood, p. 107. [99] Co. Court Minutes, A, 27. [100] Co. Court Minutes, A, 17. [101] Guild, p. 307. [102] Land Records, 1788-1793, p. 6. [103] Haywood, p. 139. [104a] Minutes, Committee of the Cumberland Association, file T44, TN Hist. Soc. [104b] Land Records, 1788-1793, p. 21. [105] Land Records, 1788-1793, p. 27. [106] American State Papers, I, 322. [107] The Roll. [108] American State Papers, I, 322. [109a] Deed Book, A, 47. [109b] Co. Court Minutes, A, 1. [109c] Deed Book, A, 247. [109d] Will Book, II, 3. [110a] Haywood, p. 224. [111] Deed Book, A, 47. [112a] Co. Court Minutes, A, 4. [112b] Deed Book, A, 329-330,334. [112c] Haywood, p. 243. [113] Co. Court Minute, A, 17. [114] See TN DAR Roster. [115a] Deed Book, A, 177; see also, TN DAR Roster. [115b] Hill family records, compiler's file. [116] The Roll. [117] The Roll. [118] Land Records, 1788-1793, p. 22. [119] The Roll. [120] The Roll. [121] The Document, file T44, TN Hist. Soc. [122] The Document, file T44, TN Hist. Soc. [123] The Document, T44, TN Hist. Soc. [124a] The Document, T44, TN Hist. Soc. [124b] State Record of NC, XXIV, 629-630. [124c] The Roll. [125a] Family date, compiler's file. [125b] The Document, T44, TN Hist. Soc. [126b] Minutes, Committee of the Cumberland Association, file T44, TN Hist. Soc. [125d] Ibid. [125e] State Record of NC, XXIV, 629-630. [125f] The Roll. [125g] Land Record, 1788-1793, p. 13. [125h] Deed Book, A, 208. [126] Haywood, p. 235. [127a] Haywood, p. 89. [127b] Arnow, Seedtime On The Cumberland, p. 219. [127c] Family tradition, compiler's file. [127d] The Document, T44, TN Hist. Soc. [127e] State Record, XXIV, 629-630. [127f] Minutes, Committee of the Cumberland Association, T44, TN Hist. Soc. [127g] Ibid. [127h] Ibid. [127i] Land Records, 1788-1793, p. 22. [128a] Haywood, p. 95. [128b] Co. Court Minutes, A, 3. [129] Haywood, pp. 245-246,248. [130a] Deed Book, A, pp. 82,320. [130b] Ibid., pp. 14-15. [130c] Deed Book, A, 327-328. [130d] Co. Court Minutes, A, 9. [130e] Marriage Book, 1, p.46. [131] Land Records, 1788-1793, p. 3. [132a] Land Records, 1788-1793, p. 10. [132b] Deed Book, A, 155. [133a] Haywood, pp. 94-95. [133b] The Document, T44, TN Hist. Soc. [134a] Minutes, Committee of the Cumberland Association, file T44, TN Hist. Soc. [134b] Ibid. [134c] Deed Book, A, 111. [134d] The Roll. [135] The Roll. [136a] The Roll. [136b] Marriage Book, 1, p. 4.

DAVIDSON COUNTY

H

(see bibliography following)

[137a] Family tradition, compiler's files. [137b] State Record of NC, XXIV, 629-30. [138] Marriage Book, 1, 3. [139] Deed Book, A, 250. [140a] Haywood, pp. 133-34. [140b] Kelly, Children Of Nashville, p. 42. [141] Guild, p. 307. [142a] The Document, T44, TN Hist. Soc.. [142b] Haywood, p. 133. [142c] State Record of NC, XXIV, 629-30. [143] See TN D.A.R. Roster. [144a] Haywood, p. 143. [144b] Deed Book, A, 350. [144c] The Tax Roll. [144d] Deed Book, A, 244. [146] Marriage Book, 1, 3. [147a] See TN D.A.R. Roster. [147b] Deed Book, A, 342. [147c] TN D.A.R. Roster. [148a] The Tax Roll. [148b] Deed Book, A, 342 & 279, respectively. [149a] Land Records, 1788-1793, p. 25. [149b] Co. Court Minutes, A, 29. [150] Family tradition, compiler's files. [151] The Tax Roll. [152] Deed Book, A, 260. [153] Land Records, 1788-1793, p. 10. [154] Haywood, p. 134. [155] Haywood, pp. 134-35, 223. [156] The Tax Roll. [157a] Minutes, Committee of the Cumberland Association, file T44, TN Hist. Soc. [157b] Deed Book, A, 94. [158a] Family tradition, compiler's files. [158b] State Record of NC, XXIV, 629-30. [158c] Haywood, p. 381. [159] Land Records, 1788-1793, p. 19. [160] Co. Court Minutes, A, 28. [161] Marriage Book, 1, 4. [162] Deed Book, A, 333. [163] Haywood, p. 91. [164] Land Records, 1788-1793, p. 3. [165] Haywood, p. 255. [166] Wills & Inventories, I, 95. [167a] Deed Book, A, 230 & 289, respectively. [167b] Wills & Inventories, I, 95. [168] Land Records, 1788-1793, p. 26. [169] The Tax Roll. [170] Land Records, 1788-1793, p. 3. [171] Land Records, 1788-1793, p. 19. [172a] See TN D.A.R. Roster. [172b] Ibid. [172c] Carr, p. 13. [172d] TN D.A.R Roster.

I

(see bibliography following)

[1] The Tax Roll. [2] Deed Book, A, 351. [3] Haywood, p. 142. [4] Co. Court Minutes, A, 29. [5] Deed Book, A, 334. [6] Deed Book, A, 316. [7] Deed Book, A, 98.

J

(see bibliography following)

[1a] Co. Court Minutes, A, 2. [1b] Haywood, p. 257. [2] Deed Book, A, 303. [3] The Document, file T44, TN Hist. Soc. [4] Deed Book, A, 303. [5a] The Tax Roll. [5b] Deed Book, A, 180. [6] The Tax Roll. [7] Land Records, 1788-1793, p. 1. [8a] Haywood, p. 143.

210

DAVIDSON COUNTY

J

(see bibliography following)

[8b] The Tax Roll. [8c] Deed Book, A, 99. [9] Deed Book,
A, 315. [10] The Document, file T44, TN Hist. Soc. [11]
The Document, file T44, TN Hist. Soc. [12] Land Records,
1788-1793, p. 22. [13] Deed Book, A, 212. [14] Co. Court
Minutes, A, 33. [15] Family tradition, compiler's files.
[16] Deed Book, A, 16. [17a] Donelson's Journal. [17b]
Haywood, pp. 102-03, 107. [17c] The Document, file T44,
TN Hist. Soc. [17d] Wills & Inventories, I, 11. [17e]
State Record of NC, XXIV, 629-30; see also, Haywood, p.
125; & Carr, p. 12. [18] Haywood, pp. 102-03. [19] Land
Records, 1788-1793, p. 16. [20a] Haywood, p. 107. [20b]
Family tradition, compiler's files; see also, Carr, p.
13; Haywood, p. 109. [20c] Haywood, p. 127. [20d] State
Records of NC, XXIV, 629-30. [21] Carr, p. 13. [22] Land
Records, 1788-1793, p. 14, (assignee of the heirs of Andrew
Littleworth). [23] The Tax Roll. [24] Land Records,
1788-1793, p. 24. [25] Land Records, 1788-1793, p. 23.
[26a] The Document, file T44, TN Hist. Soc. [26b] Haywood,
p. 135. [26c] Minutes, Committee of the Cumberland
Association, file T44, TN Hist. Soc. [26d] Ibid. [26e]
State Record of NC, XXIV, 629-30. [27] Land Records,
1788-1793, p. 23. [28] Land Records, 1788-1793, p. 2.
[29] Haywood, p. 126. [30] Co. Court Minutes, A, 8. [31]
State Record of NC, XXIV, 629-30. [32a] Family tradition,
compiler's files. [32b] The Document, file T44, TN Hist.
Soc. [32c] Haywood, p. 143. [32d] Marriage Book, 1, 1.
[34a] Family tradition, compiler's collection. [34b] The
Document, file T44, TN Hist. Soc. [34c] Minutes, Committee
of the Cumberland Association, file T44, TN Hist. Soc.
[34d] Ibid. [34e] Deed Book, A, 119-20. [34g] Co. Court
Minutes, A, 1. [34h] Deed Book, A, 323. [35a] Deed Book,
A, 114. [35b] Deed Book, A, 279. [36] Haywood, p. 245.
[37] Co. Court Minutes, A, 28. [38] State Records of NC,
XXIV, 629-30. [39] The Tax Roll. [40] Minutes, Committee
of the Cumberland Association, file T44, TN Hist. Soc.
[41] Land Records, 1788-1793, p. 24. [42] Carr, p. 13.
[43] State Record of NC, XXIV, 629-30. [44] Deed Book,
A, 307. [45] Minutes, Committee of the Cumberland
Association, file T44, TN Hist. Soc. [46] Deed Book, A,
276. [47] State Record of NC, XXIV, 629-30. [48] The
Tax Roll. [49a] The Tax Roll. [49b] Land Records,
1788-1793, p. 5. [50] American State Papers, I, 232. [51]
Haywood, p. 245; also, Putnam, p. 295. [52] Deed Book,
A, 44. [53] Land Records, 1788-1793, pp. 19,28. [54a]
The Tax Roll. [54b] Haywood, pp. 248-49; also, Ramsey,
p. 482. [54c] Land Records, 1788-1793, p. 17. [54d] Deed
Book, A, 259.

DAVIDSON COUNTY

K

(see bibliography following)

[1] Deed Book, A, 75. [2] Land Records, 1788-1793, p. 6. [3] American State Papers, I, 323. [4] American State Papers, I, 322. [5] The Document, file T44, TN Hist. Soc. [6a] Family tradition, compiler's file. [6b] Minutes, Committee of the Cumberland Association, file T44, TN Hist. Soc. [6c] Ibid. [6d] State Record of NC, XXIV, 629-30. [7] State Record of NC, XXIV, 629-30. [8] Haywood, p. 127. [9] Haywood, p. 256. [10a] Carr, p. 14; also, Haywod, p. 131. [10b] State Record of NC, XXIV, 629-30. [11] Carr, p. 14. [12a] Family tradition, compilers' files. [12b] State Record of NC, XXIV, 629-30. [12c] Will Book, I, 63. [13a] Family tradition, compiler's file. [13b] State Record of NC, XXIV, 629-30. [13c] Wills & Inventories, I, 39. [13b] Ibid., p. 58. [14] Haywood, p. 125. [15a] See TN DAR Roster; also, Tax Roll. [15b] TN D.A.R. Roster. [16] Guild, p. 307. [17] Guild p. 307. [18] The Document, file T44, TN Hist. Soc. [19a] First Records of Davidson Co., p. 478, TN Hist. Soc. [19b] Co. Court Minutes, A, 9,29. [20] Co. Court Minutes, A, 44. [21] Co. Court Minutes, A, 3. [22] Haywood, p. 125. [23a] See TN D.A.R. Roster. [23b] Carr, p. 7. [23c] Co. Court Minutes, A, 9. [23d] Deed Book, A, 164. [23e] TN D.A.R. Roster. [24] The Document, file T44, TN Hist. Soc. [25] The Document, file T44, TN Hist. Soc. [26] Haywood, p. 256. [27] Could this Maj. Kirkpatrick mentioned in Overmountain Men, by Alderman, be the same Capt. Kirkpatrick mentioned in Haywood, p. 256? [28a] See TN D.A.R. Roster; also, Davidson Co. Tax Roll. [28b] Marriage Book, 1, 3. [28c] Deed Book, A, 282. [29] Haywood, p. 91. [30] Haywood, p. 91. [31] Deed Book, A, 267.

L

(see bibliography following)

[1] Land Records, 1788-1793, p. 21. [2] Land Records, 1788-1793, p. 26. [3] The Tax Roll. [4] Marriage Book, 1, 31. [5] Co. Court Minutes, A, 25. [6] Marriage Book, 1, 2. [7a] The Tax Roll. [7b] Co. Court Minutes, A, 16. [7c] Deed Book, A, 69, 74. [7d] Deed Book, A, 177. [7e] Land Records, 1788-1793, p. 19. [8] Haywood, p. 107. [9] Deed Book, A, 241. [10] Land Records, 1788-1793, p. 16. [11] Haywood, p. 126. [12a] State Record of NC, XXIV, 629-30. [12b] Will Book, I, 4. [13] State Record of NC, XXIV, 629-30. [14] Land Records, 1788-1793, p. 21. [15] Deed Book, A, 259. [16] Guild, p. 307. [17a] Co. Court Minutes, A, 3.

DAVIDSON COUNTY

L

(see bibliography following)

[17b] Land Records, 1788-1793, p. 14. [18] Deed Book, A, 251. [19a] The Document, file T44, TN Hist. Soc. [19b] Minutes, Committee of the Cumberland Association, file T44, TN Hist. Soc. [19c] State Record of NC, XXIV, 629-630; see also, Louise Lynch, Loose Records Of Williamson Co., TN, p. 96. [20] Land Records, 1788-1796, p. 24. [21] Land Records, 1788-1793, p. 22. [22] Land Records, 1788-1793, p. 28. [23] The Document, file T44, TN Hist. Soc. [24a] The Document, file T44, TN Hist. Soc. [24b] See James Leeper. [24c] Deed Book, A, 306. [25a] See TN DAR Roster. [25b] The Document, file T44, TN Hist. Soc. [25c] Draper, 32s, p. 314; see also, Gambill, Kith And Kin. [26] Deed Book, A, 306. [27] Gambill, Kith And Kin..p. 14. [28] Minutes, Committee of the Cumberland Association, file T44, TN Hist. Soc. [29] Kelly, Children Of Nashville, p. 12; also, Haywood, p. 219 which refers to him as "Lafour." [30] Land Record, 1788-1793, p. 19. [36] The Roll. [37] Deed Book, A, 47. [38a] See TN DAR Roster. [38b] Deed Book, A, 216. [39] Deed Book, A, 323. [40] The Roll. [41] Wills & Inventories, I, 96. [42] Putnam, p. 161. [43] The Roll. [44a] Haywood, p. 88. [44b] Carr, p. 7. [44c] The Document, file T44, TN Hist. Soc. [44d] Minutes, Committee of the Cumberland Association, file T44, TN Hist. Soc. [44e] Ibid. [44f] Ibid. [44g] Deed Book, A, 216. [44h] Co. Court Minutes, A, 26 [45] Deed Book, A, 57. [46] Land Records, 1788-1793, p. 14. [47a] Deed Book, A, 178. [47b] Will Book, II, 17. [48] Deed Book, A, 195. [49a] Family tradition, compiler's file. [49b] The Document, T44, TN Hist. Soc. [49c] Minutes, Committee of the Cumberland Association, file T44, TN Hist. Soc. [50a] Haywood, pp. 198,232. [50b] Deed Book, A, 156. [50c] The Roll. [50d] Haywood, p. 232. [50e] Co. Court Minutes, A, p. 5. [51] Co. Court Minutes, A, 11-12. [52] Wills & Inventories, I, 293. [53] Deed Book, A, 256. [54] See TN DAR Roster. [55] The Roll. [56] Haywood, p. 256. [57] Deed Book, A, 188. [58] Deed Book, A, 23. [59] The Document, file T44, TN Hist. Soc. [60a] Family tradition, compiler's file. [60b] The Document, file T44, TN Hist. Soc. [60c] State Record of NC, XXIV, 629-630. [60d] Co. Court Minutes, A, 9,17. [60e] Land Records, 1788-1793, p. 20. [61] Co. Court Minutes, A, 3,9. [62] The Roll. [63a] Deed Book, A, 263. [63b] Co. Court Minutes, A, 8. [64a] Minutes, Committee of the Cumberland Association, file T44, TN Hist. Soc. [64b] Deed Book, A, pp. 25 & 312, respectively. [64c] Haywood, p. 223. [64d] The Roll. [65] Co. Court Minutes, A, 44. [66a] The Document, file T44, TN Hist. Soc. [66b] Minutes, Committee of the Cumberland Association, file T44, TN Hist. Soc. [66c] Deed Book, A, 233. [67a] Haywood, pp. 131-132.

L

(see bibliography following)

[67b] Draper, 6xx, p. 50-12. [67c] State Record of NC, XXIV, 629-30. [68a] Will Book, II, 63,274. [68b] Ibid. [69a] Minutes, Committee of the Cumberland Association, file T44, TN Hist. Soc. [69b] Co. Court Minutes, A, 29. [70] Co. Court Minutes, A, 29. [71] State Record of NC, XXIV, 629-30. [72] Minutes, Committee of the Cumberland Association, file T44, TN Hist. Soc. [73] Carr, p. 13. [74] The Tax Roll. [75a] Co. Court Minutes, A, 38. [75b] Ibid., p. 29. [76] The Tax Roll. [77] Haywood, p. 91. [78a] The Tax Roll. [78b] Deed Book, A, 217. [79a] The Document, file T44, TN Hist. Soc. [79b] Minutes, Committee of the Cumberland Association, file T44, TN Hist. Soc. [80a] Land Records, 1788-1793, p. 17. [80b] Deed Book, A, 43; see also, TN D.A.R. Roster. [81] Deed Book, A, 10.

M

(se bibliography following)

[1a] The Document, file T44, TN Hist. Soc. [1b] Minutes, Committee of the Cumberland Association, file T44, TN Hist. Soc. [1c] Ibid. [1d] Ibid. [1e] Ibid. [2a] Family tradition, compiler's files. [2b] The Document, file T44, TN Hist. Soc. [2c] Deed Book, A, 159. [2d] State Record of NC, XXIV, 629-30. [3a] The Document, file T44, TN Hist. Soc. [3b] State Record of NC, XXIV, 629-30. [4] The Tax Roll. [5] The Tax Roll. [6] The Tax Roll. [7] The Tax Roll. [8] Co. Court Minutes, A, 17. [9a] Carr, pp. 13,19. [9b] Minutes, Committee of the Cumberland Association, file T44, TN Hist. Soc. [9c] Ibid. [9d] Ibid. [9e] Co. Court Minutes, A, 17,28-29. [10a] The Tax Roll. [10b] Will Book, I, 107. [11] Deed Book, A, 288. [12] Deed Book, A, 261. [13] The Document, file T44, TN Hist. Soc. [14a] The Tax Roll. [14b] Co. Court Minutes, A, 29. [15] Land Records, 1788-1793, p. 21. [16] Co. Court Minutes, A, 5. [17] Deed Book, A, 126. [18] Minutes, Committee of the Cumberland Association, file T44, TN Hist. Soc. [19] Guild, p. 307. [20a] Land Records, 1788-1793, p. 2. [20b] Haywood, p. 345. [21a] Haywood, p. 340. [21b] Guild, p. 307; also, Haywood, p. 370. [22a] Haywood, p. 405. [22b] Will Book, II, 74. [23] See Thomas McCrory. [24a] Guild, p. 307. [24b] Will Book, I, 44. [25] Land Records, 1788-1793, p. 2. [26] Land Records, 1788-1793, p. 1. [27] Deed Book, A, 346. [28] Wills & Inventories, I, 92. [29a] Co. Court Minutes, A, 3. [29b] Wills & Inventories, I, 92. [30a] The Document, file T44, TN Hist. Soc. [30b] The Tax Roll. [30c] Deed Book, A, 245. [30d] Marriage Book, I, 31.

DAVIDSON COUNTY

M

(see bibliography following)

[**31a**] The Document, file T44, TN Hist. Soc. [31b] The Tax
Roll. [**32**] Wills & Inventories, I, 93. [**33**] Land Records,
1788-1793, p. 28. [**34**] Land Records, 1788-1793, p. 23.
[**35**] The Roll. [**36a**] Land Records, 1788-1793, p. 9. [**36b**]
Deed Book, A, 249. [**37**] Co. Court Minutes, A, 117. [**38**]
Deed Book, A, 32. [**39a**] TN DAR Roster. [39b] Deed Book,
A, 344. [39c] TN DAR Roster. [**40**] Co. Court Minutes, A,
16. [**41**] The Roll. [**42a**] Minutes, Committee of the Cumberland Association, file T44, TN Hist. Soc. [42b] First Records
of Davidson Co., p. 478, TN Hist. Soc. [42c] The Roll.
[42d] Deed Book, A, 162. [**43**] American State Papers, I,
324. [**44a**] Minutes, Committee of the Cumberland Association,
file T44, TN Hist. Soc. [44b] The Roll. [44c] Deed Book,
A, 34. [**45a**] Minutes, Committee of the Cumberland Associa-
tion, file T44, TN Hist. Soc. [44b] The Roll. [44c] Deed
Book, A, 34. [**45a**] Minutes, Committee of the Cumberland
Association, file T44, TN Hist. Soc. [45b] The Roll. [45c]
Deed Book, A, 151,187. [45d] Will Book, II, 44. [**46**] The
Roll. [**47**] Deed Book, A, 277. [**48**] Ramsey, p. 482; see
also, Haywood, p. 256. [**49a**] Deed Book, A, 254. [49b]
The Roll. [**50a**] TN DAR Roster. [50b] The Roll. [50c] Deed
Book, A, 131. [50d] Deed Book, A, 183-84. [50e] TN DAR
Roster. [**51**] Deed Book, A, 253,261. [**52**] The Roll. [**53**]
The Roll. [**54a**] Deed Book, A, 177. [54b] The Roll. [**55**]
The Roll. [**56**] Marriage Book, 1, 31. [**57a**] Deed Book,
A, 177. [57b] Deed Book, A, 173-74. [**58a**] The Document,
file T44, TN Hist. Soc. [58b] Deed Book, A, 164. [58c]
Guild, p. 307; see also, American State Papers, I, 323.
[**59**] Deed Book, A, 169. [**60**] The Document, file T44, TN
Hist. Soc. [**61a**] The Document, file T44, TN Hist. Soc.
[61b] State Record of NC, XXIV, 629-30. [**62**] The Document,
file T44, TN Hist. Soc. [**63**] The Document, file T44, TN
Hist. Soc. [**64a**] Co. Court Minutes, A, 1. [64b] Haywood,
p. 256. [**65**] The Roll. [**66**] The Roll. [**67**] Land Records,
1788-1793, p. 10. [**68**] The Roll. [**69**] The Roll. [**70**]
The Document, file T44, TN Hist. Soc. [**71**] The Roll. [**72**]
Co. Court Minutes, A, 17. [**73**] The Document, file T44,
TN Hist. Soc. [**74a**] See TN DAR Roster. [74b] The Roll.
[74c] Deed Book,A, 16. [74d] TN DAR Roster. [**75**] Co. Court
Minutes, A, 1. [**76**] Co. Court Minutes, A, 11-12. [**77a**]
Land Records, 1788-1793, p. 14. [77b] Co. Court Minutes,
A, 17. [**78**] Co. Court Minutes, A, 27. [**79a**] Haywood, p.
126. [79b] Haywood, p. 131. [**80**] Deed Book, A, 169. [**81a**]
Family tradition, compiler's files. [81b] State Record
of NC, XXIV, 629-30. [81c] Co. Court Minutes, A, 1. [**82a**]
Haywood, pp. 88-93. [82b] The Document, file T44, TN Hist.
Soc. [82c] Carr, pp. 14,19; see also, Haywood, pp. 96-7;
108,218,248,366,449-50,481. [82d] Minutes, Committee of
the Cumberland Association, file T44, TN Hist. Soc. [82e]
Ibid. [82f] Co. Court Minutes, A, 9. [**83**] Minutes, Committee
of the Cumberland Association, file T44, TN Hist. Soc.

DAVIDSON COUNTY

M

(see bibliography following)

[84] Deed Book, A, 225. [85] The Roll. [86] Wills & Inventories, I, 2. [87a] Minutes, Committee of the Cumberland Association, file T44, TN Hist. Soc. [87b] Deed Book, A, 238. [88] Marriage Book, 1, p. 4. [89] Marriage Book, 1, p. 31. [90] The Roll. [91a] The Roll. [91b] Deed Book, A, 126. [92] Deed Book, A, 210. [93] Chancery Court Records, Williamson Co., TN, June 24, 1824 (John & Geo. Mayfield vs. Wm. Haggard). [94] Co. Court Minutes, A, 27. [95] Marriage Book, 1, p. 4. [96] Co. Court Minutes, A, 17. [97a] The Roll. [97b] Co. Court Minutes, A, 1. [97c] Ibid., p. 11. [97d] Deed Book, A, 185. [98a] The Document, file T44, TN Hist. Soc. [98b] Haywood, p. 135. [98c] Minutes, Committee of the Cumberland Association, file T44, TN Hist. Soc. [98d] The Roll. [98e] Haywood, p. 246. [98f] Deed Book, A, 11. [98g] Deed Book, A, 163. [98h] Deed Book, A, 288 & 317, respectively. [99a] Deed Book, A, 31. [99b] Co. Court Minutes, A, 29. [100a] Land Records, 1788-1793, p. 16. [100b] Haywood, p. 230. [101] American State Papers, I, 323. [102] Land Records, 1788-1793, p. 24. [103] American Historical Magazine & Tennessee Historical Quarterly, 1896-1902, Vol. II, 90; see also, Haywood, p. 222. [104a] Carr, p. 7. [104b] Minutes, Committee of the Cumberland Association, file T44, TN Hist. Soc. [105] Carr., p. 49. [106] Deed Book, A, 209. [107a] Haywood, p. 134. [107b] Minutes, Committee of the Cumberland Association, file T44, TN Hist. Soc. [107c] Haywood, p. 134. [108a] Minutes, Committee of the Cumberland Association, file T44, TN Hist. Soc. [108b] Deed Book, A, 16. [109] Minutes, Committee of the Cumberland Association, file T44, TN Hist. Soc. [110] The Document, file T44, TN Hist. Soc. [111a] Carr, p. 7. [111b] Haywood, p. 134. [112a] The Document, file T44, TN Hist. Soc. [112b] Deed Book, A, 148. [112c] Haywood, p. 244. [113] Haywood, p. 139. [114] State Records of NC, XXIV, 629-630. [115a] The Document, file T44, TN Hist. Soc. [115b] State Record of NC, XXIV, 629-630. [115c] Will Book, II, 63. [116a] Co. Court Minutes, A, 27. [116b] Ibid., p. 22. [117] Deed Book, A, 170. [118] Haywood, p. 127. [119] Will Book, II, 63. [120] Co. Court Minutes, A, 17. [121] Family tradition, compiler's file. [122] Haywood, p. 249. [123a] Family tradition, compiler's file. [123b] State Records of NC, XXIV, 629-630. [123c] The Roll. [123d] Haywood, p. 405. [124a] Family tradition, compiler's files. [124b] Haywood, p. 125. [124c] State Record of NC, XXIV, 629-630. [124d] Will Book, I, 16. [124e] Deed Book, A, 145. [124f] Haywood, p. 340. [124g] Co. Court Minutes, 1810. [125] Chancery Court Records, Williamson Co., TN, June 24, 1824 (John & Geo. Mayfield vs. Wm. Haggard).

DAVIDSON COUNTY

M

(see bibliography following)

[126] Margaret, widow of Southerlin Mayfield, when later making final settlement of the estate is mentioned as having married John Gibson. [127a] Deed Book, A, 96-7. [127b] Ramsey, p. 482; see also, Haywood, pp. 248-49. [127c] Will Book, II, 48. [128] Deed Book, A, 123. [129] The Roll. [130] Co. Court Minutes, A, 20. [131] Deed Book, A, 317. [132a] The Roll. [132b] Land Records, 1788-1793, p. 10. [133a] Deed Book, A, 40. [133b] Deed Book, A, 317. [133c] Co. Court Minutes, A, 1. [134] Minutes, Committee of the Cumberland Association, file T44, TN Hist. Soc. [135] Deed Book, A, 223. [136] The Roll. [137] Deed Book, A, 287. [138a] Carr, p. 12; see also, Haywood, p. 125. [138b] State Record of NC, XXIV, 629-30. [139] Haywood, pp. 142,256. [140] Land Records, 1788-1793, p. 3. [141] The Document, file T44, TN Hist. Soc. [142] The Document, file T44, TN Hist. Soc. [143] Marriage Book, 1, 5. [144] Wills & Inventories, I, 47,77. [145] Marriage Book, 1, 4. [146a] The Roll. [146b] Deed Book, A, 156. [147] Land Record, 1788-1793, p. 19. [148a] The Document, file T44, TN Hist. Soc. [148b] Minutes, Committee of the Cumberland Association, file T44, TN Hist. Soc. [148c] Ibid. [148d] First Records of Davidson Co., p. 478, TN Hist. Soc. [148e] Deed Book, A, 34. [148f] Deed Book, A, 68,223. [148g] Deed Book, A, pp. 68 & 237, respectively. [148h] The Roll. [149a] Deed Book, A, 136-39. [149b] Land Records, 1788-1793, p. 3; see also, Deed Book, A, 226,260,263-65,336, 345. [149c] Family tradition, compiler's files. [150a] See TN DAR Roster; also, Haywood, p. 91 (see also, pp. 72, 219). [150b] Donelson's Journal. [150c] The Document, file T44, TN Hist. Soc. [150d] State Record of NC, XXIV, 629-30. [150e] Co. Court Minutes, A, 20. [150f] TN DAR Roster. [150g] TN DAR Roster. [151] Minutes, Committee of the Cumberland Association, file T44, TN Hist. Soc. [152] Deed Book, A, 212. [153] Carr, p. 14; see also, Haywood, p. 131. [154] The Roll. [155] The Document, file T44, TN Hist. Soc. [156] The Document, file T44, TN Hist. Soc. [157] The Document, file T44, TN Hist. Soc. [158] Deed Book, A, 209. [159a] The Document, file T44, TN Hist. Soc. [159b] Deed Book, A, 46. [159c] Will Book, I, 47. [159d] Will Book, II, 62. [160] The Document, file T44, TN Hist. Soc. [161] Deed Book, A, 346. [162] The Document, file T44, TN Hist. Soc. [163] Deed Book, A, 145. [164a] The Document, file T44, TN Hist. Soc. [164b] Deed Book, A, 113-14. [165a] The Roll. [165b] Deed Book, A, 48. [166] The Document, file T44, TN Hist. Soc. [167] The Document, file T44, TN Hist. Soc. [168] Land Record, 1788-1793, p. 10. [169] Marriage Book, 1, 47. [170] Co. Court Minutes, A. 33. [171] The Doc-

217

DAVIDSON COUNTY

M

(see bibliography following)

ument, file T44, TN Hist. Soc. [172] Co. Court Minutes, A, 20. [173] State Record of NC, XXIV, 629-630. [174a] Land Record, 1788-1793, p. 1. [174b] Ibid., p. 23. [175] The Document, file T44, TN Hist. Soc. [176] The Document, file T44, TN Hist. Soc. [177] Wills & Inventories, I, 1. [178a] The Roll. [178b] Land Records, 1788-1793, p. 21. [179a] Haywood, pp. 98,218. [179b] Minutes, Committee of the Cumberland Association, file T44, TN Hist. Soc. [179c] First Records of Davidson Co., TN Hist. Soc. [179d] State Record of NC, XXIV, 629-630. [179e] Deed Book, A, 270. [179f] Land Records, 1788-1793, p. 5. [179g] Guild, p. 307. [180] Haywood, p. 139. [181a] Haywood, p. 98. [181b] State Record of NC, XXIV, 629-630. [181c] Deed Book, A, 162,269. [182] Deed Book, A, 227. [183] Haywood, p. 142. [184] Deed Book, A, 196. [185a] The Document, file T44, TN Hist. Soc. [185b] Haywood, p. 126. [186] Land Records, 1788-1793, p. 22. [187] The Roll. [188a] See TN DAR Roster. [188b] Co. Court Minutes, A, 38. [188c] See TN DAR Roster. [189] The Document, file T44, TN Hist. Soc. [190] Marriage Book, 1, p. 26. [191] Haywood, p. 126. [192] The Roll. [193a] Marriage Book, 1, p. 4. [193b] Deed Book, A, 331. [194] Deed Book, A, 350. [195] Land Record, 1788-1793, p. 26.

N

(see bibliography following)

[1] Haywood, p. 240. [2a] The Roll. [2b] Land Record, 17881793, p. 4. [2c] Co. Court Minutes, A, 5. [2d] Marriage Book, 1, p. 32. [3] The Roll. [4a] Co. Court Minutes, A, 3,9. [4b] Haywood, p. 340. [5a] Donelson's Journal. [5b] Minutes, Committee of the Cumberland Association, file T44, TN Hist. Soc. [5c] The Roll. [6] Haywood, p. 245. [7] Carr, p. 13. [8a] See TN DAR Roster. [8b] Carr, p. 7. [8c] Carr, pp. 12,13; also, Haywood, p. 125 (see also) p. 95. [8d] State Record of NC, XXIV, 629-630. [8e] TN DAR Roster. [9] The Roll. [10] Minutes, Committee of the Cumberland Association, file T44, TN Hist. Soc. [11] Family data; compiler's files; also, Draper, 6xx96, p. 32. [12] Robertson fam. data; compiler's files. [13] Donelson's Journal. [14] Wills & Inventories, I, 300. [15] Wills & Inventories, I, 302. [16] Wills & Inventories, I, 300. [17] Wills & Inventories, I, 300. [18] Wills & Inventories, I, 300. [19] Co. Court Minutes, A, 39. [20] Haywood, p. 128. [21] Wills & Inventories, I, 11. [22] Donelson's Journal.

DAVIDSON COUNTY

N

(see bibliography following)

[23] Deed Book, A, 246. [24a] Land Records, 1788-1793, p. 2. [24b] Co. Court Minutes, A, 1. [24c] Marriage Book, 1, 3. [24d] Co. Court Minutes, A, 17. [24e] Deed Book, A, 179. [25] Marriage Book, 1, 46. [26a] Deed Book, A, 21. [26b] The Roll. [27] Co. Court Minutes, A, 1. [28] Deed Book, A, 147. [29] Co. Court Minutes, A, 7. [30] The Document, file T44, TN Hist. Soc. [31] Deed Book, A, 133. [32] Land Record, 1788-1793, p. 28. [33] The Document, file T44, TN Hist. Soc. [34] The Roll. [35] State Record of NC, XXIV, 629-30. [36] American State Papers, I, 322. [37a] Family tradition; compiler's files. [37b] Minutes, Committee of the Cumberland Association, file T44, TN Hist. Soc. [37c] State Record of NC, XXIV, 629-30. [37d] Deed Book, A, 108. [38] Haywood, p. 142. [39] Haywood, p. 142. [40] Haywood, p. 142. [41] Haywood, p. 243. [42] Haywood, pp. 142, 256. [43] The Document, file T44, TN Hist. Soc. [44] Co. Court Minutes, A, 9.

O

(see bibliography following)

[1] Land Records, 1788-1793, p. 24. [2] Land Records, 1788-1793, p. 25. [3] Guild, p. 307. [4] The Roll. [5a] Marriage Book, 1, 4. [5b] Co. Court Minutes, A, 4. [6] Land Records, 1788-1793, p. 21. [7] Wills & Inventories, I, 3. [8] The Roll. [9] Co. Court Minutes, A, 28. [10] Land Records, 1788-1793, p. 22. [11] The Roll. [12a] Haywood, pp. 95-96. [12b] Minutes, Committee of the Cumberland Association, file T44, TN Hist. Soc. [12c] Ibid. [12d] Ibid. [12e] State Record of NC, XXIV, 629-30. [12f] Deed Book, A, 167. [12g] The Roll. [12h] Haywood, p. 142. [12i] Will Book, II, 17. [13a] Land Records, 1788-1793, p. 25. [13b] Co. Court Minutes, A, 18. [14] The Roll. [15] The Roll. [16] The Document, file T44, TN Hist. Soc. [17] Co. Court Minutes, A, 8,17.

219

DAVIDSON COUNTY

P

(see bibliography following)

[1] Land Records, p. 23. [2] Carr, p.12. [3a] Land Records, 1788-1793, p. 20. [3b] Ibid., p. 28. [4] Land Records, 1788-1793, p. 23. [5] Land Records, 1788-1793, p. 29. [6] The Document, file T44, TN Hist. Soc. [7] Land Records, 1788-1793, p. 10. [8] Haywood, p. 101. [9] The Roll. [10a] The Roll. [10b] Co. Court Minutes, A, 4. [11a] Will of Lewis Payne (Wills & Inventories, I, 26). [11b] Deed Book, A, 217. [11c] The Roll. [12] Land Records, 1788-1793, p. 2. [13a] Deed Book, A, 76. [13b] The Roll. [13c] American State Papers, I, 324. [14] The Roll. [15] Haywood, p. 237. [16] Deed Book, A, 147. [17a] Deed Book, A, 147. [17b] The Roll. [18] Deed Book, A, 37. [19] Land Records, 1788-1793, p. 4. [20] Land Records, 1788-1793, p. 27. [21] The Document, file T44, TN Hist. Soc. [22] Buchanan data; compiler's files. [23] The Document, file T44, TN Hist. Soc. [24] State Record of NC, XXIV, 629-30. [25] Haywood, p. 126. [26] Deed Book, A, 193. [27a] The Document, file T44, TN Hist. Soc. [27b] The Roll. [28] Land Records, 1788-1793, p. 4. [29a] Land Records, 1788-1793, p. 25. [29b] Will Book, II, 85. [30] Haywood, p. 126; see also, State Records of NC, XXIV, 629-30, for Legislative Act granting his heirs land. [31] Haywood, p. 237. [32] The Roll. [33] The Document, file T44, TN Hist. Soc. [34a] Deed Book, A, 109. [34b] Ibid. [35] Deed Book, A, 302. [36] Arnow, Flowering Of The Cumberland, p. 240. [37a] Deed Book, A, 36-37. [37b] Land Records, 1788-1793, p. 14. [38a] The Roll. [38b] Co. Court Minutes, A, 12. [39] The Document, file T44, TN Hist. Soc. [40a] Donelson's Journal; see also, Haywood, p. 107. [40b] State Record of NC, XXIV, 629-30. [41] State Record of NC, XXIV, 629-30. [42a] See TN DAR Roster. [42b] Haywood, p. 125. [42c] Will Book, I, 45. [42d] TN DAR Roster. [43] Co. Court Minutes, A, 1,4. [44] Land Records, 1788-1793, p. 27. [45] Land Records, 1788-1793, p. 17. [46] Deed Book, A, 197. [47] Deed Book, A, 230. [48] Territorial Papers, IV, 996. [49] The Document, file T44, TN Hist. Soc. [50a] Family tradition, compiler's files. [50b] State Record of NC, XXIV, 629-30. [50c] Marriage Book, I, 6. [51] Land Records, 1788-1793, p. 21. [52] Co. Court Minutes, A, 29. [53] Co. Court Minutes, A, pp. 8 & 28, respectively. [54a] The Document, file T44, TN Hist. Soc. [54b] Haywood, pp. 230,243. [55a] Minutes, Committee of the Cumberland Association, file T44, TN Hist. Soc. [55b] First Records of Davidson Co., p. 478, TN Hist. Soc. [55c] Deed Book, A, 234. [55d] The Roll. [55e] Co. Court Minutes, A, 17,28. [56] Co. Court Minutes, A, 17. [57] Co. Court Minutes, A, 28. [58] The Roll. [59] Land Records, 1788-1793, p. 2. [60a] Minutes, Committee of the Cumberland Association, file T44, TN Hist. Soc. [60b] Haywood, pp. 142-43. [61] Haywood, p. 227. [62a] The Document, file T44, TN Hist. Soc.

DAVIDSON COUNTY

P

(see bibliography following)

[62b] Deed Book, A, 143. [63] Land Records, 1788-1793, p. 28. [64] Land Records, 1788-1793, p. 28.

Q

(see bibliography following)

[1a] The Document, file T44, TN Hist. Soc. [1b] Haywood, p. 130. [1c] State Record of NC, XXIV, 629-630. [1d] Minutes, Committee of the Cumberland Association, file T44, TN Hist. Soc. [2] Land Records, 1788-1793, p. 19.

R

(see bibliography following)

[1] The Document, file T44, TN Hist. Soc. [2] The Document, file T44, TN Hist. Soc. [3a] Haywood, pp. 88,96-98,124-125,142, 231-232,238-240,249,366,368-370,382,384. [3b] Ibid. [3c] Minutes, Committee of the Cumberland Association, file T44, TN Hist. Soc. [4] Haywood, p. 240. [5] The Document, file T44, TN Hist. Soc. [6] Haywood, p. 142. [7] Land Records, 1788-1793, p. 28. [8] The Roll. [9] Draper, 30s,81, p. 242. [10] Draper, 30s,81,p. 242. [11a] Family tradition; compiler's file. [11b] Carr, p. 13. [11c] Minutes, Committee of the Cumberland Association, file T44, TN Hist. Soc. [11d] State Record of NC, XXIV, 629-630. [11e] Ramsey, p. 482; see also, Haywood, pp. 243,256. [11f] Land Records, 1788-1793, p. 19. [12a] Family notes; compiler's file. [12b] Minutes, Committee of the Cumberland Association, file T44, TN Hist. Soc. [12c] Deed Book, A, 107. [12d] The Roll. [12e] Co. Court Minutes, A, 17,29. [13] Deed Book, A, 26. [14a] Draper MSS 55,61. [14b] The Roll. [14c] Will Book, I, 69. [15a] Family tradition, compiler's collection. [15b] State Record of NC, XXIV, 629-630. [16] The Document, file T44, TN Hist. Soc. [17] The Document, file T44, TN Hist. Soc. [18a] The Document, file T44, TN Hist. Soc. [18b] Deed Book, A, 39. [19a] Minutes, Committee of the Cumberland Association, file T44, TN Hist. Soc. [19b] Ibid. [19c] State Record of NC, XXIV, 629-630. [19d] The Roll. [20] The Document, file T44, TN Hist. Soc. [21] The Roll. [22] The Roll. [23a] Deed Book, A, 121-122. [23b] Will Book, II, 80. [24a] Minutes, Committee of the Cumberland Association, file T44, TN Hist. Soc. [24b] First Records of Davidson Co., p. 478, TN Hist. Soc. [25] Family tradition, in the

DAVIDSON COUNTY

R

(see bibliography following)

compiler's files. [26] Land Records, 1788-1793, p. 27. [27] The Document, file T44, TN Hist. Soc. [28] The Document, file T44, TN Hist. Soc. [29] Carr, p. 13. [30] Haywood, p. 127. [31] The Document, file T44, TN Hist. Soc. [32] Minutes, Committee of the Cumberland Association, file T44, TN Hist. Soc. [33a] Haywood, p. 127. [33b] State Record of NC, XXIV, 629-30. [34] Haywood, pp. 235,243. [35] Haywood, pp. 106-07. [36] Haywood, p. 133. [37] Land Records, 1788-1793, p. 5. [38a] Will Book, II, 5. [38b] Co. Court Minutes, A, 31-32. [39a] Deed Book, A, 313. [39b] Co. Court Minutes, A, 1,5. [40a] Minutes, Committee of the Cumberland Association, file T44, TN Hist. Soc. [40b] Co. Court Minutes, A, 31-32. [40c] Family tradition, compiler's files. [40d] Will Book, II, 5. [41a] Family tradition, compiler's file. [41b] State Record of NC, XXIV, 629-30. [41c] Haywood, pp. 223-24; see also, pp. 138,218,243. [42] Haywood, p. 240. [43] Featherstonehaugh, Excursion, I, 205. [44a] See TN DAR Roster. [44b] Co. Court Minutes, A, 29. [44c] TN DAR Roster. [45] Haywood, p. 230. [46] The Document, file T44, TN Hist. Soc. [47] Co. Court Minutes, A, 31-32. [48a] The Roll. [48b] Co. Court Minutes, A, 4. [49] Deed Book, A, 211. [50] Deed Book, A, 238. [51] Deed Book, A, 354. [52a] Deed Book, A, 304. [52b] The Roll. [53] Family tradition, compiler's files. [54a] See TN DAR Roster. [54b] Haywood, p. 256. [54c] The Roll. [54d] Will Book, II, 77. [54e] TN DAR Roster. [55] Deed Book, A, 34. [56] Carr, p. 16. [57] Deed Book, A, 303. [58] Deed Book, A, 303. [59a] See TN DAR Roster. [59b] The Document, file T44, TN HIst. Soc. [59c] State Record of NC, XXIV, 629-30. [59d] The Roll. [59e] Deed Book, A, 11. [59f] American State Papers, I, 323. [59g] TN DAR Roster. [59h] Family tradition, compiler's files. [59i] TN DAR Roster. [60] Haywood, p. 128. [61] State Record of NC, XXIV, 629-30. [62a] Nashville Banner newspaper, Nov. 23, 1921; see also, Haywood, pp. 343,402. [62b] Will Book, 3-4, July 15, 1816. [63] Haywood, p. 386. [64] The Roll. [65a] Family tradition, compiler's file: see also, Haywood, p. 95. [65b] Ramsey, p. 194. [65c] Minutes, Committee of the Cumberland Association, file T44, TN Hist. Soc. [65d] Ibid. [65e] State Record of NC, XXIV, 629-30. [65f] Haywood, p. 230; see also, Deed Book, A, 79, which mentions his "heirs." [65g] Wills & Inventories, I, 53. [66] Haywood, p. 245; see also, Nashville Daily News, Sept. 27, 1902, p. 14, which gives the site of his grave. [67a] The Roll. [67b] Haywood, p. 383. [68] Co. Court Minutes, A, 9-10. [69] Land Records, 1788-1793, p. 26. [70] Haywood, p. 236.

DAVIDSON COUNTY

R

(see bibliography following)

[71] Land Records, 1788-1793, p. 19. [72] Marriage Book, 1, 5. [73] Haywood, p. 235. [74] Co. Court Minutes, A, 4. [75] Deed Book, A, 64. [76] Land Records, 1788-1793, p. 11. [77a] Deed Book, A, 182. [77b] The Roll. [77c] Deed Book, A, 182. [78] Wills & Inventories, I, 77. [79] Land Records, 1788-1793, p. 2. [80] Land Records, 1788-1793, p. 11. [81] Deed Book, A, 302. [82a] The Document, file T44, TN Hist. Soc. [82b] State Record of NC, XXIV, 629-30. [82c] The Roll. [82d] Co. Court Minutes, A, 17. [82e] Deed Book, A, 174. [83a] Haywood, p. 98. [83b] The Document, file T44, TN Hist. Soc. [83c] State Record of NC, XXIV, 629-30. [83d] The Roll. [84] The Roll. [85] Donelson's Journal. [86] Co. Court Minutes, A, 10. [87] Land Records, 1788-1793, p. 9. [88] The Roll. [89] Co. Court Minutes, A, 17,28. [90] Haywood, p. 91. [91] Deed Book, A, 344. [92] Deed Book, A, 210. [93] Marriage Book, 1, 47. [94] The Document, file T44, TN Hist. Soc. [95a] The Document, file T44, TN Hist. Soc. [95b] Land Records, 1788-1793, p. 9. [96] Co. Court Minutes, A, 4.

S

(see bibliography following)

[1] Minutes, Committee of the Cumberland Association, file T44, TN Hist. Soc. [2] Land Records, 1788-1793, p. 19. [3] Co. Court Minutes, A, 28. [4] Co. Court Minutes, A, 28. [5] Deed Book, A, 49. [6a] Minutes, Committee of the Cumberland Association, file T44, TN Hist. Soc. [6b] Deed Book, A, 12; see also, p. 68. [6c] Haywood, p. 416. [7] Haywood, pp. 139, 380. [8] Land Record, 1788-1793, p. 10. [9] Deed Book, A, 64. [10a] Deed Book, A, 341. [10b] Co. Court Minutes, A, 17. [10c] Wills & Inventories, I, 24. [11] Deed Book, A, 55. [12] The Document, file T44, TN Hist. Soc. [13a] The Roll. [13b] Deed Book, A, 115. [14a] Land Records, 1788-1793, p. 16. [14b] Deed Book, A, 115. [15] Deed Book, A, 57. [16] State Record of NC, XXIV, 629-30. [17] Land Record, 1788-1793, p. 25. [18] State Record of NC, XXIV, 629-30. [19] Co. Court Minutes, A, 29. [20] Deed Book, A, 250. [21] Deed Book, A, 54. [22a] Land Records, 1788-1793, p. 4. [22b] Co. Court Minutes, A, 14. [22c] Land Records, 1788-1793, p. 12. [23a] Co. Court Minutes, A, 6. [23b] Ibid., p. 1. [23c] Haywood, p. 361. [24a] Haywood, p. 143. [24b] State Record of NC, XXIV, 629-30. [24c] Deed Book, A, 150. [24d] Guild, p. 307. [25] State Record of NC, XXIV, 629-30. [26] Haywood, p. 237.

DAVIDSON COUNTY

S

(see bibliography following)

[27a] The Document, file T44, TN Hist. Soc. [27b] Deed Book, A, 181. [27c] The Roll. [27d] Deed Book, A, 126. [28] Deed Book, A, 181. [29a] The Document, file T44, TN Hist. Soc. [29b] The Roll. [29c] Deed Book, A, 242. [30a] Deed Book, A, 181. [30b] The Roll. [30c] Deed Book, A, 181. [30d] Land Records, 1788-1793, p. 13. [30e] Co. Court Minutes, A, 18. [31] The Document, file T44, TN Hist. Soc. [32] The Roll. [33] Co. Court Minutes, A, 7. [34a] Deed Book, A, 175. [34b] Co. Court Minutes, A, 29. [35a] Haywood, pp. 94-5. [35b] Land Records, 1788-1793, p. 3. [36a] The Document, file T44, TN Hist. Soc. [36b] Minutes, Committee of the Cumberland Association, file T44, TN Hist. Soc. [36c] Ibid. [36d] American State Papers, I, 323. [37] Putnam, p. 161. [38] Co. Court Minutes, A, 42. [39a] The Document, file T44, TN Hist. Soc. [39b] The Document, file T44, TN Hist. Soc. [39e] State Record of NC, XXIV, 629-30. [39f] The Roll. [40] The Roll. [41a] Minutes, Committee of the Cumberland Association, file T44, TN Hist. Soc. [41b] Ibid. [41c] Deed Book, A, 41. [42] Co. Court Minutes, A, 28. [43a] The Roll. [43b] Deed Book, A, 289. [43c] Co. Court Minutes, A, 142. [44a] See TN DAR Roster. [44b] Co. Court Minutes, A, 28. [44c] Deed Book, A, 153. [44d] Haywood, p. 257. [45] Deed Book, A, 285. [46] Deed Book, A, 155. [47a] Haywood, p. 235. [47b] Deed Book, A, 159. [47c] Co. Court Minutes, A, pp. 8,17,28. [48] The Document, file T44, TN Hist. Soc. [49] The Document, file T44, TN Hist. Soc. [50] Land Records, 1788-1793, p. 7. [51a] Haywood, p. 125. [51b] State Record of NC, XXIV, 629-30. [52a] Minutes, Committee of the Cumberland Association, file T44, TN Hist. Soc. [52b] The Roll. [53] Land Records, 1788-1793, p. 3. [54] Haywood, p. 134. [55] Land Records, 1788-1793, p. 11. [56] The Document, file T44, TN Hist. Soc. [57a] Land Records, 1788-1793, p. 25. [57b] Co. Court Minutes, A, 29. [58a] Deed Book, A, 130. [58b] Wills & Inventories, I, 83. [58c] Will Book, II, 63. [59] Deed Book, A, 318. [60] Deed Book, A, 318. [61] The Document, file T44, TN Hist. Soc. [62] Deed Book, A, 74. [63a] Co. Court Minutes, A, 10. [63b] See James Thompson's Deed, Book B, 242, for these relationships. [64] The Roll. [65] Marriage Book, I, 3. [66] Land Records, 1788-1793, p. 13. [67] Land Records, 1788-1793, p. 3. [68] Land Records, 1788-1793, p. 24. [69] Co. Court Minutes, A, 15. [70] First Records of Davidson Co., p. 478, TN Hist. Soc. [71a] The Roll. [71b] Deed Book, A, 186. [71c] Deed Book, A, 86. [72] Haywood, p. 88. [73] Co. Court Minutes, A, 19. [74] The Roll. [75] Land Records, 1788-1793, p. 19. [76] Marriage Book, 1, 3. [77] Co. Court Minutes, A, 17. [78] The Document, T44, TN Hist. Soc. [79] The Roll. [80] Haywood, p. 243. [81] Co. Court Minutes, A, 17. [82a] Marriage Book, 1, 2. [82b] Land Records, 1788-1793, p. 19.

DAVIDSON COUNTY

S

(see bibliography following)

[83] Minutes, Committee of the Cumberland Association, file T44, TN Hist. Soc. [84a] Haywood, pp. 94-5. [84b] Minutes, Committee of the Cumberland Association, file T44, TN Hist. Soc. [84c] State Record of NC, XXIV, 629-30. [85a] Haywood, p. 223. [85b] Deed Book, A, 306. [85c] Haywood, pp. 103, 137, 218, 319, 330, 386. [86] The Roll. [87] Land Record, 1788-1793, p. 54. [88] State Record of NC, XXIV, 629-30. [89] Land Record, 1788-1794, p. 4. [90] Land Record, 1788-1793, p. 5. [91] The Roll. [92] The Roll. [93] The Roll. [94] Haywood, p. 256. [95] Co. Court Minutes, A, 29. [96a] The Document, file T44, TN Hist. Soc. [96b] Minutes, Committee of the Cumberland Association, T44, TN Hist. Soc.. [97] Haywood, p. 243. [98] Deed Book, A, 61. [99] The Roll. [100] Haywood, p. 227. [101] Haywood, p. 232. [102] Deed Book, A, 167. [103] Deed Book, A, 169. [104] Land Records, 1788-1793, p. 19. [105a] Minutes, Committee of the Cumberland Association, file T44, TN Hist. Soc. [105b] State Record of NC, XXIV, 629-30. [105c] _American State Papers_, I, 324. [106] Haywood, pp. 49, 88-90. [107] Land Records, 1788-1793, p. 28. [108] Land Records, 1788-1793, p. 10. [109] Haywood, p. 91. [110a] Haywood, pp. 88, 129. [110b] The Document, file T44, TN Hist. Soc. [111] Putnam, p. 296; (Haywood, p. 249, says the killed were 2 sons of Stovall.) [112] Donelson's Journal. [113a] Donelson's Journal. [113b] Haywood, p. 224. [113c] Co. Court Minutes, A, 27. [113d] The Roll. [113e] Co. Court Minutes, A, 7. [114] State Record of NC, XXIV, 629-30. [115a] The Roll. [115b] Deed Book, A, 113. [116a] Haywood, pp. 98,126. [116b] The Document, file T44, TN Hist. Soc. [116c] State Record of NC, XXIV, 629-30. [116d] The Roll. [116e] Deed Book, A, 290. [117a] The Document, file T44, TN Hist. Soc. [117b] The Roll. [118a] The Document, file T44, TN Hist. Soc. [118b] Haywood, pp. 125-26. [118c] State Record of NC, XXIV, 629-30. [119a] Wills & Inventories, I, 97. [119b] Land Records, 1788-1793, p. 24; see also, TN DAR Roster. [120a] Co. Court Minutes, A, 1. [120b] Land Records, 1788-1793, p. 19. [121] Haywood, p. 91. [122a] Co. Court Minutes, A, 29. [122b] Ibid., p. 42. [123] Land Records, 1788-1793, p. 28. [124] Minutes, Committee of the Cumberland Association, file T44, TN Hist. Soc. [125] The Document, file T44, TN Hist. Soc. [126] Land Records, 1788-1793, p. 6. [127a] The Roll. [127b] Will Book, II, 3. [128a] See TN DAR Roster. [128b] Haywood, pp. 95-6, 132, 138. [128c] Guild, p. 317. [128d] First Records of Davidson Co., p. 478, TN Hist. Soc. [128e] State Records of NC, XXIV, 629-30. [128f] TN DAR Roster. [129] Carr, p. 14.

225

DAVIDSON COUNTY

T

(see bibliography following)

[1] Deed Book, A, 106. [2] Co. Court Minutes, A, 2. [3a]
The Roll. [3b] Co. Court Minutes, A, 5. [4] First Records
of Davidson Co., p. 478, TN Hist. Soc. [5] Co. Court Minutes,
A, 29. [6] Deed Book, A, 309. [7] Co. Court Minutes, A, p.
5. [8] Deed Book, A, 73. [9a] The Document, file T44, TN Hist.
Soc. [9b] Haywood, p. 128. [10a] Co. Court Minutes, A, 29.
[10b] Land Records, 1788-1793, p. 21. [11] Deed Book, A, 345.
[12a] Deed Book, A, 95. [12b] The Roll. [13a] Haywood, p.
88. [13b] Minutes, Committee of the Cumberland Association,
file T44, TN Hist. Soc. [13c] Ibid. [14a] The Document, file
T44, TN Hist. Soc. [14b] Haywood, p. 133. [14c] State Records
of NC, XXIV, 629-630. [15] Deed Book, A, 192. [16a] Family
tradition, compiler's file. [16b] Minutes, Committee of the
Cumberland Association, file T44, TN Hist. Soc. [16c] State
Records of NC, XXIV, 629-630. [16d] Haywood, p. 243. [18a]
Deed Book, A, 284. [18b] The Roll. [19] Haywood, p. 243.
[20] Deed Book, A, 169. [21a] First Records of Davidson Co.,
p. 478, TN Hist. Soc. [21b] State Records of NC, XXIV, 629-630.
[21c] The Roll. [21d] Deed Book, A, 174. [21e] Co. Court
Minutes, A, 7; see also, John Sadler. [22] The Roll. [23a]
The Document, file T44, TN Hist. Soc. [23b] Minutes, Committee
of the Cumberland Association, file T44, TN Hist. Soc. [23c]
Ibid. [23d] State Records of NC, XXIV, 629-630. [23e] Haywood,
p. 142. [23f] Will Book, I, p. 13; (Division, p. 36). [24]
Land Records, 1788-1793, p. 13. [25a] Deed Book, A, 86-87.
[27] Co. Court Minutes, A, 5. [28] The Roll. [29] The Document,
T44, TN Hist. Soc. [30] The Document, file T44, TN Hist. Soc.
[31a] American State Papers, I, 322; see also, Haywood, pp.
343,386. [31b] See James Thompson in TN DAR Roster; also,
Family Bible, TN Hist. Soc. collection; also, family data,
compiler's files. [32a] State Record of NC, XXIV, 629-630.
[32b] Deed Book, A, 164. [32c] The Roll. [33] The Roll. [34a]
The Document, file T44, TN Hist. Soc. [34b] Deed Book, A,
148. [34c] The Roll. [35] The Document, file T44, TN Hist.
Soc. [36a] See TN DAR Roster. [36b] The Document, file T44,
TN Hist. Soc. [36c] State Record of NC, XXIV, 629-630. [36d]
Deed Book, A, 26. [36e] The Roll. [36f] TN DAR Roster . [36g]
American State Papers, I, 322. [36h] TN DAR Roster. [37a]
Land Records, 1788-1793, p. 1. [37b] Deed Book, A, 97. [37c]
American State Papers, I, 324. [38a] Deed Book, A, 287. [38b]
The Roll. [38c] Co. Court Minutes, A, 17. [39a] The Document,
file T44, TN Hist. Soc. [39b] State Record of NC, XXIV, 629-630.
[39c] Marriage license written by Andrew Ewing now in the Loose
Mss Collection of the TN Hist. Soc. (not recorded in the County
Marriage Book. [39d] The Roll. [39e] Deed Book, B, 241.

DAVIDSON COUNTY

T

(see bibliography following)

[40] Guild, p. 307. [41] The Roll. [42a] Haywood, p. 98, 346. [42b] Ibid. [42c] Deed Book, A, 127. [43] Deed Book, A, 283. [44] The Document, file T44, TN Hist. Soc. [45] The Document, file T44, TN Hist. Soc. [46a] The Document, file T44, TN Hist. Soc. [46b] First Records of Davidson Co., p. 478, TN Hist. Soc. [47] The Document, file T44, TN Hist. Soc. [48a] The Document, file T44, TN Hist. Soc. [48b] Minutes, Committee of the Cumberland Association, file T44, TN Hist. Soc. [49a] The Document, file T44, TN Hist. Soc. [49b] Minutes, Committee of the Cumberland Association, file T44, TN Hist. Soc. [50] The Roll. [51] Land Records, 1788-1793, p. 19. [52a] The Roll. [52b] Land Records, 1788-1793, p. 6. [52c] Haywood, p. 416; see also, Haywood, pp. 98,257,379,416. [53a] The Document, file T44, TN Hist. Soc. [53b] Minutes, Committee of the Cumberland Association, file T44, TN Hist. Soc. [53c] Ibid. [53d] First Records of Davidson Co., p. 478, TN Hist. Soc. [53e] Deed Book, A, 12, 124. [53f] The Roll. [54a] Co. Court Minutes, A, 28. [54b] Haywood, p. 257. [55] Co. Court Minutes, A, 29. [56] Land Records, 1788-1793, p. 19. [57a] The Roll. [57b] Deed Book, A, 27. [57c] Land Records, 1788-1793, p. 5. [58] Co. Court Minutes, A, 5. [59] Haywood, p. 141. [60a] Deed Book, A, 228. [60b] Haywood, p. 235. [61] Marriage Book, 1, p. 3. [62] Land Records, 1788-1793, p. 19. [63a] Collins, _Kentucky_. [63b] The Document, file T44, TN Hist. Soc. [63c] State Record of NC, XXIV, 629-30. [64] Haywood, p. 136. [65a] Minutes, Committee of the Cumberland Association, file T44, TN Hist. Soc. [65b] Co. Court Minutes, A, 18. [65c] Haywood, p. 222. [66] Land Records, 1788-1793, p. 24. [67a] See TN DAR Roster. [67b] Deed Book, A, 38. [67c] TN DAR Roster. [67d] Ibid. [68] Land Records, 1788-1793, p. 25. [69] Land Records, 1788-1793, p. 12. [70] Land Records, 1788-1793, p. 19. [71] Minutes, Committee of the Cumberland Association, file T44, TN Hist. Soc. [72a] The Document, file T44, TN Hist. Soc. [72b] Haywood, p. 139 (see appendix also). [72c] Haywood, p. 133. [72d] Putnam, p. 151. [73] Haywood, p. 143. [74] Guild, p. 307. [75a] Deed Book, A, 269. [75b] Land Records, 1788-1793, p. 20. [76] The Document, file T44, TN Hist. Soc. [77a] The Document, file T44, TN Hist. Soc. [77b] Minutes, Committee of the Cumberland Association, file T44, TN Hist. Soc. [77c] Ibid. [78] Land Records, 1788-1793, p. 26. [79a] State Record of NC, XXIV, 629-30. [79b] Marriage Book, 1, 31. [80a] TN DAR Roster. [80b] Deed Book, A, 149. [80c] TN DAR Roster. [81] Putnam, p. 161.

DAVIDSON COUNTY

T

(see bibliography following)

[82] State Record of NC, XXIV, 629-630. [83a] Carr, p. 13. [83b] State Record of NC, XXIV, 629-630. [84a] Haywood, pp. 107,127. [84b] The Document, file T44, TN Hist. Soc. [85] Land Records, 1788-1793, p. 5.

U

(see bibliography following)

[1] Land Records, 1788-1793, p. 28.

V

(see bibliography following)

[1] Land Records, 1788-1793, p. 26. [2] Deed Book, A, 224. [3] Will Book, I, pp. 24,46. [4] Deed Book, A, 162.

W

(see bibliography following)

[1a] Land Records, 1788-1793, p. 16. [1b] Marriage Book, 1, p. 2. [2] The Roll [3a] The Roll. [3b] Co. Court Minutes, A, 1,7 . [4a] The Roll. [4b] Deed Book, A, 157. [5] Co. Court Minutes, A, 29. [6a] Minutes, Committee of the Cumberland Association, file T44, TN Hist. Soc. [6b] State Record of NC, XXIV, 629-630. [6c] The Roll. [6d] Deed Book, A, 150. [7] Haywood, p. 107. [8] Co. Court Minutes, A, 28. [9] The Roll. [10] Haywood, p. 243. [11] Co. Court Minutes, A, 3. [12] Ramsey, p. 482. [13] Land Records, 1788-1793, p. 22. [14] Haywood, p. 248 (see Walters, ____). [15] Haywood, p. 224. [16a] See TN DAR Roster. [16b] Co. Court Minutes, A, 4. [16c] Land Records, 1788-1793, p. 16. [16d] The Roll. [16e] Deed Book, A, 104-106. [17] Co. Court Minutes, A, 37. [18] Land Records, 1788-1793, p. 19. [19] The Document, file T44, TN Hist. Soc. [20] Haywood, p. 256. [21] Minutes, Committee of the Cumberland Association, file T44, TN Hist. Soc. [22a] Guild, p. 317. [22b] Haywood, p. 139. [23a] Family data; compiler's files; see also, Haywood, p. 98. [23b] The Document, file T44, TN Hist. Soc. [23c] Family data; compiler's files. [23d] Minutes, Committee of the Cumberland Association. [23e] First Records of Davidson Co., p. 478, TN Hist. Soc. [23f] State Record of NC, XXIV, 629-630. [23g] Carr, p. 7.

DAVIDSON COUNTY

W

(see bibliography following)

[23h] The Roll. [23i] Co. Court Minutes, A, 7. [23j] Deed Book, A, 154,163. [24] Land Records, 1788-1796, p. 2. [25] The Document, file T44, TN Hist. Soc. [26] Land Records, 1788-1793, p. 14. [27a] Minutes, Committee of the Cumberland Association, file T44, TN Hist. Soc. [27b] State Record of NC, XXIV, 629-630. [27c] American State Papers, I, 322. [28] Marriage Book, 1, p. 32. [29] The Document, file T44, TN Hist. Soc. [30a] Minutes, Committee of the Cumberland Association, file T44, TN Hist. Soc. [30b] First Records of Davidson Co., p. 478, TN Hist. Soc. [30c] Co. Court Minutes, A, 25. [30d] The Roll. [31a] Land Records, 1788-1793, p. 16. [31b] Deed Book, A, 72. [32a] Haywood, pp. 95-96, 131. [32b] The Document, file T44, TN Hist. Soc. [32c] Draper, 32s, p. 314. [32d] State Record of NC, XXIV, 629-630. [32e] Land Records, 1788-1793, p. 20. [33] Co. Court Minutes, A, 17. [34] Deed Book, A, 334. [35] The Roll. [36] Guild, p. 307. [37] Deed Book, A, 252-253. [38] Deed Book, A, 264. [39] Land Records, 1788-1793, p. 25. [40] The Document, file T44, TN Hist. Soc. [41] Marriage Book, 1, p. 4. [42] American State Papers, I, 323. [43a] American State Papers, I, 323. [43b] Haywood, p. 245. [44] Haywood, p. 142. [45a] Deed Book, A, 279. [45b] Haywood, p. 238. [46] The Roll. [47a] Haywood, pp. 98,128-129. [47b] The Document, file T44, TN Hist. Soc. [47c] Minutes, Committee of the Cumberland Association, file T44, TN Hist. Soc. [47d] First Records of Davidson Co., p. 478, TN Hist. Soc. [47e] Deed Book, A, 157. [47f] Co. Court Minutes, A, p. 1 . [47g] Wills & Inventories, I, 302. [47h] Clayton, History Of Davidson County, p. 370. [48] Deed Book, A, 94. [49] Land Records, 1788-1793, p. 15. [50] Marriage Book, 1, p. 3. [51] Land Records, 1788-1793, p.7. [52] See TN DAR Roster; see also, Fulcher, Williams Family History (Brentwood: Family History Center, 1978). [53] American State Papers, I, 324. [54a] Haywood, p. 98. [54b] The Document, file T44, TN Hist. Soc. [54c] State Records of NC, XXIV, 629-630. [54d] The Roll. [54e] Land Records, 1788-1793, p. 14. [54f] Haywood, p. 256. [54g] Guild, p. 307. [55a] Co. Court Minutes, A, 35. [55b] American State Papers, I, 324. [56] Land Records, 1788-1793, p. 23. [57] Deed Book, A, 144. [58] The Roll. [59] Land Records, 1788-1793, p. 4. [60] The Roll. [61] The Roll. [62a] See TN DAR Roster. [62b] Deed Book, A, 304. [62c] Land Records, 1788-1793, p. 27. [62d] Haywood, p. 245. [62e] Co. Court Minutes, A, 9. [62f] TN DAR Roster. [63] American State Papers, I, 323. [64a] American State Papers, I, 322. [64b] Land Records, 1788-1793, p. 11. [65a] Land Records, 1788-1793, p. 16. [65b] Co. Court Minutes, A, 31. [65c] Co. Court Minutes, A, 17,29. [66a] The Document, file T44, TN Hist. Soc.

DAVIDSON COUNTY

W

(see bibliography following)

[66b] Deed Book, A, 173. [66c] Co. Court Minutes, A, 3,9. [66d] Co. Court Minutes, A, 28. [67] The Document, file T44, TN Hist. Soc. [68a] The Document, file T44, TN Hist. Soc. [68b] Deed Book, A, 160. [68c] Co. Court Minutes, A, 17. [69] Land Records, 1788-1793, p. 21. [70] Haywood, p. 230,247. [71a] See TN DAR Roster. [71b] Co. Court Minutes, A, 3. [71c] Land Records, 1788-1793, p. 20. [71d] See TN DAR Roster. [72] Land Records, 1788-1793, p. 20. [73] Land Records, 1788-1793, p. 20. [74] Land Records, 1788-1793, p. 16. [75a] State Record of NC, XXIV, 629-630. [75b] The Roll. [76a] See TN DAR Roster. [76b] Haywood, p. 98. [76c] State Record of NC, XXIV, 629-630. [76d] Co. Court Minutes, A, 8. [76e] TN DAR Roster. [77] American State Papers, I, 322. [78] Land Record, 1788-1793, p. 5. [79] Co. Court Minutes, A, 9. [80] The Document, file T44, TN Hist. Soc. [81] Deed Book, A, 224. [82] Deed Book, A, 222. [83] The Roll. [84] Land Records, 1788-1793, p. 3. [85] Putnam, p. 168. [86] Land Records, 1788-1793, p. 5.

X

(none)

Y

(see bibliography following)

[1] Co. Court Minutes, A, 28. [2] Deed Book, A, 66. [3] Land Records, 1788-1793, p. 5. [4] Marriage Book, 1, p. 4.

Z

(see bibliography following)

[1] Land Record, 1788-1793, p. 14. [2] Land Record, 1788-1793, p. 13.

- - -

230

Part Two

SUMNER COUNTY

A

(see bibliography following)

[1a] The Roll. [1b] Co. Court Minutes, I, 5. [1c] Ibid.,
p. 30. [2] Co. Court Minutes, I, 4. [3] Co. Court Minutes,
I, 15. [4] John Trotwood Moore, Editor, Tennessee The Volunteer
State 1769 - 1923, Vol. I, (Nashville: The S. J. Clarke
Publishing Co. 1923), p. 871. [5] Deed Book, A, 55. [6] Deed
Book, A, 216. [7] Co. Court Minutes, I, 8. [8a] The Roll.
[8b] Co. Court Minutes, I, 2. [9] Marriage Records, 1787-1794.
[10] Co. Court Minutes, I, 2. [11] Marriage Records, 1787-1794.
[12] Co. Court Minutes, I, 3. [13] Marriage Records, 1787-1794.
[14] Davidson Co. Deed Book, A, 189. [15] Carr, p. 7.

B

(see bibliography following)

[1] Haywood, p. 230. [2a] Co. Court Minutes, I, 7. [2b] Ibid.,
p. 23. [3a] The Roll. [3b] Co. Court Minutes, I, 3. [3c]
Co. Court Minutes, I, 14. [4] Haywood, p. 125. [5] Will Book,
I, 17. [6] Co. Court Minutes, I, 30. [7] Co. Court Minutes,
I, 21. [8] American State Papers, IV, 465. [9] See TN DAR
Roster; also, Clark's North Carolina Records, Vol. 22, p. 452.
[10] Carr, p. 22. [11] Haywood, p. 21. [12a] The Roll. [12b]
Co. Court Minutes, I, pp. 3,4. [12c] Ibid., p. 5. [13] Carr,
p. 21; also, Haywood, pp. 21,90. [14a] The Roll. [14b] Co.
Court Minutes, I, 2. [14c] Ibid., p. 13. [15a] The Roll.
[15b] Co. Court Minutes, I, 1. [16] Colonial & State Record
of NC, Vol. 21, pp. 427-428; mentioned in a letter from James
Robertson and Anthony Bledsoe to Gov. Johnson, Jan. 4, 1788.
[17] Moore, Tennessee The Volunteer State 1769 - 1923, I, 874.
[18] Co. Court Minutes, I, 25. [19] The Roll. [20] Haywood,
p. 243. [21] Marriage Records, 1787-1794. [22] Davidson Co.
Deed Book, A, 11. [23a] The Roll. [23b] Co. Court Minutes,
I, 6. [23c] Marriage Records, 1787-1794. [24a] See TN DAR
Roster. [24b] The Roll. [24c] Marriage Records, 1787-1794.
[24d] Co. Court Minutes, I, 8. [25] Deed Book, A, p. 2. [26]
Haywood, p. 88. [27a] See TN DAR Roster. [27b] Carr, p. 19.
[27c] The Roll. [27d] Co. Court Minutes, I, 1. [27e] Ibid.,
p. 2. [27f] Ibid., p. 5. [27g] Marriage Records, 1787-1794.
[27h] Haywood, p. 247; see also, Carr, pp. 22,90. [27i] Will
Book, I, 2. [27j] Ibid. p. 19. [27k] Ibid., pp. 19,26. [271]
TN DAR Roster; see also, Haywood, pp.
54,245,247,248,254,340,376,380,404,& 415 for further information.
[28a] Haywood, pp. 91,92; see also, pp. 381,401,415,504. [28b]
Minutes, Committee of the Cumberland Association, file T44,
TN Hist. Soc. [28c] Carr, p. 19. [28d] The Roll. [28e] Co.
Court Minutes, I, 1. [28f] Ibid., p. 2. [28g] Ibid., p. 3.

SUMNER COUNTY

B

(see bibliography following)

[28h] Co. Court Minutes, I, p. 5. [28i] Ibid., pp. 6,7.
[28j] Ibid., pp. 2,9. [28k] Ibid., p. 22. [28l]. Ibid.
p. 24. [28m] Ibid., p. 22. [28n]. Ibid., p. 22. [28o]
Ibid., p. 1. [28p]. Carr, p. 90; see also, Will Book, I,
19. [29a] Marriage Records, 1787-1794. [29b] Haywood,
pp. 386,428. [30] Haywood, p. 415. [31] Co. Court Minutes,
I, 4. [32a] Co. Court Minutes, I, 9. [32b] Ibid., p. 23.
[32c] Will Book, I, 13. [33a] The Roll. [33b] Co. Court
Minutes, I, 3,4. [33c] Ibid., p. 5. [33d] Ibid., p. 3.
[34] The Roll. [35a] The Roll. [35b] Ibid. [35c] Co.
Court Minutes, I, 2. [36] Carr, pp. 22,90. [37] Co. Court
Minutes, I, 4. [38] Co. Court Minutes, I, 2. [39a] The
Roll. [39b] Ibid. [39c] Co. Court Minutes, I, 2. [40a]
The Roll. [40b] Ibid. [40c] Co. Court Minutes, I, 1. [40d]
Ibid., pp. 3,6. [41a] Moore, I, 874. [41b] Co. Court
Minutes, I, 6. [41c] Carr, pp. 22,90. [42] Co. Court
Minutes, I, 6. [43] Marriage Records, 1787-1794. [44a]
Co. Court Minutes, I, 1. [44b] Ibid., p. 1. [44c] Ibid.,
p. 3. [45] Will Book, I, 7. [46] Co. Court Minutes, I,
23. [47] Moore, I, 874. [48] Moore, I, 874.

C

(see bibliography following)

[1] Marriage Records, 1787-1794. [2a] See TN DAR Roster.
[2b] Co. Court Minutes, I, 28. [2c] TN DAR Roster. [3]
Marriage Records, 1787-1794. [4] The Roll. [5] Haywood,
p. 247; see also, Carr, p. 22. [6a] The Roll. [6b] Co.
Court Minutes, I, 1. [6c] Ibid., p. 2. [6d] Ibid., p.
7. [6e] Ibid., p. 7. [6f] Ibid., p. 8. [7] Marriage
Records, 1787-1794. [8] Marriage Records, 1787-1794. [9a]
See TN DAR Roster. [9b] Davidson Co. Deed Book, A, 208.
[9c] Davidson Co. Court Minutes, A, 28. [9d] Davidson Co.
Deed Book, A, 207. [9e] TN DAR Roster. [10] Marriage
Records, 1787-1794. [11a] Co. Court Minutes, I, 24. [11b]
Marriage Records, 1787-1794. [12a] The Roll. [12b] Co.
Court Minutes, I, pp. 2-4;25. [13] Marriage Records, 1787-
1794. [14a] Carr, pp. 13,19. [14b] The Roll. [14c] Co.
Court Minutes, I, 2. [14d] Ibid., pp. 3,4. [14e] Will
Book, I, 2. [14f] Will Book, I, 3. [15] Moore, I, 874.
[16a] The Roll. [16b] Co. Court Minutes, I, pp. 2,15. [16c]
Will Book, I, 18. [17a] The Roll. [17b] Davidson Co. Court
Minutes, A, 9. [18a] The Roll. [18b] Co. Court Minutes,
I, pp. 4,5; see also, p. 9. [18c] Ibid., p.7. [18d] Ibid.,
p. 19. [18e] Ibid., p. 28. [19] Co. Court Minutes, I,
25. [20] Will Book, I, 10. [21] Co. Court Minutes, I,
3. [22] Co. Court Minutes, I, 6. [23] Co. Court Minutes,
I, pp. 5,8. [24] Co. Court Minutes, I, 6. [25] Marriage
Records, 1787-1794.

232

SUMNER COUNTY

C

(see bibliography following)

[26a] Co. Court Minutes, I, 4. [26b] Ibid., p. 5. [26c] Will Book, I, 2. [27a] The Roll. [27b] Co. Court Minutes, I, 26. [27c] Marriage Records, 1787-1794. [28] Co. Court Minutes, I, 22. [29] The Roll. [30] Co. Court Minutes, I, 13. [31a] The Roll. [31b] Co. Court Minutes, I, 3-4. [32a] The Roll. [32b] Co. Court Minutes, I, 3,6. [32c] Will Book, I, 4. [33a] The Roll. [33b] Co. Court Minutes, I, pp. 3,4,6. [33c] Ibid., p. 13. [34] Co. Court Minutes, I, 25. [35] Will Book, I, 11. [36] The Roll.

D

(see bibliography following)

[1] Co. Court Minutes, I, 8. [2] Co. Court Minutes, I, 17. [3a] Will Book, I, 10. [3b] Marriage Records, 1787-1794. [4] Will Book, I, 15-16. [5] Co. Court Minutes, I, 13. [6] Carr, pp. 22,90. [7a] Co. Court Minutes, I, 1. [7b] Will Book, I, 19. [8] Will Book, I, 11. [9a] The Roll. [9b] Co. Court Minutes, I, 1. [9c] Ibid., p. 3. [9d] Ibid., pp. 3-4. [9e] Ibid., p. 5. [9f] Ibid., p. 5. [9g] Will Book, I, 6. [9h] Co. Court Minutes, I, 5. [10] Carr, pp. 22,90. [11] Co. Court Minutes, I, 2. [12] Co. Court Minutes, I, 4. [13] Co. Court Minutes, I, 9. [14] Co. Court Minutes, I, 9. [15] Carr, p. 22. [16a] The Roll. [16b] Co. Court Minutes, I, 2. [16c] Ibid., p. 5. [16d] Carr, p. 90. [17] Co. Court Minutes, I, 23. [18] Will Book, I, 13. [19] Will Book, I, 47. [20a] The Roll. [20b] Co. Court Minutes, I, 3,25. [21] See TN DAR Roster. [22a] Carr, p. 91. [22b] The Roll. [22c] Co. Court Minutes, I, 25. [22d] Will Book, I, 2. [22e] Ibid., p. 7. [22f] Ibid., p. 9. [22g] Ibid., p. 10. [22h] Marriage Records, 1787-1794. [23] Will Book, I, 2. [24a] The Roll. [24b] Co. Court Minutes, I, 1. [24c] Ibid., p. 1. [24d] Ibid., p. 1. [24e] Ibid., p. 2. [24f] Ibid., pp. 4-5. [24g] Ibid., p. 13. [24h] Ibid., p. 22. [24i] Ibid., p. 17. [24j] Ibid., p. 23. [25a] The Roll. [25b] Co. Court Minutes, I, 1. [25c] Ibid., pp. 3,4,6. [26a] The Roll. [26b] Co. Court Minutes, I, 1. [26c] Ibid., pp. 2,6. [27a] The Roll. [27b] Co. Court Minutes, I, 2,6. [27c] Will Book, I, 10. [27d] Marriage Records, 1787-1794. [28] Co. Court Minutes, I, 3. [29] Will Book, I, 6. [30] Co. Court Minutes, I, 22.

233

SUMNER COUNTY
E

(see bibliography following)

[1] Carr, p. 91. [2] Marriage Records, 1787-1794. [3] Marriage Records, 1787-1794. [4] Moore, I, 874; see also, Carr, pp. 21,99. [5a] Co. Court Minutes, I, 25. [5b] Will Book, I, 10. [6] Co. Court Minutes, I, 8. [7] The Roll. [8a] The Roll. [8b] Co. Court Minutes, I, 20. [9] The roll.

F

(see bibliography following)

[1] Co. Court Minutes, I, 9. [2] Carr, pp. 21,91. [3] Co. Court Minutes, I, 21. [4] Co. Court Minutes, I, 15. [5] Marriage Records, 1787-1794. [6] Marriage Records, 1787-1794. [7a] Co. Court Minutes, I, 1. [7b] Ibid., p. 1. [7c] Ibid., p. 3; see also, pp. 4,6. [7d] Will Book, I, 17. [8a] The Roll. [8b] Co. Court Minutes, I, 1. [8c] Ibid., pp. 4,6. [8d] Marriage Records, 1787-1794. [8e] Ibid. [9] Carr, p. 94. [10a] The Roll. [10b] Co. Court Minutes, I, 3. [10c] Co. Court Minutes, I, 23. [10d] Will Book, I, 7. [10e] Moore, I, 874. [11a] Co. Court Minutes, I, 4. [11b] Ibid., p. 5. [11c] Marriage Records, 1787-1794. [12a] Co. Court Minutes, I, 25,26. [12b] Ibid., p. 26.

G

(see bibliography following)

[1] Co. Court Minutes, I, 22. [2a] The Roll. [2b] Co. Court Minutes, I, 21. [3] Marriage Records, 1787-1794. [4] Carr, p. 22. [5a] Document, file T44, TN Hist. Soc. [5b] The Roll. [5c] Co. Court Minutes, I, 5. [6a] Co. Court Minutes, I, 21. [6b] Marriage Records, 1787-1794. [7] Marriage Records, 1787-1794. [8] Marriage Records, 1787-1794. [9] Will Book, I, 4. [10] The Roll. [11] Co. Court Minutes, I, 4,6,15. [12] Co. Court Minutes, I, 21. [15a] The Roll. [15b] The Roll. [15c] Co. Court Minutes, I, 1. [15d] Ibid., p. 1. [15e] Ibid., pp. 4,21. [15f] Will Book, I, 3.

SUMNER COUNTY

H

(see bibliography following)

[1] The Roll. [2] Will Book, I, 18. [3] The Roll. [4a] Co. Court Minutes, I, 1. [4b] Ibid., p. 1. [4c] Ibid., p. 2. [5a] Co. Court Minutes, I, 25. [5b] Will Book, I, 2. [5c] Carr, p. 24. [6a] Co. Court Minutes, I, 4. [6b] Marriage Records, 1787-1794. [6c] Ibid. [7a] The Roll. [7b] Co. Court Minutes, I, 1. [7c] Ibid., p. 25. [7d] Carr, p. 99. [8a] Carr, p. 22. [8b] Carr, p. 23. [9] Carr, p. 22. [10] Carr, p. 22. [11a] Carr, p. 22. [11b] Moore, I, 874. [12] Carr, p. 22. [13] Carr, p. 22. [14a] Co. Court Minutes, I, 3. [14b] Ibid., pp. 14,15. [14c] Will Book, I, 10. [14d] Marriage Records, 1787-1794. [15a] Carr, p. 60. [15b] The Roll. [15c] Carr, pp. 22,23. [15d] Will Book, I, 10. [16] The Roll. [17] The Roll. [18] Co. Court Minutes, I, 21. [19] Will Book, I, 14. [20a] The Roll. [20b] Co. Court Minutes, I, 6. [20c] Ibid., p. 20. [21a] The Roll. [21b] Co. Court Minutes, I, 3. [21c] Ibid., p. 2. [21d] Ibid., p. 3. [21e] Ibid., p. 13; see also, p. 15. [22a] Co. Court Minutes, I, 1. [22b] Ibid., p. 13. [23] Co. Court Minutes, I, 15. [24] Will Book, I, 9. [25] Carr, p. 23. [26a] The Roll. [26b] Co. Court Minutes, I, 2. [26c] Marriage Records, 1787-1794. [27] Co. Court Minutes, I, 18. [28a] The Roll. [28b] Co. Court Minutes, I, 3. [29a] The Roll. [29b] Co. Court Minutes, I, 1. [29c] Ibid., pp. 4,15. [29d] Will Book, I, 11. [30a] The Roll. [30b] Co. Court Minutes, I, 1. [30c] Ibid., p. 1. [30d] Ibid., p. 3. [30e] Ibid., p. 5. [31a] Carr, p. 21. [31b] Co. Court Minutes, I, 4. [32] Carr, p. 23. [33] Marriage Records, 1787-1794. [34] Will Book, I, 18. [35] The Roll. [36] Co. Court Minutes, I, 1. [37] Will Book, I, 17. [38a] Co. Court Minutes, I, 17. [38b] Ibid., p. 24. [38c] Carr, p. 91. [38d] Carr, p. 99. [39a] Carr, p. 99. [39b] Marriage Records, 1787-1794. [39c] Ibid. [40a] The Roll. [40b] Co. Court Minutes, I, 10. [40c] Ibid., p. 13. [41a] The Roll. [41b] Co. Court Minutes, I, 1. [41c] Ibid., pp. 2,3. [41d] Ibid., p. 5. [41e] Ibid., p. 6. [42] Marriage Records, 1787-1794. [43] Marriage Records, 1787-1794. [44] Co. Court Minutes, I, 4. [45a] Will Book, I, 7. [45b] Co. Court Minutes, I, 29. [46] The Roll. [47] Co. Court Minutes, I, 21. [48a] The Roll. [48b] Co. Court Minutes, I, 4. [48c] Ibid., p. 20. [49a] Will Book, I, 7. [49b] Co. Court Minutes, I, 29. [50] The Roll [51] Co. Court Minutes, I, 21. [52a] The roll. [52b] Co. Court Minutes, I, 9. [52c] Ibid., p. 20. [52d] Moore, I, 874. [53a] Co. Court Minutes, I, 1. [53b] Co. Court Minutes, I, 3,4. [53c] Carr, p. 22. [54] Marriage Records, 1787-1794. [55] Co. Court Minutes, I, 21. [56] The Roll. [57] Marriage Records, 1787-1794. [58] Co. Court Minutes, I, 16. [59] Marriage Records, 1787-1794. [60] Carr, p. 22. [61a] Co. Court Minutes, I, 1. [61b] The roll. [61c] Co. Court Minutes, I, 9,15.

SUMNER COUNTY

H

(see bibliography following)

[61d] Carr, pp. 23,98. [62] Co. Court Minutes, I, 18. [63a] The Roll. [63b] Co. Court Minutes, I, 1. [63c] Ibid., pp. 2,3. [64a] Co. Court Minutes, I, 5. [64b] Ibid., p. 8. [65] Marriage Record, 1787-1794. [66a] The Roll. [66b] Co. Court Minutes, I, 3,4. [66c] Ibid., p. 9. [66d] Will Book, I, 14. [67a] The Roll. [67b] Co. Court Minutes, I, 3. [67c] Ibid., pp. 3,4,6. [67d] Marriage Records, 1787-1794. [68a] The Roll. [68b] Co. Court Minutes, I, 10. [68c] Ibid., p. 13. [68d] Ibid., p. 15. [68e] Marriage Records, 1787-1794. [68f] Carr, p. 21. [68g] Carr, p. 91. [69a] Co. Court Minutes, I, 1. [69b] Ibid., p. 2. [70a] The Roll. [70b] Co. Court Minutes, I, 21. [71a] The Roll. [71b] Will Book, I, 19. [72a] The Roll. [72b] Co. Court Minutes, I, 25. [73] The Roll. [74] Co. Court Minutes, I, 18. [75] Will Book, I, 18. [76] Will Book, I, 10. [77] Marriage Records, 1787-1794.

J

(see bibliography following)

[1] Co. Court Minutes, I, 14,15. [1b] Will Book, I, 9. [2a] The Roll. [2b] Co. Court Minutes, I, 4. [2c] Co. Court Minutes, I, 9,15. [3] Co. Court Minutes, I, 14/15. [4] Marriage Records, 1787-1794. [5] Will Book, I, 4. [6a] Co. Court Minutes, I, 24. [6b] Ibid., p. 14. [7] Co. Court Minutes, I, 24. [8] Carr, p. 21. [9a] The Roll. [9b] Co. Court Minutes, I, 4.

K

(see bibliography following)

[1] Co. Court Minutes, I, 1. [2] Co. Court Minutes, I, 8. [3] Co. Court Minutes, I, 8. [4a] Co. Court Minutes, I, 5. [4b] Ibid., p. 6. [5] Will Book, I, 3. [6a] The Roll. [6b] Co. Court Minutes, I, 1. [6c] Ibid., p. 2. [6d] Ibid., p. 2. [6e] Ibid., pp. 3,6. [7] Co. Court Minutes, I, 13. [8] Co. Court Minutes, I, 25. [9a] The roll. [9b] Co. Court Minutes, I, 1. [9c] Ibid., p. 4. [9d] Carr, pp. 22,90. [10] Co. Court Minutes, I, 1. [11a] The roll. [11b] Co. Court Minutes, I, 3. [11c] Ibid., p. 19. [12a] Co. Court Minutes, I, 1. [12b] Ibid., p. 1. [12c] The roll. [12d] Co. Court Minutes, I, 1. [12e] Ibid., p. 1. [12f] Ibid., p. 2. [12g] Ibid., p. 5. [12h] Ibid., p. 19. [12i] Ibid. .[13a] The Roll.

SUMNER COUNTY

K

(see bibliography following)

[13b] Co. Court Minutes, I, 2,6,21. [14a] The Roll. [14b] Co. Court Minutes, I, 4. [15a] The Roll. [15b] Co. Court Minutes, I, 2. [15c] Ibid., pp. 4,6. [15d] Ibid., p. 9. [15e] Ibid., pp. 13,20.

L

(see bibliography following)

[1a] Co. Court Minutes, I, 26. [1b] Ibid., p. 29. [2] Co. Court Minutes, I, 15. [3] Will Book, I, 18; see LANIER. [4a] Co. Court Minutes, I, 7. [4b] Ibid., p. 7. [5] See TN DAR Roster. [6] Carr, pp. 22,23,93. [7] Marriage Records, 1787-1794. [8] Carr, p. 23. [9] The Roll. [10] The roll. [11] Co. Court Minutes, I, 13. [12a] The Roll. [12b] Co. Court Minutes, I, 1. [12c] Ibid., p. 24. [13] Co. Court Minutes, I, 8. [14] Co. Court Minutes, I, 5. [15a] Moore, I, 874. [15b] Will Book, I, 24,35. [16a] Co. Court Minutes, I, 1. [16b] Ibid., p. 1. [16c] Ibid., p. 4. [16d] Will Book, I, 11. [17a] The Roll. [17b] Co. Court Minutes, I, 2. [17c] Will Book, I, 1. [18] The Roll. [19a] Co. Court Minutes, I, 3-5. [19b] Marriage Records, 1787-1794. [19c] Moore, I, 874; see also Will Book, I, 1 (Bondsman for Thomas Martin as Sheriff in 1788); also, Will Book, I, 11 (witness to deed of John D. Hannah 1790). [20a] The Roll. [20b] Moore, I, 874. [21] Will Book, I, 17. [22] Will Book, I, 19. [23a] Co. Court Minutes, I, 1. [23b] Ibid., p. 1. [23c] Ibid., p. 2. [24a] The Roll. [24b] The Roll. [24c] Co. Court Minutes, I, 1.

Mc

[1a] Will Book, I, 14. [1b] Co. Court Minutes, I, 30. [2] Moore, I, 874. [3a] Carr, p. 99. [3b] Moore, I, 874. [4] Will Book, I, 14. [5] Co. Court Minutes, I, 21. [6] Marriage Records, 1787-1794. [7] Co. Court Minutes, I, 15. [8] Co. Court Minutes, I, 8. [9] The Roll. [10] Co. Court Minutes, I, 13. [11a] The Roll. [11b] Co. Court Minutes, I, 1. [11c] Ibid., p. 1. [11d] Ibid., p. 4. [11e] Ibid., p. 19. [11f] Ibid., p. 20. [11g] Will Book, I, 4. [12a] The Roll. [12b] Co. Court Minutes, I , 29. [12c] Ibid., p. 30. [12d] Will Book, I, 3. [13] Co. Court Mintes, I, 9. [14] Will Book, I, 6. [15] Co. Court Minutes, I, 6. [16] The Roll. [17a] The Roll. [17b] Co. Court Minutes, I, 1. [17c] Ibid., p. 3. [17d] Ibid., p. 5. [17e] Will Book, I, 17. [17f] Carr, p. 98. [18] Haywood, p. 136. [19] Co. Court Minutes, I, 18.

SUMNER COUNTY

Mc

(see bibliography following)

[20] Co. Court Minutes, I, 30. [21a] The Roll. [21b] Co. Court Minutes, I, 7. [21c] Ibid., p. 25. [22] Will Book, I, 6.

M

[1] The Roll. [2] Co. Court Minutes, I, 19. [3a] Co. Court Minutes, I, 1. [3b] Ibid., p. 1. [3c] Ibid., p. 1. [3d] Ibid., p. 6. [3e] Ibid., p. 13. [4a] Co. Court Minutes, I, 5. [4b] Marriage Records, 1787-1794. [5a] The Roll. [5b] Co. Court Minutes, I, 1. [5c] Ibid., p. 1. [5d] Ibid., p. 4. [5e] Ibid., p. 5. [5f] Will Book, I, 9. [6a] The Roll. [6b] Ibid. [6c] Co. Court Minutes, I, 6. [7] Marriage Records, 1787-1794. [8a] The Roll. [8b] The Roll. [8c] Co. Court Minutes, I, 2. [8d] Ibid., p. 8. [8e] Will Book, I, 1. [9] Carr, p. 24. [10] Co. Court Minutes, I, 13. [11] Co. Court Minutes, I, 21. [12] The Roll. [13] Co. Court Minutes, I, 14,15. [14a] The Roll. [14b] Co. Court Minutes, I, 1. [14c] Ibid., p. 1. [14d] Ibid., p. 2. [14e] Ibid., p. 4. [14f] Ibid., p. 7. [14g] Ibid., p. 13. [15] Carr, p. 97. [16] The Roll. [17a] Co. Court Minutes, I, 4. [17b] Ibid., p. 5. [18] Co. Court Minutes, I, 18. [19a] The Roll. [19b] Co. Court Minutes, I, 4,6. [19c] Ibid., p. 22. [20] Carr, p. 21,90. [21] Will Book, I, 2. [22] Carr, p. 22. [23a] The Roll. [23b] Carr, p. 23. [24] The Roll. [25a] Haywood, p. 227. [25b] The Roll. [25c] Co. Court Minutes, I, 1. [25d] Ibid., p. 1. [25e] Ibid., p. 2. [25f] Ibid., pp. 4,9. [25g] Carr, pp. 22-23; also, Haywood, p. 230. [26a] The Roll. [26b] Co. Court Minutes, I, 5. [27a] The Roll. [27b] Ibid., p. 1. [27c] Ibid., p. 9. [27d] Carr, p. 22. [28a] The Roll. [28b] Co. Court Minutes, I, 3,15. [28c] Ibid., p. 19. [29] Co. Court Minutes, I, 30. [30] Moore, I, 874. [31] Co. Court Minutes, I, 22. [32] Co. Court Minutes, I, 22. [33] Co. Court Minutes, I, 24. [34] Will Book, I, 2. [35] Marriage Records, 1787-1794.

N

(see bibliography following)

[1a] Carr, p. 22. [1b] Will Book, I, 7. [2] Co. Court Minutes, I, 8. [3] Co. Court Minutes, I, 8. [4a] The Roll. [4b] Co. Court Minutes, I, 3. [4c] Ibid., p. 5. [4d] Ibid., p. 9. [4e] Ibid., pp. 14/15. [4f] Ibid., p. 24. [4g] Carr, pp. 22, 90.

SUMNER COUNTY

N

(see bibliography following)

[5] Will Book, I, 10. [6a] Marriage Records, 1787-1794. [6b] Carr, p. 22. [7] <u>American State Papers</u>, I, 313. [8] Carr, p. 22. [9] Will Book, I, 7. [10] Will Book, I, 7. [11] Will Book, I, 12. [12] Will Book, I, 2. [13a] The Roll. [13b] Co. Court Minutes, I, 1. [13c] Ibid., p. 1. [13d] Ibid., pp. 2,3. [13e] Ibid., p. 5. [13f] Ibid., p. 7. [13g] Ibid., p. 19. [14a] The Roll. [14b] Co. Court Minutes, I, 1. [14c] Ibid., p. 4. [14d] Ibid., p. 14/15. [14e] Ibid., p. 24.

O

(see bibliography following)

[1] Co. Court Minutes, I, 30. [2a] Co. Court Minutes, I, 5. [2b] Ibid., p. 13. [2c] Ibid., p. 14/15. [2d] Marriage Records, 1787-1794. [3] The Roll. [4] The Roll. [5a] The Roll. [5b] Co. Court Minutes, I, 4,6. [5c] Ibid., p. 17. [6] Will Book, I, 7. [7] Co. Court Minutes, I, 24.

P

(see bibliography following)

[1] Carr, p. 21. [2a] Will Book, I, 9. [2b] Marriage Records, 1787-1794. [2c] Ibid. [2d] Will Book, I, 26. [3a] The Roll. [3b] Co. Court Minutes, I, 1. [4a] The Roll. [4b] Will Book, I, 19. [5] Co. Court Minutes, I, 18. [6] Co. Court Minutes, I, 30. [7] Co. Court Minutes, I, 24. [8a] Will Book, I, 10. [8b] Marriage Records, 1787-1794. [9] Carr. p. 21. [10] Carr, p. 91. [11] Carr, p. 94. [12a] The Roll. [12b] Co. Court Minutes, I, 1. [12c] Ibid., p. 2. [12d] Ibid., p. 3. [12e] Ibid., p. 4. [12f] Ibid., p. 8. [12g] Ibid., p. 8. [12h] Carr, p. 94. [13] Carr, p. 94. [14] Marriage Records, 1787-1794. [15] Will Book, I, 4,7. [16] Moore, I, 874. [17] Carr, pp. 21,90. [18] Co. Court Minutes, I, 16,30. [19a] Co. Court Minutes, I, 1. [19b] Co. Court Minutes, I, 16,30. [20a] Co. Court Minutes, I, 7. [20b] Will Book, I, 1. [21] Will Book, I, 18. [22] Will Book, I, 17. [23] <u>American State Papers</u>, I, 323.

SUMNER COUNTY

R

(see bibliography following)

[1] Co. Court Minutes, I, 26. [2a] The Roll. [2b] Co. Court Minutes, I, 3. [2c] Carr, p. 22. [3] The Roll. [4] Carr, p. 22. [5] Co. Court Minutes, I, 20. [6] Carr, p. 93. [7] The Roll. [8] Will Book, I, 19. [9a] The Roll. [9b] Co. Court Minutes, I, 2,10. [9c] Co. Court Minutes, I, 13. [9d] Marriage Records, 1787-1794. [10] Co. Court Minutes, I, 22. [11a] Co. Court Minutes, I, 2,6,24. [11b] Marriage Records, 1787-1794. [11c] Ibid. [12] Co. Court Minutes, I, 30. [13] Co. Court Minutes, I, 30. [14] Co. Court Minutes, I, 8. [15] Co. Court Minutes, I, 18. [16] Co. Court Minutes, I, 14,15. [17] Carr, p. 97. [18a] Carr, p. 13. [18b] Carr, pp. 12,13a. [18c] Draper, W6XX, 110-111, 43,525. [18d] The Roll. [18e] Will Book, I, 2. [18f] Ibid., p. 10. [18g] Carr, p. 97. [19] Will Book, I, 4. [20] Will Book, I, 4. [21] Marriage Records, 1787-1794. [22] Will Book, I, 4; see also, Co. Court Minutes, I, 26. [23] Will Book, I, 4. [24] Will Book, I, 4. [25a] The Roll. [25b] Co. Court Minutes, I, 4,6. [25c] Ibid., p. 26; see also, Will Book, I, 4. [26] Marriage Records, 1787-1794. [27] Marriage Records, 1787-1794.

S

(see bibliography following)

[1] Will Book, I, 17. [2a] Carr, p. 22. [2b] Moore, I, 874. [3a] Co. Court Minutes, I, 15. [3b] Will Book, I, 6. [4] Marriage Records, 1787- 1794. [5] Co. Court Minutes, I, 22. [6] Co. Court Minutes, I, 24. [7] Moore, I, 874. [8] Carr, pp. 22,23,93. [9] Will Book, I, 6. [10] Co. Court Minutes, I, 22. [11] The Roll. [12] Co. Court Minutes, I, 21. [13] Co. Court Minutes, I, 22. [14a] Will Book, I, 18. [14b] Ibid., p. 19. [15a] The Roll. [15b] Carr, p. 91. [15c] Will Book, I, 19. [16] Will Book, I, 18. [17a] Co. Court Minutes, I, 20. [17b] Ibid., p. 30. [18a] Carr, p. 21. [18b] The Roll. [18c] Co. Court Minutes, I, 1. [18d] Ibid., p. 2. [18e] Ibid., p. 24. [18f] Will Book, I, 1. [18g] Ibid., p. 2. [19] Moore, I, 874. [21] The Roll. [22] Co. Court Minutes, I, 25. [23a] The Roll. [23b] Co. Court Minutes, I, 21. [24a] The Roll. [24b] Co. Court Minutes, I, 2. [24c] Ibid. [24d] Ibid., pp. 14,15. [24e] Ibid., p. 24. [24f] Will Book, I, 2. [24g] Ibid., p. 19. [25] Marriage Records, 1787-1794. [26a] Carr, p. 23,93. [27] Marriage Records, 1787-1794. [28a] The Roll. [28b] Co. Court Minutes, I, 1. [28c] Ibid., p. 5. [28d] Ibid., p. 13. [28e] Ibid., p. 17. [29a] The Roll. [29b] Carr, p. 21. [29c] Carr, p. 23. [30] Co. Court Minutes, I, 8.

SUMNER COUNTY

S

(see bibliography following)

[31] Co. Court Minutes, I, 8. [32] Co. Court Minutes, I, 6. [33a] The Roll. [33b] Co. Court Minutes, I, 4. [33c] Ibid., p. 7. [33d] Ibid., pp. 14,15. [33e] Ibid., p. 20. [34a] Co. Court Minutes, I, 21. [34b] Carr, p. 93. [35] Carr, p. 22. [36] Carr, p. 22. [37a] Co. Court Minutes, I, 1. [37b] Ibid., p. 6. [38a] The Roll. [38b] Moore, I, 874. [39] Marriage Records, 1787-1794. [40] The Roll. [41a] The Roll. [41b] Co. Court Minutes, I, 1. [41c] Ibid., pp. 7, 14/15. [41d] Ibid., p. 4. [42a] The Roll [42b] Co. Court Minutes, I, 1. [42c] Ibid., pp. 3,4.

T

(see bibliography following)

[1] Co. Court Minutes, I, 30. [2] Co. Court Minutes, I, 15. [3] Co. Court Minutes, I, 18. [4] Will Book, I, 1. [5a] The Roll. [5b] Co. Court Minutes, I, 1. [5c] Ibid., p. 14/15. [5d] Will Book, I, 14. [6a] Will Book, I, 7. [6b] Ibid., p. 13. [6c] Ibid., p. 14. [7a] The Roll. [7b] Co. Court Minutes, I, 4. [8a] The Roll. [8b] Co. Court Minutes, I, 25. [8c] Will Book, I, 7. [9] Marriage Records, 1787-1794. [10a] The Roll. [10b] Co. Court Minutes, I, 3,4. [11a] Co. Court Minutes, I, 2. [11b] Ibid., p. 8. [12] Will Book, I, 12. [13] Will Book, I, 7. [14] Will Book, I, 14. [15a] The Roll. [15b] Co. Court Minutes, I, 1. [16c] Ibid., pp. 2,9. [16d] Ibid., p. 18. [16e] Ibid., p. 19. [17] Moore, I, 874. [18] Co. Court Minutes, I, 26.

V

(see bibliography following)

[1] Co. Court Minutes, I, 25.

W

(see bibliography following)

[1a] Co. Court Minutes, I, 24. [1b] Will Book, I, 12. [1c] Ibid., pp. 15,16. [2] Co. Court Minutes, I, 24. [3a] Co. Court Minutes, I, 24. [3b] Will Book, I, 14. [3c] Co. Court Minutes, I, 24. [3d] Ibid., p. 30. [4a] Co. Court Minutes, I, 25. [4b] Marriage Records, 1787-1794. [5a] The Roll.

SUMNER COUNTY

W

(see bibliography following)

[5b] Co. Court Minutes, I, 3. [5c] Ibid., p. 5. [5d] Ibid., p. 19. [6a] The Roll. [6b] Co. Court Minutes, I, 1. [6c] Ibid., p. 4. [7] Carr, p. 22. [8] The Roll. [9] Co. Court Minutes, I, 22. [10] Marriage Records, 1787-1794. [11a] Will Book, I, 7. [11b] Ibid., p. 14. [12a] Will Book, I, 13. [12b] Ibid., p. 7. [13a] Co. Court Minutes, I, 30. [13b] Will Book, I, 7. [13c] Ibid., p. 12. [13d] Carr, pp. 21,99. [14a] The Roll. [14b] Marriage Records, 1787-1794. [14c] Ibid. [15] Will Book, I, 7. [16] Marriage Records, 1787-1794. [17] Co. Court Minutes, I, 1. [18] Carr, p. 91. [19a] The Roll. [19b] Co. Court Minutes, I, 3. [19c] Ibid., 8. [19d] Ibid., p. 13. [19e] Ibid., pp. 13,20. [19f] Ibid., p. 17. [19g] Ibid., p. 24; see also, Carr, p. 21. [19h] Will Book, I, 6,15. [19i] Ibid., p. 19. [19j] Ibid., p. 21. [20a] The Roll. [20b] Co. Court Minutes, I, 1. [20c] Ibid., p. 2. [20d] Ibid., p. 14. [20e] Ibid., p. 21. [20f] Ibid., p. 24. [20g] Ibid., p. 24. [20h] Will Book, I, 14. [20i] Marriage Records, 1787-1794. [21a] The Roll. [21b] Co. Court Minutes, I, 3. [22a] The Roll. [22b] Co. Court Minutes, I, 5. [22c] Ibid., p. 16. [22d] Ibid., p. 19. [22e] Marriage Records, 1787-1794. [25] Moore, I, 874. [26a] The Roll. [26b] Co. Court Minutes, I, 2,3. [26c] Will Book, I, 12,19. [26d] Carr, p. 22. [27a] Carr, p. 21. [27b] The Roll. [27c] Co. Court Minutes, I, 1. [27d] Ibid., p. 1. [27e] Ibid., p. 2. [27f] Ibid., p. 3. [27g] Ibid., p. 4. [27h] Ibid., p. 5. [27i] Ibid., p. 6. [27j] Will Book, I, 12. [27k] Ibid., p. 19. [271] Carr, p. 94. [28a] Co. Court Minutes, I, 17. [28b] Will Book, I, 12. [28c] Ibid., p. 19. [29] Moore, I, 874. [30] Co. Court Minutes, I, 23.

Y

(see bibliography following)

[1a] The Roll. [1b] Co. Court Minutes, I, 6. [1c] Ibid., p. 21. [2] The Roll. [3] Co. Court Minutes, I, 24.

- - -

TENNESSEE COUNTY

A

(see bibliography following)

[1] Moore, I, 864.

B

(see bibliography following)

[1] Moore, I, 864,865.   [2] Moore, I, 864.   [3] Mss: "A return of persons killed, wounded, & taken prisoner from Miro District since the 1st of Jan'y 1791" (copy in compiler's file); see American State Papers, I, 324.   [4] Moore, I, 865.

C

(see bibiliography following)

[1] Moore, I, 864,865.

E

(see bibliography following)

[1] Moore, I, 865.

F

(see bibliography following)

[1] Moore, I, 864,865.   [2] Carr, p. 25.

G

(see bibliography following)

[1] Mss: "A return of persons killed, wounded, & taken prisoner from Miro District since the 1st of Jan'y 1791," (copy in compiler's file); see American State Papers, I, 324.   [2] Moore, I, 864.

TENNESSEE COUNTY

H

(see bibliography following)

[1] Mss: "A return of persons killed, wounded, & taken prisoner from Miro District since the 1st of Jan'y 1791," (copy in compiler's file); see American State Papers, I, 324. [2] Moore, I, 864. [3] Haywood, p. 13; see also, Carr, p. 16.

J

(see bibliography following)

[1] Moore, I, 864. [2] Moore, I, 864.

K

(see bibliography following)

[1] Carr, p. 25.

Mc

(see bibliography following)

[1] Moore, I, 865.

M

(see bibliography following)

[1] Haywood, p. 134. [2] Moore, I, 864. [3] Moore, I, 864.
[4] Moore, I, 864.

N

(see bibliography following)

[1] Moore, I, 864. [2] Moore, I, 865. [3] Moore, I, 865.
[4] American State Papers, I, 324.

TENNESSEE COUNTY

P

(see bibliography following)

[1] American State Papers, I, 323. [2] American State Papers, I, 324. [3] Moore, I, 865. [4] Moore, I, 864,865.

R

(see bibliography following)

[1] Moore, I, 864. [2] Carr, p. 25.

S

(see bibliography following)

[1a] Moore, I, 865. [1b] Carr, p. 22. [2] Carr, p. 25. [3] Moore, I, 865. [4] Moore, I, 865. [5] Carr, p. 25. [6] Moore, I, 865.

T

(see bibliography following)

[1] Moore, I, 864. [2a] Moore, I, 171,864. [2b] Carr, p. 13.

W

(see bibliography following)

[1] Moore, I, 865.

- - - -

BIBLIOGRAPHY

County Records - **DAVIDSON COUNTY**

Deed Book, A. - (microfilm of original; Tennessee State
   Library and Archives, Nashville.)
Land Records, 1788-1793. - (W.P.A. typescript; Tennessee
   State Library and Archives, Nashville.)
County Court Minutes, A. - (W.P.A. typescript; Tennessee
   State Library and Archives, Nashville.)
Will Book, I. - (microfilm of original; Tennessee State
   Library and Archives, Nashville.)
Marriage Book, I. - (microfilm of original; Tennessee State
   Library and Archives, Nashville.)
Wills & Inventories, I, 1784-1794. - (W.P.A. typescript;
   Tennessee State Library and Archives, Nashville.)
The Roll - (copies of original tax rolls; Tennessee State
   Library and Archives, Nashville.)

County Records - **SUMNER COUNTY**

Deed Book, A. - (microfilm of original; Tennessee State
   Library and Archives, Nashville.)
County Court Minutes, I. - (microfilm of original; Tennessee
   State Library and Archives, Nashville.)
Will Book, I. - (microfilm of original, Tennessee State
   Library and Archives, Nashville.)
Marriage Records, 1787-1794 - (microfilm of original marriage
   bonds; Tennessee State Library and Archives, Nashville.)
The Roll - (copies of original tax records; Tennessee State
   Library and Archives, Nashville.)

Other Sources

American Historical Magazine - American Historical Magazine
   & Tennessee Historical Quarterly, 1896-1902, Vol.
   II. (Nashville).
American State Papers - American State Papers, Indian
   Affairs, I.
Arnow - Harriett L. Arnow. Seedtime On The Cumberland
   (New York: Macmillan & Co., 1963).
Carr - John Carr. Early Times In Middle Tennessee
   (Nashville: E. Stevenson & F. A. Owen, 1857).
Carter - Claresa Edwin Carter. The Territorial Papers
   Of The Territory South Of The River Ohio, 1790-1796,
   IV, (Washington, D. C.: 1976).

BIBLIOGRAPHY

(continued)

Clayton - W. W. Clayton, History Of Davidson County. (1880).

Collins - Collins, Kentucky, I. (1882).

Donelson's Journal - John Donelson's, "Journal of a Voyage, intended by God's Permission, in the good Boat Adventure, from Fort Patrick Henry on Holston River to the French Salt-Springs on Cumberland River, kept by John Donelson." file T35, Ac. No. 195, collection of the Tennessee Historical Society, Nashville.

The Document - Cumberland Compact, file T44, collection of the Tennessee Historical Society, Nashville.

Draper - Lyman C. Draper Manuscripts, Microfilm Edition. State Historical Society of Wisconsin.

Family data/tradition - unsubstantiated stories and traditions in the family files from compiler's collection.

Featherstone - Featherstone, Excursion, I.

Fulcher - Richard C. Fulcher, The Williams Family History (Brentwood, TN: privately published, 1978).

Gambill - Nell McNish Gambill, The Kith And Kin Of Capt. James Leeper And Susan Drake, His Wife. (n.p., n.d.).

Guild - J. C. Guild, Old Times In Tennessee. (Nashville: Tavel, Eastman & Howell, 1878).

Haywood - John Haywood, Civil And Political History Of Tennessee. (Knoxville: Heiskell & Brown, 1823).

Keith - A. B. Keith, ed., The John Gray Blount Papers, I, (Raliegh: NC State Department of Archives & History, 1952).

KELLY - Sarah Kelly, Children Of Nashville.

Kentucky Gazette Newspaper.

Lynch - Louise Lynch, Miscellaneous Records Of Williamson County, Tennessee. Vols. 1-4.

_____. County Court Of Williamson County, Tennessee Lawsuits, 1821-1872, Books 2-8. [Franklin, TN: 1974].

MOORE - John Trotwood Moore, Tennessee The Volunteer State, 1769-1923, I, (Nashville: The S. J. Clarke Publishing Co., 1923).

Nashville Banner Newspaper.

Nashville Whig Newspaper.

NC State Record - State Record Of North Carolina, XXIV.

Putnam - A. W. Putnam, History Of Middle Tennessee. (Nashville: Southern Methodist Publishing House, 1859).

Ramsey - J. G. M. Ramsey, Annals Of Tennessee (Kingsport: Kingsport Press, 1853).

TN DAR Roster - Edythe R. Whitley, Rosters And Soldiers - The Tennessee Society Of The American Revolution. Vols. 1 & 2.

APPENDIX

In the loose Williamson County, Tennessee Court records are found several lawsuits with depositions appended thereto, which more clearly identify some of the settlers or settlers' families mentioned in the previous enumerations.

BRESHEARS, Kissiah - wife of John Tucker (see hereafter).

BURBROOK, Ezekiel - was 80 years old in 1826, and a resident of Simpson County, Kentucky, when he gave his deposition regarding his acquaintance with William Leaton (see hereafter).

CAZEEN, ____ - husband of Sarah Tucker, is mentioned in Williamson County, Tennessee Court Records in 1821, having died and his widow Sarah is said to be living in the territory of Illinois. (See John Tucker, hereafter).

CAZEEN, Sarah - daughter of John Tucker (see hereafter).

DONALDSON, John, Sr. - made his deposition in 1828, recorded in Williamson County, stating he surveyed with James Robertson and Jonathan Robertson, his son, and Bartley W. Pollock [sic], and Joseph Neal, the Survey of William Mebane for 7,200 acres. He further stated he was acquainted with Mebane in Orange Co., North Carolina. (Williamson County Loose Records)

DEMOR, John - married Hannah Tucker, daughter of John Tucker (see hereafter), and moved to the Illinois territory.

EDMONDSON, Thomas - was aged 58 in 1818, when he gave his deposition in Williamson County Court, stating that he was acquainted with David Hay, deceased, formerly of Nashville in 1785. He also mentioned David Hay's brother, Joseph Hay, deceased. (Loose Records).

ELLIOTT, John - mentioned as the brother of William Elliott, and once resident of Orange Co., North Carolina; and having purchased land grant from McVey, according to the deposition of John Hill recorded in Williamson County, 26 January, 1822. (Loose Records).

ELLIOTT, William - brother of John Elliott (see abovementioned).

EWING, William - was aged 50 in 1828, when he gave his deposition in Williamson County Court regarding William Leaton (see hereafter).

GOWER, Able - mentioned in the lawsuit (William Leaton vs. Thomas McCrory's heirs and the heirs of N. P. Hardeman), brought in Williamson County, 12 May, 1826. He was said to have been "defeated" (killed) when getting corn in the early part of the year 1781, at Clover Bottom, along with John Robertson and William Leaton (see hereafter).

APPENDIX

(continued)

HAGGARD, Edmund - son of John Haggard (see hereafter).
HAGGARD, John (Jr.) - son of John Haggard (see hereafter).
HAGGARD, John (Sr.) - according to Williamson County Court
  records, he died intestate, leaving Samuel, Edmund, and
  John Haggard, his sons and only heirs. He and John Campbell
  and Benjamin Joslin had made a contract with Southerlin
  Mayfield to go live with Mayfield at this station for 2
  years to clear 10 acres of ground each and buld a new
  station. The station was built, and the men moved their
  families in it. While they were burning the logs to plant
  the first crop, and putting up a wolf pen about 1/2 mile
  from the station, when Indians ambushed the party.
  Southerlin Mayfield was one of those killed, and in a few
  days, at the request of Mrs. Mayfield, all the settlers
  left the station. Joslin stated that Haggard was killed
  a few days before or after Mayfield. (Loose Records).
HAGGARD, Samuel - son of John Haggard (see beforementioned).
HAY, David - mentioned in the deposition of Thomas Edmondson
  recorded in Williamson County Court, 6 Mar. 1818, in which
  Edmondson states that he was acquainted with David Hay,
  deceased, formerly of Nashville in 1785, and David Hay's
  brother, Joseph, deceased. (Loose Records).
HAY, Joseph - brother of David Hay (see abovementioned).
HAYNES, Stephen - married Mary Tucker, daughter of John Tucker
  and Kissiah Breshears (see hereafter).
HERROD, Jane - wife of John Tucker (see hereafter).
HILL, John - his deposition, dated 26 Jan. 1822, recorded
  in Williamson, TN County Court, stated he was acquainted
  with the brothers, John and William Elliott for 40 years
  and knew them in Orange County, North Carolina. (Loose
  Records).
LEATON, Elizabeth - (see Elizabeth Robertson.)
LEATON, Hugh - son of William Leaton (Sr.) [see hereafter].
  Hugh was the father of William Leaton (see hereafter),
  who died ca. 1782, according to his son's deposition (see
  hereafter). Ezekiel Burbrook, Sr., stated in deposition
  that Hugh died about 1782.
LEATON, James - son of William Leaton (Sr.) [see hereafter].
  He went to the Mississippi country shortly after the
  Revolution and was never heard of again. His father went
  and searched for him but could not find him.
LEATON, John - son of William Leaton (Sr.) [see hereafter].
  According to the deposition of Edward Tompkins, dated 12
  February 1819, filed in a lawsuit in Williamson County
  Court, John Leaton was Edward Tompkins' half-brother.
  Tompkins stated that William Leaton, father of John, was

APPENDIX

(continued)

LEATON, John - (continued).
married to his mother, and that he was present at the wedding. He further stated that he saw John Leaton 1 or 2 days after he was born, and saw him nursing his mother. (Loose Records).

LEATON, Rebecca - daughter of William Leaton (Sr.) [see hereafter].

LEATON, William - son of William Leaton (see hereafter), enlisted in the (Revolutionary) War and was killed by Indians during the time that Charleston was taken by the British, according to a deposition of his sister, Elizabeth (Robertson), in Court in Williamson County, Tennessee, in the lawsuit (William Leaton vs. Thomas McCrory heirs and heirs of N. P. Hardeman). The Court record also records that William Leaton was a single man in the summer or fall of the year 1780, when killed by Indians near the Clover Bottom on Stone's River, along with John Robertson and Able Gower, when getting in corn. His heirs became entitled to a preemption on the Harpeth River of 640 acres. (Loose Records).

LEATON, William "Billy" - son of Hugh Leaton (see abovementioned), was aged 48 at the time of giving his deposition in June 1828, in the lawsuit (William Leaton vs. Thomas McCrory's heirs and heirs of N. P. Hardeman), heard in Court in Williamson County, Tennessee. He stated in his deposition that his father Hugh Leaton had died when William was about 2 years old. He remembered Hugh's father to be William Leaton, who told him that he had married a woman in South Carolina. William also stated that he was uncertain whether his grandfather, William, had actually married, as he had heard that he just lived with the woman. William stated that he was the son of Mrs. Robinson which indicated that his mother had remarried. (Loose Records).

LEATON, William - according to various depositions recorded in the lawsuit (William Leaton vs. Thomas McCrory's heirs and heirs of N. P. Hardeman) brought to Court in Williamson County, Tennessee, William was the father of James, John, Hugh, William, Elizabeth, and 3 unnamed daughters. His wife died during the Revolution. He came to the Cumberland in 1780, and raised corn at Bledsoe's Lick in that year. John Buchanan testified that William Leaton lived in the French Lick Station. Years later William told his daughter, Elizabeth, according to her deposition, that he had taken up with a woman in a fort and had children by her. The woman's name was Tompkins, and she had two sons by a prior marriage, Archibald and Edward Tompkins. Edward Tompkins made his deposition in the above proceedings, stating he

APPENDIX

(continued)

LEATON, William (continued)
was present at the marriage of his mother to William Leaton, and identified the couple's child as being John Leaton. Edward had accompanied William Leaton to the Cumberland country in 1780. William file a preemption claim with William McCutchen, the brother of James McCutchen, whose deposition is also filed in the above-mentioned lawsuit. James McCutchen thought that his brother William had purchased a part of William Leaton's claim. Years later, William Leaton's daughter, Elizabeth, saw him, and she said he was "poorly." She stated he told her he had settlements of land in Kentucky that he wanted to go to see and had left it so that the children of the woman he had taken up with would get the land. She further stated that she understood her father lived with 3 women after the death of his (first) wife. William Leaton, son of Hugh Leaton, testified he was employed in 1798, to go to North Carolina where "old William" lived and purchase the right to a 640 acre tract of land. He said that William was still living in 1814.

LEWIS, Joel - in a deposition recorded in Court in Williamson County, Tennessee, in the lawsuit (Letitia, Alfred, Nancy, Jesse, and Mary Ann, persons of color held in slavery vs. Abraham P. Maury, 13 June 1837, Mrs. Miriam Myra Crabb stated that she married Joel Lewis, a brother of William T. Lewis, and lived in North Carolina 6 or 7 years. She stated that she came to "Tennessee" in the fall that Buchanan's Station was taken and settled in the neighborhood of Nashville, and lived as neighbors with William T. Lewis several years. She mentioned a sister of William. (Loose Records).

LEWIS, Miriam Myra - wife of Joel Lewis, afterward apparently remarried to Crabb (see Joel Lewis above.)

LEWIS, William T. - brother of Joel Lewis (see above).

MARION, John - was aged 64 years and a resident of Bedford County, Tennessee, 22, June 1824, when he made a deposition recorded in Court in Williamson County, Tennessee, concerning his acquaintance with Southerlin Mayfield. He said he came to this country in Sept. 1785. He mentioned that Thomas Nolin (sic) was killed a few days after he came to this country. (Loose Records).

McCUTCHEN (variously, McCUTCHEON, McCUTCHIN), James - was aged 70 years and a resident of Giles County, Tennessee, on 12 Sept. 1828, when he gave his deposition which was recorded in the Court records of Williamson County, Tennessee. In it he stated he came to the French Lick in 1782, and he mentioned his brother, William McCutchen. (Loose Records).

McCUTCHEN, William - brother of James McCutchen (see above).

APPENDIX

(continued)

McFARLIN, James - husband of Phoebe Tucker, daughter of John Tucker (see hereafter).

MEBANE, William - his claim of 7200 acres was surveyed by John Donaldson and others according to Donaldson's deposition recorded in the Court records of Williamson County, Tennessee. Donaldson stated he knew Mebane in Orange County, North Carolina. (Loose Records).

NEAL, Joseph - helped John Donaldson, Sr. (see beforementioned) survey William Mebane's grant.

NEGROS - several generations of one former slave family are chronicled in depositions recorded in Court records of Williamson County, Tennessee in the lawsuit (Letitia, Alfred, Nancy, Jesse, and Mary Ann, persons of color held in slavery vs. Abraham P. Maury) dated, 13 June 1837. According to those depositions, JANE SCOTT was the progenitor of this family, "a woman of color," was purchased from a man named Blunton by William T. Lewis. She was said to be free. She remained in Lewis' possession many years and had a large family. She was brought by Lewis to the Cumberland settlements ca. 1782, and it was thought that when she decided to sue for her freedom, she was sent off to either Natchez or the lower country somewhere. Her children were: Priscilla, Kisiah, Sally, and Gabriel. PRISCILLA was given to Governor Claiborne. KISIAH, who was lame, was called "limping or hopping Kizzy." She had several children. SALLY, had 2 children: Jo and Rebecca. Sally was drowned in the Holston River on the way to the Cumberland Settlements. She was supposedly drowned intentionally, according to a letter from the man who hired her. GABRIEL was only mentioned as the child of Jane Scott in the depostions. JO was given to Dr. Claiborne, who married William T. Lewis' daughter. Thomas Crutcher was thought to have been purchased from Claiborne. REBECCA was also given to Dr. Claiborne. She raised and suckled Micajah Claiborne. She had two children: Alfred and Letitia. When Thomas Crutcher purchased her from Claiborne, he sent her to Natchez where she was sold. ALFRED was thought to have died in Nashville. LETITIA came into the possession of Abram P. Maury. Other plaintiffs in the lawsuit abovementioned included NANCY, JESSE, and MARY ANN, whose relationship to the family is unclear. (Loose Records).

NOLIN (variously, NOLAN, NOLAND), Thomas - mentioned in John Marion's deposition (see beforementioned) has having been killed. (see p. 92).

APPENDIX

(continued)

NORRIS, Nicholas - husband of Nancy Tucker, daughter of John
Tucker (see hereafter).
POLLOCK, Bartley W. (sic) - helped John Donaldson, Sr., survey
William Mebane's grant (see p. 97).
ROBERTSON, Elizabeth - daughter of William Leaton, at the
age of 85 years, while residing in Simpson County, Kentucky,
gave her deposition regarding the Leaton family which was
recorded in the Court records in Williamson County,
Tennessee. (See William Leaton, beforementioned).
STOVALL, Bartholomore - at the age of 69 years, while a
resident of Bedford County, Tennessee, he gave a deposition
which was recorded in the Court records of Williamson County,
Tennessee. In it he stated he was acquainted with Southerlin
Mayfield 2 or 3 years before his death, and he knew John
Haggard before he was killed in Sept. 1793. (Loose Records).
TOMPKINS, Archibald - step-son of William Leaton (see
beforementioned).
TOMPKINS, Edward - step-son of William Leaton (see
beforementioned).
TUCKER, Enoch - son of John Tucker (see hereafter), moved
to the Illinois territory.
TUCKER, Hannah - daughter of John Tucker (see hereafter);
married John Demor and moved to the Illinois territory.
TUCKER, Henry - son of John Tucker, moved to the Illinois
territory.
TUCKER, John - mentioned in Court records in Williamson County,
Tennessee, as "late of Robertson County, Tennessee; died
in 1801 or 1802, intestate. Many years ago John Tucker
was lawfully married in the state of North Carolina to
Kissiah Breshears, and they lived together for many years.
They had two children, a boy and a girl. The boy died
when he was about 2 years old. The girl was named Mary,
and she married Stephen Haynes during the lifetime of her
father. She is still living as is John's widow, Kissiah.
Shortly after the birth of the second child, John Tucker
left his wife and came to the part of North Carolina that
is now Tennessee and never returned to his wife. Here
he lived with Jane Herrod in a state of adultry for several
years and had several children by her: Enoch Tucker, Henry
Tucker, Hannah Tucker, Sarah Tucker, Nancy Tucker, Phoebe
Tucker, and Riggs Tucker. Hannah married John Demor and
is now living. Nancy married Nicholas Norris and is living.

APPENDIX

(continued)

TUCKER, John - (continued)
Phoebe married James McFarlin and is still living. Jane Herrod, Enoch Tucker, Henry Tucker, James McFarlin and Phoebe his wife, John Demor and Hannah his wife, and Sarah Cazeen whose husband is dead have all moved to the territory of Illinois. Nicholas Norris and Nancy his wife lives in Dickson County, Tennessee, and Riggs Tucker, a minor, lived in Robertson County, Tennessee. In 1802, Jane Herrod produced a paper purporting to be the last will of John Tucker and Peter Spence appeared to prove the said will." See John Tucker's sketch in the main text of this work, and note the discrepancy regarding Jane (Jenny) Herrod. (Loose Records, ca. 1821).
TUCKER, Mary - daughter of John Tucker and Kissiah Breshears, married Stephen Hayes. (See John Tucker, beforementioned).
TUCKER, Nancy - daughter of John Tucker (see beforementioned).
TUCKER, Phoebe - daughter of John Tucker (see beforementioned).
TUCKER, Riggs - son of John Tucker (see beforementioned).
TUCKER, Sarah - daughter of John Tucker (see beforementioned).

- - - -